Exploring the Vault: Masonic Higher Degrees 1730–1800

EXPLORING THE VAULT

Masonic Higher Degrees 1730-1800

JOHN BELTON & ROGER DACHEZ

Westphalia Press
An Imprint of the Policy Studies Organization
Washington, DC

EXPLORING THE VAULT: MASONIC HIGHER DEGREES 1730–1800

All Rights Reserved © 2024 by Policy Studies Organization
© UK John Belton & Roger Dachez

Westphalia Press
An imprint of Policy Studies Organization
1367 Connecticut Avenue NW
Washington, D.C. 20036
info@ipsonet.org

ISBN: 978-1-63391-948-8

Interior design by Jeffrey Barnes
jbarnesbook.design

Daniel Gutierrez-Sandoval, Executive Director
PSO and Westphalia Press

Updated material and comments on this edition
can be found at the Westphalia Press website:
www.westphaliapress.org

This book is dedicated to those Brothers
who were members of the
Union French Lodge No. 98,
and who carried the degrees of free-masonry
from London and over the seas to Europe.

Table of Contents

Preface

"Reunite what is scattered." John Belton and Roger Dachez have taken this traditional Masonic injunction literally and gone to the archives to gather an impressive collection of documents scattered across Europe and the Atlantic. Breaking with a teleological perspective that reconstructs the origins of the Ancient and Accepted Scottish Rite as if it were an ineluctable process, they reconstruct, in a succession of chapters that will keep the reader on the edge of his seat, the various paths taken by in a history that is constantly enriched by new discoveries. Breaking with the idea inherited from Harry Carr that nothing happened on the high-rank front across the Channel between 1730 and 1760, they happily shake up our chronological laziness. In so doing, they revisit whole swathes of Masonic history, and above all rethink Masonic movements in eighteenth-century Europe. The Jacobite exile is no longer studied as a passive transfer from the British Isles to France, but is revisited from below. It is now embodied in so many individual trajectories set in context. Hector Maclean of Duart (1703–1750), Grand Master of the Grand Lodge of Paris, knew very little about British Masonry. Born in France, he was much more familiar with French lodges. Conversely, Lodge no. 98, which became Union French Lodge in 1739 when it moved from the Kings Arms tavern to the Union Coffee House, established itself from London outwards as a remarkable Masonic nursery whose members had a decisive influence from the Holy Roman Empire to the United Provinces (now the Netherlands), and through the printed word throughout Europe, since their publications shaped the Masonic culture of the time. Brothers La Tierce, Coustos, Steinheil and La Chapelle, who left their names in the pantheon of early eighteenth-century Freemasonry, are well known separately, but here we will discover Lanse (Thomas Lansa) and many other little-known brothers, as well as the importance of musical and artistic circulations as vectors of Masonic exchange.

To challenge a long-standing historiographical tradition and challenge the authority of the vulgate, it was necessary to go to the sources—*Ad Fontes*! in the words of the humanists and reformers of the sixteenth century. It was also necessary to draw on the critical and philological experience forged over several decades of landmark research and publications. John Belton, author of *The English Masonic Union of 1813* and a member of some of the best research circles on Freemasonry, has also written a postscript to the French version of *Franc-maçonnerie, l'histoire retrouvée* by David Taillades. As for Roger Dachez, his Masonic bibliography fills entire bookshelves, where he combines the power of argument, the sense of formula that he is known for both orally and in writing, with an unparalleled erudition and an ever-renewed scholarly curiosity. On a personal note, his *Invention de la franc-maçonnerie: Des opératifs aux spéculatifs,* to be read in its second edition, is the book of the last fifteen years that has most impressed me in the field we hold dear. And here it is the same all-encompassing method of investigation that hits the nail on the head. But a four-handed book cannot be improvised. To be successful, you need to combine and share methods and fieldwork. This book is therefore the fruit of several years' work and intellectual collaboration. Readers, whether English-speaking or French-speaking, will go from one discovery to the next. If they thought they had been warned that nothing much had happened between 1730 and 1760, they will discover that, on the contrary, this was a seminal period marked by a profusion of experimentation and exchange. It was then that Freemasonry spread across the continent and overseas. While the reader may have been familiar with a "national" history of the Masonic order, he will discover that he needs to change scale, because Freemasonry, more than any other form of sociability, was fundamentally transnational in the eighteenth century. This is why following individual itineraries and the spread of lodges was both difficult and yet essential.

This book is an investigation in which the authors not only share their findings with readers. As the chapters progress, they pick up traces and clues that they record, observe, comment on and compare. This history is first and foremost an archaeology, and in it John Belton and Roger Dachez demonstrate both their taste for archives and their desire to (re)construct a narrative. Their analyses invite readers not only to question a number of certainties, but also to push their own thinking. This is the hallmark of successful books that are destined to become benchmarks. They do not need to challenge their predecessors, because history is cumulative knowledge. One can acknowledge one's debts and pay an intellectual tribute to the great ancients, while recognising their limitations. We can also question some of their perspectives, while highlighting the pioneering aspects of their work. This approach to the work of the historian has become sufficiently rare that it deserves to be applauded. Too many authors have tried, particularly on this side of the Channel, to enter the arena by announcing with great effect that everything that had been written before them had *ipso facto* been demonetised and that they were going to revolutionise the state of our knowledge thanks to their unique science. Their books have often aged badly. Here, on the contrary, the authors honour themselves with a scientific modesty that only their unrivalled mastery of their subjects has enabled them to achieve, and the result is both stimulating and particularly convincing.

This book is not the end of an investigation, but rather an invitation to continue it, as each chapter offers original perspectives and revisits a fragmented and piecemeal history. Its publication in two languages is to be welcomed as an invitation to dialogue on the basis of a shared and accessible science. The writing is effective, never jargony, but rejects anachronisms and the brilliance of artificial constructions, taking a back seat to the Masonic work and its craftsmen in order to highlight them. The result is delightful.

Pierre-Yves Beaurepaire
Professor of Modern History at the Université Côte-d'Azur (Nice)
Member of the Institut Univ

Introduction

One has only to pick up a book on the history of Freemasonry and one is presented with huge gaps in the story of how things developed in the eighteenth century. Whether that book was written by Robert Freke Gould, Knoop and Jones, Harry Carr, or Bernard E Jones in England or, in France, Thory, Pierre Chevalier, Pierre Mollier or Louis Trébuchet, seems to make no difference. Probably it is possible to set out a coherent eighteenth-century history of the first three degrees in any country but the problems start to arise as soon as one considers the higher degrees.

This problem of huge gaps in the masonic history between 1730 and ca. 1800 has not been addressed until now; and the question has to be—why is that the case? There are two possible reasons for this. The first is that there has been a tendency for researchers to just consider events in one Grand Lodge territory, or alternatively and often even more restrictively to only consider one degree in one territory. But one should consider the mythical Scots Master degree as well, and it is only really since the return of masonic documents from the Russian archives that new evidence appeared to prompt research and extend understanding of that.

Typically, if we take the Royal Arch in Ireland as an example, there is a mention of the Royal Arch being carried in procession in Youghal in 1722, then Dassigny's book in 1744—and then the first English mention of the degree being obtained by Thomas Dunkerley in the naval port of Portsmouth in 1757, followed by Charter of Compact of the Excellent Grand and Royal Arch Chapter of Jerusalem in 1766. So there is little comprehension to any English reader of how the Royal Arch developed between 1744 and 1766 or indeed from 1766 till almost the end of the century—when some rituals start to appear in manuscript form. The absence of any English language ritual for the Royal Arch poses a real intellectual problem in trying to trace the history.

The other traditional escape is to treat all higher degrees only in the context of them being all amalgamated into the Ancient and Accepted Scottish Rite—that too simply allows those difficult eighteenth century questions to be avoided. And we accept the validity of the histories written on the Ancient & Accepted Scottish Rite, but of course they only start in 1800.

The objective of this book is to try and uncover what took place during the eighteenth century by looking at all the available evidence.

Scope

1. The investigations of the authors start in 1730 with the publication of *Masonry Dissected*. This point was chosen simply because this was **the first** occasion that the third degree is displayed with a complete catechism in print for the first time and it proved so popular that it ran to several editions very quickly. We do not deny that there were hints of a third degree before —but only in 1730 did it clear to the whole masonic world that Hiram was slain and that the Word was lost.

2. Our researches examine the degrees and developments that follow, and include the Harodim, Ecossais, Royal Arch and Knights Templars.

3. In essence our researches stop around 1800 when governing bodies for all the surviving degrees started to be created. This British process started in Scotland in 1800, followed by England in 1813 and finally Ireland between 1805 and the 1830s. But of course, the process was different in France where most of high degrees arose between 1740 and 1770, without a preconceived plan or apparent coherence, and also developed differently in different cities across France (e.g., Paris, Bordeaux, Lyon, Marseilles).

4. Different degrees found differing acceptances in different countries in Europe; and developments did not take place in unison.

5. Not all the degrees which sprang into life are included, although several are mentioned. So the 'Excellent and Superexcellent Masons' which are part of the full Royal Arch series, the degrees of Retribution, the Mark Degree, and Knights of the Sword and East are not examined in full detail.

6. The Ancient and Accepted Scottish Rite is quite deliberately not mentioned. When it sailed out of Bordeaux on its way to the Caribbean, in the form of a primitive system that had only 25 grades, it took on a different life of its own. It is also a story that has already been extensively researched, in reality we are considering the period prior to that event when those degrees were developing.

But back to the Scots Masters degree. The return of documents from the Russian archives in 2000 has started an exploration of the Scots Masters degree, by leading European researchers, and this has excited interest in these early years. In the last few years this enthusiasm has spread (in France) to looking at the origins of the Royal Arch degree—and several recent issues of Renaissance Traditionelle (volumes 197, 198, 199, & 200) have been devoted to these early higher degrees.

So the undercurrent of developing thought on the early years of the rise of the 'higher degrees' has proved infectious, and also captured the attention of the authors.

What was clear was that **all** the traditional approaches to masonic research had failed, but that the Maitre Ecossois had already demonstrated that for the determined there was more evidence to be found. But it was clear that the return of the archives from Russia around 2000 theories had really not advanced much beyond that of Robert Freke Gould and his *History of Freemasonry*. Thus it was clear that some novel approaches would be required if any substantive progress was to be made.

In the past Harry Carr and WCF Jackson had been of the view that there were no ritual exposures between *Masonry Dissected* in 1730 and that rash of exposures of the Craft degrees such as Boaz and Jachin in 1760. It should not be forgotten, however, that the publication in 1751, in London, of *Le Maçon D*émasqué, a French-language exposure of a ritual supposedly practised in London, perhaps demonstrates that Masonic practices on the two sides of the Channel were perhaps not very different and that consequently, French sources can reasonably be viewed as filling the silence of the English archives. **But if one looks outside the first three degrees, then the statement by Carr that nothing ritual happened was clearly wrong if one included other degrees.** We know that in London there were Scots Masters, Royal Arch and Harodim of Kilwinning being worked—and that these degrees had been spreading into Europe.

And Carr was even more wrong because he translated a number of French exposures of the 1740s into English and thus should have accepted that the masonic world had not stopped changing.[1] In effect, he was denying his own statement. Then the thought occurred to both of us that all the research to date had been limited within the narrow confines of the three degrees and in one single nation at a time. The first shaft of our enlightenment was that just as trade and culture flowed across borders, so ideas and thought also travelled as easily as a virus does, even if in the eighteenth century it only travelled by boat or horse. Thus our initial conclusion was that to improve the chances of success a holistic approach would be beneficial. So I sold the idea to my French friend and brother Roger Dachez; who had other attributes to bring to the hunt. He also was a scientist, with a forensic approach, and he was willing to consider new ideas and adopt a hard analytical approach—so now there were two of us on board. Now we could look at how all these new 'higher degrees' developed across France, England, Ireland, Scotland; and that we might also look towards the Netherlands and Germany too.

---

1   Harry Carr, *Early French Exposures*, published Quatuor Coronati Lodge (1971), p. xi.

The next thought was to accept that if little progress had been made in unravelling the masonic innovations of the eighteenth century that radically new and different approaches were going to be needed.

The typical story has previously been presented as odd facts from several places and the reader is asked to accept that there are gaps in the continuity and to do so utterly without question.

The past century has failed to provide any answers.

Largely research into the history of freemasonry has been conducted with a narrowness of approach. Maybe the history of one lodge, or one province; typically it would also be limited to a single nation's freemasonry or more normally just the three Craft or Blue degrees in one nation. The English, and the French equally as often, also believe that they are the font of all wisdom and progress. All these 'sins of research.' The authors have adopted a different approach.

Taking a HOLISTIC approach to research

From the beginning to the end of our researches we have endeavoured to look at particular degrees, particular issues and particular successes and failures across the nations of England, Ireland, Scotland, France and being prepared also to look at the Netherlands and Germany. Each of these nations can claim innovations; but only by looking at the full panorama was it possible to gain a fuller and broader perspective. But this in itself was not sufficient to gather together all the available clues.

The reality is that freemasonry progressed at different speeds in different countries, some degrees were accepted and prospered in some places and faded away and vanished in others. So our aim was to 'follow our noses,' and the story moves across Europe (just as the key players also moved across Europe).

We decided that we had also to adopt a different approach by

Taking a FORENSIC approach to discovering evidence.

The reality is that much past research, and many printed documents of the day contains genuine gems of information, but because the writer was only taking a very narrow focussed approach these facts were not made use of. This has required a considerable volume of reading around each subject. In doing this we have been able to resolve or clarify various issues that had evaded answer in the past. So we can now explain the degree of 'Passing the Chair'— and discovered that an answer lies within Ahiman Rezon, explain lodges without warrants that appeared in the engraved lists and more.

We have for example been able to discover the earliest ritual for Installing a Master in France. Before 1745, as we shall see later, there was in Paris a degree called "Ecossais des 3 JJJ," which corresponded in its symbolic and ritualistic content to the "secrets confined to the Chair" and documented in England only about fifteen years later. This Parisian degree itself qualified its holder to preside over a lodge of the first three degrees! Can we not therefore assume that, in a more or less similar form, it was already known in London or elsewhere in England? And in Scotland we have been able to tell the story of how the first Grand Conclave appeared in 1810 and to be followed by the Supreme Grand Royal Arch Chapter took form in 1817, and the Irish influences as well.

Much of the failure is because today's researchers have simply repeated the quotations of those who had gone before them, and had blindly assumed that yesterday's researchers had given them all the evidence, and in their turn they had assumed that Robert Freke Gould, in his amazing History of Freemasonry, had offered them all the evidence. The failure to read has been endemic and meant that little progress has been made.

Calling a spade a spade

As the research progressed it became clear that one element of confusion among what we read was the habit of translating every title of a publication into the language of the text. Firstly, this may confuse the reader into thinking that the publication was from the country of its title. There are two issues: first, the almost complete ignorance in Britain of French higher degrees; and second, the habit of the French to throw around the words 'Maitre' and 'Ecossais' and to translate all foreign variants into 'Ecossais.'

Methodology

Quotations

That tendency of researchers to simply repeat the quotations offered by those that have gone before. We have endeavoured to go back to the source and examine each quote; and often we have found quotes to have been truncated and that other key statement simply became ignored. So we have tended to make quotes somewhat longer if needed. And it is perhaps worth giving one typical example.

Laurence Dermott in his first 1756 Ahiman Rezon refers to the Royal Arch, and the standard quote is:

> "that Part of Masonry commonly called the Royal Arch (which I firmly believe to be the Root, Heart, and Marrow of Free-Masonry)."

What is never quoted from the same paragraph, is below:

This is the Case of all those who think themselves Royal Arch Masons, without passing the Chair in regular Form, according to the ancient Custom of the Craft: To this I will add the Opinion of our Worshipful Brother Doctor *Fifield D'Assigny,* printed in the Year 1744. "Some of the Fraternity (fays he) have expressed an Uneasiness at this Matter being kept a Secret from them (since they had already passed through the usual Degrees of Probation) I cannot help being of Opinion, that they have no Right to any such Benefit until they make a proper Application, and are received with due Formality: And as it is an organised Body of Men who have passed the Chair, and given undeniable Proofs of their Skill in Architecture, it cannot be treated with too much Reverence; and more especially since the Characters of the present Members of that particular Lodge are untainted, and their Behaviour judicious and unexceptionable: So that there cannot be the least Hinge to hang a Doubt on, but that they are most excellent Masons."

Thus by failing to properly read around, or even to the end of a paragraph, those researchers failed to identify that a mere five years into the life of the Antients Grand Lodge, there was clearly a pressing demand by those who had not 'passed the chair' to get the Royal Arch degree—and that the only evidence Dermott could use in addition were Dassigny's words from 1744 to try and stop 'the rules being broken.' And suddenly the perspective of events has been altered.

We have come across numerous examples of additional information never being 'seen' because of the tendency simply to requote from previous author's works; and we acknowledge that we too have found ourselves sometimes guilty of the same sin.

Providing the Panorama

Because we live in the world of railways, cars, and planes, it is all too easy to consider that a rapid flow of ideas did not start to happen until the second half of the nineteenth and then the twentieth centuries, but that simply ignores the evidence of trade or of refugees from religious persecution. When men travel they take ideas and books with them, and these dangerous novelties spread rapidly.

We took the view that we could possibly build a clearer picture of masonic developments in the eighteenth century. Of course there may be times when the authors do not agree (and we will tell you that) or when we have not found an answer to a big question; if we can prompt others to find answers then we are happy. Equally, we may be proved wrong; and if that happens we will be delighted.

The huge empty gap in knowledge between Masonry Dissected in 1730 and what follows until the end of the eighteenth century has long deserved to be investigated—and this has been our objective. It has been a labour of love and has lasted almost four years of intensive research. We offer the discoveries resulting from our labours and thoughts to the readers. We hope other researchers will be encouraged to see the development of freemasonry in the 18th century as an area for their attention.

In some cases, our conclusions are radical. And precisely for that reason we have felt it appropriate on occasions to provide somewhat longer quotes that authors have done in the past. We have taken the view that the problem of the past was that all too often there was a lack of perspective. Additionally we are only too well aware that challenging an accepted view of history that we will be attacked for doing so; thus, we have endeavoured to provide clarity for our conclusion. There is of course little that is more annoying but to find huge claims being made with no evidence and even no footnotes either. Where needed we have added extra details and even a couple of lists to support our conclusions

This book is not, and really cannot be, a standard historical text; what it tries to do is to paint pictures which illustrate of those events which have remained largely unnoticed. By pulling together disparate events and travels we hope the reader will feel we have completed our objective. We are aware that we have not probed all the cracks and corners of the European masonic eighteenth century—but we do hope that others will be able to flesh out our discoveries.

But perhaps most of all we invite all readers to join with us in reading about the pan-European activities of the members of the Union French Lodge No.98. And we name this group of eighteenth century professionals all of European origins, as one of the key forces that spread free-masonry across Europe in the 1730s and 1740s. Do enjoy a new view of the masonic 18th century.

The Growing Pains of the Grand Lodge of England after 1730

If the laxity of control [of ritual] in a matter so important as the means of recognition appears at variance with all our ideas of a strong and efficient government, we must not forget that for, at least, the first forty years of its existence as a governing body of the English Craft showed neither strength in organisation not efficiency in management. John Heron Lepper[1]

Reading the minutes of Grand Lodge in which the two 1730 exposures *The Mystery of Freemasonry* and *Masonry Dissected*, it is clear that Grand Lodge did not approve of what was being written. The earlier chapter on Masonry Dissected covers the reactions of Grand Lodge, but in 1730 they were equivocal and unclear. But the next question is what did they approve of? Again there was no official or printed version of any ritual to assist the brothers in their lodges.

This chapter will consider the administrative problems that faced the Moderns, and made managing the organisation very difficult. It is probably also true that there was no example of how to effectively manage any voluntary organisation with branches randomly scattered across the land.

1. The need to circulate Minutes of GL Meetings

The meeting of Grand Lodge on 14 May 1731 was an interesting one, and the minutes speak for themselves.

> It was observed that the Minutes of the Quarterly Communication had not been delivered at the several Lodges in due time, the writing them taking up so much of the Secretary's time, and printing them being thought inconvenient, Several things were offered to the Consideration of the Grand Lodge thereupon, in order to remedy those Inconveniences for the future as also to lessen the Expence to the Grand Master.
> Bʳ Pine proposed that the Minutes of each Quarterly Communication should for the future be etched by him who is a Mason and very well known to the Grand Lodge and might be trusted with anything relating to the Craft.

---

1   John Heron Lepper, The Traditioners. *AQC* (1943) vol.56, pp. 138-204. This paper was instrumental in setting out developments between 1730 and 1766, and is the only work on the subject. It is excellent and most highly commended to any researcher.

B^r Pine being called up, and asked how long he should be about such a thing. He said he would undertake to etch the Plate and have them printed off in three days.

The Question being put

It was Resolved that B^r Pine should for the future etch I the Minutes as aforesaid, and that the Secretary of the I Grand Lodge should attend at the printing them off and when the Number directed were done, he was to bring the said Minutes and the Plates to the Grand Master or his Deputy in order to have the Plates destroyed.[2]

2. Recording the names of all members of Lodges

The very start of the first minute book is a list of Lodges and their members[3] dated 23 November 1723, and clearly this was already considered vital information.

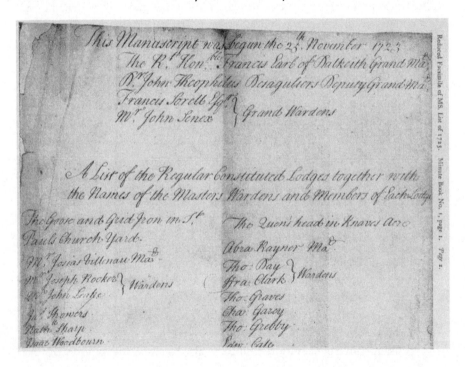

And on 19 February 1724 the GL agreed the following: "It is the Grand Ma^{rs} Order that every Mar or Warden bring with them the List of every Member belonging to his Lodge at the next Quarterly Meeting." Whether they did or not is not recorded in the proceedings.

---

2   *QCA* vol.10 pp. 206-207.

3   *QCA* vol.10 p. 2.

At the meeting of 21 November 1724 it was ordered "And that all Lodges that have or hereafter remove do forthwith send an Account thereof to the Grand Master." There is no record of these returns in the Proceedings.

The next listing appears in the end of the first minute book and is dated 17 March 1731, with the heading:

> List of the Names of the Members
> of all the regular Lodges as they
> were returned in the Year 1730.
> The R^t Hon^{bl} Thomas Lord Lovell
> being then Grand Master

However this listing was perhaps **the** (only?) record of all the members of Lodges. This is because it purports to be the record relating to the year 1730, but it also includes the Lodge meeting at Prince Eugens Head Coffee House (later the Union French Lodge No.98) which only received its warrant on 17 August 1732. Having seen this the last entry onto the list was for a Lodge meeting at the Virgin's Inn, Derby which received its warrant on 14th September 1732.

The authors acknowledge their debt to the transcriber of these details, for without it we would have no idea who the members were of what later became the Union French Lodge.

3. Organising the Grand Feast and admission

Two quotes suffice to make the point. The first is that in April 1724 they had a plan:

> That his Grace Charles Duke of Richmond be declared Grand
> Ma^r. at the Next Annuall Meeting 1
> > It is the Grand Ma^{rs} Order that the following Regulations
> > be Observed at the next Annuall meeting.
> 1st That no Wine be opened till Dinner be Laid on the Table.
> 2d That the Money or Ticketts be return'd to the Stewards about
> 14 Days before Midsummer. I
> 3d That the Members of Each Lodge Sitt together as much as
> possible
> at the Grand Feast. I
> 4th That the Price of Each Tickett shall be ten Shillings.
> 5th That the Company shall have no Wine from the Stewards after
> Eight of the Clock at Night. (QCA vol.10, p.57)

However just a few years later, in December 1727, the whole organisation of this annual event had collapsed and the second quote specifically explains what needed to be done. The words of the then Grand Master are better than any comment the authors can add. What is below is just a taste, the Grand Master was 'Not Amused' at all. His words need no further comment.

> You may remember (Brethren) that at the last Quarterly Communication, (which is the proper time for that purpose) Care was taken to a Degree of exactness of Every Step preparatory to the Grand Feast you then determined to hold on St John's day next. And that particular provision was made and direction given for tickets to be made out and returned at least fourteen clays before that day.
>
> This you were sensible was perfectly necessary to the end that those concern'd to provide for you might have some measure to go by in the doing of it, without wch I it is really impracticable to do it, with any Decency, if at all.
>
> Accordingly 500 Tickets were immediately made out by me to be and lodg'd in the hands of Your present Secretary, with directions to be distributed in due time proportionably among the several Lodges, recorded in the Grand Book.
>
> And had that been effectually done, perhaps Your present trouble had been saved.
>
> But Brethren when the day of Return came I found a very inconsiderable one.
>
>
>
> The Acco^t stands thus.
> Paid for 81
> Standing out.. ..111
> Remain 308
> *[total]*   500
>
>
>
> and upon visiting some Lodges, a reason for it, which, whether it surprized or concerned me most I can't well say (viz) That either they had no Tickets at all sent 'em or not a sufficient Number. I have heard too, another Reason given, why so few Tickets have been as yet taken, which whether I am rightly informed in or no, is better known among You (i.e.) That some Brethren intend to take 'em at the Hall door. (*QCA* vol.10 pp. 78-79)

4. Recording the lodges places of meeting, giving lodges a permanent number (and later a name)

When John Revis became Grand Secretary in 1734 there were 127 lodges, but by 1740 this had grown to 187. Combine this with the number of Lodges moving from inn to inn and one can appreciate why any Grand Secretary would want to keep a numbered list so as to keep track of lodges and of their contributions to charity. The re-numbering of 1770 followed the appointment of James Hesseltine as Grand Secretary, that of 1780 the appointment of William White. One might reasonably conclude that each new Grand Secretary cleaned out the cupboard of his predecessor and put his own house in order. The difficulty is that until the 1770s the lists were largely in *Pocket Companions* which were privately published, and even when they adopted the *Freemason's Calendar* Grand Lodge did not fully control the publication.

Curiously, it was only in 1768 when the Grand Lodge of England was seriously raising money to build a 'grand' masonic hall in Great Queen Street that they started always using the lodge numbers in their Proceedings. Perhaps as always it was the accountants who finally forced the secretariat to adopt better working practices.

5. Irregular Makings and visitations.

On the 21ˢᵗ November 1724 the minutes of Grand Lodge contained the following statement:

> That if any Brethren shall meet Irregularly and make Masons at any place within ten miles of London the persons present at the making (The New Brethren Excepted) shall not be admitted even as Visitors into any Regular Lodge whatsoever unless they come and make Such Submission to the Grand Maʳ and Grand Lodge as they shall think fit to impose upon them.

And there were numerous similar references at later dates. Perhaps Grand Lodge considered irregular makings rather more of a threat than worrying about ritual.

In summary all these matters illustrate the problems of running any voluntary society, especially Masonry, and especially in the early 18ᵗʰ century. Perhaps we should feel pity for the Grand Secretary, often alone, trying to keep things in order, and which explains that as they got older and less active that matters got worse. It is clear that Grand Lodge had many other considerations that bothering about the precise words the brethren used in their work. When these situations were added to the organisational woes of having indifferent Grand Masters, then the Craft decayed. But that is a later chapter.

6. William Preston states in 1775 that the Rituals were changed in 1739

The date of 1739 is often stated to have been the date when Grand Lodge changed its ritual practices. As you can read above there is NO evidence for this in the Proceedings and the ONLY source so far found is Preston's Illustrations. There is one single sentence (below in bold) which implies some changes, but it is not repeated by Preston, but appears only in the 1775 edition of the Illustrations. (Curiously by the 8th edition of 1792 Preston has changed his comment on the year 1739 to be the start of the Antients Grand Lodge activities).

William Preston was initiated in an Antients Lodge in 1764, but soon moved to the Moderns and from 1768 till 1777 was Assistant to the Grand Secretary. He joined the Lodge of Antiquity in 1774 and was eventually expelled from the Grand Lodge of England in 1779 for a public procession and his unwillingness to apologise. He then formed the Grand Lodge South of the River Trent which lasted until 1790 when he was readmitted into the Moderns Grand Lodge once more. His writings often reflect his changing allegiances, and should be interpreted with caution.

The quote below is from the 1775 2nd Edition of *Illustrations of Freemasonry*, and it is worth noting that in the 1772 1st Edition there is no mention at all of either Raymond as Grand Master, or 1739, nor do any of these issues appear. The 1775 quote is below:

> Lord Raymond succeeded the marquis of Carnarvon in May 1739. His Lordship, in several communications, redressed many grievances complained of, and ordered the laws to be strictly enforced against some lodges, on account of irregularities which then prevailed.* Several lodges were constituted by his Lordship.
>
> > * Several persons, disgusted at some of the proceedings of the Grand Lodge at this time, renounced their allegiance to the Grand Master, and, in opposition to the original laws of the Society, and their solemn ties, held meetings, made masons, and, falsely assuming the appellation of a Grand Lodge, even presumed to constitute lodges. **The regular masons, finding it necessary to check their progress, adopted some new measures.** Piqued at this proceeding, they endeavoured to propagate an opinion, that the ancient practices of the Society were retained by them, and totally abolished by the regular lodges, on whom they conferred the appellation of Modem Masons, By this artifice they continued to impose on the public, and introduced several gentlemen into their assemblies; but of late years, the fallacy being detected, they have not been so successful.[4]

Sadly Preston's claim cannot be substantiated, even though it is clear that some changes took place the date they were made is unknown.

What is clear is that Grand Lodge found it hard to keep its affairs in order, and other matters such as Scotts Masters or Harodim of Kilwinning were probably not high on their agenda.

---

4   William Preston, *Illustrations of Masonry*, 1775, pp. 258-259.

MASONRY

DISSECTED:

BEING

A Universal and Genuine

DESCRIPTION

Of all its BRANCHES from the Original to this Present Time.

As it is deliver'd in the

Constituted Regular Lodges

Both in CITY and COUNTRY,

According to the

Several Degrees of ADMISSION.

Giving an Impartial ACCOUNT of their Regular Proceeding in Initiating their New Members in the whole Three Degrees of MASONRY.

VIZ.

I. ENTER'D 'PRENTICE, } { II. FELLOW CRAFT.
{ III. MASTER.

To which is added,

The Author's VINDICATION of himself.

The SECOND EDITION.

By SAMUEL PRICHARD, *late Member of a* CONSTITUTED LODGE.

LONDON:

Printed for J. WILFORD, at the *Three Flower-de-Luces* behind the *chapter-house* near St. Paul's. 1730. (Price 6 d

14

1730 Samuel Prichard's Masonry Dissected

*M*asonry Dissected burst upon the scene in 20th October 1730 with five reprints and a pirated edition in a few weeks—thus it arrived with all the energy of a radical new social manifesto. In total there were about twenty editions published in England between 1730 and 1760.[1] Harry Carr in writing about Masonry Dissected said:

> There is no doubt that the book enjoyed a phenomenal success, both immediate and long-term, and that all the major historians are agreed that Masonry Dissected was largely responsible for the stabilisation of the English ritual in its formative years under the first Grand Lodge.[2]

And that is as much as Harry Carr has to say on the effect that MD had upon the masonic world. Gould in his History of Freemasonry simply stated that it was published and popular—and that is it. Other authors fail to ask themselves what effect this document had upon Freemasonry

The authors take the view that

Masonry Dissected, first advertised for sale on Tuesday 2 October 1730, was the single most important masonic document of the eighteenth century, if not the most significant in the shaping of the breadth of freemasonry as we know it today.

It was also republished in other languages and in other countries. In print the masons of 1730 were able to read, for the first time, that at the completion of the Temple of Solomon the architect Hiram Abiff was slain, and that the Word was lost, and a substitute word put in its place.

And of course it is only *after* the Word is lost that there is going to be a need to discover what the 'Word that was lost' had been. And likewise all the degrees that follow the slaying of Hiram can only be created 'after his (ritual) death.' Chronologically this can only be after 1730.

Quite why researchers have missed this obvious probable conclusion is unclear; but it is starkly obvious to us that those who examined Masonry Dissected did so ONLY in the context of the three Craft degrees, and gave no thought whatsoever to any other or 'higher' degrees that developed later.

---

1 See list at chapter end.

2 Harry Carr, *World of Freemasonry* (1984), p. 142.

Pre-1730 Clues to the Hiramic Legend

While *Masonry Dissected* was the seminal published document, it would be unrealistic to think that it came out of nowhere, and that part(s) of its content was not used in several places prior to October 1730. Bits and pieces have previously been well researched and some even claim to date the start of the third degree to 1725. But the authors choose the key document to be Samuel Prichard's *Masonry Dissected*, which laid out the ritual in a format which is familiar even to this day.

Clearly both printer and publisher had made a commercial judgement that they would recoup their investment and maybe help put bread on their tables. That is they were of the opinion that the content would resonate with a potential audience. This would indicate that the ideas within were not completely novel or unheard of and that many would want to know more. And so it proved to be.

But it is essential however to state that in those days there was no fixed ritual, nothing publicly printed in any volume which set a standard text. With lodges outside London being perhaps hundreds of miles apart there would be little chance of any conformity, indeed considerable variation was likely. Grand Lodge even struggled to produce its own minutes and to distribute them, and most of its publishing was delegated in its entirety to private printers, so perhaps we should not be surprised that ritual was not high up in its priorities. However, if one goes through the published catechisms before 1730 then are some clues.

One part of the Hiramic legend, which is that is the name of the principal architect in the construction of Solomon's Temple in Jerusalem stems from the earliest Old Charges. In the earliest ones in the 15th century, the *Cooke* and *Regius* manuscripts the presence of a master artificer is named as 'King Son of Tyre,' with the name of Hiram or Hiram Abiff only appearing in Old Charges of the 16th century.[3]

In Andersons Constitutions of 1723 we can read that:

> .....Solomon was much oblig'd to Hiram, or Huram, King of Tyre, who sent his Masons and Carpenters to Jerusalem, and the Firs and Cedars of Lebanon to Joppa the next Sea-port.

> But above all, he sent his Namesake Hiram, or Huram the most accomplish'd Mason upon Earth....[4]

But that is all we get, apart from a copious set of footnotes relating to the biblical references in the second book of Chronicles and the first book of Kings in the Old Testament. And it is worth relating the small sections that occur in various

---

3   David Taillades, A New Approach to the Old Charges, *AQC* vol.133 (2020).

4   James Anderson, *Constitutions 1723*, pp. 10-11.

exposures after the formation of Grand Lodge in 1717/1721. By 1725 there is a hint of other ritual thoughts taking place in *The Whole Institutions of Freemasons Opened* (Dublin, 1725):

> Yet for all this I want the primitive word, I answer it was God in six terminations, to wit I am, and Johova is the answer to it . . . or else Excellent and Excellent, Excellency is the answer to it . . . for proof read the first of the first of St. John.

And around three years later (ca.1726) in an advertisement in a London paper, entitled *Antediluvian Masonry*, publicising a series of lectures read (in part)

> There will likewise be a lecture giving a particular description of the Temple of Solomon ... with, the whole History of the Widows Son killed by the Blow of a Beetle, afterwards found three Foot East, three foot West, and three foot perpendicular....[5]

And the Wilkinson ms of ca.1727 offers us the curious regarding Hiram's death

> Q. What is the form of your Lodge?
>
> A. An Oblong Square
>
> Q. Why so
>
> Q. The Manner of our Great Master Hirams Grave.

While these small insights are fascinating the authors take the view that **they are insufficient** to be able to state that a Third, or Master Masons, Degree was actually being practiced prior to 1730.

We also need to remember that it is with Masonry Dissected that we know that a candidate had taken his obligation of the degree before he entered the lodge room where he learned more about freemasonry through a series of questions and answers. This does not relate well to what we now understand as 'working a degree.'

The Responses of Grand Lodge to the 1730 Exposures

In the Minutes of the meeting on 28th August 1730 it is recorded that

> Dr Desaguliers stood up and (and taking notice of a printed Paper lately published and dispersed about the Town, and since inserted in the News Papers, pretending to discover and reveal the Misteries of the Craft of Masonry) recommended several things to

---

5   Knoop, Jones & Hamer, *Early Masonic Pamphlets* (1945), p. 192.

the Consideration of the Grand Lodge, particularly the Resolution of the last Quarterly Communication for preventing any false Brethren being admitted into regular Lodges and call themselves Honorary Masons.

The Deputy Grand Master seconded the Doctor and proposes several rules to the Grand Lodge to be observed in their respective Lodges for their Security against all open and Secret Enemies to the Craft.[6]

But this was not actually a response to the publication of MD but instead a response to the publication on another exposure entitled *The Mystery of Free-Masonry* of August 1730,[7] and in which there is no hint of a third degree.

By December it was Prichard whose publication was berated in Grand Lodge, but by the Deputy Grand Master (Nathaniel Blackerby, and not the redoubtable Dr Desaguliers), and the worst he could say was to describe Masonry Dissected as 'a foolish thing not to be regarded.' How wrong he was because the brothers regarded it well and adopted it, and its essence is with masonry to this day. What was said is below:

> The Deputy Grand Master took notice of a Pamphlet lately published by one Pritchard who pretends to have been made a regular Mason: In violation of the Obligation of a Mason w[ch] he swears he has broke in order to do hurt to Masonry and expressing himself with the utmost Indignation against both him (stiling him an Impostor) and of his Book as a foolish thing not to be regarded. But in order to prevent the Lodges being imposed upon by false Brethren or Impostors: Proposed till otherwise Ordered by the Grand Lodge, that no Person whatsoever should be admitted into Lodges unless some member of the Lodge then present would vouch for such visiting Brothers being a regular Mason, and the Member's Name to be entred against the Visitors name in the Lodge Book, which Proposal was unanimously agreed to.[8]

There was a printed response from Grand Lodge against *Masonry Dissected*, indirectly in the form of *A Defence of Masonry* also published in 1730. It is long and wordy and really an attempt at justifying Masonry. The matter of the Death

---

6   Proceeding Grand Lodge of England 28th August 1730, *QCA* vol.10 (1913), p. 128.

7   The Mystery of Freemasonry in, Knoop, Jones & Hamer, *Early Masonic Catechisms* (1943). It was printed in the *Daily Journal* on 13 August 1730 under the name of 'The Grand Whimsy of Masonry, as a broadside as The Mystery and Motions of Free-Masonry. The name used is that applied in Knoop, Jones & Hamer.

8   Proceeding Grand Lodge of England 15th December 1730, *QCA* vol.10 (1913), pp. 135-136.

of Master Hiram was made out to be a theme borrowed from elsewhere. It was republished in Anderson's Constitutions of 1738, together with an additional section called *Brother EUCLID'S Letter to the Author Against Unjust Cavils*. From these two documents one can learn that Grand Lodge did not approve of either Bro Prichard's publication nor of the innovation of the death of Master Hiram—not in 1730, and it would seem neither in 1738.

How the Hiramic theme developed after 1730

The records of English masonry leave very few clues as to how things developed in terms of the general acceptance of the Prichard Third Degree and its Hiramic Legend, and recourse to other published materials is necessary to gather what is available. Sections that relate to the Hiramic Legend are given below.

The position of Grand Lodge was clearly stated in Andersons Constitutions of both 1723 and 1738, and clearly indicates the change in 'official opinion.' The change in wording is significant.

In 1723 in Charge IV of Masters, Wardens, Fellows and Apprentices part of the clause reads

> Only *Candidates* may know, that no *Master* shall take an *Apprentice*, unless he has sufficient Imployment for him, and unless he is a perfect Youth, having no Maim or Defect in his Body, that may render him uncapable of learning the *Art*, of serving his *Master's* Lord, and of being made a *Brother*, and then a *Fellow-Craft* in due time, even after he has served such a Term of Years as the Custom of the Country directs; and should be descended of honest Parents; that so, when otherwise qualify'd, he may arrive to the Honour of being the WARDEN, and then the *Master* of the *Lodge*....[9]

By the time of the second edition of the Constitutions in 1738 we can find the same caveats on fitness of a Candidate but by then the words change:

> ....he May become an *Enter'd Prentice*, or a *Free-Mason* of the lowest degree, and upon his due Improvements a *Fellow-Craft* and a *Master-Mason*, capable to undertake a Lord's Work.

> The WARDENS are chosen from among the *Master-Masons*, and no Brother can be a *Master* of a *Lodge* till he has acted as a *Warden* somewhere....[10]

---

9 Anderson's Constitutions (1723), p. 51.

10 Anderson's *Constitutions* (1738), p. 145.

In 1723 the wording is very similar to that of the Old Charges and there is only mention of two degrees, but *by 1738 there is an unequivocal statement that there are three degrees,* and the progress is through Apprentice, Fellowcraft and Master Mason, and (only) then possibly to be a Warden and Master of a Lodge. While there is much that can be said of these two Charges the crucial point to make here is that between the appearance of Masonry Dissected in October 1730 and the 1738 Constitutions that Grand Lodge had been forced to concede that the degree of Master-Mason was *de facto* the third degree of Freemasonry. The practices of the English Brothers and their acceptance of the Hiramic legend had left them no other option but to concede.

Hiram gets a mention in *Book M: or Masonry Triumphant* in 1736, and published at Newcastle-upon-Tyne, in the north-east of England, but there is no mention of his death.[11]

What Pennel had to say in 1730 (his Constitutions are adaptions of Anderson 1723) for Clause IV shows that he thought there was a difference between being a Master and a Master of a Lodge

> And no Master should take an Apprentice unless he has sufficient Employment for him, and unless he be a perfect Youth, having no Maim or Defect in his Body, that may render him uncapable of learning the Art, of serving his Lord, of being made a Brother, and a Fellow-Craft, and in due time a Master; and when qualify'd, he may arrive to the Honour of being Warden, then Master of a Lodge....[12]

Pennel's changes have often been considered by writers to have been due to carelessness, but the words are entirely logical. The authors do not have an answer to this conundrum.

Probably the next appearance of Hiram is in the 1738 edition of Andersons's Constitutions, where soon after the completion of the Temple Anderson states:

> ...But their Joy was soon interrupted by the sudden Death of their dear Master HIRAM ABIFF, whom they decently interr'd in the Lodge near the Temple according to antient Usage. (p.14)

> ...when the wise King SOLOMON was **Grand Master** of all *Masons at Jerusalem,* and the *learned* King HIRAM was Grand

---

11 *Book M* (Lecture I p. 5). This glorious Edifice thus built under the Care and Direction of Heaven (King Solomon being Grand Master of the Lodge at Jerusalem and the inspired Hiram Abif, Master of the Work) became the Wonder of all Travellers ... The same appears in William Smith's *Pocket Companion* of 1735 and 1736. It might be that the HRDM degree was not concerned with Hiram but was simply a higher degree?

12 John Pennell, *Constitutions* (1730) Printed by J Watts for John Pennell, Dublin. p. 51.

Master at Tyre, and inspired HIRAM ABIF, had been Master of Work.... (p.15)

...and many particular *Lodges* were constituted under the *Grand Master* SOLOMON, who annually assembled the **Grand Lodge** at *Jerusalem* for transmitting their Affairs to Posterity: tho' still the Loss of good HIRAM ABIFF was lamented. (p.16)

By the time of the 1757 Constitutions edited by John Entick the essence remained the same, although the text itself had become noticeably more 'masonified.'

SOLOMON was highly pleased with this Answer of the Tyrian King, and in Return for his generous Offers, ordered him a yearly Present of 20,000 Measures of Wheat, and 20,000 Measures of fine Oil for his Household - besides the same Quantity of Barlcy, Wheat, Wine and Oil, which he engaged to give Hiram's Masons, who were to be employed in the intended Work of the Temple Hiram was to send the Cedars, Fir, and other Woods, upon Floats to Joppa, there to be delivered to whom Solomon should direct, in order to be carried to Jerusalem. He sent him also a Man of his own Name, a Tyrian by Birth, but of Israelitish Descent, who was a second Bezaleel, and honoured by his King with the Title of Father; and in 2 *Chron.* 13., is called HIRAM ABIF, the most accomplished Designer and Operator upon Earth, who in Solomon's Absence filled the Chair as Deputy Grand Master, and in his Presence was the Senior Grand Warden, or principal Surveyor and Master of the Work. (p.18)

And later it is recorded that the completion was interrupted by the sudden death of Hiram Abif.

THE Temple of JEHOVAH being finished, under the Auspices of the wise and glorious King of Israel, SOLOMON, the Prince of Architecture, and the GRAND-MASTER Mason of his Day, the Fraternity celebrated the Cape-Stone with great Joy; but their Joy was soon interrupted by the sudden Death of their dear and worthy Master HIRAM ABBIF nor less was the Concern of King Solomon, who, after some Time allowed to the Craft to vent their Sorrow, ordered his Obsequies to be performed with great Solemnity and Decency, and buried him in the Lodge, near the Temple, according to the ancient Usages among MASONS and long mourned for his Loss. (p.24)

And yet when we do get more exposures, we have to wait until the period 1760–1769 of which the most successful were 'Three Distinct Knocks' (1760) and 'Jachin and Boaz' (1762).

In Tubal-Kain of 1759 published in Dublin we can read

> Ex. Where are you going?
> R. To the West.
> Ex. What are you going to do there?
> R. To seek for that which was loft and is now found?
> Ex. What was that which was lost and is now found?
> R. The Master-Mason's Word,
> Ex. How was it lost?
> R. By three great Knocks, or the Death of our Master Hiram.

And slightly later in the London exposure of 1760 *Three Distinct Knocks* or *Jachin and Boaz* of 1762. Where the candidate is introduced to the death of Hiram as follows.

> Mas. What was said to you then, Brother?

> Ans. He told me that I represented one of the greatest Men in the World, our grand Master Hiram, who was kill'd just at the Finishing of the first Temple, as you shall hear... (and then the legend is related).

The conundrum that remains is that in all the official records Hiram merely dies soon after the completion of the Temple—*but* both in 1730 in Masonry Dissected and later in the 1760s exposures he is slain by three ruffians who administer three blows. So the options are either to accept the Grand Lodge view of matters which is a simple death or alternatively what the brothers actually worked—the much more dramatic ritual of Hiram being slain.

The generally accepted view today of the gap between 1730 and 1760 where there are no exposures is commented on by Harry Carr as follows:

> Indeed, there are simply *no records of new developments* in English ritual during the 30 year gap, from 1730 to 1760 and throughout that period Prichard's work held the field.[13]

That might be true if one only looked ONLY at the Craft degrees but if one looks at other degrees, and if one casts ones net rather wider than England to include Ireland, Scotland, France, Netherlands, and Germany then it

---

13 Harry Carr, *World of Freemasonry*, Samuel Prichard's Masonry Dissected, 1730 (1984), pp. 104-144, quote p. 143.

becomes clear that the ritual desert that Harry Carr saw, was in reality one of the richest, wildest, and most creative few decades in masonic history.

This alternative viewpoint does not seem to have been considered by any other researchers, but the events followed each other in close and rapid succession, and will be related in the chapters that follow. The authors have been forced to ask themselves whether these two alternatives are merely two ways of expressing the same event or whether there might not be two different ways of creating a 'Hiramic legend.' One obvious decision was to check what had taken place in France between 1730 and 1760.

Masonry Dissected in Europe

Masonry Dissected became known in Europe as early as 1733, with a Dutch translation printed in Utrecht. Five years later, a French version appeared under the title : *La Reception Mystérieuse des Membres de la Société des Francs-Maçons contenant une Relation generale & sincere de leurs cérémonies. By Samuel Prichard, formerly Member of a Chamber of the same Confraternity. Translated from the English, clarified by critical remarks. Followed by Some Other Curious Pieces, relating to Great Britain, with Historical & Geographical Observations. In London by the Company of Booksellers.* It is not known who initiated this publication – perhaps French Freemasons in London. It was republished in Brussels in 1743. It is in fact a compilation, since it includes the text of the Réception d'un Frey-Maçon, the disclosure of Hérault which had appeared in 1737, as well as comments by the translator. There are also a few oddities in the Masonic vocabulary, but these can be explained by the fact that this French translation, despite the statement in its title ("Traduit de l'Anglais"), was not based on the English original but on the previous Dutch translation – which is easy to see by comparing it with the first translation of 1733!

The fact remains that no other French version was ever published, and it should therefore be emphasised that *Masonry Dissected* was hardly known directly in France. Later French Masonic disclosures (in particular *Le Catéchisme des francs-maçons*, in 1744, and Le *Sceau rompu*, in 1745) were, however, inspired by it—particularly in certain passages of the catechisms, which sometimes simply repeated Prichard's text. But in these publications, Prichard's legacy was quickly reworked and enriched by French innovations.

An 20th century opinion from the Netherlands

After the appearance and the process of acceptance that followed the publication of Samuel Prichard's *Masonry Dissected* it did not take long before efforts to answer the questions appeared. In fact only two and a half years later the 'Scot's Masons' Lodge No.115 appeared in London, and from there came the Scots

Masters degree(s) spread out across Europe. Perhaps the oddest thing was that Lodge No.115 left not a single name or single detail for a researcher to cling to. But we have found clues of both Craft masonry and other degrees being taken into Europe by members of the Lodge No.98 which met at Prince Eugene's Coffee House, and later at the Union Coffee House. These brothers were wandering European professional and skilled men and they took masonry with them to France, Spain, Holland and the German States—and maybe even further, but that is another topic for research.

As part of the research we came across several mentions of an article by Dr P H Pott which appeared in *Le Symbolisme* No.365 of 1964. It has only proved possible to ascertain that Dr Pott was the Librarian of Orde van Vrijmetselaren onder het Grootoosten der Nederlanden, and that he authored several books in Dutch. But he has some interesting observations that are worth quoting here

While it was in England that the idea that Hiram was assassinated and the Word becoming lost took hold and which is the Pott alternative c), then perhaps another alternative appears in Anderson's Constitutions of 1738 where he states that after the completion of the Temple that "But their Joy was soon interrupted by the sudden Death of their dear Master Hiram Abiff," and this corresponds to Pott alternative a).

> Precisely, the myth of the Master's degree furnished all the possibilities for the development of other ways of working F. M. Indeed, the dramatic event which occurs at the grade of Master does not permit the completion of the construction of the temple; the works are interrupted, the Master remains unrevenged, and the Masters Word remains lost.

If one considers this more precisely, one can say that the event occurring at the rank of Master brings about certain consequences which are not followed up:

> a) The death of Hiram Abiff disrupts the order of things. It implies the liquidation of an abnormal situation, and, as a result, the search for, arrest and punishment of those guilty of the attack, that is to say, in the final analysis, the exercise of justified revenge on them;

> b) The death of H.A. entails the cessation of the work. A new architect must be found who is as competent as possible and who will be able to continue the work and complete the construction as well as possible;

> c) The assassination of H.A. has led to the loss of the (Master's) Word and every effort must be made to recover it.

From the moment we feel the need to develop the symbolic grades, we will find a direct opportunity to do so within one of the consequences given above for the grade of Master. In fact, this is precisely what happened. We can witness the growth of types of degrees in masonry which base their ritual on one of the consequences mentioned. In the Elu degrees, it is the first consequence that is exploited. For the "Scottish" grades of apprentice and journeyman, this is the second. In the Ecossais grades of Master (Knight of St. Andrew), but also in the grades of Knight of the Sword or of the East, of Knight of the Holy Royal Vault and of Sovereign Prince Rose Cross, it is the third consequence which – in its horizontal as well as vertical sense—forms the starting point for the development of other important types of Masonic work.

In practice, this means that each of these consequences has given rise to new and specific ritual forms. Thus, in the middle of the 18th century, mainly in France, a number of other ways of working began to appear, based in one way or another on the symbolic grades.

They manifested themselves as a graft on the trunk of the symbolic grades and each followed its own path of development, entwining and stifling each other. As it was desirable to ensure a gradual ascent, attempts were made to classify all these different types of work into specific 'systems' and, in order to achieve this, they had to be pruned and brought into line with each other. The result was subordination from one 'grade' to another, which not only cost (it goes without saying) a great deal of time, but also a great deal of fighting and bickering between the different masonic rank systems that existed side by side. Within each of these systems, there are ways of working which are very similar to some existing in other systems. It was not the systems that developed first, and then the ways of working in the various successive grades. The ways pre-existed and were, as best they could, placed in a certain relationship and consequently, classified in a predetermined way.

> One of the most important systems was the Rite of Perfection, comprising twenty-five grades. From this, two well-known systems developed rapidly, one reducing the number of grades to seven (this is the French Rite) and the other by increasing the number by the addition of the so-called "philosophical" grades in a system of 33 grades: the Ancient and Accepted Scottish.

> We must keep in mind the times in which these developments took place. People appealed to privileges OR to a supposedly higher authority, and they had to prove it with documents; it was the rancour of ambition over legitimacy. As a result, in the absence of such documents, they became fabricated as a large ladder. Today we are only

25

able describe them as forgeries.[14]

The thoughts of Dr Pott some half a century ago serve well to enable researchers to separate and add structure to the huge number of degrees that arose during the 18th century.

Summary

While *Masonry Dissected* in 1730 was instrumental in giving brothers a printed form of ritual that they found acceptable or at least with a better story than they had before. Now **the Proposition we put to the reader is that in 1730, and for the first time, there was a publicly known LOSS of the word. And almost immediately various (unknown and initially English) writers clearly considered this an invitation to set about achieving the RECOVERY of The Word.**

A partial listing of printings of Masonry Dissected

Knoop and Jones in Early Masonic Catechisms state "Some thirty numbered editions of the pamphlet printed in England and eight printed in Scotland have been traced."[15] Probably the most interesting discovery was that it is often stated that there were no exposures between 1730 and 1760; it is only correct if it is described as 'no *new* exposures.' It actually reached twenty editions by 1770 in England and by 1748 we can see a 4th (Scottish) edition by 1748.

It seems reasonable to conclude that Masonry Dissected served as a guide to ritual and a structure of the degrees in both England and Scotland and in France, Germany, and Holland.

1730 Daily Journal advertised 1st edition on 21 October, the 2nd edition on 21 October and 3rd edition on 31 October 1730.

1730 Masonry Dissected pub J Wilford, London 1st ed

'1730' Reprint in Paris soon after London

1731 Masonry Dissected pub J Wilford, London

1736 Der Zunfft der Freyen Maurer, Leipzig, Germany

1736 Die Kunst der Freyen Maurer (no date, no place)

1737 Masonry Dissected pub T Cooper, London 7th ed

---

14 Dr PH Pott, Etude de l'Histoire de la Franc-Maconnerie. *Le Symbolisme* No.365, Mai-Juin 1964, pp. 311-313.

15 Knoop & Jones, *Early Masonic Catechisms* p. 207.

1739 & 1742 Masonry Dissected pub T Cooper, London 8thed

1744 *Die zergliederte Frey-Mauerey*] in Johann Küenens Übersetzung von [Andersons] *Verordnungen ... der hochlöbl. Bruderschaft derer angenommenen Freymaurer ... Dritte weit-vermehrte Auflage*, Franckfurt und Leipzig, bey Michael Blochbergern, 1744, S. 15-35.

1745 Masonry Dissected,pub J Robinson, London 9thed

ca. 1745 Masonry Dissected, 12thed (inc. List of Lodges)

1748 Masonry Dissected, pub William Gray, Edinburgh 4thed

The contents "includes Protestation against the Mason Word attested by five Masons given in their Lodge at Torphichan"

1749 Masonry Dissected, pub probably Newport, Rhode Island, USA

1770 Masonry Dissected, pub Charles Corbett, London 20thed

1774 Masonry Dissected pub S Chandler, London

1788 Masonry Dissected, Nicolas Prichard & pub Byfield & Hawksworth, London 21sted.

1788 *Die zergliederte Frey Maurerey ...*, (Masonry Dissected) Frankfurt und Leipzig,

1810 *Jachin and Boaz: or The Free Mason's Catechism to which is subjoined The Mason Word*, by Samuel Prichard, Glasgow. Despite its title, this *is* a Scottish reprint of *Masonry Dissected*, and printed as late as ca. 1810.

CH. 4

Decline, Decay & Recovery of the Grand Lodge of England 1738-1766

When one reads many of the histories of the Grand Lodge of England, or flip through many pages in John Lane's *List of Lodges* it is all too easy just to think that Grand Lodge in London went from triumph to further triumph while marching ever onwards. Sadly that was not the case and from around 1739 until the 1760s Grand Lodge shrank as lodges, especially in London, handed in their warrants and Grand Masters were increasingly absent, and with fewer meetings of Grand Lodge.

John Heron Lepper and 'The Traditioners'

Historians have written very little of these difficult times, but one who did was John Heron Lepper in his paper *The Traditioners* in AQC in 1956.[1] This paper is absolutely recommended to anyone interested in this period of British free-masonry. But Lepper does not perhaps have the same star rating as Gould in the minds of many researchers, so it is worth just briefly running through Lepper's achievements.

Lepper was born in Belfast in 1878, and went to school for some period in Scotland before going to Trinity College, Dublin, where he became Senior Moderator in Modern Literature. He became a barrister in Northern Ireland and later literary editor for Cassels the London publishers. He was initiated in 1901 in Ulster and then joined other lodges, also being a founder in 1913 of the Lodge of Research No.200 in Dublin. But in London the joined Quatuor Coronati Lodge in 1922 and became its Master in 1924. Significantly for us he then became the Librarian for the Library in Great Queen St, London from 1943 till his death in 1952. He was well equipped to write the paper, and the archives we 'next' to his office.

He writes about 'Traditioners' and describes them as:

> Such Freemasons as these, while " Modern " in their allegiance, were "Antient" in their working. Therefore it is misleading and confusing to have to allude to them as "Modern" Masons *tout court*, and to employ such a designation as "Antient-ritual-practising-Modern"

---

1   John Heron Lepper, The Traditioners. *AQC* vol.66 pp. 138-204. This paper is highly recom-mended to the reader (particularly pp. 131-154) because of the detail it offers on the fall and the eventual decline into better health.

Masons would be a calamity to any author aspiring to write in English, and that Bren gun of an adjective may be left as treasure trove for some future Teutonic historian of the Craft.

Greatly daring, I suggest an old English word to describe such Craftsmen; TRADITIONER is the one I have chosen, as uncommon enough to allow of its being used Masonically in this sense, just as ANTIENT or ATHOLL has now a special connotation with Masonic students.

I suggest the term as an honourable designation for the Brethren who upheld two great traditions, loyalty to their Grand Lodge, the senior governing body in the world, and loyalty to the ancient forms of Freemasonry, matters, as we are still taught, that admit of no innovation. These Traditioners rendered to their Caesar allegiance, tribute money, and service, but not a jot more of compliance than suited their consciences; and, above all, were careful to turn a deaf ear to the voice of the charmer who said he knew a ritual better and more refined than they had learnt in youth (pp. 139-140).

But 1943 was the year when he also became an employee of the Grand Lodge of England, so perhaps he felt that tact was required. Lepper avoids the social and political issues of the times—of then and his own life. However Ireland was 'colonised' by the English, and no matter how refined life in Dublin was, the English considered the Irish inferior. And when Lepper writes of Scotland we need to remember that in 1745 Bonnie Prince Charlie marched south into England, so the Scots were not popular in England. Scotland was occupied by the English Army (colonised?) and the wearing of tartan banned until 1823.

It is also essential to remember that there was no published ritual until 1730, and no other guidance after that until further exposures after 1760; and also numerous lodges which had been happily working, but not affiliated to the Grand Lodge in London. They could therefore do as they chose, and they did, and there was no guidance from London. One must remember that there is traditionally resentment against governance from those in power in London amongst those from Northern England, Scotland, Ireland, and Wales, but the Irish have traditionally received scant welcome in England.

The Decline of the London Grand Lodge 1739–1762 —Disinterested Grand Masters?

Perhaps the one greatest sign of decay was the manner in which, after 1730, the 'traditional' installation day of St John (the Baptists) Day were abandoned.

The 29th day of January 1730

The R[t] Hon[ble] the Lord Kingston Grand Master having appointed this day for holding the Grand Annual Feast according to ancient Custom the same was conducted in the following manner.

The Lord Kingston Grand Master attended by his Grand Officers waited on the Duke of Norfolk the Grand Master elect at his Grace's House in S' James' Square at Eleven o'thc Clock in the Morning. where they were met by many Persons of Quality and Gentry being Masons, who has coaches in Town and about one o' the. Clock made the following Procession to Merchant Taylors Hall in the City where they Dined.[2]

The event got grander year by year and the date of the installation meeting passed further away from the 27th December. Sadler says it best:

"Our first Grand Master (Anthony Sayer) was elected and installed on St. John Baptist's Day, 1717, and this day was adhered to by the Grand Lodge for the installation of his successors until 1725, when ' being unprovided with a new noble Grand Master, the officers were continued six months longer'. Lord Paisley was, however, installed on the 27th December following; Lord Inchiquin on the 27th February, 1727; Lord Coleraine on the 27th December in the same year; and Lord Kingston on the 27th December, 1728 ... The eighteen installations between 1730 and 1753 appear to have taken place on a day best suited to the convenience of the noble personage most concerned, and not one on either of the popular Saints' Days. The Antients from the very first seem to have been most scrupulous in selecting one or other of these days for their Grand ceremonials."[3]

And John Heron Lepper sums up the final low point precisely:

None of these Scottish chiefs distinguished himself as an inspiring leader, to say the least of it; but the nadir of the Grand Lodge was probably reached in the time of Lord Byron, who was elected Grand Master on the 30th April, 1747, and continued in office till the 20th March, 1752, when he handed over to Lord Carysfort.

Lord Byron attended only three meetings of Grand Lodge during his reign of five years; but this was not a bad average, for during the

---

2   *QCAntigrapha*. vol.10. Minutes of the GL of Freemasons of England 1723–1739, p. 116. 29 January 1730.

3   Thomas Sadler, *Masonic Facts and Fictions*. p. 163.

same period there were no more than nine assemblies of the governing body: the Grand Feast, 30th April, 1747; 16th December, 1747; 7th March, 1748; 22nd December, 1748; 26th May, 1749; 25th June, 1750; 4th September, 1751; 24th October, 1751: and 16th March, 1752. Lord Byron had an additional excuse for nonattendance, for during most of the time he had been out of England.[4]

Not only were incoming Grand Masters not respecting the traditional day for installation; they also started to have ever grander processions through the streets of London from their residence to the place of the meeting and the fast that followed. The first example is quoted below, but the practice got 'grander' year by year—eventually producing copycat events like the march of the Scald Miserables. One was detailed in the London Daily Post of March 20, 1742:

> Yesterday, some mock Freemasons marched through Pall Mall and the Strand as far as Temple Bar in procession, first went fellows on jackasses, with cows' horns in their hands, then a kettle drummer on a jackass having two butter firkins for kettle-drums; then followed two carts drawn by jackasses, having in them the stewards with several badges of their Order; then came a mourning-coach drawn by six horses, each of a different colour and size, in which were the Grand Master and Wardens; the whole attended by a vast mob. They stayed without Temple Bar till the Masons came by, and paid their compliments to them, who returned the same with an agreeable humor that possibly disappointed the witty contriver of this mock Scene, whose misfortune is that, though he has some merit, his subjects are generally so ill chosen that he loses by it as many friends as other people of more judgment gain.

But it showed that the excessive opulence of masonic processions was perceived by the public to be so gross that they held mock processions ridiculing the masons.

It was perhaps inevitable that this decay would also have brought with it discontent. Indeed there is a statement reflecting the Brethren's annoyance which appeared in the *Multa Paucis* of ca.1763 which reads as follows:

> *N.B.* Grand Master *Byron* was very inactive. Several Years passed by without his coming to a Grand Assembly, nay even neglected to nominate his successor.

---

4   John Heron Lepper. The Traditioners. *AQC* vol.56 (1943), p.150. This paper is highly recommended to the reader (particularly pp. 131-154) because of the detail it offers on the fall and the eventual decline into better health.

up over against Somerset House, in the STRAND on the twenty Seventh of April An° 1742.

Part of a long engraving of the Scald Miserables procession 1742

The Fraternity, finding themselves entirely neglected, it was the Opinion of many old Masons to have a consultation about electing a new and more active Grand Master, and assembled for that Purpose, according to an Advertisement, which accidentally was perceived by our worthy Brother *Thomas Manningham*, M. D. who, for the Good of Masonry, took the trouble upon him to attend at this Assembly, and gave the Fraternity the most prudent Advice for their future Observance, and lasting Advantage. They all submitted to our worthy Brother's superior Judgement, the Breach was healed.[5]

Alas the accuracy of this statement made as part of the notes in *Multa Paucis* on the Grand Assembly of 1747 has yet to be proved (or disproved) by any other evidence, but it could easily have happened.

Discontent and Decay

Lepper is certainly correct in identifying this group as he does. After all the choice was between the Huguenot Protestant correctness of Dr Desaguliers the scientist and the ordinary mason in the majority of lodges. So Lepper's definition

---

5   *The Complete Freemason, or Multa Paucis for Lovers of Secrets*, ca. 1763-1764. p.105.

remains valid. He also makes the point that both Ireland and Scotland worked close to 'the Antient tradition,' and we agree with that conclusion. The matter became very visible because there was an agreement made in 1772 between the three Grand Lodge of, the Antients in England and the Grand Lodges of Scotland and Ireland that they would 'recognise each other' (this was done by the regular exchanging of minutes). And this situation continued until 1813 when the two English Grand Lodge merged.

The authors decided not to change Lepper's use of the word 'Traditioner,' because that would simply complicate understanding. But it is clear that within masonry 'a governing elite' was not in touch with a growing numbers of masons, nor with changes within society or the economic migrants who flocked to English cities. This resulted in the Antients Grand Lodge being created in 1751.

There was however another group, one which Lepper was not concerned with, and that is the innovative brothers in London who followed up on Samuel Prichard's *Masonry Dissected* and invented the Scots Masters degree, the Royal Arch degree, and the Harodim of Kilwinning degree(s) et al.

If one looked at the key active members of the Grand Lodge of England then it is clear that a number of them were members of the Royal Society, and they were also keen to support the Hanoverian King George. But they would also have been very aware of the still present religious tensions that remained in English Society. After all the Catholic James II departed in 1689, to be replaced by the Protestant joint monarchs of William III and Mary II who reigned from 1689–1702. It is probable that the creation of a masonic Grand Lodge in London was also seen as being one way of strengthening the Hanoverian dynasty. It is likely that taking new aspects pf Freemasonry back to biblical Old Testament history might introduce ideas that ran counter to the Protestant desire to see a plainer religion practiced in whitewashed churches and the intent of those governing masonry in London to see that as being desirable.

What was clear was that in 1730 Dr Desaguliers and Grand Lodge were opposed to the publication of masonic exposures, but were unable to prevent their publication. The position of the Grand Lodge of England to oppose the practice of 'other degrees' remained firm. While England opposed the growth and spread of 'higher degrees,' similar problems were also being experienced in Ireland, Scotland, and in North America. These problems were not resolved until a variety of other masonic bodies were created in all these countries to bring eventually a structure and order into freemasonry. These bodies are mostly still recognizable today. The situation in Europe was completely different.

Masonic Decline in England after 1738 till around 1760

If one looks at *Lanes List of Lodges* it is all too easy to think that freemasonry progressed continuously from strength to strength, but that has not always been the reality. John Lane also produced a companion volume – a *Handy Book to the List of Lodges*[6]and at the rear he tabulated the number of lodges by year. It does not of course take account of defunct lodges that had not been erased but the figures are indicative. Looking at the growth of freemasonry after 1730 we can see that between then and 1738 the number of lodges more than doubled, both in London and in the rest of the country. In essence it was in 1738 when the second Book of Constitutions was published (and in which the degree of Master Mason was officially acknowledged) and of course there was a 1740 re-numeration of the lodges when all trace of 'Masters Lodges' finally vanished. So we can safely conclude that these were times when freemasonry was popular and expanding. But that growth was not going to continue.

Year	London	Country	Foreign	Total	
1729	46	13	2	61	
1738	104	48	11	168	
1741	115	56	18	189	Peak year
1750	69	68	26	163	
1760	99	88	61	248	
1766	120	160	81	381	
1771	157	164	100	421	Peak year

Number of Moderns Lodges in the Grand Lodge of England.
Ex Lane Handy Book to the List of Lodges.

But some facts are startling if one has not seen them before. Between 1740 and 1750 only two new lodges were warranted in London while the number of lodges shrank from 115 in 1740 down to 69 in 1751, and only peaking again in 1771 when the London total reached a peak of 157 lodges.

It is worth reflecting that by 1791 there were 501 lodges and by 1813 it had grown to 569; however, that number fell to 388 in the first post Union list of 1814 after all the defunct lodges (especially foreign ones) who had not communicated for years were removed.

1747–1752 – The Low Point of the Grand Lodge of England

Perhaps Lord Byron's time as Grand Master was the lowest point. He was installed in 1747 and installed his successor five years later. Meetings were rare

---

6   John Lane, *Handy Book to the List of Lodges*, 1889.

and Lord Byron himself only attended twice. While the Deputy and Grand Secretary probably did what they could there was no leadership. Here one must mention the formation in 1739 of the Antients 'Grand Committee' and which culminated in 1751 with the formation of the Antients Grand Lodge, and which was active in creating more lodges, including those Irish and Scots who had migrated to London, together with those of the classes who were less 'establishment.' One must also remember that then the Irish were considered by (most) English to be socially inferior, and for that reason were not accepted into society or into English Lodges.

In *Multa Paucis for Lovers of Secrets* was published in 1764 and contains, in the chronology, and sandwiched between words on the arrival of Lord Byron as Grand Master in 1752 and the installation of his successor in 1754:

> N. B. Grand Master Byron was very inactive. Several Years passed .by without his coming to a Grand Assembly, nay even neglected to nominate his successor.
>
> The Fraternity, finding themselves intirely neglected, it was the Opinion of many old Masons to have a consultation about elect-ing a new and more active **Grand Master** and assembled for that Purpose, according to an Advertisement, which accidentally was perceived by our worthy Brother Thomas Manningham, M. D. who, for the Good of Masonry, took the trouble upon him to at-tend at this Assembly, and gave the Fraternity the most prudent Advice for their future Observance, and lasting Advantage. They all submitted to our worthy Brother's superior Judgement, the Breach was healed.[7]

Sadly it comes without a date or the name of the paper and it could not be found in the newspaper archive in 2021; but the mere fact that more than a decade later the dissatisfaction of those times had been sufficiently remembered to cause the words to be printed.

The Seeds of Recovery

It was probably the appointment of Thomas Manningham who was Deputy Grand Master from 1752 to 1757 who started to bring the rules and regula-tions of Grand Lodge back into better order. But it was probably the election of Washington Shirley, the third Earl Ferrers, in 1752. He had become an admiral in the navy and clearly a better grasp of good order and administration. He was in turn replaced by Lord Blayney who was Grand Master from May 1764 until April 1767.

---

7 *The Complete Free Mason or Multa Paucis for Lovers of Secrets,* (1764), p. 105.

It was Lord Blayney who was the first 'Modern' to realise that the growth of other degrees was inevitable and would continue. And that he could bring some order into freemasonry by creating, on 22nd July 1766 the "Grand & Royal Chapter of the Royal Arch of Jerusalem."

But it is most likely that all the problems and difficulties of discovering how to run a voluntary organisation that spread its tentacles across England was too novel, and the social and political complexities to pressing to easily succeed. The decline in membership was primarily responsible for the absence of Pocket Companions between 1736 and 1754, and the absence of any ritual exposures between 1730 and 1760. If there is only a small market, then for a printer or publisher there can only be a small profit.

This did not stop a few innovators from exploring the events surrounding the building and rebuilding of the Temple at Jerusalem and creating a wealth of new degrees. Sadly we did not know who they were, and we apologise that we still have no clues as to who those London masonic innovators were. That is a challenge that we leave to those who follow us.

The Arrival of Cadwallader Lord Blayney

In 1762 the fifth Earl Ferrers, Washington Shirley, became Grand Master. He was the younger son of the third Earl Ferrers and thus had to make his own way in life, which he did by joining the Royal Navy and where he attained the rank of Admiral. So he reached the rank of Admiral and would have seen freemasonry in action on many places while in the navy, and of course he brought to his freemasonry (one assumes) both strategy, task, and personal skills. He served for two years and in his place Cadwallader Lord Blayney was elected as Grand Master.

One is justified in asking how we go from an English Admiral to an Irish soldier as Grand Master.[8] The answer is probably simple because the Blayney estates were in County Monaghan and it was there that a younger branch of the Shirley family had settled.

Where Blayney was made a mason is unknown, it could have been an Irish military lodge or maybe in America where he was a visitor at Royal Exchange Lodge (now St Johns No.1) Boston, Massachusetts in 1745. Back in London he was installed at the first Master of the New Lodge at the Horn Tavern (No.313) on 4th April 1764 and on the 8th May 1765 elected Grand Master, upon the recommendation of Earl Ferrers.

---

8   John Heron Lepper, 'The Traditioners,' *AQC* vol.56 (1943), pp. 153-160. This examined the life of Lord Blayney at length.

Blayney continued to be Grand Master until the 27th April, 1767, when he was succeeded by the young Duke of Beaufort; and during those three years his behaviour enables us to draw, with some certainty, inferences about his sentiments and motives: he seems to have aimed at two objects, good repute and extended power for the Body of which he was Grand Master, and the restoration of the Antient forms of ritual in those Lodges that had discarded them.

As regards the first of these aims, while Blayney undoubtedly strove for reconciliation and the consequent re-establishment of the original Grand Lodge as the sole Masonic authority in this country, he may also have owned the higher ambition of erecting it as the supreme Masonic authority in the world; if so, he was entitled to his dream.

That Blayney did not wholly succeed in his aims is beside the point. While it is easy for us to see now, with the added wisdom of nearly two centuries behind us, that the two matters of ritual and supreme authority in England were so interdependent as to be inseparable, to have held such a point of view in the seventeen-sixties postulates so much vision and intellectual power that I find it hard to give Blayney all the credit for the idea. Without the slightest wish to disparage my countryman, my suggestion is that he was inspired by brains much more astute than his own; but in any case no small *kudos* is duo to a man in high place who accepts and acts on good advice with tact, dignity, and firmness, all of which qualities distinguished Blayney during his term of office.

The first hint of his leanings in ritual matters comes with his re-appointment of Colonel John Salter as Deputy Grand Master; for Salter was also a Military Mason, who rose from the ranks to die a Major-General, and, as I have already stated, it can be taken as axiomatic that all Military Masons were Antient in the matter of ritual, whatever their Constitution.* According to Noorthouk, Blayney was out of England for the whole of 1764 and most of 1765, so Salter's office was no sinecure.[9]

Moderns and Antients in competition

The year in which Lord Blayney became Grand Master was the year in which Laurence Dermott published the 2nd Edition of *Ahiman Rezon*. So Blayney as well as reinvigorating the Grand Lodge of England had to compete for members

---

9   John Heron Lepper, 'The Traditioners,' *AQC* vol.56 (1943), p. 156.

from the Antients who were seeking members from a broader section of society and had also included the Royal Arch as a unique part of their offering. So Blayney took the sensible step of also creating the possibility for Moderns brothers to take the Royal Arch degrees and he also took Thomas Dunckerley into the Grand Chapter. While Dunckerley was active in travelling round the country for the next thirty or so years in many cases while he was Provincial Grand Master in eight counties, there were only one or two Chapters in that county. There is also a telling quote by the Grand Secretary Samuel Spencer in his famous quote in a letter that the Moderns were 'Neither Arch, Royal Arch, or Antient.' Thus we can conclude there were different factions within the Grand Lodge of England and one of those accepted that the Royal Arch was something masonic and another that rejected all other degrees than the three Craft degrees. And outside the Grand Lodge there were the Antients. The matter was put into sharp focus in 1772 when the Grand Lodges of the Antients, Ireland and Scotland agreed to be in 'Constant Cooperation' with each other. They agreed to exchange all their proceedings—so some form of recognition, and one which excluded the Moderns.

1730-1740 Masters Lodges

115		Scotts Mason Lodge, Devil Temple Bar	2ᵈ and 4ᵗʰ Munday	
116		Masters Masons Lodge, Butcher Row	2ᵈ and 4ᵗʰ Friday	
117		Masters Masons Lodge, Strand	1ˢᵗ Munday Maʃʰ Lodge D. 3⁴ Munday in ʃ Winter	

ex Hughans facsimile Engraved List of Lodges 1734 (pub 1889)

The name 'Scott's Mason Lodge No.115' has acquired an almost mythical status among those who search for the early roots of higher degrees. While one can read in Robert Freke Gould's *History of Freemasonry* about the Scots Masters degree it is only the discoveries of the past decade that have brought further light to this degree.

But that enigma is itself within a further enigma, that of 'Masters Lodges.' The doyen of *Lists of Lodges*, John Lane, devoted a paper to this subject in volume 1 of AQC.[1] No attempt to consider the development of masonry can be without a consideration of Masters Lodges. The idea of a Masters Lodge seems to commence *only* after the publication of Masonry Dissected by Samuel Prichard in December 1730.

In the years between 1730 and 1738 there were 73 new lodges created in London, and of those 16 (22%) described themselves in the Engraved Lists variously as Masters Lodges, Master Masons Lodges, (one) English Masons Lodge and a Scott's Masons Lodge, this latter held at The Devil, Temple Bar, London.

There is little evidence surviving which sheds any light at all on exactly what

---

1   Lanes List of Lodges is available as a pdf from archive.org and updates lists can be interrogated at https://www.dhi.ac.uk/lane/ Lane also produced a supplementary guide to help users of his first edition, this contains plenty of detailed information and tables of the number of lodges by year. *Handy Book to the Lists of Lodges* (1889).

'Masters Lodges' did when they met. But it provides valuable context to take a look at the challenges experienced by the Grand Lodge of England (GLE) from its start in 1717 or 1721 through to around 1740. Gaining an understanding of the challenges faced by the Grand Lodge is important because otherwise it is simply too easy to judge then by the standards that apply to the organisation of Grand Lodge today—that is some 300 years later.

Grand Lodge kept no record of its activities until 1723 when William Cowper the first Grand Secretary (1723-1726), He was followed by Edward Wilson February 1726–1727, William Reid December 1727–1733 and John Revis March 1734–1757.

Some of the challenges they faced are recorded in the first Minute Book[2] and some of them are listed below.

> And the Question was moved.
> That it is not in the Power of any person, or Body of men, to make any Alteration or Innovation in the Body of Masonry without the Consent first obtained of the Annual Grand Lodge.
> And the Question being put accordingly: Resolved in the affirmative.
> (24 June 1723 p.50)

> 2ⁿᵈ That no Brother belonging to any Lodge within the Bills of Mortality be admitted to any Lodge as a visitor unless personally known to some Brother of that Lodge where he visits and that no Strange Brother however Skilled in Masonry be admitted Without taking the Obligation over again, unless he be introduced or vouched for by Some Brother known to, and approved of by the majority of the Lodge. And whereas Some Masons have met and formed a Lodge without the Grand Maᵗʳ leave.
> Agreed: That no such person be admitted into Regular Lodges. (19 February 1724 p.56)

It is important to remember that even though the Grand Lodge only saw its 'territory' as being in London, there were in the City other lodges not affiliated, and other Masons were able to gain admission without proper checks. And of course there were no 'Grand Lodge Certificates' in those early days. This problem of unregistered Brothers seeking entrance remained a perennial problem that was repeatedly referred to. And indeed it is all related the ongoing problems of creating and managing efficient record keeping.

---

2 The Minutes of the Grand Lodge of Freemasons of England 1723–1739. *QCA* Vol.10 (1913). https://www.quatuorcoronati.com/wp-content/uploads/2016/12/QCA_VOL-10-compressed.pdf

That if any Brethren shall meet Irregularly and make Masons at any place within ten miles of London the persons present at the making (The New Brethren Excepted) shall not be admitted even as Visitors into any Regular Lodge whatsoever unless they come and make Such Submission to the Grand Ma^r and Grand Lodge as they shall think fit to impose upon them. (21 November 1724 p.59)

The two quotes below, both from the Grand Lodge meeting of 17th April 1728, serve to introduce the next part of the story:

> Then most of the Lodges present delivered the Dates of the time of their being Constituted into Lodges, in order to have Precedency in the printed Book.

> The Grand Master having appointed Brother William Reid to be Secretary to the Grand Lodge, the Deputy Grand Master signified his Lordship's pleasure of the same to the Brethren, and further acquainted them that his Lord^p notwithstanding such appointment, would not insist upon Brother Reid's being Secretary without their Unanimous Consent.
> To which they all agreed Nemine con.

Every Grand Secretary's Nightmare

The minutes in the first and second Minute Book are a contrasting mix of matters of charity, finance but occasionally also of administration. The fact that the Grand Secretary wrote all the copies of minutes needed in his own hand seems bizarre and the next fact that the Grand Master had to pay the bill for all these copies seems odd. And of course while the number of Lodges in 1728 was circa 57, by 1731 it had grown to 83 and by 1739 further to 175 lodges. It indicates some increasing degree of disorder, and one must also wonder at the cost of delivery, especially where it was to Lodges outside London.

> It was observed that the Minutes of the Quarterly Communication had not been delivered at the several Lodges in due time, the writing them taking up so much of the Secretary's time, and printing them being thought inconvenient, Several things were offered to the Consideration of the Grand Lodge thereupon, in order to remedy those Inconveniences for the future as also to lessen the Expence to the Grand Master.
> Br Pine proposed that the Minutes of each Quarterly Communication should for the future be etched by him who is a Mason and very well known to the Grand Lodge and might be trusted with anything relating to the Craft.

Br Pine being called up, and asked how long he should be about such a thing. He said he would undertake to etch the Plate and have them printed off in three days.

The Question being put

It was Resolved that Br Pine should for the future etch the Minutes as aforesaid, and that the Secretary of the Grand Lodge should attend at the printing them off and when the Number directed were done, he was to bring the said minutes and the Plates to the Grand Master or his Deputy in order to have the Plates destroyed. (14 May 1731 p.207)

John Pine (1690–1756)[3] was an engraver with a thriving practice and is perhaps best remembered by Freemasons for his frontispiece to Andersons Constitutions 1723, and his skills were appreciated by Grand Lodge where he at one time held the office of Marshall. But on his own account he also published engraved lists of lodges. These must have had great utility for many brothers because lodges changed their place of meeting with some frequency and then the only alternative to a printed list was word of mouth. But he always seemed willing to help.

The first quotation offers a newer technology to solve the problem by speeding up the process. However it did not solve the problem, because two years later the complaints were regarding slow or non-delivery especially to country lodges.[4]

Complaint being made by several Masters of Lodges that the Minutes and Proceedings of Quarterly Communications and Grand Lodges had not been sent to their respective Lodges as usual to the great Discouragement to Masonry in general, but especially to the Country Lodges.

The Dep Grand Master observed that the number of Lodges being so much increased That the Expence of sending the Minutes to each particular Lodge is become a Charge too burthensom for any Grand Master Therefore Proposed. That the Consideration of that matter should be referred to the next Committee of Charity also to ascertain the Charge of every Grand Master for the future, who arc to consider thereof and report their Opinion therein at the next Quarterly Communication. Agreed Nemine con. (13 December 1733 p.237)

---

3   Andrew Prescott, John Pine—Sociable Craftsman, *MQ Magazine* No.10, July 2004. http://www.mqmagazine.co.uk/issue-10/p-07.php

4   Ironically the self-same problem remains to this day. The Quarterly Communications are now only available as a pdf and sent electronically—but getting a copy is impossible and both emails and letters of complaint to Grand Lodge remain unanswered.

Bro Pine's name crops up again. This time regarding the number of changes he had to make to his engraved lists because of the changes by Lodges of the day or place of meetings. This highlights the fact that the engraved lists were a commercial production by the printer and not a publication of Grand Lodge. But the Grand Secretary must have faced a nightmare every meeting trying to work out who had paid dues or made a contribution of the charities—what a Secretary needed was a list!

> The Proposal of Bro: John Pine for his being paid by every Lodge that should remove from one house to another 2 s. 6d & by every Lodge that should change the times of their Meeting for the Trouble & Expense of making the necessary alterations in the engraved List of Lodges referred from the said Committee was unanimously agreed to. (13 April 1739, p.314)

This issue was first addressed in 1729 when William Read got his list up to date and it was agreed that each lodge would keep the same number until the next remuneration undertaken by the Grand Secretary. So when a lodge was removed there would now be a gap in the numbering of any published lists of lodges in for some years. Perhaps more to the point of this research, the Grand Secretary would not allocate any new numbers until the next renumeration. The lists of lodges were engraved and published by the printer, on his own account and for his own profit; thus for any new lodges the engraver simply added them to the bottom of his list and allocated the next number to that lodge. If you were a newly formed Lodge then literally a note from the lodge to the printer (enclosing 2s 6d) was probably sufficient to be on the next annual list of lodges. Just for the record after 1729 there were renumerations in 1740, 1745, 1770, 1780, 1781, 1814, 1834, 1832, and 1863.

Master's Lodges with no Warrants

If we have demonstrated that the administration of Grand Lodge was lacking in the period after the publication of Masonry Dissected in 1730, we must add in that both before and after this date Grand Lodge struggled with irregular making of Masons, and who it was unable to refuse entrance to its Quarterly Communications, then other matters would also not be under control.

It is interesting to note that all the lodges who were shown in the engraved lists as being Masters Lodges were formed AFTER 1730. It is assumed by all who have investigated this that they were a facility to allow Lodges on dates other than their normal meeting dates to confer the 'new third degree'—we see no reason to disagree with this conclusion. By avoiding official working days they presumably avoided censure by any visiting masonic dignitaries. Sadly no evidence has ever been found either to prove or disprove this theory, but to us it seems a likely explanation.

However after 1739 all the Masters Lodges vanished from the Engraved Lists, so in effect the official renumeration published in 1740 marked the end of 'Masters Lodges' in any published lists. But there were other significant changes because when Anderson rewrote his Constitutions in 1738 he both acknowledges both the Master Mason degree and the death of Hiram.

In Charge IV we can read "...he may become an Enter'd Prentice, or a Free-Mason of the lowest degree, and upon his due improvement a Fellow Craft and a Master Mason" and goes on to say "The Wardens are chosen from among the Master Masons" (p.145).

And in the Traditional History we can read that after the completion of the Temple of Solomon that "But their Joy was soon interrupted by the sudden Death of their dear Master HIRAM ABIFF,..." (p.14).

While Grand Lodge might have ranted about Masonry Dissected in 1730, by the end of the decade they had lost the battle, and the choice made by the Brethren was to accept and to prefer the 'new' degree of Master Mason, the death of Hiram Abiff and the Loss of the Word had prevailed. Maybe the need for Masters Lodges had simply disappeared, so their removal from the Engraved Lists was a formality.

But in the Lists there remain four 'Masters Lodges' that were without warrants from Grand Lodge to authorise their work—they were shown on John Pine's engraved list for 1734 as:

> 115 Scott's Masons Lodge, Devil, Temple Bar 2nd and 4th Munday
> 116 Masters Masons Lodge, Butcher Row 2nd and 4th Friday
> 117 Masters Masons Lodge, Strand 1st Munday Mastrs Lodge Do
> 3rd Munday in Winter
> 120 Oate's Coffee House, MASTERS LODGE, Great Wild Street
> 1st and 3rd Sunday

So we can see from the 1734 list that the entries for lodge 115, 116, and 117 were added between the warrant dates of new warranted lodge 114 (23rd March 1733) and 118 (26th July 1733) – so in a three month period. Likewise the lodge at Oates Coffee House was added to the engraved list between 1st August and 22nd December 1733. These four very odd additions appeared, and no satisfactory explanation has ever been offered. What can be said?

Masters Masons Lodges Nos. 116 and 117

In the Proceedings of Grand Lodge for 24 June 1735, "An address from the Body of Gentlemen who had served the Society in the Quality of Stewards directed to the Grand Lodge was then read praying certain Privileges in consideration of such their Services &c." The minutes went on to repeat their three claims, and those are repeated below.

The position of Steward was then, and still is today, a sought after honour. And the Stewards sought some privileges

1. That they might meet monthly or otherwise as a Lodge of Master Masons (under the denomination of the Stewards Lodge) and be enrolled among the number of the Lodges as usual with the times of their Meeting.

2. That they might be so distinguished (since all the Grand Offices are for the future appointed to be chosen out of their Number; and in order to qualify themselves to the right discharge of these Officers. When called to the same) send a Delegation of twelve from the whole body of Stewards to each Quarterly Communication, all the twelve to have Voices, and all that come to pay half a crown apiece towards the Expense of that Occasion.

3. That no person who had not served the Society as a Steward might be permitted at a Quarterly Communication or elsewhere to wear their coloured Ribbands or Aprons, but.....[5]

They were granted some of these privileges but on 11 December 1735, there was a counter petition presented by several Masters of Lodges against the privileges granted to the Steward's Lodge at the last Quarterly Communication and read and then put to the vote and the minutes tell an interesting story:

> In the course of collecting the votes on this occasion there appeared so much confusion that it was not possible for the Grand Officers to determine with any certainty what the Numbers on either side of the Question were, they were therefore obliged to dismiss the Debate and close the Lodge. [6]

Whatever one might think this was clearly one group aiming to take greater control of Grand Lodge, and it clearly did not meet with general approval. Such minutes always present events in a somewhat sanitised way, but clearly there was great disorder to the extent that the only option was to close the meeting. Such

---

5   *Minutes of the Grand Lodge of Freemasons of England*, QCA vol 10: 257.

6   *Minutes of the Grand Lodge of Freemasons of England*, QCA vol 10: 263.

chaos is rare, so the event was clearly volatile.

There are however entries for two 'Masters Masons Lodges' recorded, no.116 meeting at the Bear and Harrow in Butchers Row, and no.117 at the King's Arms in the Strand.

No.116 first appeared in the 1733 Engraved List. Lane tells us that there was no date of formation, and that it never paid for a Constitution (warrant), that it had no dates for a general meeting and never attended Grand Lodge. It was struck out in ink on the Official List in 1736.

No.117 appeared only in the 1734 and 1735 Engraved Lists. Again there is no date of foundation, it never paid for a Constitution, and never attended Grand Lodge. It had no days for a general meeting. It had vanished from the 1736 Engraved List. Lane notes that the Lodge that took its place was the Stewards Lodge which met at the Shakespeare's Head in Covent Garden—and its warrant was granted on 25 June 1735—the day immediately following the Quarterly Communication at which the Stewards were accorded their privileges. So here were two Lodges in the Engraved Lists that really were only for Master Masons —and whose purpose was not to confer the third degree. It was allocated the same number 117, and then in 1792 "placed at the head of the list by order of the Grand Lodge" and without a number—a position it retains to this day.

As a side note, the Steward's job was to facilitate the Annual Installation and the Feast, and it was a sought after position. These Stewards Lodges still exist today, and members wear not a regular blue trimmed apron but one edged in red (the authors cannot guess whether this use of red was then seen as a mark of superiority as it was in France).

There is no information found on the lodge at Oate's Coffee House, only that it was struck out in 1836. That seems to deal satisfactorily with those two problem lodges.

Scotts Masons Lodge No.115

Removing these three 'intruders' from the four lodges without warrants just leaves No.115 Scotts Masons Lodge for consideration. John Lane's thoughts, are worth repeating, because they represented the commonly held view until recently:

> FIRST, as to No. 115, the " Scott's Masons Lodge," at the Devil
> Tavern, Temple Bar. It appears, for the first time, in Rawlinson's
> List of 1733, and next in Pine's Engraved List of 1734, without a
> date. It never paid for a Constitution, but, from its position and
> number, was evidently placed on the Roll in 1733. It continued at

the Devil Tavern, meeting on the "2d & 4ᵗʰ Monday," until 1736, when it removed to "Daniel's Coffee House, Temple Bar." We have seen that it never attended Grand Lodge, and it was erased (i.e., struck out in ink), from the Official List in 1736.

Now, at the same "Devil Tavern within Temple Bar," Lodge No. 8 (of 25th April, 1722), was located from 1729 to 1736, meeting on the "1st and 3d Monday," i.e., on alternate Mondays to No. 115, and, like No.115, it removed to "Daniel's Coffee House, within Temple Bar," in 1736, where it met on the 1st Monday only.

I consider the fact of the meetings of both Lodges having been held at the same place from 1733 to 1736, and that both removed in the same year to another place in common, must be more than a mere coincidence; for it suggests a very strong presumption that both Lodges were composed of the same members, one of them being designated by the peculiar, and as yet unexplained, name of a "Scott's Masons Lodge."[7]

Lodge No.8 was also known as the French Lodge and has in the past been linked with No.115, simply because they both met in the same tavern (but with no evidence). The chapter dealing with the Union French Lodge will clarify matters.

The Union French Lodge No.98, at Prince Eugene's Coffee House, St Albans Street. Constituted August 1732, renumbered No.87 in 1740, and surrendered its warrant in 1753. The lodge met variously at:

Prince Eugen's Coffee House, St. Albans Street	1732
Duke of Lorraine, Suffolk St	1733
King's Arms, Picccadilly	1736
Union Coffee House Upper end of Haymarket	1739
Hoop & Grapes, Greek St, Soho	1741
Cardigan, Charing Cross	1742
Greyhound, Strand	1743
Meuse Coffee House	1745
Lebeck's Head, Strand	1745

One cannot lose sight of the fact that ALL the Masters Lodges that were named in the Engraved Lists only existed in London, so clearly other conditions applied in London which did not apply elsewhere in the country. Maybe it is sufficient to ponder that in London Lodges were under a somewhat closer scrutiny by

---

7   John Lane, Masters Lodges *AQC* vol.1, p. 174. Lane does give a list of members of No8 and attempts to link Lodges No. 8 & 115. However we present other evidence which points strongly to Union French Lodge no.98 as being the focus of distribution both of Craft masonry and higher degrees to other countries.

Grand Lodge, and that Masonic politics were more active.

Postscript

The paper much referred to in this chapter was delivered by John Lane on the Festival of St John meeting of Quatuor Coronati Lodge in 1888. In response part of WJ Hughan's comments are worth repeating—for he sets forth the conundrum which has remained for over 130 years.

> Bro. Hughan quoted from the "*St. James' Evening Post*," of Dec. 19th, 1738, as follows, being an early instance of a Masters' Lodge being held:- "We hear that on Sunday last there was a numerous meeting of Master Masons at the Bear Tavern in the Strand, who have agreed to hold a Master Masons' Lodge there for the future, every Sunday night on extraordinary business!"
>
> Those familiar with Bro. Gould's grand Masonic History would he aware that our W.M. fixes 1740 as the year when the "Scots' degrees" were fabricated, so that the "Scotts" Masons Lodge of 1733 had no connection with that novelty.
>
> In 1741 we meet with the "Royal *Order* of Scotland" in London; in 1746, our Bro. Goldney (in his excellent History), tells us of brethren *made* Scotts' Masons at Salisbury; Bro. W. Logan has traced the "Highrodiam" in the same year, at Durham; and Bro. R. Hudson, the "Harodim" at Sunderland, in 1756. The Royal Arch is alluded to so early as 1744, in print. All these degrees, however, came years after 1733, the period of advent of No. 115.[8]

That represents the conundrum that has faced masonic researchers ever since 1888. It has however proved possible to prove that several key players were all members of the Lodge meeting at Prince Eugene's Coffee House, later called the Union French Lodge No.98—see later.

Addendum: There were two times when 'Masters Lodges' were noted, and this was the first occasion—in London between 1733 and 1739. The other occasion was between 1770 and 1800, and they appeared in various cities in England. The cause of the later 1770–1800 Masters Lodges has not been investigated in this book.

---

8   WJ Hughan, comments on a paper by John Lane 'Masters Lodges' in *AQC* vol.1 (1888), p. 176. Hughan is wrong in his claim that the 'Royal Order of Scotland' was active in London in 1741 —it was then called the HRDM of Kilwinning. See the relevant chapter for details.

The H.R.D.M., Pocket Companions and Book M

It seems important to look at various intermingling events and people, because that offers some light on how things may have developed. The role of Pocket Companions is not generally appreciated, and BookM and the Harodim of the North-East of England are probably unknown to French readers, and indeed to most British readers. It is probably that all were in some way interrelated, but over three centuries evidence has gone missing. We have tried to collate what there is and dispose of ill-considered opinions, and thus to be able to paint and alternative masonic landscape. Wherever we turned in our researches we came across fascinating individuals who travelled and carried freemasonry with them, and those in this chapter are no exception.

William Smith (b.1698– d.1741)—Inventor of the Pocket Companion for Free-Masons & Editor of Book M[1]

William Smith remains an enigma, and strangely the masonic researchers who have attempted to explore the field come to differing conclusions. But we cannot ignore him because his Pocket Companions were a real innovation and BookM offers a new light upon masonic values. Perhaps firstly we need to consider the William Smith who published in late 1734 a Book of Songs, and then early the next year published the first *Pocket Companion* in London and also in Dublin in the same year. And the 'second' William Smith who compiled *BookM: or Masonry Triumphant* in 1736 having been 'made free' in Swalwell Lodge the previous year. And the 'third' William Smith who became a member of Swalwell Lodge in the County of Durham. The probability is that they were one and the same.

It is worth listing The William Smith publications because that provides a context for the chapter.

1734 A Collection of Songs of Masons. pub London. No printer or author named; but the page numbering starts at 48 and the type matches exactly the same pages in the 1735 Pocket Companion.

1735 A Pocket Companion for Free-Masons. pub London. E. Rider, Blackmore Street, near Clare-Market. Oddly the lodges are all renumbered and NOT in the order of the engraved lists or the Collection of Songs.[2]

---

1   A scan of an original *BookM* can be downloaded at https://collections.lib.utah.edu/details?id=2 39506

2   The lodges listed in the Songbook name the Scotts Masons Lodge as 115 and name two more

1735 A Pocket Companion for Free-Masons, pub Dublin E. Rider and sold at the Printing House Georges-Lane; T Jones Clavendon-Street; and J. Pennel[3] at the Hercules, St Patrick-Street.

1736 BookM: or Masonry Triumphant. Pub Newcastle upon Tyne by Leonard Umfreville and edited by William Smith.

1736 The Free Masons Pocket Companion.[4] Pub London John Torbuck in Clare–Court, near Drury-Lane.

1738 The Free Masons Pocket Companion. Pub London John Torbuck. This edition included 'A Defence if Freemasonry.'

If they were one and the same then we can credit William Smith being the first brother to offer masonic knowledge to the ordinary brother in the form of a *Pocket Companion*, because this was an innovation that spread from England to both to Ireland and Scotland. If it was the same William Smith who spread the Harodim tradition of lectures on the history and values of Masonry through *BookM: or Masonry Triumphant*, and thus maybe also one of the key persons who spread the Harodim degree from Durham to London?

If so then it established another link, rather than just Joseph Laycock, between the Harodim of the North East of England and London. So if you follow the words below they will explain more about William Smith.

It is Cecil Adams in AQC 45 (1932) who provides copious detail on the subject of Pocket Companions, an invention of William Smith. This was the start of making masonic information available to ordinary Brother. One had to pay half a guinea (£0.55) for a copy of Andersons Constitutions 1738 but only 2 shillings (£0.10) for a Pocket Companion. But as to Smiths origins read on.

In the *Presbyterians of Ulster 1680-1730*[5] one can find "an Ulster Bookseller in Dublin, William Smith." In *Nations and Nationalism, France, Britain and Ireland*[6] (1995) "John Smith, has a contact in Amsterdam, his cousin William Smith," and also as Wm Smith Bookseller at the Hercules, Dame's St, Dublin.

—this shows that it was published in December 1934. The list of lodges in the 1735 Pocket Companion has all the lodges with different numbers – something that Smith corrected for all the later editions. This perhaps indicates some typesetting disaster at the printer, and the recovery still not being correct?

3   Note that John Pennel, also a printer, had published the first Irish Book of Constitutions in 1730

4   The list of lodges has corrected numbering and is updated

5   Robert When, *Presbyterians of Ulster 1680–1733* (2013).

6   Michel O'Dea, Kevon Whelan, *Nations & Nationalisms: France, Britain, Ireland and the Eighteenth-Century Context* Vol.86 No. 341 Spring 1997, p. 152.

THE

PREFACE.

AT the Defire of a great many of the Brethren I have compriz'd the Hiftory,
(which for the moft part is extracted
from our excellent Conftitution Book) Charges,
Regulations, Songs, Account of Lodges, and
feveral other Articles in MASONRY, not to be
found in any one of our Books yet publifhed, in a
fmall Volume eafily portable, which will render
what was before difficult to come at, and trouble-
fome to carry about, of more extenfive Ufe. For
it has been often remark'd that great Numbers,
efpecially of the younger Mafons, (who have been
defirous of knowing every thing relating to the
Craft) have been a long time fruftrated in their
Purfuits for want of fomething of this Kind, which
they might have recourfe to at any time. I need
not fay more in relation to the Book itfelf, but muft
here beg leave to exhort the Brotherhood, that a-
voiding all Innovations they adhere ftrictly to the
antient Practices of the ORDER when all the fo-
cial Virtues fhone confpicuoufly amongft us, and the
World admir'd us rather for our Veracity, Bro-
therly Love, and Relief of one another, than for
thofe invalueable Secrets which we have ever kept,
or thofe Fabricks which we have erected for the
Convenience

Then in *Ireland & French Enlight-enment 1700-1800*[7] by G Gragett & G Sheridan (1999) that:

> John Smith was in partnership with his cousin, William Bruce, from 1725 to 1738. They carried on a thriving trade in French and Dutch books, John's uncle William Smith, travelling to Holland to buy stock for the bookshop of Smith and Bruce on the Blind Quay, Dublin. This link was maintained until William returned to Dublin in 1727.

The information all points to the conclusion that the William Smith the Dublin book dealer was the same William Smith who authored the Pocket Companions and BookM. But it is worth looking in a bit more detail at the Pocket Companions because they too were innovations.

In the Preface Smith writes that:

> At the Desire of a great many of the Brethren I have compriz'd the History, (which for the most part is extracted from our excellent Constitution Book) Charges, Regulations, Songs, Account of Lodges, and several other Articles in Masonry, not to be found in any one of our Books yet published, in a small Volume easily portable, which will render what was before difficult to come at, and troublesome to carry about, of more extensive use. For it has been often remark'd that great Numbers, especially of the younger Masons, (who have been desirous of knowing everything relating to the Craft) have been a long time frustrated in their want of something of this Kind, which they might have recourse to at any time.

When one reads Andersons Constitutions of 1723 one gets, probably quite

---

7   G Gragett & G Sheridan, *Ireland & French Enlightenment 1700-1800* (1999), p.175.

rightly, the idea that Anderson was writing this to establish the credentials of Grand Lodge, and possibly also to demonstrate his own knowledge. The thought that the Constitutions were to enlighten the ordinary Brother, let alone 'younger Masons' probably did not occur to Grand Lodge; but this radical thought did come to William Smith. Anderson speedily brought his complaint to the Grand Lodge in February 1735 and they resolved that:

> It was thereupon Resolved, and Ordered That every Master and Warden present shall do all in their Power to discountenance so unfair a Practice, and prevent the said Smith's Books being bought by any Members of their respective Lodges.[8]

But near the back of the book is a three page item entitled '**A Short Charge to be given to new admitted Brethren**' which is also an innovation. It starts with the words:

> You are now admitted by the unanimous Consent of our Lodge, a *Fellow* of our Antient and Honourable SOCIETY; *Antient*, as having subsisted from time immemorial....

And it goes on:

> There are three general Heads of Duty which *MASONS* ought always to inculcate, *viz.* to *God,* our *Neighbours,* and *ourselves.*
>
> *To GOD* , in never mentioning his Name but with that reverential Awe which becomes a Creature to bear to his Creator, and to look upon him always as the *Summum Bonum* which we came into the World to enjoy; and according to that View to regulate all our Pursuits.
>
> *To our Neighbours,* in acting upon the Square, or doing as we would be done by.
>
> *To Ourselves,* in avoiding all Intemperances and Excesses, whereby we may be rendered incapable of following our Work, or led into Behaviour unbecoming our laudable Profession, and in always keeping within due Bounds, and free from all Pollution.[9]

This Charge has been seen and noted by other researchers, but strangely none of

---

8' *The Minutes of the Grand Lodge of Freemasons of England. QC Antigrapha* vol.10, p. 144, Communication of 24 February 1735.

9 This charge after Initiation first appears, not in Andersons Constitutions (1723) but in William Smiths Pocket Companion printed in London, pp. 43-35, and is repeated precisely as above in Book M: Or Masonry Triumphant 1736; the essence of this charge id still worked today in English Emulation Ritual (1986), p.99.

them have thought it to be important. The authors take a completely different point of view.

When Masonry Dissected appeared in 1730 freemasonry for the first time had a clear detail of each degree, but only in the form of a catechism. This charge in the first 1735, and in subsequent editions of the Pocket Companion is the first ever appearance in masonic ritual ceremonial of an oratorical text, and one which was concerned only with morals and ethics—the key values of freemasonry. With a few changes it is still used today, because the words written still flow off the tongue as easily as they first did then, some 290 years ago. It also appeared in BookM in the following year.

What else can we say about William Smith, perhaps we might find this quote from Laurence Dermott's Ahiman Rezon of 1756 of interest because Smith's Pocket Companion was one of his reference books:

> . . . I placed the following Works round about me, so as to be convenient to have Recourse to them as occasion should require, viz. Doctor Anderson and Mr. Spratt directly before me, Doctor D'Assigny, and **Mr. Smith** on my Right-hand, Doctor Desagulier and Mr. Pennell on my Left-hand, and Mr. Scott and Mr. Lyon behind me...[10]

Book M; Or Masonry Triumphant (1736)

Before commenting on, or presenting details of, the contents of Book M it is perhaps helpful to relate the purpose that the editor William Smith stated within the Preface to the Book.

> The following sheets I have published for the use of the Brethren inhabiting these Northern Counties; that the whole sum of their Duty, as Masons, continually about them, that they may be deter'd from doing any Thing contrary to the laudable Profession.

But it is also clear that the County of Durham while it was not without lodges did not, until the arrival of Joseph Crowley in 1732 or 1733, and then his appointment as Provincial Grand Master probably in 1734, or the constitution of the Lodge[11] of *Two'fencing Master's, Swalwell, in the Bishopric of Durham, 1st Monday June 24, 1735* have a single lodge which was part of the Grand Lodge of England. And the second lodge was only constituted on 8 March 1736. And Lecture IV of BookM is the oration read at that occasion.

---

10 Laurence Dermott, *Ahiman Rezon*, London (1756), pp. vi-vii.

11 A new Lodge is typically Consecrated, but where a lodge is pre-existing then the ceremony would be the one of Constituting a Lodge.

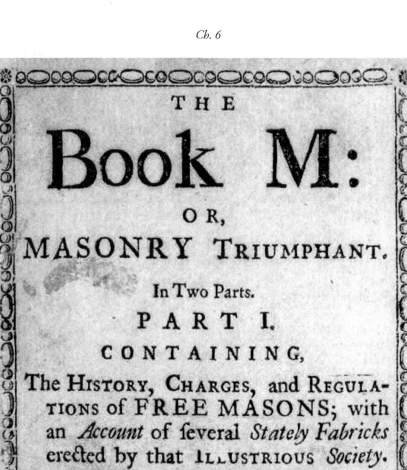

THE
Book M:
OR,
MASONRY TRIUMPHANT.

In Two Parts.

PART I.

CONTAINING,

The HISTORY, CHARGES, and REGULATIONS of FREE MASONS; with an *Account* of several *Stately Fabricks* erected by that ILLUSTRIOUS *Society.*

PART II.

Containing,

The SONGS usually sung in LODGES, PROLOGUES and EPILOGUES spoken at the *Theatres* in *LONDON* in Honour of the CRAFT; with an Account of all the Places where REGULAR LODGES are held.

Be wise as Serpents, yet innocent as Doves.

Newcastle upon *Tyne,*
Printed by LEONARD UMFREVILLE and COMPANY. M.DCC.XXXVI.

We cannot know exactly what masonic practices were so far distant from London, but the whole approach of Book M demonstrates that they were not only concerned with the formalities which are what largely appear in Anderson Constitutions but were also concerned about the values and ethics of Masonry.

Part I of BookM is masonic, and the lecture titles are below; while Part II consists of Songs Sung in Lodge, Prologues and Epilogues, and finally a list of Lodges

Lecture I.   An History of Freemasonry.

Lecture II.   On the Grand Principle, TRUTH.

Lecture III.   On Masonry. (especially the Grand Principles (Charity. To Walk Circumspectly, Live Temperately, nor ... injure our Brethren, Fidelity, Obedience to Superiors in Masonry, all things be done in Decency, Set a bright example of Goodness to the World)

Lecture IV.   Read at Gateshead, 8th March, 1736.

Lecture V.   Read in London, before a great assembly

Lecture VI.   On Ancient Buildings. (a long list and all English except five from Scotland).

Lecture VII. Collection of Memorables by Wm. Smith. (including notably the Seven Wonders of the World)

BookM: Lecture IV

In the middle of this lecture are two curious verses, and the source is stated "as the following old Verses relate." What is unusual in these two verses is that they have survived almost intact and remain today as part of the degree of the Rosy Cross (or Red Cross) in the Royal Order of Scotland some 250 years later. One might well postulate that these verses were perhaps ritual even back in 1736! Equally the sword and trowel also start to appear in rituals, and remained so to this day.

> After that the great *Nebuchadnezzar* had destroyed the Temple, and all the other glorious Edifices at *Jerusalem,* and carried away the *Jews* Captive to *Babylon, in* order to assist him in those pro-digious Works which he design'd there, as his Palace, hanging Gardens, Bridges, Temple, &c. all which he erected to display the Might of his Power, and the Glory of his Dominion, as well as to make it the Centre to which the Desires of the Earth thou'd tend, that Mankind, being allur'd thither by the Charms of the Place, he might have the better Opportunity of securing his wide extended Empire to his Posterity.

But, how vain is humane Forecast! for the Kingdom was soon snatch'd from his Race, and given to *Cyrus* the *Persian,* who, Seventy Years after their Captivity, restor'd the *Jews to* their Country, and commanded *Jerusalem* and the Temple to be rebuilt; in which Work, the M A S O N S being distres'd, did as the following old Verses relate:[12]

Book M Lecture 4 (1736)	Royal Order of Scotland[13] (1980)
When Sanballat Jerusalem *distress'd With sharp Affaults in* Nehemiah's *Time, To War and Work the* Jews *themfelves address'd,*	When Sanballat Jerusalem distressed With sharp assaults in Nehemiah's time, The Jews themselves for war or work addressed,
And did repair their Walls with Stone and Lime. One Hand the Sword against the Foe did shake, The other Hand the Trowel up did take.	And did repair their walls with stone and lime. One hand the Sword against the foe did shake, The other hand the Trowel up did take.
Of valiant Minds, lo, here a worthy Part, That quailed not with Ruin of their Wall; But Captains *bold did prove the* M A S O N S *Art: Which doth infer this Lesson unto all, That, to defend our Country dear from Harm, To War or Work we either Hand should arm.*	Oh valiant minds, lo! here's a worthy part, The Jews quailed not at ruin of their wall, But, champion-like, improved Freemason's Art; Which does infer this lesson unto all, That, to defend our country dear from harm, For war or work we either hand should arm.

But it is also worth noting that the theme of the return of the Jews from Babylon to Jerusalem, and discovering vaults and rebuilding, becomes a repeating part of many of the degrees that come between the Third Degree and the Knights Templars. **We believe its appearance in BookM is the earliest masonic appearance of these verses and theme.** It is not that Anderson did not mention the Second Temple, he did, but the detail and differences in emphasis are significant.

The Sanballat verses are referred to as 'old Verses'; so where did those lines originate? Oddly they were significantly earlier and for example can be found in Whitney's *Book of Emblems* published in 1586:

---

12 William Smith, *BookM*. Lecture IV, p. 20.

13 Ritual text ex https://www.stichtingargus.nl/ This is the 1980 wording as used in the Netherlands.

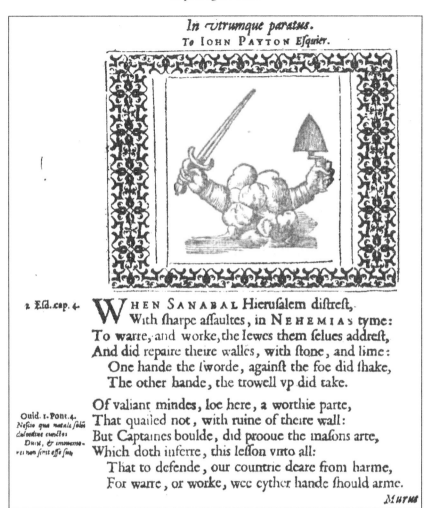

2 E.d.cap. 4.

WHEN SANABAL Hierufalem diftreft,
With fharpe affaultes, in NEHEMIAS tyme:
To warre, and worke, the Iewes them felues addreft,
And did repaire theire walles, with ftone, and lime:
One hande the fworde, againft the foe did fhake,
The other hande, the trowell vp did take.

Of valiant mindes, loe here, a worthie parte,
That quailed not, with ruine of theire wall:
But Captaines boulde, did prooue the mafons arte,
Which doth inferre, this leffon vnto all:
That to defende, our countrie deare from harme,
For warre, or worke, wee eyther hande fhould arme.

MUTUS

Lecture V

Lecture V contains a paragraph about an oddly shaped stone which after its makers were punished, was later found to be the final Cape Stone (or Coping Stone) to enable the building to be completed. The final punishment of 'Let the Names of those be erased out of the Book M would seem to imply that this was already known to the readership of Book M. It is a theme well known to any Mark Mason.

> These, with all other Articles in *Free Masonry*, have been handed down to us by a very singular and faithful Method, which (as heretofore) will continue on through all succeeding Ages, 'till that high Time, when all *faithful Brethren*, who have been obedient to the Rules and Charges given them by their Lord and Supreme Master,

shall receive the Reward of their Labours from his Divine Hand, and be translated into his Rest; whilst those *wicked Masons,* who rejected the **Lapis Augularis** [**Angularis**], which (now to their great Confusion) they see is become the *Cape Stone;* ſhall receive Punishment instead of Reward, for spoiling the Work of the grand Architect, by introducing Confusion instead of Order, and blending the two Opposites of Light and Darkness together. These erect vain Fabricks, according to their own depraved Imaginations, supporting them by Ignorance, Debility and Deformity, which, when the Tempests blow, come down with mighty Ruin on the Builders Heads, Let the Names of those be eras'd out of the Book M, and their Devices scatter'd as Dust before the Winds,....[14]

These examples from the works of William Smith serve to highlight not only his skills of authorship, but also to demonstrate that his words are still in use in masonic ritual to this day more than 280 years later. It is perhaps also odd to discover so early the rejection of the misshapen stone that was then needed to complete the building—whether that predates 1736 we leave to other researchers to consider.

Perhaps the most remarkable material are the verses about Sanballat and the use of the sword and trowel theme. It is a complete part of the Royal Order of Scotland ritual to this day, it can be found for example on the tracing board of the Cana Chapter in Lancashire (and this was one of the first chapters constituted by the English Grand Chapter in 1769) as a crossed sword and trowel on their chapter tracing board, and also anyone familiar with the Irish Knight Masons or the 'Degrees of the Captivity' in the Lodge and Council within Scottish Grand Chapter. It is interesting to see that these verses, spoken in public at the constitution of a lodge were surely already known to brothers in Durham, but were not repeated by Smith in any of his other publications.

Where does the term Harodim originate

In a masonic context it appears in Anderson's 1723 Constitutions as his 3,600 Princes which he further details in I Kings v.16.[15]

Tools, though there were, employ'd about it no leſs than 3,600 *Princes,* * or *Maſter-Maſons,* to conduct the Work according to *Solomon's* Directions, with 80,000

---

14 *Book M: or Masonry Triumphant* (1736), Lecture V, p. 23.

15 James Anderson. Constitutions, 1723, p. 10.

> * *In* 1 Kings v. 16. *they are call'd* הרדים Harodim, *Rulers or Provosts affisting King* Solomon, *who were set over the Work, and their Number there is only* 3,300 : *But* 2 Chron. ii. 18. *they are called* מנצחים Menatzchim, *Overseers and Comforters of the People in Working, and in Number* 3,600 ; *because either* 300 *might be more curious Artists, and the Overseers of the said* 3,300, *or rather, not so excellent, and only Deputy-Masters, to supply their Places in case of Death or Absence, that so there might be always* 3,300 acting Masters *compleat ; or else they might be the*

It is perhaps best to start by relating that Anderson, when talking about those who built the Temple, refers to Princes, and in a footnote gives other descriptors as being Harodim, *Rulers or Provosts*. By the time of the 1738 Constitutions that emphasis had changed and the first class of Masons is now described (without footnotes) as:

1. **Harodim**, Rulers or Provosts, call'd also **Menatzchim**, *Overseers* and Comforters of the People in Working, that were expert *Master Masons* in number 3600.[16]

Given Anderson's proclivities to add words and extend footnotes one might choose just to see this as Anderson merely trying to extract the most remuneration for his task. But the story of the Harodim, and of Scot's Masons is full of the emphasis of them being Rulers. Provosts and Masters. Indeed it is perhaps that sense of superiority which led to the idea of there being 'Higher Degrees'—an idea that has persistently prevailed ever since.

The problem issue regarding origin

In the normal sense of finding factual evidence to decide events, in this case we have evidence of a distant and originally operative lodge working something different, a means for the flow of information between the north and London, and the 1736 publication of BookM. BookM emphasises that the masonry worked in Durham was much more oratorical, much more concerned with morals and ethics than in London.

All we have in London is the arrival of the name 'Scots Masters Lodge' in the engraved lists in 1733. By chance we also have some records for the Union French Lodge. And we also know that Coustos took the idea of a plaque with a name upon it to France around 1736, and Fabris sought the Maitre Ecossois degree for use in Berlin in 1740.

Probably the 'Sanballat theme,' and an oratorical approach went from Swalwell

---

16 Jams Anderson. Constititutions, 1738, p. 11.

in the north to London in the south. But it seems that other themes were also developing in London during those same years. In less than a decade we suddenly have a series of degrees appearing:

The Order of Harodim of Kilwinning (active 1741/1743–1750).

The Royal Arch (active in Ireland 1743–1745, but with versions from both London and York arriving in Dublin ca 1744).

Scots Master (Maitre Ecossois in Berlin 1742, Maitre Ecossais in Paris 1744).

Perhaps all that can be said is that the ideas of the Harodim were practised in Durham from the early 1730s, and maybe earlier (for which (sadly) no evidence remains). The evidence in London is at best scant and limited to three newspaper advertisements (the earliest in 1743), together with the papers given to William Mitchell in 1750 which also by good luck have survived.

But we should really consider the appearance *in print* of BookM far away from London as representing a new strand of freemasonry and something of significance. It introduces the ideas of lectures and orations to brethren, but it also does more than that, it introduces through the Sanballat poem and the sword and trowel theme in a public oration at the constitution of a new lodge. It is highly likely that such material was included precisely because it was part of what the audience would already understand as being masonic in the north-east of England at that time.

The *Pocket Companions* have been much ignored by researchers, but they were invented by William Smith and they were the only item that an ordinary brother could purchase for a couple of shillings to learn more about freemasonry in the mid eighteenth century. There has been considerable speculation regarding William Smith and his activities. But the Swalwell Lodge records record him being a member, and then his name being attached to Book M then of course material from the Pocket Companion also appears in Book M. This matter is unlikely ever to be forensically proven,[17] and perhaps even just accepting that a new approach to the explaining of Freemasonry was introduced under the name of one William Smith between 1734 and 1738 is sufficient.

Likewise BookM has also not been appreciated as part of the masonic culture of England. We wish to challenge that idea and consider it should be placed full centre in sources that were published after Masonry Dissected. If nothing else **what BookM does do is to place the Sanballat poem and the theme of the**

---

17 Philip Crossle. Comments on Cecil Adams paper on Pocket Companions in *AQC* vol.45 at great length (pages 218-229) and careful thought. He does not provide a final answer, I commend these pages to anyone who wants to take up the challenge.

sword and trowel firmly into masonic ritual tradition from the year 1736. It is thus the first reference in print in England to the presence of any masonic ritual practices in the higher degrees of freemasonry.

The Ambrose Crowley Ironworks and Joseph Laycock

It was the Ironworks which brought Laycock to Durham. They used the locally mined iron ore and coal to manufacture essential supplies for the Royal Navy. And it was an Ambrose Crowley who established the iron works there; he acquired the site ca. 1680 and completed the ironworks in 1690, but to discover Ambrose Crowley some 50 years later sending Joseph Laycock to Swalewell is a tall stretch of the imagination. However it is possible to establish the ownership of this via some family tree work.[18] Ambrose Crowley I (born in 1608 and died 1680); his son Ambrose Crowley II was born 1635 in Rowley Regis, Staffordshire and died 1720 in Stourbridge, Worcs, and is generally considered to have been involved in the iron trade.

His son Ambrose Crowley III[19] born 1657 in Stourbridge, Worcs and died 1713. This was the Ambrose Crowley who created the ironworks at Winlaton, but clearly could not have been the Ambrose Crowley who sent Joseph Layock to Northumberland in the 1730s. Luckily the family tree tells us that he had a son John Crowley (1689–1728) who married a Theodosia Gascoyne and they had four children, the oldest who was called Ambrose Crowley IV. John was an ironmaster and merchant, Member of Parliament, Alderman of London, but died young. His wife together with others family members carried on the business. Ambrose Crowley IV (1717–1754) is not apparently in the business but aged around 15 could he really be the Ambrose who sent Joseph Laycock north to Northumberland?

The Crowley family set up an enterprise which made ironmongery, products such as chains and anchors for the British Navy, and had factories in the north east and in a large warehouse on the south bank of the Thames in London,[20] and the company also ran a fleet of sailing barges to carry his products south. This meant that his distant enterprises could quickly and easily communicate with each other.

One Joseph Laycock became, around 1732–1733, the manager of a large business, the Crowley Iron Works, making materials for the British Navy such as

---

18 An extensive chronology entitled 'The Descendants of Ambrose Crowley' is available at www. pennyghael.org.uk/Crowley.pdf

19 See https://en.wikipedia.org/wiki/Ambrose_Crowley

20 We also know that later the HRDM of KLWNNG was active in the South Bank by the 1750s. This of course might just be coincidence.

chains and anchors. Production was based in the county of Durham (which had both coal and iron ore) and delivered by the companies regular boat service to its wharf on the South Bank of the River Thames.

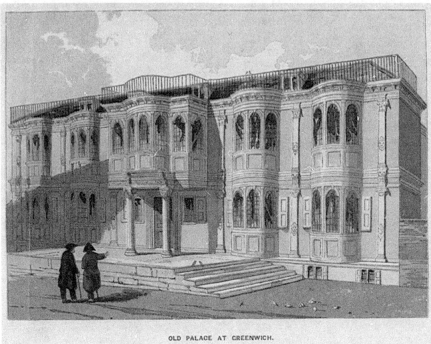

OLD PALACE AT GREENWICH.

Laycock was also made Provincial Grand Master for Durham in 1734 or 1735 by the Grand Lodge of England and we know of his existence and activities until around 1741 when there was another brother appointed to that position. Apart from the minutes of Swalwell Lodge we (sadly) know little more masonically about Laycock.

Crucially we have copies of *BookM or Masonry Triumphant*. This contains the Sanballat poem which remains part of the Royal Order of Scotland ritual to this day, and also examines the morals and ethics of freemasonry. Notably the editor was one William Smith, whose name will appear elsewhere

Masonic Developments between 1733 and 1744

The whole of 'the action' regarding the early mentions of higher degrees all takes place between 1733 and around 1744—so some 280 to 290 years ago. Sometimes the evidence is slight, but in almost every case is less that one would hope for. It goes from the first mention of a 'Scotts Masons Lodge' No.116, but then no further information. When it comes to the Harodim of Kilwinning we have three newspaper advertisement and Mitchell's patent and that is all. And while all is quiet in London in respect of the Royal Arch, which then appears in the south of Ireland in 1743 and in Dublin again in 1744. But again we simply consider that the records have simply got lost over the centuries.

And in France a multiplicity of higher degrees appeared, and we find "Maîtres Ecossais" are mentioned in the Grand Lodge General Regulations, Paris, in December 1743. And one should not ignore the formation of the Loge Ecossois in Berlin either.

Looking at all of this it is clear that a great amount of masonic ritual activity was actually taking place. The standard English traditional view, held by most masonic researchers is that expressed by Harry Carr and is that because there were no exposures between 1730 and 1760 there were no developments. But they only looked at the Craft (Blue Degrees) and only in England. We have chosen to take a broader approach, and find much had actually happened.

Our conclusion is that the appearance of Masonry Dissected in 1730, and its numerous reprints, was responsible for all this activity. And key to that was the loss of 'the Word' when Hiram was slain. This seems to have offered an intellectual challenge to various groups of brothers to resolve the loss.

What we do not know

Regarding the Harodim we do not know what the ritual of the degree was that was worked in Durham, we only know that it was worked for many decades afterwards. The major difficulty is to find evidence from the decade that follows

Masonry Dissected and we have not found much. We have at all times endeavoured to use only evidence from the time we are looking at—and ignore later evidence. This inevitably leaves gaps, and we are happy to encourage others to find other evidence to fill those gaps.

We do know that Joseph Laycock played a key role in developing freemasonry in Durham. For the man the personal evidence is poor. All we know is that he was said to have been born around 1810 in Wetherby, Yorkshire; and that he was probably the man in charge of the Crowley Ironworks in Durham by 1732. His death is said to have been in 1840, but there is again no real extant evidence. Both masonic sources and local history statements are equally vague and unclear.

Quite how the Harodim degree travelled south is not clear. We consider the best probability is that it was via the persons of Joseph Laycock or William Smith; and almost certainly by sea to London on Crowley owned boats, but that is only our assumption of probability.

It has also been proposed that the Harodim degree travelled north from London to Swalwell. While that cannot be totally excluded as a possibility we think it much less likely.

Sadly the history of the Harodim has been addressed at times in a manner where claims made without footnoting the sources of evidence for those claims. The Harodim history has been fully addressed by Jan Snoek in volume 3 of British Freemasonry but regarding his two sections titles "I). In London, no later than 1732" and "II). In the North of England, no later than 1733" he relies solely upon Trevor Stewart's paper of 1996[21]—and some of the claims in this paper are not footnoted and so far searches have failed to locate that evidence (see addendum to this chapter).

Thus the question, did the Harodim start in the North East of England or in London, remains unanswered. The authors consider the probability of a northern origin much more likely.

And to mark the occasion there was also the publication of *Book M*, presumably to celebrate the event, and the members of all the local Durham Lodges were able to subscribe to a copy. While it contained material from Anderson's 1723 Constitutions it contained a selection of lengthy lectures which Jan Snoek considers typical of the Harodim style and tradition.[22]

---

21 Jan Snoek, British Freemasonry Volume. 3, p. 20; and Trevor Stewart, The H.R.D.M.: A Fourth visitation to a Curious 18th Century Masonic Phenomenon from the North-East Region of England. *Ars Macionica*, vol.6 (1996).

22 British Freemasonry ed Robert Peter. Volume 3, Harodim Material and Higher Degrees ed Jan Snoek. pp. xx-xxi. Note that Snoeks attributes cover the total time span of the Harodim, but we

Extracts of BookM will be referred to later, but of note is the fact that some of the content appeared in print for the first time and some still remains in the ritual of the Royal Order of Scotland to this day. Post 1736 The Harodim Degrees were worked for the following century in the county of Durham, and Waples records all those occasions.

But the big question is just what connects the earlier Harodim in Durham with the Harodim in London? And it seems to be individuals that make such a connection. Every article on the early Durham Harodim starts with the statement "Early in the eighteenth century Mr. Joseph Laycock came from Wetherby, in Yorkshire, to Winlaton to take the management of the factory."[23] And it is often coupled with the 'fact' that he was born 'about 1710.' So we are also being asked to believe that Laycock came straight from Wetherby to manage the smelting and smithing enterprise of Ambrose Crowley in Winlaton—at the unlikely young age of 22? Equally all previous researchers seem not to have noticed this anomaly, nor noticed that Ambrose Crowley (III) had died in 1713.

But Laycock was a real person because he managed to establish his masonic credentials with Swalwell Lodge and convince Grand Lodge in London to make him Provincial Grand Master in 1734. Sadly little information seems to remain of Laycock's labours at the factory.

The Harodim of Kilwinning in London

We can find William Mitchell in London in 1750 signing and collecting his patent and papers to take back to the Netherlands the signed statement by the Grand Master in his patent to Mitchell which includes the words that '1750 was the ninth year of his Provincial Grand Mastership.'[24]

> GIVEN under my hand and the Seal of my Office at London this twenty-second day of July A.D.1750, A.M.H. 5753 and in the **Ninth Year of my Provincial GRAND MASTERSHIP** [bold added by author]
> ENTER'D in the Grand Register By Command of the Provl Grd Mastr the 22: Day of July 1750: 5753

Assuming this is correct then one can assume that the order was active in London around 1741. And this is followed by three newspaper advertisements.

---

are only looking at the formative time period.

23 William Bourn, *History of the Parish of Ryton* (1896).

24 The master texts are Robert Strathern Lindsay's *The Royal Order of Scotland*, ed by AJB Milborne (1971) and the follow up by George Draffen, *The Royal Order of Scotland: The Second Hundred Years* (1977).

The Brethren of the Scotch H—D—M. or Antient and Honourable Order of K----n----g, are desir'd to meet the Grand Master of the said Order, and the test of his Grand Officers, at the Sign of the Swan in Great Portland-Street, near Oxford-Market, on Wednesday next, at Three o'Clock in the Afternoon precisely, to celebrate the Day. By Order of the Grand Master.

E. W. Grand Sec.

1743 Advertisement in the Daily Advertiser 26th November

1750 The text of the petition of William Mitchell in July Provincial Grand Master of the Most Ancient and Hon^le Order of the H.R.D.M. of K.L.W.N.N.G. in S.B.[25]

R.L.F.   P.G.M. in S.B.

The Brethren of the H.R.D.M., are desired to take Notice, that the Grand Lodge and Grand Chapter of the Order are removed from the White Swan in Great Portland-Street, near Oxford Market, to Brother Field's, the Thistle and Crown in Chandos Street, near St. Martin's Lane.

Note, The Grand Chapter meets on the first, and the Grand Lodge on the fifth Sunday in each Month at Six in the Evening.

By Command of the P.G.M.

N.B.L.T.Y.   Grand Secretary

1750 Advertisement in the Daily Advertiser 1st August 1750

On Wednesday next, being the third Wednesday in this month, will be held the Grand Chapter of the Order of H.R.D.M., at the Crown and Bull, in Playhouse Yard, Black Fryers, where the Brethren of that Order are desired to attend, Yours

W.S.   Gd T.R.S.A.A.

1753 Advertisement in the Daily Advertiser 27th November 1753

---

25   There was a habit after the 1707 union to refer to Scotland as being North Britain, and here it is London being in S.B.–South Britain. This practice ceased in the mid 19th century.

This 1753 advertisement seems to have been either the end of the order in London or simply that other evidence did not survive.

Mitchell returned to Holland only to find that the Loge de Juste had chosen to adopt the Scots Master degrees rather that the Harodim / KRC degree, and then around 1753 we find that Mitchell has returned to Scotland

1754 Mitchell starts to recruit in Edinburgh, but it was only in July 1767 when the Grand Lodge of the Order was formed from the Edinburgh Chapter that it changed its name (and its ritual) from Harodim of Kilwinning to The Royal Order of Scotland.

Absence of (reliable) evidence—Harodim, Scots Masters & Royal Order of Scotland.

"Early in the eighteenth century Mr. Joseph Laycock came from Wetherby, in Yorkshire, to Winlaton to take the management of the factory." Source: Unknown and Oft Repeated, always unsourced

There is an old saying that 'absence of evidence is not evidence of absence' and vica versa, and that applies to the ritual developments that we know took place in London between 1733 and 1743/1750. Those who have gone before us in investigating this period found exactly the same, but they have been few and perhaps the best effort was the paper by J Shum Tucket in 1919.[26]

There have been a few stars in this wilderness, namely Robert Lindsey's Royal Order of Scotland, the labours of William Waples on the Harodim in two papers in AQC 60 & 62 and other recent discoveries relating to the Scots Masters degree in France, Germany and Holland. These recent discoveries and various papers published by Jan Snoek, Pierre Mollier, Reinhard Markner and Joseph Wages among others have brought some life back into the field. It seems to be proving that when one is able to follow events into other countries then the chance seems to be that various pieces of evidence which alone have no value can be brought together and some conclusions reached.

But it is the Harodim that is most challenging. Every article on the Harodim starts with the statement "Early in the eighteenth century Mr. Joseph Laycock came from Wetherby, in Yorkshire, to Winlaton to take the management of the factory."[27] And it is often coupled with the 'fact' that he was born 'about 1710'. The date of his birth remains a matter of conjecture. Equally all previous researchers seem not to have noticed this, neither noticed that Ambrose Crowley (III) had been dead for years.

---

26 JES Tuckett, The Origin of Additional Degrees. *AQC* vol. 32 (1919), pp. 5-55.

27 William Bourn, History of the Parish of Ryton (1896).

A Recent paper on the Harodim is Disclaimed

Sadly the two most recent papers, 'A Fresh Look at the Harodim' by Neville Barker Cryer[28] and 'The H.R.D.M.: A Fourth Visitation' by Trevor Stewart,[29] are utterly without footnotes. And the conclusions in Stewart's paper were also adopted by Jan Snoek in his introduction to the 'Harodim Materials' in Volume 3 of British Freemasonry.[30]

The authors state that the new claims made in these two papers cannot be used by them at all, simply because they are not footnoted, nor whether it just seemed logical to then at the time; and it has not proved possible to substantiate their claims. The problem is that we know from the lodge minutes that Laycock was in Lodge in Swalwell in March 1732 and various other facts for which there are sources. However Stewart makes various new claims under the heading 'A Hypothetical Reconstruction or Sketch of the Sequence of Events in the Spread of H.R.D.M. in the North East of England,' as a series of points. These new unsourced claims, listed with Stewart's numbering are commented upon:

5. *'Joseph Laycock born in about 1710 in Wetherby in North Yorkshire is initiated in the old unattached lodge in York City.'*

I have been unable to find any evidence for these events. The Winlaton & District Local History Society state 'John Laycock came from Yorkshire to be factory manager for Crowleys in Winlaton.' I will settle for that. There is no evidence that he was initiated in York.

6. *'In 1732 Bro Laycock travels to London, to take up employment in Crowley's London branch in Rotherhithe'* and *'In the Rotherhithe area is a masonic Lodge which works what they call 'Scots Masonry, similar to that which he had been used to in York.'*

These are all new claims and sadly no sources are given, and no evidence has been found. And of course we already know from the minutes of Swalwell Lodge that he was received in March 1732

And he also says that the HRDM *'goes under various names: Scottish Master, Ecossais, Harodim, Heredom etc'*—this seems just confusing. There is no doubt

---

28 NB Cryer, A fresh Look at the Harodim *AQC* vol. 91, pp. 116-155.

29 Trevor Stewart, The H.R.D.M.: A Fourth Visitation to a Curious 18th Century Masonic Phenomenon from the North East Region of England, *Ars Macionica* vol.6 (1996). Stewart, a friend of one author, has been asked if he could provide any evidence in support of his claims. Alas he could not, and in this paper they are all removed

30 Robert Peter (ed) British Freemasonry. Volume 3 by Jan Snoek. The statements made on pages xii-xii in relation of the HRDM in N.E. England probably need to be treated with considerable caution.

that London was a focus for other degrees, but there is no evidence that they were simply different names for the same thing. In Durham it seems to have been called Harodim and in London H_D_M or H.R.D.M., and that is understandable

7. We read *'Bro. Laycock is initiated into this H.R.D.M. and, on learning that he is to travel back up North to take charge of the Winlaton branch of Crowley's enterprise, this Body appoints him to be the Provincial Grand Master of the H.R.D.M. with authority to rule over H.R.D.M.activities in the several unattached Lodges in the area.'*

This comes to the very heart of the issue, because Stewart makes the assumption that there is already in 1732 a 'Grand Harodim body' in London, and that it initiates Laycock, and that it also appoints him as Provincial Grand Master for the area. Alas there is no (that is zero) evidence for any of these statements. No other researcher has ever suggested this.

'He is given a special 'jewel' to wear as the Provincial Grand Master of this superior form of Freemasonry. A picture of it is included as Plate no. 13.' Here Stewart writes the following *'The H.R.D.M. 'jewel' is also of silver, was made by a Bro. Edmund Loewenstock in London and was hall-marked 1732. It is marked centrally and clearly "PGM."'*

Seeking evidence for the origin of the jewel also proved a failure. While there is a picture, its quality is very poor indeed, and disastrously there is no picture at all of the hallmark, no year letter and no makers mark. Searching the records of makers marks it did not prove possible to find one for an Edmund Loewenstock around 1732—but curiously there was a silversmith of similar name in the 1882 London Commercial Directory for the firm of Abraham, David Loewenstark as goldsmiths and masonic jewellers. During the Covid pandemic of 2020/2021 it has not proved possible to trace this jewel.

8. Presumably relating to 1732, Stewart writes: *'On hearing that Bro. Laycock (who was presumably thought to be a sufficiently well-educated man) is to travel North, the Premier Grand Lodge appoints him to be the Provincial Grand Master of all Craft Lodges in the County of Durham with the remit that he was to bring the several unattached Lodges known to be operating there under their control.'*

While the evidence is not in the actual Proceedings of Grand Lodge, the later statements in Book of Constitution all point to Laycock being made PGM is 1734/35 and not in 1732.

Firstly there is an assumption made that the HRDM started in London and was taken north by Laycock, and that in 1732 some 'Grand body' was already confidently in existence, and understanding the concept of Provincial Grand Master seems unlikely. Alas I am not aware of ANY traces of Scots Masters in 1732, or earlier, in London, the name only first occurs and is dateable to mid 1733 in an Engraved List of Lodges for the year.

Stewart's alternative is that Laycock took the H.R.D.M. north with him in 1732, where it then took root. But there is no evidence (of which we are aware) for a body of H.R.D.M. in London in the year 1732 nor that they gave Laycock any sort of 'H.R.D.M. Provincial Grand Mastership.' These matter have been personally discussed with Stewart and he has not been able to provide any evidence to support any of the key claims he makes because he no longer has his notes—as researchers we have no choice but to ignore the validity of these claims, and they do not enter our text. Because the chapter on Harodim in *British Freemasonry* volume three accepts Stewarts conclusions that also needs to be treated with caution when it also accepts these claims. For avoidance of all doubt we feel the need to explain these differences here. There is a clear need to just stick to proven evidence, and to ignore claims made without any evidence. To do otherwise would simply distort further research.

We have thought long and hard, because we agree with Stewart that what was orated in public, in 1735–36 was going to already have been known and be acceptable to, and accepted by, the masons who listened to it. This indicates to us a reasonable probability that the H.R.D.M. had been established for some years in the North East and probably originated there.

One other remaining unanswered question is the date of birth of Joseph Laycock, usually stated to be ca. 1710. That he was accepted into Swalwell Lodge in 1732 as well as being in charge of the huge engineering enterprise at the age of ca. 22 seems very unlikely. We have found no answer to provide a more realistic date.

Some Additional Early Harodim Chronology

It is worth adding a skeletal chronology for the reader, but we do commend the work of William Waples to all who are interested.

29 September First Swalwell minute book starts and is 'operative' in content (AQC60).

1731 Laycock left London for Winlaton to manage the Crowley Works (AQC 62 p. 107) (AQC 60).

March 1732 Laycock recorded as 'Accepted Mason' in Swalwell Lodge (AQC 62).

1733 New Minute Books started for Swalwell Lodge. This seems to mark a change from 'operative' to speculative work, although the operative side continued for some decades.

1733 In a 'Memorandum of Sundry Persons – Names of persons who were made free in the Society' under the date 24ᵗʰ June 1733 the name Joseph Laycock appears. Further down the same list on 3ʳᵈ March 1735 the name William Smith is written. Smith was the compiler and editor of *BookM: or Masonry Triumphant*. William Waples[31] does not explain further what this act means and all we can do is guess or assume that such men were already freemasons. (AQC 62) (AQC 60).

1734 Laycock appointed/elected Senior Warden of Swalwell Lodge (Minute Book).

1734 Appointed Provincial Grand Master for Durham in 1734 (AQC 62). This is as per UGLE and Book M. There is a controversial claim that Laycock was made PGM earlier for which the evidence is poor.

24 February 735. Wm Smith Pocket Companion condemned by GLE. (AQC 62)

3 March 1735 Mr William Smith made free of the lodge. (AQC 60)

March 1735 Constituted the Swalwell Lodge as PGM. (AQC 62)

27 March 1735 Appointed Senior Warden of Swalwell Lodge. (AQC 60)

24 Jun 1735. Lodge constituted by Mr Joseph Laycock, Prov GM and Kenrick Jones as Master. (AQC 62)

1736 Constituted the Lodge at Gateshead as PGM. (AQC 62)

1736 Book M published in Newcastle. Author/editor William Smith; printer Leonard Unfreville

24 June **1741** (Edward Alport appointed as his replacement – see Newcastle Courant 24 June 1741). (AQC 62)

1741 London (P)GM who signed Mitchell warrant declared in 1751 that he had been (P)GM for 10 years.

1743 Kendrick Jones made PGM. (AQC 60 p. 150)

7 July **1745** Joseph Laycock died and buried at Whickham. (AQC 60 plus research)

---

31 William Waples, The Swalwell Lodge, *AQC* vol.62 (1949); and An Introduction to the Harodim in *AQC* vol.60 (1947). The Harodim were Waples' lifetime interest and the quality of his work is general very reliable.

Robert Strathern Lindsay's book '*The Royal Order of Scotland*'[32]

There is no doubt that without this volume it would have been almost impossible to do our researches, and we thank him for that. George Draffen's 'The Royal Order of Scotland—The Second Hundred Years' published in 1977 is also an invaluable companion.

Lindsay however always refers to the early days (prior to 1767) as the 'Royal Order' when from ca. 1741 because until then it was the 'Harodim of Kilwinning.' This might lead one to think that these two bodies were always one and the same, and this was not true and only causes confusion.

There were great events in 1766–1767, and Lindsay tells us:

> From 31st October 1766 to 4th July 1767, none of the Minutes are signed and William Mitchell is not recorded amongst those present at the Meetings....
>
> ....Up to 4th July the regulations for the Royal Order at Edinburgh were "The Laws, Rules and Orders" current at London in 1750.[33]

That the body changed its name, changed it annual festival date from St Andrews Day to 4th July, named the King of Scotland as perpetual Grand Master are almost passed over as being insignificant—but certainly not worth a headline in bold.

It also seems that Lindsay was not aware of Ramsay's Orations nor the presence of a Harodim degree being worked in Durham in the 1730s nor of BookM. What is clear is that the Harodim arrived in London probably in the 1730s; and if the word Harodim had not occurred elsewhere then the idea might be credited to London. That a Harodim degree was worked in Swalwell Lodge and that BookM contains the Sanballat poem seems significant.

The problem with Lindsay's book is that he sees the freemasonry of the 18th century as being governed by, and conforming to, the same set of rules that were rigorously applied in the 20th century. His facts are sound, but his conclusions are sometimes doubtful. His major intellectual problem is to see the earlier Harodim of Kilwinning as being the same as that of the Royal Order post 1767—and that reduces the understanding of the reality of yesteryear for researchers.

---

32 Robert Strathern Lindsay, The Royal Order of Scotland. Edited after the authors death by AJB Milbourne (1971).

33 Lindsay, *The Royal Order of Scotland*, p. 69.

The HRDM in London and William Mitchells patent for The Hague of 1750

The HRDM in London is as odd and obscure in origin as the Scots Masters and the Royal Arch. The evidence is often as transitory as, in this case, three newspaper advertisements (1743, 1750 and 1753), in the case of the Scots's Masters a few entries in Engraved Lists of Lodge (1734, 1735) and in the case of the Royal Arch all we really have is Dassigny's statement that there were two forms in Dublin—one coming from York and followed by another from London. But the Harodim of Kilwinning must qualify to be among the first higher degrees whether it was in Durham or in London.

What is curiously, and sadly, absent are the identities, of the freemasons who created these various degrees. They must surely have been educated men who had their own libraries, or access to learned libraries. In the case of the H.R.D.M. of Kilwinning the best clues are the beginning and end of the patent given to William Mitchell.

> SIR ROBERT R. L. F. Knight of the Order of the
> R.Y.C.S. Warder of the Tower of R.F.S.M.N.T.
> President of the Judges and Council of the Great S.N.H.D.R.M.
> and Provincial Grand Master of the H.R.D.M. of K.L.W.N.N.G. in
> S.B.: &cᵃ: &cᵃ: &cᵃ
> .....
> GIVEN under my hand and the
> Seal of my Office at London
> This twenty-second day of July
> A.D. 1750 A.M.H. 5753 and in
> The Ninth Year of my Provincial
> GRAND MASTERSHIP[34]

From this we learn that even in 1750 The HRDM contained both a Great Sanhedrin and another part requiring a Provincial Grand Master, and is stated to have been active since 1741.

There also exists a copy of a letter sent to Mitchell to collect his documentation from "attend me at the house of Bro Lewis S.N.C.R.T.Y. the sign of the Gold Horseshoe in Cannon Street in Southwark...."

So who were these brothers; Sir Robert and Bro Lewis? So far the list of possible brothers is blank, but it is likely that nobody has yet tried hunting out the

---

34 These quotes are taken from Robert Lindsey, *The Royal Order of Scotland*, pp. 39 & 41. The abbreviations are simply the proper names with all the vowels removed and substituted with a full stop. Thus H.R.D.M. = Harodim; R.F.S.M.N.T. = Refreshment; S.N.H.D.R.M.= Sanhedrim (sic); H.R.D.M.= Harodim; K.L.W.N.N.G. = Kilwinning.

individually name persons. Lewis as a given name is not common and in the minutes of Grand Lodge the name only occurs twice —and one was that of Lewis Mercy who was a member of the same lodges as John Coustos (see below for more information on Mercy).

Both the Scots Masters and H.R.D.M. share one other co-incidence, that the documents given to Mitchell, and the documents that arrived in Berlin were exceptionally detailed in terms of rules and practices which would seem to have been indicative of well-run organisations. One can only assume that the minutes and other records have simply vanished over time.

The full text of the patent given to Mitchell is in Lindsay's book 'The Royal Order of Scotland,' but as it does not contain any ritual clues—it is just organisational and administrative.

It is interesting to note that the Lodge de Juste in the Netherlands chose not to wait for its patent to work the Harodim of Kilwinning degrees, but instead chose to use the Maitre Ecossais degrees instead. The lodge in the Netherlands clearly knew that it had a choice of other degrees.

The Royal Order in Scotland 1757–1836

William Mitchell returned from Den Hague and settled in Edinburgh, where it seems he taught French. Upon his return to Den Hague it suffices to say that he did not activate his patent for 'The Seven United Provinces' before returning around 1753. Once he had established his business in Edinburgh he did what every brother would do and joined a lodge. It seems he joined a lodge with the title 'The Scots Lodge' in the Canongate which changed its name around 1760 to Lodge St. Andrew's around 1760. Thus we discover that Mitchell was its Right Worshipful Master for the years 1762–1764. Its earlier records are sadly lost.[35]

However records have been found belonging to Lodge St David and record Mitchell's visits there and the dates are informative.

i)   In 1753, visits on 12th September and 10th October. At the first of these Mitchell is recorded as wearing 'his proper Clothing and Jewels; and is described as 'The Most Worshipful Br Mitchell, Grand Master of the Seven United provinces and 'Provincial Grand Master from London Kilwinning over all Europe Brittain (sic) excepted.

ii) In 1754, visits on 9th January, 23th February, 1st, 13th, 22nd, and 25th March, 24th June, 30th August and 11th September.

---

35   Robert Strathern Lindsay, *The Royal Order of Scotland,* Ed. AJB Milborne (1972), p. 60.

iii) In 1755 visits on 9th April and 8th October.

iv) In 1756 Mitchell was present on 9th June as part of a deputation from the Royal Order, but including Mitchell, it could not have exceeded four in number as no more in Scotland were then members of the Order.

v) On June 19th 1764, the minutes record "We were visited on this occasion by the Rt Worshipfull Br. Mitchell & a number of the Brethren of the Royal Order in plain clothing.[36]

Lindsay fails to add in a couple of later items. One of which refers to a visitation in March 1765 'by Br Jas Ker, and a considerable number of the Knights and Brethren of the Royal Order of Scots Masonry. Two years later, in 1767, the Royal Order made a generous donation of nine guineas to the Lodge St David in thanks for being able to meeting in their lodge room. Later the Royal Order had sought additional rights over meetings and furniture and this produced a huge argument, in which the Order left this meeting place. The other thing that Lindsay omitted from his book were details of certain members of Lodge St David who were key members of the Royal Order. That table[37] is below.

Some Members of Lodge St. David connected with the Royal Order of Scotland.

	Office held in Lodge St. David.	In Royal Order.
James Ker, Keeper of the Records in Laigh Parliament Ho	Secretary	Succeeded Wm. Mitchell as Grand Master, 1767 to 1776.
William Baillie, Advocate, first Lord Polkemmet	R.W. Master 1768-1769 Jun. Gd. Warden of Scot. 1769-70	Grand Master 1776-1778.
William Charles Little, Advocate of Liberton.	Depute Master, 1783 Sub. Gd. Mr. of Scot. 1782-83	Depute Gd. Master, 1777. Grand Master, 1778.
David Earl of Leven & Melville	R.W. Master, 1758 to 1763 Gd. Master of Scot. 1759-1760	Depute Gd. Master, 1778. (Characteristic in R.O."Rectitude")
Gavin Wilson, The Poetical Shoemaker	Poet Laureate	Characteristic in R.O." Description"
John Osburn Brown, W.S.	R.W. Master, 1795 & 1799	Stated to be the two members of Lodge St. David who revived the R.O. in 1839
Houston Rigg Brown	R.W. Master, 1800 to 1804 and 1808 to 1819.	
George Murray, Accountant	Treasr. Sub. Master	Grand Treasr. admitted 1839 To whose exertions the Order perhaps
John Brown Douglas, W.S.	R.W. Master, 1842-43-44	Grand Secty. admitted 1839 owes its present existence (Murray Lyon)
John Donaldson Boswall of Wardie. Captain R.N.	R.W. Master, 1838 to 1841	Deputy Governor, 1840.

36 Ibid., 66.

37 A M Mackay, Notes on the Royal Order of Scotland in Notes & Queries in *AQC* vol. 22 (1909), pp. 59-61.

So we can now see the precise date when Mitchell retired (or resigned) in 1767. After that the leadership of the Royal Order was entirely in the hands of members of St David from 1767 to 1778, and again from 1813–1819 and later 1839–1856. For Lindsay states that he sees the periods between 1805–1812 and 1820–1838 as being blank. I think there is some uncertainty on that matter because Murray Lyon in his History of the Lodge of Edinburgh tells us that Deuchar was RWM of Mary's Chapel from 1810–1814, in 1824 and in 1835 and that "in 1825 he (Deuchar) inaugurated a movement for the resuscitation of the Royal Order of Scotland."[38] It is sad that nothing has so far been found to prove that claim, but given Deuchar's propensity to adopt other degrees it is perfectly possible.

Of course what started out as H.R.D.M. or the H.R.D.M. of Kilwinning, and which travelled from London to Den Haag and back to Edinburgh, did at some time have to change its name to the Royal Order of Scotland and add to its legend to become truly Scottish. It seems most likely that this happened in 1767 and was associated with or just after Mitchell's resignation.

That was the year that Mitchell left the order, the year in which Lodge St David and the order fell out over the use of the lodge room and furniture, and the year in which the Laws of the R.L. H.R.D.M. were approved on 5th January 1767. There is a footnote on the first page which states that "The King of Scotland is perpetual Grand Master of this order and therefore not mentioned among the Elective Officers."

And in Article 2 the date of the Annual Meeting date was changed from St Andrews Day to the 4th July—thus introducing the 'Bruce tradition' was introduced.[39] But clearly this was the point at which the Royal Order departed from the main tradition of masonry to become a separate and distinct Scottish order, which it has stayed to this day. Thus it ceases to become part of our investigations, but still unique and Scottish.

A French aside

The history of the Royal Order seems always to have been fractured, and on several occasions to seems to vanish only to appear again. A chapter in Paris was chartered by Edinburgh on 4th October 1786, and its records became the property of the French masonic historian Thory, and from him to Dr Charles Morrison.

---

38 David Murray Lyon, *History of the Lodge of Edinburgh, Mary's Chapel No.1* (1900 Tercentenary Edition), p. 310.

39 The date of 4th July seems obscure but is introduced by Lindsay on pp. 70-72 where he discusses the 1767 Laws of the Order.

In July 1842 in Edinburgh two brethren were admitted and a Dr Charles Morrison was affiliated. He had been resident in Paris and in 1822 was admitted to the Order in Chapter "Du Choix" in 1822. The Edinburgh Chapter did not remit most of his fee for affiliation and it may be that he had also brought back with him from France a copy of the original ritual of 1786. It was the same Dr Charles Morrison whose services were used to enable a Charter for a Supreme Council to be formed in Scotland in 1846. Once this was done Morrison went back to France never to return to Scotland.

There seems always to have been a close connection between the Royal Order and the Supreme Council for Scotland because from 1855 part of the essential requirements to join the Supreme Council was membership of the Royal Order. This practice continued until at least the 1870s and it was used by the Supreme Council as an excuse to explain why the Scottish Supreme Council could not sign the Concordat proposed by the English Supreme Council.

Musings

Origins of Lodge St David No.36. It appears that in June 1736 three brethren made application to Lodge Cannongate Kilwinning Lodge No.2 which in turn had been chartered by Mother Kilwinning in 1677. They referred this to Mother Kilwinning and a charter was granted for 'Canongate Kilwinning from Leith' on 24th June 1736, which was subsequently altered to Lodge St. David Edinburgh, by decision of Grand Lodge.[40]

Belton once visited Lodge St David (probably circa 2000), and purely by chance, it was on the occasion of a fraternal visitation by the Lodge of Industry No. 48 UGLE. And with some pride they explained that such annual fraternal visitations had been taking place for over 100 years. One might think nothing of that except that this lodge was Swalwell Lodge, 'home of the Harodim', removed to Newcastle and became the Lodge of Industry! Were it not for the fact that the focus of the Royal Order in Scotland was firmly with the brothers of St David's one might think no further. There has to be scope for some fascinating research.

As to the role of Mother Kilwinning, there is always a permanent denial of participation in other or higher degrees. The reply surely has to be "methinks thou dost protest too much" (to slightly misquote William Shakespeare). Exactly what role the H.R.D.M. of Kilwinning played in London from around 1733 to around 1743 remains as unclear as the role of the Scotts Master Lodge no.115 in the 1730s.

---

40 W J Hughan, Lodge St David No.36, Edinburgh. *The Masonic Illustrated*, July 1904, p. 222.

The Harodim—A disambiguation

Among all the masonic words that of the 'Harodim' used to mostly get a blank stare when mentioned. But that changed in 2016 when the amazing four volume series *British Freemasonry* was published, and in this case especially volume 3 which is entitled *Rituals II – Harodim Material and Higher Degrees*.

The Harodim Material listed by Prof Snoek is as follows into what he describes as 'nine distinct, yet related appearances'[41] which are as follows:

    I) In London, no later than 1732

    II) In the North-East of England, no later than 1733

    III) In the Earliest Lodges in Paris: The Ritual Herault of 1737

    IV) Le Parfait Macon 1744

    V) The Adoption Rite 1744

    VI) In London, no later than 1741/1750 (Harodim of Kilwinning)

    VII) The Royal Order of Scotland 1754–1767

    VIII) Lambert de Lintot's Rite of Seven Degrees and his Royal Order Charter of 1783.

    IX) William Preston's Order of Harodim, founded 1787

It just shows how rapidly interest has been lit up, that a mere seven years later it seems like time to review this list. Appearances I, II, VI and VII are all re-arranged and details corrected in the chapters that follow.

The impossibility that we discovered of following developments in one country is shared with Snoek because he found that he had to include French developments in his list of Harodim developments. He is absolutely right and we have also chosen to engage even more actively in that approach.

Appearances VIII and IX are really beyond the time scope of this study, but they are probably matched in France by Les Plus Secret Mysteres of 1766 and perhaps also in the 13-degree collection Conversations Allegoriques of 1763 and 1767. There was a popularity of collections of rituals which favoured collections where the rituals were in prime numbers of 7 or 13. It is also important to remember that the tale of the Knights Templar as a real medieval order was part of the imagination of history within the society of the later eighteenth century and the Masonic Knights Templars built upon that and were very Christian.

---

41 Peter Robert, ed, *British Freemasonry* volume 3, pp. xii-xvi.

All the Ecossais degrees are placed by Snoek under the heading High[er] Degrees, and it does feel uncomfortable to find Le Parfait Macon categorised as Harodim and the Royal Arch as a Higher Degree. So perhaps the valuable idea of Harodim, while valuable is stretched rather too far for our purposes(?).

Snoek lists a (long) set of characteristics as being typical of the Harodim, but for the purposes of focussing in on the period up to around the mid 1740s a shorter (selected) set of criteria seem more relevant.

- The rituals are catechetical, and usually contain long lectures.

- It is interesting that the first piece of catechetical ritual was introduced by William Smith (also of BookM) in his Pocket Companion of 1735. This is "A Short Charge to be given to New Admitted Brethren" (p. 43) and it still part of the first-degree ritual today (albeit slightly modified).

- The themes do not involve the building of King Solomons Temple, but do often focus on the exploration of the remains of the first Temple, often finding a vault, and within that a metal plaque bearing the name of God. Themes can also move into explorations of the remains of the third (Herod) Temple by Scottish Crusaders.

- Themes around the rebuilding of the Temple by Zororobel are also part of this general theme.

- The most persistent theme is that of rebuilding the walls of Jerusalem with a trowel in one hand and the sword in the other. This of course first appeared in a masonic context in BookM as the Sanballat poem.

- The Seven Wonders of the World are also often present, and presumably are drawn from the Old Charges or Andersons Constitutions.

From the 1740s onwards other themes appear, and it is perhaps simple to leave them intact as separate themes rather than call them all Harodim. Two of the main themes are:

> Degrees of Retribution (to avenge those who slew Hiram the Architect)
> Degrees of Captivity (the return of the Jews from Babylon to rebuild the Temple with the permission of Cyrus. The start of this is contained in Le Parfait Macon of 1744).

It is probably true to say that human imagination, and a delight to be able to create 'just one more degree' resulted in a huge number of degrees being created and by the end of the eighteenth century there came a time when it became essential to bring some order and simplification by creating orders to take re-sponsibility for different segments of rituals.

But perhaps the most important development, one which becomes a key part of all French ritual texts is that the catechism sections are almost all accompanied by explanations of events and on the required morals and ethics expected of candidates. This of course then came back into English printed ritual styles from the 1760s.

So we are grateful to adopt Snoek's category of 'Harodim,' but we have redefined it somewhat to fit a somewhat different view of how things developed, and ap-plied a shorter timescale to it which ends around 1750.

1733-1749 Scots Masters Degree in England

A mere three years after the publication of *Masonry Dissected*, we can see in the Engraved List of 1734 that something called the Scott's Masons Lodge was meeting at the Devil Tavern on Temple Bar in London. It entered the Rawlinsons's list of 1733 as number 115, then also was in Pine's 1734 list, but in reality it never applied for a warrant. This was possible because the list was the property of the engraver and publisher, and all that was required was to go to his office and ask for the entry, pay the fee, and he would simply add the new lodge number and meeting place; the Grand Secretary was not involved.

But we can be quite precise as to the date of its first appearance. It was between the date when lodge No.114 was warranted on 23rd May 1733 and the next listed warranted lodge, the Lodge of Relief No.118 in Bury, Lancashire warranted on 3 July 1733; when they would have gone to the engraver of the list to get their entry added. It seems that they were struck off the list in 1736, so there are no further entries appear, but we know from their 1741 warranting of a lodge in Berlin that they stayed doing their 'Scots Masters' degrees in London.

The Scotts Masons Lodge is recorded in Lanes Lists as meeting in two places:

Devil Tavern, Temple Bar 1733–1736 and

Daniel's Coffee House 1736–onwards

There are two aspects of this worth considering; the first is what was called a Scott's Masons' Lodge in London, and secondly the delivery of the Scott's Masters Degree outside London, and we have dealt with the easy part above.

Scots Master outside London

Eric Ward in 1962[1] gives detailed notes on the known occurrence of the Scots Masters degree being conferred. And it seems it was always done to a group of Brothers together at the same meeting and recorded in the normal lodge minute book. In his paper he gives examples at the Bear in Bath in October 1735, January 1746 and on other occasions until 1758, and at Salisbury in 1766. It may well be that this degree was more widely spread, but the availability of minutes is limited and such extra-curricular activities may not have been well recorded.

---

1   Eric Ward, *Early Masters' Lodges and their Relation to Degrees*. *AQC* 76 (1962), pp. 172-173. And William Waples mention of Durham is on p. 147 in the same article.

Antiquity No.2	17 June 1740 (9 made S:M inc the WM)
Rummer, Bristol	18 July 1740
	15 August 1740 (mention)
	7 November 1740 (5 made SM)
Bear, Bath	October 1735 (made 10)
and also present were	S:M, S:S:W and S:J:W: who presumably conferred the degree.
	8 January 1746 (2 made S:M)
	22 November 1754 (made 5 S:M)
	17 February 1756 (5 made S:M)
	14 April 1758 (9 made S:M)
Salisbury	19 February 1746 (5 made S:M)

Mentions like this are only those where minutes books still exist, and have been searched, and many separate minute Books will not have survived. However they do demonstrate that the degree continued to be worked, although all the records relate only to the south of England, and all the places are on the main highway between London and Bristol. Bristol was the main port for travel and trade with Ireland and Bath was a fashionable Georgian spa resort.

There is no evidence at all relating to whatever Scots Masters degree was worked in London from circa 1733, only one early occasion, in 1735 of it being worked in Bath, and all other occasions were in 1740 or later. These few meetings have for decades been put forward by researchers as evidence of the degree. That is true, but there is no evidence of its popularity or acceptance more broadly across England.

Compare this with the great surge of popularity with which Masonry Dissected was greeted in 1730, and the multiple editions that were rapidly printed. Until further evidence appears, it seems that at present, there is nothing more to be said regarding the Scots Masters degree in England.

The Union French Lodge No. 98 of London

Note that in 1740 the lodge changed its number from 98 to 87 as a result of the remuneration. It was warranted on 17 August 1732 and surrendered its warrant in 1753.

Any attempt to discover who was behind all this activity in 'higher degrees' seems to have been plagued with difficulty. But perhaps a good start are the words of Paul Tunbridge:

> Of the thirty known members of the Union French Lodge No. 98, which was constituted at Prince Eugene's Coffee House at St. Alban's Street in 1732, all but two were Frenchmen. This Lodge took its name at the time of its removal in 1739 to the Union Coffee House, at the upper end of the Haymarket. The Master of this Lodge in 1732 was Mr. Lewis Mercy who was probably the composer of the music for the Fellow-Craft's song in Anderson's *Constitutions* of 1723. The Lodge was erased in 1753.[2]

Tunbridge's paper is 24 pages long, he mentions three other names to which we will refer, but nowhere mentions their involvement with and membership of Lodge No. 98. So it seems best to start by relating the names of the members of the lodge that met at the Rainbow Coffee House in York Buildings No.73 (warranted17 July 1730) who together were the founders (with others) of the lodge meeting at Prince Eugen's Head Coffee House No. 98 (warranted 17 August 1732).

Mr Lewis Mercy	Masr
Mr [Thomas] Lanse	Warden
Mr Protin	Warden
Mr Friard	[Secretary]
Mr St Jean	

---

1 John Pine, List of the Regular Lodge according to their Seniority & Constitution. The entry for lodge No. 98.

2 Paul Tunbridge, "Climate of European Masonry 1730–1750." *AQC* Vol.81, p. 91.

Mr Vincent La Chapelle
Mr Delahaye
Mr Coustos

There are a few others who claimed membership of the lodge and we only have their actions as proof positive of being members (listed in alphabetical order). There may be others yet to be discovered.

Jacopo Fabris
Louis-François Marquis de la Tierce
Philipp Friederich Steinheil

The participants who appear in this chapter all carried freemasonry from London into Europe, and each in their own various ways. And they had various professional occupations apart from being freemasons, including flautist, composer, artist, stage machinery designer, jeweller, diplomat, celebrity chef and tutors of nobility.

All those we name belonged to No. 98 and none to lodge No. 8. So let us examine where lodge No.98 met during its existence:

Prince Eugene's Coffee House, St. Albans Street	London 1732
Duke of Lorraine Suffolk Street	London 1733
Kings Arms, Piccadilly	London 1736
Union Coffee House, Upper End of Haymarket	London 1739
Hoop & Grapes, Greek Street	London 1741
Cardigan, Charing Cross	London 1742
Greyhound, Strand	London 1743
Meuse Coffee House	London 1745
Lebeck's Head, Strand	London 1745[3]

In England Lodges were known by the name of the place they met, and every time when they moved that name changed. While an engraved list might give them a number that also could change as other lodges older than them returned their warrants. Luckily there was one set of lists of members of lodges which covered the correct years for our researches. It has been simply stated to be the list of members as supplied to grand lodge in the year 1731 and follows the meeting of 17th March. But it also includes the members of Lodge No. 98 which was warranted on 17th August 1732 and only finishes even later with the lodge 'Ship without Temple Bar' which received its warrant on 8th September 1732.

---

3   *Lanes List of Lodges*, p. 59.

This list therefore appears to be the list of all members of lodges starting in 1731 but being continued as the list of members until September 1732, with no corrections being made for deaths, resignations, or new members etc. In this case it is likely that only the founding members are given in the list, and that all other members who joined after were never recorded. This probably accounts for the presence of brothers stating they were members but not being recorded in the (only extant) list.

Pierre Mollier in two articles printed in *Maçonnerie* in January and February 2015 makes a connection between the Scots Masons Lodge (No.115) and the Union Lodge because both met at the Devil Inn at Temple Bar in London. Jan Snoek also makes similar claims. There is a Lodge (actually No.8) which did meet at the Devil Tavern from 1727 to 1735 and The Scots Masons Lodge did meet at both those places at much the same time. Sadly though it was the 'Union French Lodge' No.98 which was the Lodge that spread both lodges and freemasonry into Europe, and not No.8. It is of course a mistake that can be made so easily—but this clarification is important so that any further work on the members of this unusual lodge starts by looking at the right 'Union Lodge.' There is ZERO evidence of any member of the Union Lodge No. 8 taking masonry into Europe but much of the activity of the members of lodge No. 98 was taking masonry into Europe. We must resign ourselves to the reality that it is most unlikely that any evidence relating the Scotts Masons Lodge No. 115 will ever be found.

The Epitaph for the claims for Union Lodge No. 8

De la Tierce, a self-declared member of the Union French Lodge No. 98, in his 1742 book *Histoire, Obligations...* (etc) which includes an approbation[4] page for his translation of Andersons Constitutions 1723 into French which was completed in 1733 and signed by '*Le Frere* Friard' (and we know he was the secretary of the lodge No. 98).

Friard's exact words are below in the original French includes the following which describe the lodge exactly:

> ...The venerable Master, the Wardens, the Compagnons & the Apprentices of the French Lodge of Free-Masons situated at London in Suffolk Road at the sign of the Duke of Lorraine...

And this was precisely the meeting place of the lodge at that time, and described exactly according to the custom of the time. So here the spurious and oft stated claim for Union Lodge No.8 to be the source of the masonic expansion into Europe ends.

---

4   De la Tierce, *Histoire Obligations et Statuts de la Tres Venerable Confraternity des Francs-Macons.* Pub Varrntrap, at Frankfort sure Meyn (1742), p. 21.

APPROBATION.

L'An de la Maçonnerie cinq mille sept cens trente trois, le troisieme mardi du mois d'Août, le haut & puissant Seigneur Mylord JACQUES LION Comte de STRATHMORE & de KINGHORN, Seigneur de GLAMES, étant le très-vénérable Grand-Maitre de toutes les Loges du Royaume d'Angleterre, le vénérable Maitre, les Surveillans, les Compagnons & les Apprentifs de la Loge Françoise des Francs-Maçons size à Londres dans la Ruë de Suffolck à l'Enseigne du Duc de Lorraine, après avoir attentivement ouï la lecture d'un Manuscript intitulé HISTOIRE DES FRANCS-MAÇONS &c. ont unanimement déclaré qu'il ne contenoit rien, qui ne fût conforme aux Loix, aux Statuts, aux Réglemens & aux Usages de la très-ancienne & très-vénérable Confraternité.

Le Frère FRIARD, *Sécrétaire* avec paraphe.

The name of Union Lodge seemed to spread across Europe, and to find resonance in other cities in Europe and this might have some significance. Strangely it only became known as the Union French Lodge in 1739 when it moved from the Kings Arms to the Union Coffee House—so it got its name from the Coffee House where it met and not because it was forming 'masonic unions.' Sometimes research provides unexpected answers.

The Members of Lodge No. 98 who have been traced and tracked

Lewis Mercy[5]—first master of the Union French Lodge

Wallace McLeod noted that there were two musicians in the Union French Lodge and that their details were recorded in the Grove Dictionary.

> Professor Gordon R. Silber has pointed out that two more members of Coustos's lodges in London were apparently musicians of note who merit an entry in Stanley Sadie (ed.) The New Grove

---

5   Mercy's flute music is available on YouTube and also on CD, Tactus TC691302.

Dictionary of Music and Musicians (London, 1980). At any rate the names coincide and the dates are right.

> Mercy, Lewis[6] (c. 1695–c. 1750), member, Lodge No. 75, London, 1730; Master, Lodge No. 98, London, 1732; 'English composer and recorder player of French origin'; in the service of the Earl of Carnarvon (father of the Grand Master for 1738) 'probably before 1720' (The New Grove Dictionary of Music and Musicians (London, 1980) (Grove, volume 12, p. 178).

> Snow, Valentine, member, Lodge No. 75, London, 1730; Snow, Valentine (possibly before 1702–1770), 'English trumpeter,' for whom 'Handel wrote the obbligato trumpet part in Messiah' (1741) and other works; sergeant-trumpeter to the king, 1753–1770 (Grove, volume 17, p. 428).[7]

It seems this group of brothers were not only musical, but that they operated in a world where they were well connected to key figures of their day. There are repeated mentions of Handel for example, which demonstrate the social circles they were associated with.

Mr Lanse (aka Thomas Lansa) Warden

Little is known except that he was clearly a musician and/or a composer, and probably a professional. Quite often he is credited with authorship of songs. More is said in a section on masonic songs as an addendum to this chapter. The 1749 edition of Chansons Originaires throws light on the various editions of songs of a quality Lansa did not approve of, but it is clear that several members of the Union French Lodge were keen to promote the 'craft' of masonic singing.

Mr Protin	Warden – no discovered details
Mr Friard	[Secretary] – no discovered details
Mr St Jean	no details discovered
Mr Vincent La Chapelle	(see later in this chapter)

Mr Delahaye – no discovered details

---

6   Also see Wikipedia "Merci was born around 1695 in England, probably into a French-English family, and died in London around 1750. He was engaged around 1720 in the musical chapel of James Brydges, Earl of Carnarvon and Duke of Chandos. In 1730 he married Ann Hampshire and settled in Covent Garden. In collaboration with the recorder maker Thomas Stanesby (1692–1754), he tried to improve the recorder, which at that time was in danger of disappearing in favour of the transverse flute."

7   Wallace McLeod, More Light on John Coustos, *AQC* vol.95, p. 119.

Mr Coustos. Jean Coustos was a jeweller by trade, a founder member of No. 9. He left London for Paris and set up the Villeroy—Coustos Lodge. This lodge closed because of the Herault action and then Coustos travelled to Lisbon in Portugal perhaps with the idea of travelling to Brazil. While practicing his free-masonry in Lisbon he was arrested and interrogated by the Holy Inquisition. He was sentenced to serve rowing in the galleys, but by the request of the British government was soon released and returned to Britain.

Jacopo Fabris (b.1689 Venice–d. 1761 Copenhagen). When Fabris arrived in Berlin after a few years in Mannheim Fabris sought details of the Scots Masters degree, almost certainly from his London lodge and founded the Scot's Masters Lodge L'Union in Berlin on St Andrews Day 1742. Fabris was an artist spe-cialising in buildings and ruins in the landscape and an expert in perspective, and his paintings sell at auctions today at decent prices. His career took him across Europe and a summary of his life's travels is worth repeating. More im-portant at the time, but more ephemeral, was probably his skills in scenery painting in theatres and opera houses. Information is ephemeral but it does illustrate that his moves around Europe were related to employment offered by the higher levels of society. His career was pan European; Karlsruhe 1719-1721, Court Painter to the Margrave of Baden-Durlach in Karlsruhe, Hamburg 1724-1730, theatre painter at the Opernhaus and designed the sets for Handels 'Giulio Cesare' performed at Hamburg in 1725, London 1730–1736, collabo-rated with Handel, Mannheim 1736–1741, Berlin 1741–1747, Theatre Painter to Frederich the Great in Berlin and finally Copenhagen 1747–1761, Theatre Painter to Frederich V in Copenhagen.[8] He also took the Maitre Ecossois degree to Copenhagen.

Louis-François Marquis de la Tierce (b.1699–d.1782). Said to be a military en-gineer by training, and also to have been tutor to the children of Lord Stafford. He was the translator of the 1723 Andersons Constitutions into French which was completed by 1733. At the same time he was working on the words of ma-sonic songs with other members of the Union French Lodge, but it seems that he had to leave London in 1733 with these matters unfinished. He was also the 'redacteur-negre' (copy editor with the phrase implying that this was a hard task) for the 1738 edition of Andersons Constitutions. He was one of the founders of the Union Lodge in Francfort and this was at the time of the coronation of Charles III, a fortuitous timing because it brought together the key players of the Union Lodge, and Joseph Uriot who was then involved in theatre work as a comedian.. Frankfort was also a centre of the book trade at the time.

De la Tierce also adapted Andersons Constitutions with his own interpretations

---

8   Source: wikidata.org and his occupations discovered from many sources.

of freemasonry which were published in 1742 and then 1745. His role in the development of masonry in Europe as a result of his publications deserves further study.

Philipp Friederich Steinheil (b.1703–d.1763 Frankfurt) The founder and first master of the 'Frankfort Lodge of Union', Philipp Friederich Steinheil, was a German diplomat who had been *en poste* in London when he had been initiated. He was present in Grand Lodge in March 1741 at the election of the Earl of Morton as Grand Master, and gave one of the addresses. Steinheil, with his high-level London connections, was able to get *post facto* regularization of the Frankfurt Lodge by a Charter from the Grand Lodge of England, dated 8 February 1743. This states that a Bro. Beaumont, oculist to the Prince of Wales, having assured 'us that the Lodge had been constituted in due *form* under the name of Union, and as a daughter of the Union Lodge of London, we do hereby recognize it, etc. and order that the members of either Lodge be equally considered members of the other.'

But there is rather more to it that the words of an English Brother because 30 October 1744 Steinheil was elected Master of the Lodge of the Three Globes in Berlin[9] and that in 1746 he published "Die Quintessenz der ächten Freymaurerey: entworssen von einem Meister der Schottishen Bruderschaft."[10]

Steinheil does not seem to have left such a big mark as some other members of the lodge, but certainly in Frankfurt he probably was the one with the best social contacts and best placed tob provide a safe foundation for the new lodge. But it seems that like de la Tierce he too had a view of what freemasonry was at its centre. And it is worth noting what Eugen Lennhoff had to say about him:

> Saxonian secretary of the legation, became a freemason in England and came to Frankfurt am Main 1741 for the election and coronation of Charles VII. At the suggestion of the French envoy Marquis de Belleisle he met German and French freemasons, diplomats like him, 1742 to found the lodge "L'Union" (later "Zur Einigkeit"), of which he became first master of the chair.

> He wrote down a famous speech in French "about the first ideas and knowledge of the noble art of masonry," published 1746 in German in "Die Quintessenz der echten Freimaurerey," often read in lodges,

---

9 Alain Bernheim, "Did Early High or Ecossais Degrees Originate in France." *Freemasonry in Context* (2004), p. 31; and also at Pietre Stones, "High or Ecossais Degrees Originate in France" http://www.freemasons-freemasonry.com/bernheim17.html

10 Additional details can be found at https://freimaurer-wiki.de/index.php/Philipp_Friederich_Steinheil

also in the Grand Lodge of London. Steinheil is also regarded as the author of the defensive pamphlet published on the occasion of the Bernese masonic printing of 1746: "Le Franc-Maçon dans la République."[11]

It is interesting to read on the cover.

In his speech (also reproduced in the "Eklektisches Bundesblatt," 1931, no. 27), Steinheil calls Freemasonry "a union of discerning men who, strengthened by the fraternal bond and guided by the rules of moral virtue, try to form a rational society to which each of its members must contribute all that it can make useful and pleasant."

It is perhaps odd that while his presence was recorded in the minute book of the Grand Lodge in London, the fact that he spoke (at length) is not recorded. What he had to say is thus better known in Europe and unknown here in England.

And near the end our researches we discovered another name, that of Prince Anthony Esterhazy published in the London paper, the Daily Advertiser[12]:

> Daily Advertiser, 9th August, 1733. Prince Anthony Esterhazy admitted F.M. "at the French Lodge held the first and third Tuesdays of every month, at the Duke of Lorrain's Head, in Suffolk Street."

---

11 *International Masonic Encyclopaedia* by Eugen Lennhoff and Oskar Posner (1932 ed.), p. 804.

12 W Chetwode Crawley.

A thought to ponder

Could it be that the Lewis Mercy[13] who was involved with, and Master of, the Union French Lodge that same person who then appears twenty years later living at the Golden Horseshoe on the south bank of the Thames, where it seems he was living in 1750? Sadly the Licenced Victuallers records for Southwark in 1750 seem not to exist. However the possibility that this brother being involved with other known brothers was active in spreading freemasonry could be one and the same person. We leave that thought for some other curious mind to investigate.

Could he in his old age have ended up as the Grand Secretary to the Harodim of Kilwinning? Maybe some other researcher might like the challenge.

Ch 7.c The Union French Lodge & its Music

Music is a moral law. It gives soul to the universe, wings to the mind, flight to the imagination, and charm and gaiety to life and to everything. —Plato

When this research started the Union French Lodge was probably no more than the lodge that John Coustos belonged to before he went to Paris. And apart from the list of members in 1733 in the minutes of the Grand Lodge of England the sheet of paper remained stubbornly blank. Some months ago I chanced across some words by Wallace McLeod in his short paper 'More Light on John Coustos'[14] (although it took me most of a day to convert that memory into finding the words once more).

ADDENDUM

MORE MUSICIANS IN COUSTOS'S LODGE. Professor Gordon R. Silber has pointed out that two more members of Coustos's lodges in London were apparently musicians of note who merit an entry in Stanley Sadie (ed.) The New Grove Dictionary of Music and Musicians (London, 1980). At any rate the names coincide and the dates are right.

Mercy, Lewis (c. 1695–c. 1750), member, Lodge No. 75, London, 1730; Master, Lodge No. 98, London, 1732; 'English composer and recorder player of French origin'; in the service of the Earl of Carnarvon (father of the Grand Master for 1738) 'probably before 1720' (Grove, volume 12, p. 178).

---

13 Lewis Mercy, Sonatas for Flute. https://www.muziekweb.nl/Link/CDX0901 CD Tactus TC691302. Here again is another member of the French Union Lodge!

14 Wallace McLeod, "More Light on John Coustos," *AQC* volume 95 (1982), pp. 117-119.

Snow, Valantine, member, Lodge No. 75[15], London, 1730; Snow, Valantine (possibly before 1702-1770), 'English trumpeter,' for whom 'Handel wrote the obbligato trumpet part in Messiah' (1741) and other works; sergeant-trumpeter to the king, 1753–1770 (Grove, volume 17, p. 428).

Two points of interest are that the Grove Dictionary mentions that Mercy was in the service of the Earl of Carnarvon, and that Snow had a work written for him in the Messiah by George Frideric Handel. Sadie was not quite right about Carnarvon, but the clue was there.

The reality was that it was James Brydges, the first Duke of Chandos, 'who was a patron of Handel.' The duke, a flute player, had a private orchestra, consisting of 24 instrumentalists. Johnn Christoph Pepusch was the Master of Music at Cannons from 1716 and he saw the size of the musical establishment at first expand and then decline in the 1720s in response to Brydges' losses in the South Sea Bubble, a financial crash which took place in 1720.[16]

The mention of Handel was exciting because another member of the Union French Lodge who came to London 'worked for Handel,' the painter Jacopo Fabris.[17] Most of Fabris's work that remains is in terms of city landscapes with grand buildings, his paining of scenery for operas backdrops has (perhaps inevitably) vanished. However it is clear why he had come to London. And as well McLeod offers the following members:

> **Friard, Augustus and Daniel,** members, Lodge No. 75, London, 1730; Friard, -- member, Lodge No. 98, London, 1732; 'Le Frere Friard, Secretaire,' on behalf of the 'the Worshipful Master, Wardens, Fellows, and Apprentices of the French lodge of Free Masons meeting at the Duke of Lorraine, Suffolk Street, London' (that is, Lodge No. 98; see Lane, *Masonic Records,* p. 59) signed the approbation (dated August 1733) to La Tierce's translation of Anderson's *Constitutions* of 1723, which was published under the title *Histoiries obligations et sta ruts de la tres venerable confra ternite des Francs-Macons* (Frankfurt-on-Main **1742**). (See Silber, p. 172, note 8)

---

15 No. 75 met at the Rainbow Coffee House and was the lodge with the key members of the Union French Lodge. Snow seems not to have been one of the early members of No. 98 (but could possibly have joined later).

16 Wikipedia, Handel at Cannons. Viewed July 2023. The son of the Duke of Chandos, Henry Brydges, had the title of the Earl of Carnarvon (until he succeeded to his father's title).

17 Fabris's career was Karlsruhe 1719–1721, Hamburgh 1724–1730, London 1730–1736, Mannheim 1736–1741, Berlin 1741–1747 and Copenhagen 1747–1761. So he was also in London at the right time.

de la Cappell, Vincent, member, Lodge No. 75, London, 1730; La Chappelle, Vincent, member, Lodge No. 98, 1732, *chef de cuisine,* first to the British ambassador (to the Netherlands), Phillip Stanhope, Earl of Chesterfield, and then to William of Orange, later to become William IV (Jacob, p. 110, citing Dr **S, K.** Blom, 'Vincent La Chappele,' *Thoth: Tijdschrift voor vrijmetselaren,* vol. 28, 1977); Worshipful Master of the first lodge in the Netherlands, founded in the Hague in November 1734; published the first collection of masonic songs in French, *Chansons de la tres-venerable confiairie de Macons Libres* (The Hague, 1735; 'Aux depens du Sr. Vincent La Chapelle, Maitre de Lodge'). (See Silber, p. 172, note 8; p. 176.)

Lance, Thomas, member, Lodge No. 75, London, 1730; Lanse, --, member, Lodge No. 98, London, 1732; 'Le Frere de Lansa' translated into French The Master's Song and the Enter'd 'Prentice's Song, for inclusion in La Tierce's *Histoire etc.* (1742); 'le Frere Lansa' subsequently published a collection of songs, *Chansons originaires de Francs Macons* (The Hague, 1747). (See Silber, p. 172, note 8; pp. 181-2.) Laroche, member, --, Lodge No. 98, London, 1732; according to Professor Jacob (p. 131, citing unpublished manuscript sources in the University Library, Cambridge), he was one of Robert Walpole's agents, who 'spied on the Jacobites in Paris and reported back directly to Walpole.'

de La Tierce, 'Marquis' Louis Francois (1699–1782). He was one of the founders of the Lodge *zur Einigkeit* in Frankfurt, probably in 1741. In the preface to his translation of Anderson, *Histoire, etc.* (1742) La Tierce mentions that he wrote it in London in 1733 and that it was approved by the lodges there; the approbation (dated 1733) was signed by Brother Friard (see above). The book is dedicated by 'The Author to the Brethren of his Lodge' that is, 'to the Worshipful Master, Wardens, Fellows and Apprentices of the French Lodge of Freemasons constituted at London with the usual ceremonies 17 August 1732.' In the dedicatory epistle he states explicitly that he was 'received as a member of your lodge,' evidently at a date subsequent to the initial return to Grand Lodge. The book includes The Warden's Song and The Fellow-craft's Song, both translated by 'le Frere de la Tierce,' while the other two songs were translated by Brother Lansa (see above). (Silber, p. 172, note 8; pp. 178, 182; Labbe, pp. 20-1.)

But the further we have searched the more apparent it is that music and song played a large and significant part in the Lodge. To find that the three senior officers in the new lodge all came for one other lodge is an indication that they had one shared purpose in mind. And it might seem that music and songs were at the top of the list. (see Chapter 20)

John Coustos's release from the Galley—a thought

For years I have wondered quite how and why Jean Coustos got released from his sentence by the Inquisition to be a rower on the galleys. It was almost certainly the influence of the Earl of Carnarvon, Grand Master, Peer of the Realm, and Master of the Horse to Frederick Prince of Wales. The Earl had a track record of helping those who faced bad times with fortitude and there seems no reason why the principles demonstrated below could not have been applied to Coustos a few years later.

In 1728, he married Lady Mary Bruce (1710–1738), daughter of the fourth Earl of Elgin. They had two children who survived childhood, Lady Caroline Brydges (1729–1789) and James Brydges, 3rd Duke of Chandos. The Duke's second marriage was unconventional. In 1744, he married Anne Wells, a former chambermaid from Newbury in Berkshire. They had met a few years earlier in circumstances described by a witness as follows:

> The Duke of Chandos and a companion dined at the Pelican, Newbury, on the way to London. A stir in the Inn yard led to their being told that a man was going to sell his wife, and they are leading her up with a halter around her neck. They went to see. The Duke was smitten with her beauty and patient acquiescence in a process which would (as then supposed) free her from a harsh and ill-conditioned husband. He bought her, and subsequently married her (at Keith's Chapel) on Christmas Day, 1744.[18]

Or one can take a slightly different version from the Gentleman's Magazine of 1832.

> The Duke of Chandos, while staying at a small country inn, saw the ostler beating his wife in a most cruel manner; he interfered and literally bought her for half a crown. She was a young and pretty woman; the Duke had her educated; and on the husband's death he married her. On her death-bed, she had her whole household assembled, told them her history, and drew from it a touching moral of reliance on Providence; as from the most wretched situation, she had been suddenly raised to one of the greatest prosperity; she entreated their forgiveness if at any time she had given needless offence, and then dismissed them with gifts; dying almost in the very act.

---

18 *Notes and Queries*, Fourth Series, VI, 179; 27 August 1870.

Freemasonry in the Netherlands—the Seven United Provinces

This section is here because it relates the efforts of Vincent la Chapelle, a member of the Union French Lodge No. 98, and his efforts in establishing freemasonry in the Seven United Provinces of the Netherlands. But it is also relevant because it is a part of the background of William Mitchell and his HRDM patent for the Loge de Juste.

The early years of masonry in the Netherlands (then the Seven United Provinces) does involve a member of Lodge No. 98 and his employer the British Ambassador to the Netherlands. And Freemasonry also became to political tool for the British government, and perhaps a route further into a Europe full of small statelets. But it is also important to always also remember that the English merchants who traded across the North Sea also brought freemasonry with them and that two formed part of the bigger picture.

So while the Seven United Provinces or the members of Lodge No. 98 played a smaller role in the developing higher degrees they were always a force to be reckoned with. Also by forming their own Grand Lodge in 1735 they were very much 'ahead of the game,' and being an entrepot of ideas actions provided constant challenges for the Grand Lodge in London to deal with.

It seemed easier to keep all the Netherlandic story together in one place because otherwise it would become split between several chapters.

The first Lodge in Holland

Upon being advised by Jan Snoek that most of my previous version was wrong (for which I thank him) the writer set about seeing just where he had gone wrong, and in doing so a more complicated train of events appeared that should please the reader.

The first of these meetings is often stated to be the first meeting of a lodge in the Netherlands that took place in May or June 1731, even if only of the 'occasional' kind. At first sight it seems to have little to do with Netherlandic masonry, except that Richard Stanhope was actually the British ambassador to the Netherlands at Den Haag (and one Bro Vincent la Chapelle was his chef extraordinaire). The meeting in Norfolk occurred between the 4th and the 13th November 1731.

The November meeting is reported in Anderson's 1738 Constitutions. There can be little doubt that both events took place because they are reported in several places. Anderson says Desaguliers was present at the Den Haag lodge but Thory, in 1815, gives us a different picture, without Dr Desaguliers:

> "C'est en cette annee quon trouve les premieres traces de l'introduction de la Maconnerie dans les Provinces-Unies des Pays-Bas.

Une grande Assemblee de Macons se reunit a la Haye sous la presidence de *Philippe Stanhope*, comte de Chesterfield, ambassadeur d'Angleterre. L'ecuyer *Strickland* remplissait les fonctions de depute, et MM. Benjamin *Hadley* et Guill. *Ducth* celles de premier et second Gardiens. On y recoit *Francois*, duc de Lorraine, grand duc de Toscane, depuis empereur d'Allemagne."[19]

And that later in the year the Duke of Lorraine did visit England and did visit Houghton Hall and an 'occasional lodge' was held. It was recorded in *The Norwich Gazette* that under the dateline of London, November 27th, 1931 that:

We hear that during the Stay of the Duke of Lorrain at Houghton in Norfolk, a Lodge of Free and Accepted Masons was held before the Lord Lovell, Grand Master, in which Sir Robert Walpole and Count Kinski were admitted Brethren.

And on this occasion there is a third opinion as to what took place, and Daynes tells us that:

Lastly, we have the Maid's Head Lodge account, which tells us that this Lodge was summoned by the Grand Master to Houghton, and that Thomas Johnson, the then Master, made the Duke of Newcastle, the Earl of Essex, Major General Churchill and Lord Lovell's Chaplain Masons in the presence of the Duke of Lorraine and many others.[20]

It seems best to start with the quote in Andersons 1738 Constitutions:

His Royal Highness FRANCIS Duke of *Lorrain* (now *Grand Duke* of Tuscany) at the *Hague* was made an *Enter'd Prentice* and *Fellow Craft*, by Virtue of a *Deputation* for a *Lodge* there, consisting of Rev. Dr. Desaguliers Master, *John Stanhope*, Esq.; *Jn. Holtzendorf*, Esq.; *Grand Wardens*, and the other Brethren, viz. Philip Stanhope Earl of *Chesterfield* Lord Ambassador, – *Strickland* Esq.; nephew to the Bishop of *Namur*, Mr. *Benjamin Hadley* and an *Hollandish* Brother.

Our said *Royal* Brother LORRAIN coming to *England* this Year, *Grand Master* Lovel formed an Occasional Lodge at Sir *Robert Walpole's* House of *Houghton-Hall* in *Norfolk*, and made Brother LORRAIN and Brother Thomas Pelham Duke of *Newcastle* **Master Masons**. And ever since, both in the G. Lodge and in partic-

---

19 Daynes, p.140 & Thory Acta Latomorum (1815), p. 25.

20 Daynes, p. 125.

ular *Lodges,* the Fraternity joyfully remember His Royal Highness in the proper Manner.[21]

There can be no doubt that this meeting actually took place, while there must be considerable doubt regarding the 1738 statement by Anderson that the Duke of Lorraine and the Duke of Newcastle were made Master Masons in the presence of the Grand Master Lord Lovell. The dislike of *Masonry Dissected* that was made public in Grand Lodge in December 1730 makes it seem very strange that a mere one year later, the third degree of Master Mason had been in any way accepted by those controlling Grand Lodge? The details of exactly who was present at these lodges remains (sadly) inconsistent. Alas another error of memory by Anderson seems probable.

Lists of ambassadors state that Stanhope was ambassador to the United Provinces from 1728 to 1734, and other sources suggest that he had to return for a while on either health of financial reasons but return he did because he was in Den Haag for the visit of the Duke of Lorraine in the role of Ambassador. But we do know that Stanhope was appointed ambassador and left the country on 23rd April 1728. It seems that he was charged with helping negotiate the 1731 Treaty of Vienna and to 'arrange' the marriage of Princess Anne, daughter of George II to William IV Prince of Orange. [That wedding took place at St James Palace. London on 25 March 1734]. One can read that Stanhope had to return to England because of poor health or financial reasons in 1730, but it is clear that he was back in Den Haag for the arrival of the duke of Lorraine in mid-1731.

Vincent la Chapelle (c.1690 to 1703–1745)

Was born in France, and described variously as a Catholic or a Huegenot, and whose life until he arrived in London a mystery. He rose to fame as a chef seemingly in the household of the Earl of Chesterfield and became a mason all in a few years in London. All this seemed to happen rapidly because Stanhope only returned to London after the death of George I in June 1727, where he sought successfully to establish himself with the new regime.

Cookery sources suggest that la Chapelle was Stanhope's Chef between 1728 and 1732 but without offering any evidence, one source stated that he only left Stanhope after the marriage of Willem IV and Anne returning 'with them' to the Netherlands in 1734 to become chef d'office, (chef de cuisine and concierge) of the Palace of the Prince of Orange.[22]

---

21 James Anderson, *Book of Constitutions,* 2nd edition, 1738, p. 129. Also read the paper by Gilbert Daynes in *AQC* 37 (1927), THE DUKE OF LORRAINE AND ENGLISH FREEMASONRY 1N 1731, where all these events are recalled in excellent and fascinating detail. It is worth adding that Walpole was Prime Minister of the UK from 1725–1742.

22 Jan Snoek, Radermacher, Johan Cornelis / Jean Corneille (1700–1748)," in: C. Porset &

Despite this slightly uncertain chronology it was certainly quite feasible for la Chapelle to be initiated in London, and recorded as being a member of two lodges in 1731, the Lodge at the Rainbow Coffee House and the Lodge at Prince Eugen's Head (later named as the Union French Lodge).[23] At this point memory caused a reminder to ring loudly, and upon checking it was confirmed that both la Chapelle and John Coustos (who was questioned by the Inquisition in Lisbon) were both members of the same two lodges in London—and so must have known each other each other (see later / earlier in the book).

On 8th November 1734 la Chapelle formed a lodge at the tavern 'Lion d'Or' in Den Haag, with himself as Master assisted by six Brethren and on the same day they made four men masons, including Louis Dagran, a draper from Lisbon.[24] On 22nd November 1734 it seems they sent a Brother Liegois to London to secure 'une legitime constitution' but what happened to it is unknown. On 4th March 1735 they initiated Johann Cornelius Rademacher (treasurer to the Prince of Orange). Jean de Missy (historian, and Orangeist journalist) and several others. And at the next meeting on 24th June 1735 the lodge declared itself to be a Grand Lodge, elected Radermacher as its "First Grand Master of our illustrious Order in the United Provinces and of the Resort of the Generality," and promptly renamed itself the Lodge of the Grand Master of the United Provinces and of the Resort of the Generality; after which Radermacher appointed Johan Küenen his "Deputy Grand Master," and Louis Dagran his "Venerable Lodge Master".

After that, maybe around 16th October 1734 a lodge was formed in Amsterdam and soon after on 24th October a second lodge was formed in Den Haag named 'Le Veritable Zele' with Dagran as its Master upon the instructions of 'their Grand Master.' But of course there were no rules, and very few precedents, saying that they could not do this.

For example in England the first Provincial Grand Master in the Grand Lodge of England was for Cheshire and he was chosen by the brothers in the city of Chester—and Grand Lodge was not consulted. One has to realise that the English Grand Lodge was struggling even to produce minutes and send them to the increasing number of lodges spread across England—without being concerned with what was happening on the other side of the North Sea.

C. Révauger (eds): *Le Monde Maçonnique des Lumières (Europe-Amériques & Colonies). Dictionnaire prosopographique/* (3 Vols), Champion: Paris, pp. 2322-2324.

23 QCA Vol.10 Members all name: Rainbow Coffee House, pp. 183-184, and Prince Eugen's Head, pp. 192-193.The Lodge at the Rainbow Coffee House was warranted on 17 July 1730 and was then No. 75 and now Britannic Lodge No. 33. The lodge at Prince Eugen's Head was warranted 17 August 1732, named as Union French Lodge in 1739 and ceased in 1753.

24 Dr D E Boerenbeker, The Relations between Dutch and English Freemasonry from 1734 to 1771. *AQC* vol. 83, p. 149. Sadly he does not name the other brothers.

La Chapelle was as much a celebrity chef as any of those who appear on out television screens today, and he ensured his popularity by publishing a set of cookbooks. These appeared in London, under several publishers, the 1ˢᵗ edition in 1733, the 2ⁿᵈ in 1736, the 3ʳᵈ in 1744 and the 4ᵗʰ in 1751. But also, being a celebrity chef in the Netherlands, he published his series there in French: the 1ˢᵗ ed in 1735 and a second edition in 1742.

A Grand Lodge in the Netherlands

The appearance of an advertisement in the *Amsterdam Saturdaegse Courant* on 5 November 1735,[25]

> "In the presence of the Grand Master J. Cornelis Radermacher, Tresorier Generael van zyn Hooght. den Heer Prince van Oranje, and the Gedeputeerde Groot Meester Johan Kuenen ...."

And also in the *Daily Advertiser* November 1735 there was an announcement of the creation of this Netherlandic lodge stating that

> "The solemnity was honoured by the presence of their Grand Master, Mr. John Cornelis Rademaker, Treasurer of His Highness the Prince of Orange, and their Deputy Grand Master, Mr. John Cuenen...." [It is important to remember that at this time Willem IV was only Prince of Orange and not the Stadtholder of the United Provinces].

It is worth pointing out that Johan Keunan had translated the Anderson 1723 Constitutions into Dutch and the a few years later also published them in French. Given how long it took the people of the Pays-Bas to escape from the Hapsburg dynasty, it is perhaps not surprising that they also thought to take their freemasonry under their own control.

Willem III of the United Provinces was also to become King William III of England, Scotland, and Ireland, and when he died in 1702 there were complications. The succession lay in the hands of his sister-in-law and cousin Anne and that the end result of this was that a suitable stadtholder could not be found; as a result, there was a Stadtholderless period until 1748. Thus, if the British Ambassador promoted the marriage of the Anne, the daughter of George II of Britain which took place in 1731—this was high international politics. In the same way that placing an advertisement in the newspaper which indicated that Freemasonry was distinctly Orangeist could also be considered a political

---

25 Van den Brand, *De vrijmetselarij in de Republiek der Verenigde Nederlanden tot 1737, Vestiging en Verbod*, Doctoraalscriptie Geschiedenis, Rijksuniversiteit Utrecht, (1993), p. 33.

act. So to discover that after an investigation of around a month the provinces of Holland and West Friesland banned the order. And it remained banned until 1744 when it was reopened by Dagran with the approval of Rademacher. Willem IV did not become Stadtholder until 1748, but presumably his power-base was sufficiently strong allow freemasonry to open its lodges again without problems.

This Netherlands story does not end here and is completed in the chapter on the Harodim and the Royal Order of Scotland.

Vincent la Chapelle went on to publish a book of masonic songs in Den Haag in 1735?? And to be chef for John V of Portugal and Madame de Pompadour (the mistress of Louis XV) and publishing a final five volume set of Le Cuisine Moderne in Den Haag in 1742 and another in London in 1744. He died in 1745 in Apeldoorn in Holland, so if he had a 'home' anywhere then perhaps it was in the Netherlands.

La Loge de Juste, Den Haag 1751

Enlightenment thinking must have run deep in Den Haag in the 1750s because in that year a group decided that they would like to form a Lodge of Adoption. These discussions included what degrees they wanted to work and apart from the three degrees normal in a Lodge of Adoption they decided that they wanted to work the Rose Croix degree, and they decided to send two of the founders to get a patent to work the degree, and they were Bros William Mitchell and Jonas Kluck. Thus the two Brothers set out, possibly via Paris, and ended up in London in June or July 1750 and made contact with the 'Order of H.R.D.M. of K.L.W.N.N.G in South Britain,' who were based in London, and to obtain a patent. They agreed and presumably the fee was paid and the petition submitted around the 10 July. Some twelve days later, on the 22 July, Mitchell attended at the 'sign of the Golden Horseshoe' and was presented with all the paper work, which he took back to Holland with him arriving at some unknown later date.

The Lodge had taken its title from the name of the Master who was one Juste Girard, Baron Wassenair (who coincidentally was also the current Grand Master of the (Craft) Grand Lodge). The minutes of the Lodge are extant and record a meeting of 24 November 1751, in which those present agreed that in the absence of a charter they had decided instead to work the Ecossais grades of 'Architect' and 'Grand Architect.' Lindsay tells us that the records of la Loge de Juste are extant and in particular he refers to a report dated 24th November:

> (b) a draft or copy of a report by the Deputy Master de Saint Etienne
> to the Grand Master dated 24th November 1751. It refers to the fact
> that whilst waiting for a Charter, the Lodge had thought it more

prudent to work only the Degrees of Adopted Masonry but that when the expected Charter did not materialise it was decided to adopt a new form of Masonry known as Eccosais Masonry consisting of the two grades of Architect and Grand Architect, which it is intended to use in addition to the degrees of Adoptive Masonry.[26]

Lindsay goes on to say that Mitchell's name appears in the records of the meeting held on 11th April but not thereafter. The financial records also tell us that the Lodge met once in January, twice in February, three times in March, twice in April and then on the first of May. In the light of this it would seem that the lodge was acting 'under (self) dispensation.'[27] But all did not go well and the events of May 1751 are worth recounting:

> ... serious financial trouble ... turned to the Grand Master [of the Dutch masonic Grand Lodge], Juste Gerard [Baron of Wassenaer], for help ... Whatever the reason, Juste Gerard agreed to recognise this Lodge of Adoption with a founding date of 1 May 1751. He not only recognised it, but even turned it into a Grand Lodge of Adoption, becoming its Grand Master himself. The last entry in the accounts was made over two weeks after the official recognition. It brings them up to date to 16 May and shows a debt of f 208.4. To all appearances the records were made specially to be presented to Juste Gerard, who in all probability paid the debts of the newly recognised lodge. De St. Etienne would have been reimbursed at least f 169.20. Since the lodge's brand new songbook, with De St. Etienne's *Discours*, was published at this time, the Grand Lodge of the United Provinces or, more likely, Van Wassenaer himself would almost certainly have financed this as well.[28]

Probably the closing remark in this episode that the (1735) Grand Lodge collapsed as a result of mismanagement and the then Grand Master van Wassenaar resigned. His place was taken by Louis Dagran as interim Grand Master in June 1752.

But returning to Mitchell and his patent. He received it in July 1750, but he

---

26 Robert Strathern Lindsay, *The Royal Order of Scotland* edited by AJ Milborne (1972), p. 62. Lindsay does not tell us where the records are but Snoek does and they are in the Archives of Grand East of the Netherlands (GON Arch. 4686 [563–2] (dossier Loge 'La Juste').

27 The practice of working 'under dispensation' is one still widely used in North America where a new lodge often works this way before being finally 'Constituted.'

28 Malcolm Davies, *The Masonic Muse. Songs, Music, and Musicians Associated with Dutch Freemasonry: 1730–1806*, (2005), Utrecht pp. 88-89.

must have not communicated his success to Den Haag, or his letter never arrived. Either way the decision instead to add the Ecossais degrees instead of the HRDM changed the direction of Netherlandic masonry—and the exchange of letters regarding the Scots degrees with Manningham that took place in 1757 shows that the Scots Lodges had gained significant position in the Netherlands.

So finally all the efforts of Mitchell and Kluck came to nothing, but it does at least explain why Mitchell felt he could take his patent to Edinburgh and to use it there to create the Heredom of Kilwinning in Scotland.

Lindsay in providing his explanation of the troubles that Mitchell might have faced in trying to use his patent in Holland are all based upon his assumption that the patent would be used according to its wording, a rather narrow way of thinking. It is important to remember that there is a long and proud tradition of a patent being issued for one purpose being used for another, and that the origin and source of any patent is often far less important than having a beautifully written document that can be waved about. Later the case of the Knights Templars of Ireland Kilwinning Lodge will provide another example. (The practice is still in use in the 21st century with a USA example relating to the CBCS).

Ch.9

Freemasonry arrives in France (1725-1736)

reemasonry, as everyone knows, was not born in France, but it made its appearance there very early on. The history of the "grades Ecossais" in France, which will be the main subject of the following chapters, cannot be approached, nor can it be understood, without first recalling how and when Freemasonry appeared in Paris, around 1725, so who were the men who introduced it to this country, and in what form it then took?

The question is made all the more delicate by the fact that there is an almost completely obscure period in this early history of Masonry in France: it covers roughly the years 1725 to 1736. Original French Masonic documents from this period are extremely scarce—but in some cases they do provide valuable information. However, from its very beginnings, early French masonry, inheriting a cultural heritage that was already well characterised, resulting from several years of evolution in Scotland and England, already provides us with some information and clues as to what the first "Scottish" grades would be, very shortly afterwards.

Before going any further, let us briefly retrace the first stages of this genesis.

The public revelation of Freemasonry in France

One of the first public revelations of Freemasonry in France took place on 27 December 1736. It took place in an establishment called Le Grand Saint-Germain, rue du Paon—also known as rue du Paon Saint-André—in the central district of Paris, the Faubourg Saint-Germain, near the abbey of Saint-Germain-des-Prés, whose commendatory abbot[1] a few months later was to be Louis de Bourbon-Condé, future Grand Master of the regular lodges of the Kingdom of France.

But that evening, it was another Grand Master who was being celebrated. A gazetin[2] echoed the news:

> On the 27th of last month, the feast of St John the Evangelist, a general meeting of the Most Ancient and Most Honourable Society of

---

1   En vertu du Concordat de Bologne, conclu en 1516 entre le pape et le roi de France, un laïc pouvait devenir « abbé en commende » d'une abbaye sur laquelle il n'exerçait aucun pouvoir spirituel mais dont il percevait les bénéfices.

2   Les gazetins, ou « nouvelles à la main », étaient de petits journaux manuscrits, souvent réduits à seule feuille, que l'on vendait dans les rues en dépit de la censure royale, et qui donnaient toutes sortes d'informations politiques ou littéraires, assez souvent frondeuses ou polémiques.

Free Masons was held at the Grand Saint-Germain, rue du Paon, to elect a Grand Master; after the ordinary ceremonies, the Most High and Mighty Lord Charles Ratcliff [sic], Earl of Derenwater[3] [sic], Peer of England, was proclaimed with great acclamation in place of the High and Mighty Lord Hector Mac Leone [sic], Knight Baronet of Scotland, who had been continued in this honourable office by election for several years to the satisfaction of the Society; On this occasion there was a magnificent feast where many came, 60 in number, in ceremonial dress and went by carriage to the Grand Lodge, where, after the meal, the proclamation of the Grand Master and his officers was accompanied by general applause and the sound of trumpets, timpani and hunting horns followed by a vocal [and] instrumental concert; the feast having ended to the satisfaction of the whole assembly, each Lodge withdrew in the same manner as it had arrived.[4]

In these few lines appear the names of two of the founders—and for several years, the leaders—of young French Freemasonry: Charles Radcliffe and Hector Maclean. Their identities and backgrounds are worth recalling here, because it was they who gave Freemasonry its first impetus in France.

An illegitimate descendant of Charles II through his mother, Mary Tudor, Charles Radcliffe (1693–1746), 5th Earl of Derwentwater from 1731, was an unbridled fighter for the Stuart cause, to which he devoted his life until he died on the scaffold, beheaded in London in 1746. He came to France at the age of ten to be brought up with his cousin, Jacques-François-Édouard (known as Jacques III or the "Old Pretender" to his Whig enemies), and did not return to England until 1712, shortly before taking part in the final and unsuccessful Jacobite uprising of 1715, during which he was taken prisoner and sentenced to death. He escaped his scheduled execution, however, by escaping from Newgate prison to France in December 1716. He was still only twenty-three.

Throughout his life, Radcliffe travelled all over Europe, from Brussels to Paris, from Turin to Rome, making brief visits to Great Britain, as he did in 1732, to try to recover his property confiscated by the government. From 1732 until 1745, however, he seems to have remained almost constantly in France, apart from a few brief visits to Scotland. That year, in anticipation of the forthcoming

---

3 Il subsiste un doute sur la présence effective de Derwentwater à Paris à cette date. Il y est sûrement en février 1737, pour installer la loge de Bussy-Aumont, mais un gazetin de juin de la même année le dit « arrivé depuis peu à Paris » (BHVP, ms. 616, f° 324). Il reste toutefois possible qu'il ait effectué dans l'intervalle un court voyage en Grande-Bretagne.

4 Gazetin manuscrit de la Bibliothèque d'Epernay, ms 124, cité par G. H. Luquet, *La franc-maçonnerie et l'État en France au 18è siècle*, 1963, p. 146.

Jacobite expedition—which ended in the final disaster at Culloden in 1746—Radcliffe embarked. Taken prisoner in November 1745, he was again condemned to death and, this time, perished under the executioner's axe in London on 8 December 1746.

No one yet knows where or when this unrepentant adventurer, an unconditional supporter of a cause he believed to be sacred, was initiated. There is nothing to say that it was in England, and this is perhaps even the least likely, if we consider for a moment the details of his biography. Perhaps he was received into the very lodge of which he is said to be the founder, in Paris, by others who had preceded him, at a time when a lodge was assembled without giving it a name or bothering to keep a register. It is known, however, that in the years following the Duke of Wharton's visit to France, driven out of England for his reversals and inconsistencies, Derwenwater was considered the Grand Master of Freemasons, if not in France, then at least in Paris.

What knowledge did this brawler, whose life was so turbulent—and so courageous—have of the English masonry of his time? No one can say, but given his chronology, we can assume that he knew very little.

Can Maclean, Derwentwater's predecessor at the head of the French lodges, tell us more?

Hector Maclean of Duart (1703–1750), 5th baronet and 20th head of his clan, was destined for exile: in fact, he was born there! His father, Sir John, had been forced to flee England for his Jacobite activities since 1689—but he returned to Scotland in 1703, shortly after the birth of his son, and was granted a pardon the following year. Many years later, Hector Maclean was captured by the English when he returned to Scotland to prepare for the insurrection of 1745. Unlike Derwentwater, he owed his life to this fact: by virtue of the law of the land which prevailed at the time, he had been born a French subject.

This robust man, whose honesty and generosity are accepted by all, spoke half a dozen languages and possessed a vast historical, scientific and religious culture. A perennial conspirator in the Stuartist party, pensioned off by the King of France, he died in Rome—a rare occurrence in his milieu—while seeking the Pretender's approval for a new landing plan on the Scottish coast.

Here again, the same conclusion can be drawn as for Derwentwater, whose life and origins were very different: it is possible that Maclean was initiated in Scotland, but he left no trace of it in the Masonic annals and, it seems, never took advantage of it. All hypotheses are therefore open, but it is also plausible that he was received into Masonry in Paris.[5] As with Derwentwater, if he was

---

5   Alec Mellor dit qu'il le fut en 1728 à Boulogne, mais sur quoi repose cette affirmation ? (*La*

propelled to the forefront of Parisian Masonry, his initiators remained in the shadows, but it is in any case difficult to see him as an educated heir to the traditions of "old Scottish Masonry."

These were two of the main "British" founders of Freemasonry in France! Freemasonry was clearly not the main focus of their lives; France was like a second homeland for them (or even the first for one of them!), and Freemasonry across the Channel, both English and Scottish, remained essentially quite foreign to them —they hardly knew it except on French soil. They were loyal to a king rather than to a country or an ideology. They were leaders, administrators and organisers—their courageous and risky political commitments forced them to develop these qualities. But in the end, we know little about their conception of Freemasonry—apart perhaps from their attraction to the discreet network it provided them for a little over a dozen years—it is indeed remarkable to observe that they distanced themselves from it or were dismissed from it as soon as it became public. It is thus understandable that, when the first disclosure of Masonic practices was made in 1737, as we shall see, Derwentwater "railed a great deal against the French and protested that it was against his feelings that they had been admitted!"[6] Proof, no doubt, that Masonry should, in his opinion, have remained confined to the small circle of British exiles in the capital.

The adventure had in fact begun a dozen years earlier.

The first steps and the obscure years

It has often been argued that the only surviving account of the creation of the Grand Lodge of London and Westminster is that provided by James Anderson —who was not present—some thirty years later.[7] However, the documented history of the first steps of Freemasonry in France begins with an account written some fifty years after the event:

Around the year 1725,[8] Milord Dervent-Waters, the Chevalier

---

charte inconnue de la franc-maçonnerie chrétienne, Paris, 1965, p. 66). Il reste que, dès 1721 et jusqu'en 1726, Maclean était venu parfaire son éducation à Paris.

6   Lettre de Le Camus à Bertin du Rocheret, le 23 décembre 1737 (BNF, ms fr. 15176, f° 27).

7   On sait que la date classique du 24 juin 1717, et même la réalité de l'événement, ont été remis en cause par des travaux récents. *Cf.* « A Quatuor Coronati Lodge Symposium: 1717 and all That, » *AQC* 131 (2018), pp. 35-136.

8   G. Bord, à partir d'une source qu'il ne précise pas, donne le 12 juin 1726 (*La franc-maçonnerie en France des origines à 1815 – vol. 1* [seul paru] *Les ouvriers de l'idée révolutionnaire (1688-1771)*, Paris, 1908, *rep.* 1985, p. 155), mais cette date apparaît aussi dans le « Registre du Président de la Grande Loge des Maîtres de l'Orient de Paris ditte de France du 19 may 5760 [1760] au 4 février 5767 [1767] » (BnF, FM₁ 91). Pour citer un autre témoignage, plus proche de l'événement, *Le Sceau rompu*, une divulgation publiée à Paris en 1745, indique que l'établissement de la maçonnerie en France s'était produit dix-huit ans plus tôt (soit vers 1727 au plus tard). Un doute

Maskelyne, d'Heguerty, & some other Englishmen established a L∴ in Paris, rue des Boucheries,[9] at Huré's, an English caterer, in the manner of the English societies; in less than ten years, the reputation of this L∴ attracted five or six hundred brothers to Masonry, & caused other lodges to be established [...].[10]

In fact, it was in this same district of Saint-Germain-des-Prés, which was already very cosmopolitan, that the English liked to meet up, occasionally staying with guests from their own nation who had settled in Paris.

We know nothing more about the circumstances surrounding this foundation, nor its precise date. Nor do we have a list of the other founders, and we do not know how often they met at the home of their compatriot to hold their meetings.

Given the date, a number of questions remain unanswered in the current state of the documentation, for example: when did this lodge know and practise the grade of Master, the first evidence of which in London dates back to 1725, and the first public disclosure to 1730? In Paris, there is no way of telling, but thanks to the recent rediscovery of the oldest French Masonic document in the "Russian archives,"[11] we can at least say that the Grand Master was known and practised in Bordeaux as early as 1732, in a Masonic milieu where the English presence was very strong.[12] Was the same true in Paris? When and from what source?

However, as we have just seen, only twelve years later, emerging from the shadows, there were at least half a dozen lodges in Paris and about as many in the provinces. In December 1736, they had even given themselves a second Grand Master. The first Grand Master left his name on a document that tells us a great deal about the state of mind and practices of this first Freemasonry in France.

---

subsiste donc sur la date exacte de cette fondation mais la période d'incertitude demeure étroite.

9 Elle correspondait à la partie ouest de l'actuelle rue de l'École-de-médecine, qu'elle prolongeait jusqu'aux rues du Four et de Bussy (Buci), s'achevant derrière Saint-Germain-des-Prés. Elle disparut lors du percement du boulevard Saint-Germain, entre 1855 et 1866.

10 Paru dans le Supplément de l'*Encyclopédie* en 1773, sous la plume de l'astronome Jérôme Lalande (1732-1807), l'article fut republié le Grand Orient en 1777 sous le titre de *Mémoire historique sur la Maçonnerie*. Lalande avait été initié en 1765 dans loge Saint-Jean d'Ecosse à Bourg-en-Bresse, sa ville natale. Il fut, on le sait, l'un des plus grands savants de son temps et devint un des membres les plus illustres de la loge des Neuf Sœurs qui rassemblait alors toute l'*intelligentsia* maçonne à Paris et initia Voltaire en 1778.

11 Considérable ensemble d'archives maçonniques françaises, pillées par les nazis pendant la Deuxième Guerre mondiale et restituées à la France en 2000.

12 L. Trébuchet, « De nouvelles précisions sur les plus anciennes loges de Bordeaux », *Renaissance Traditionnelle*, n° 194 (2019), pp. 98-110.

Les Devoirs enjoints aux Macons Libres

A 68-page document, first published between 1964 and 1965,[13] and currently held by the Bibliothèque nationale de France,[14] provides us with valuable information about the way in which the first Freemasons in France approached masonry, and about the first elements of their organisation.

This text, entitled Devoirs enjoints aux Maçons Libres (Duties enjoined on Free Masons), is a free translation, a sort of adaptation of the text of the Obligations d'un franc-maçon ("Charges of a Free-Mason") and the Règlements généraux published in 1723 in Anderson's Constitutions. As was customary at the time, the translation is not entirely faithful to the original text, but in some significant respects takes considerable liberties with it. There is also an Approbation (as in the English text of 1723), the Ceremonial on the manner of constituting a new lodge (attributed, in the Constitutions of 1723, to the Duke of Wharton) and finally a key to the Masonic alphabet, probably the first in Masonic history to have come down to us.

The second part contains a richly informative introduction:

> General regulations, modelled on those given by the very high and powerful Prince Philippe, Duke of Warthon [sic], Grand Master of the Lodges of the Kingdom of France, with the changes which have been made by the present Grand Master Jacques Hector Macleane, Cheval[ier] Baronet of Scotland, and which were given with the approval of the Grand Lodge at the Grand Assembly held on 27 Xbre [December] 1735 day of St John the Evangelist, to serve as rules for all the Lodges of the said Kingdom.

Let us come to the Approval (pp. 58-60):

> As since the government of the Most Worshipful Grand Master the Most High and Powerful Prince Philip, Duke of Wharton, Peer of England, etc. ... there had been for some time neglected the exact observance of the rules and duties to which Freemasons are obliged, to the great prejudice of the Order of Masonry, and the harmony of the Lodges, we, Hector Macleane, Knight Baronet of Scotland, present Grand Master ... have ordered to be made such changes as We have deemed necessary in the Rules which were given by our

---

13 E. Fournial, Les plus anciens Devoirs et Règlements de la franc-maçonnerie française, Supplément au Bulletin du Grand Orient de France, 1964, pp. 3-44. Réimprimé dans *Renaissance Traditionnelle*, n°144 (2003), pp. 89-129. A. Mellor, *La Charte inconnue de la franc-maçonnerie chrétienne, Paris, 1965*.

14 Sous la cote FM₁ 94 (ancienne cote FM₄ 146).

predecessor, and having seen and examined them in the form here-inbefore transcribed, do approve them, and following the example of our most respectable predecessor, order them to be read at the reception of new Brethren, and when the Master of each Lodge shall think fit. - Given at the annual Grand Lodge held in Paris on 27 Xbre 1735 and sealed with Our seals on the said day.

[signed] Count Darnwentwater[sic][15]   By order of the Most
Respectable Grand Master :

L'abbé Moret, grand Secrétaire

These references tell us at least three things: firstly, that there was already in France a structure, as yet ill-defined, claiming to assume authority over all the lodges in the country from Paris—whatever the practical application of this claim may have been; secondly, that Philip de Wharton, the Grand Master who was contested in England in 1722–1723, would have been recognised as the Grand Master in France —which could not have happened, if the fact is proven, until 1728; finally, it follows that everything contained in the document is official and, a priori, considered and deliberated, having received the approval of an assembly supposedly endowed with the necessary powers. It is from this perspective that we must read the text.

We will only reproduce and comment on significant extracts from the first part, because it is these sections of the text that are directly relevant to our subject.

Here, first of all, is Article 1 of the Duties (corresponding General Heads I of God and Religion (p.49) in the Constitutions of 1723)[16]: This has not been translated but English readers will note the introduction of the word 'christian' into the original Anderson text.

> Un maçon libre est obligé par son état de se conformer à la loi morale, et s'il entend bien l'art, il ne sera *jamais un athée ni un libertin sans religion.*[17]

> Quoique dans les siècles passés les maçons étoient obligés d'etre de la religion du païs où ils vivoient, depuis quelque tems on a jugé & plus à propos de n'exiger d'eux que *la religion dont tout chrétien convient*, laissant a chacun leurs sentimens particuliers, cet a dire bons frères et fidèles ; d'avoir de l'honneur et de la probité, de quelque

---

15 Cette mention finale permet de supposer qu'il s'agit d'une copie effectuée en 1736, année où, comme on l'a vu, Derwentwater a de nouveau succédé à Maclean.

16 Nous avons respecté la graphie d'origine du manuscrit.

17 Ici comme dans le paragraphe suivant, les italiques sont de nous.

manière qu'ils puissent être distingués d'ailleurs : par ce moien, la maçonnerie devient le Centre et l'union d'une amitié solide et désirable entre les personnes qui sans elle seroient pour toujours séparés les uns des autres.

The general structure and structure of Anderson's text are easy to recognise. However, two major differences from the English text of 1723 are immediately apparent.

The first concerns the "stupid atheist," which has disappeared in favour of the pure and simple atheist, so to speak. In France in particular, there has been some debate about the meaning of Anderson's phrase "stupid Atheist," suggesting that it refers only to a particular kind of atheist—"intelligent atheists," on the other hand, are not covered by the ban: Maclean's unadorned translation leaves no room for this kind of diversion.

But the translation goes even further in interpreting the English text: the original formula "that religion in which all Men agree" is here simply rendered as "the religion of which Christians agree!" Remember that we are dealing with a Jacobite editor, no doubt hostile to the powers that be in London, both on the English throne and at the head of his Grand Lodge, but the reference text used is that of 1723—there was no other at the time. However, the interpretation made by a Mason of both French and British culture in 1735 is very clear—Anderson would only have meant Christian denominations as a whole, and nothing else.

Another document confirms that this interpretation was widely accepted in Paris in the small Masonic circles of the time. On 29 November 1737, Derwentwater, who had succeeded Maclean as Grand Master, was to grant Baron Scheffer, Sweden's Minister Plenipotentiary in Paris, who had been initiated the same year in the Parisian Coustos-Villeroy Lodge, a set of documents enabling the diplomat to establish lodges in Sweden.[18]

These documents included a copy of the French Rules and Duties of 1735. Now, in this new copy, we find yet another translation of Anderson's Title I. It now reads:

> In past centuries, Freemasons were obliged to profess *the Catholic religion, but for some time now, their particular sentiments have not been examined, provided however that they are Christians, etc....*

This first observation, which is not entirely unrelated to our subject, we will come back to: if it were still necessary, here is one more testimony that, for a Mason of 1735–1737, both French and British, Masonry was essentially Christian.

There is another article that deserves our attention, and this time it is of even more direct interest to us—it is article 4, corresponding to Anderson's Title IV,

---

18 Ensemble publié une première fois par A. Groussier, *Documents pour servir à l'histoire du Grand Orient de France*, 1932 (republié par E. Fournial, *op. cit.*). Actuellement conservé dans les archives de la Grande Loge de Suède, à Stockholm.

"Of Masters, Wardens, Fellows and Apprentices." As we know, in 1723 this Title described a two-grade system ("Brother" or "Apprentice," and "Fellow-Craft"), while the 1738 version confirmed a three-grade system ("Enter'd Prentice," "Fellow-Craft" and "Master-Mason")—between the two editions, the "new" grade of Master had in fact begun to be talked about, around 1725, and its essential content had been made public by Samuel Prichard, in Masonry Dissected, in 1730.

However, what is striking here, in an official text read "at the reception of the new Brethren," written at the end of 1735, is that it adheres without the slightest reservation to the two-grade system! How are we to interpret such a presentation of the grades? Can we seriously imagine that the grade of Master was not known in Paris in 1735? Or is it simply a sort of slip of the tongue, or absent-mindedness, which led the editor to adopt Anderson's text unchanged, even though the system of grades had evolved considerably since 1723?

There is no definitive answer to this last question, but we do know that by 1732, in Bordeaux at least, the grade of Master was known and practised, as has already been pointed out. In fact, in the first register of the Bordeaux lodge L'Anglaise, established on 27 April 1732—and which remained English-speaking until 1743—a register reputedly lost, recently found and in the process of being published, we can read the following entry:

> This Night was recd **Master** Mr James Bradshaw Mercht ; Bro :
> Capt Patrick Dixon of Dublin **interprentice & fellow Craft**.[19]

The oldest French Masonic document, written in English, therefore shows that as early as 1732 the three grades of apprentice, journeyman and master were known and practised in France—albeit by Masons who were either British or Irish.

---

19 L. Trébuchet, *art. cit.*

The First French Exposure:
Reception d'un Frey-Maçon (1737)

On 27 December 1736, as we have seen, a feast of Saint John was held in Paris to elect a Grand Master, Derwentwater. A "magnificent" feast was attended by more than sixty people of quality who came in ceremonial dress and carriage, "to the sound of trumpets, timpani and hunting horns followed by a vocal and instrumental concert."[1] One can be sure that the event did not go unnoticed.

As early as March 1737, Leiden reported that the brotherhood of freemasons was "making a lot of noise" in Paris. It was added, however, that "there is reason to believe that it will soon be banned by order of the Court."[2]

At this time, Louis XV, although of age, had the country governed by Fleury, and public order in the capital was placed under the control of Lieutenant de Police René Hérault. Typical of those servants of the state who had risen from the bourgeoisie to become ennobled, Hérault was a zealous but unsympathetic character.

Born in 1691 to an old Normandy family, René Hérault de Fontaine[3] was first a King's lawyer at the Châtelet and then Attorney General at the Grand Council, before becoming Master of Requests and Intendant of the Generalitate of Tours. In 1725, during a food shortage, his organisational skills worked wonders. The crowning achievement of his career came the same year, when he became a Conseiller d'Etat and Lieutenant General of the Police in Paris. Married for the first time in 1719, then widowed, he married again in 1732 to the young Marie-Hélène Moreau, barely eighteen years old. She brought with her 300,000 livres in annuities, two houses in Paris and the Séchelles estate in Picardy. The marriage contract bore the signatures of Louis XV himself and Maurepas, Minister of the King's Household, to whom Hérault was subordinate. This unattractive, prematurely aged man was renowned for his choleric temperament and soon overwhelmed his young wife with incessant fits of jealousy. Paris was teeming

---

1   GH Luquet, *La Franc-Maconnerie et L'Etat en France au XVIII Siecle* p. 146.

2   GH Luquet, *La Franc-Maconnerie et L'Etat en France au XVIII Siecle* p. 146.

3   S. Pillorget, « René Hérault de Fontaine, histoire d'une fortune », Actes du 93ème congrès national des sociétés savantes, 1971, II, 287-311 ; *Cf.* aussi : R. Dachez, « Quelques notes à propos du Lieutenant de Police René Hérault et de sa famille », *Renaissance Traditionnelle (RT)* n°72 (1987), pp. 264-268.

with cruel epigrams that left little doubt as to the infidelity of the young wife, who was said to have had more than one lover. In fact, she gave René Hérault an adulterous son by the Marquis de Contades, whose radiant character had seduced her. From this offspring, the next generation would produce the conventionalist Hérault de Séchelles.[4]

Finally exhausted by dropsy but also, it was said, by the pox, René Hérault died on 2 August 1740, aged 49, without the slightest regret; his son-in-law, Feydeau de Marville, immediately took over his office.

In his position, Hérault left behind the memory of a brutal man, who had little regard for procedure and did not hesitate to use letters of seal without a ministerial seal. Maurepas, who sometimes simply post-dated them, was even called to order by the Parliament, which included a number of Jansenists. As early as 1728, the Lieutenant de Police had been attacked for his actions in the *Nouvelles ecclésiatiques*, a newspaper that had been leading the fight against the Jesuits from Holland.

In March 1737, Hérault turned his suspicions to the Freemasons' lodges. Everything pointed to them as being worthy of suspicion. There were half a dozen lodges in Paris at the time. It was well known that many of the leading members—starting with the Grand Master—were British. And while some, like Derwentwater, were Jacobites, others were clearly Hanoverians. Henceforth, they met in the presence of subjects of the King of France—but for what purpose? For Hérault, asking the question meant answering it: nothing that could be useful to the King. Moreover, as early as March 1736, no doubt following the first echoes of the Parisian press, the subject had been raised in the King's Council, but without any immediate effect. On 17 March 1737, Fleury informed his Lieutenant de Police that no more Freemasons should be received in Paris and that innkeepers should be forbidden to receive and handle such meetings.

The Grand Lodge meeting due to take place on 24 March—at which Ramsay was to speak—was then adjourned by Derwentwater. After a few weeks' respite, the police began to take action. At the end of July, the register of the Coustos Lodge was seized and, a few days later, a search took place at the Hôtel de Bourgogne at the home of an Englishman named Bromett who worked for the Grand Lodge. A few more documents were seized. Finally, on 10 September, Superintendent Jean de l'Epinay, accompanied by police and several squads of the watch, went on duty in front of the home of Sieur Chapelot, a wine merchant in La Rapée, a

---

4 Marie-Jean Hérault de Séchelles (1759–1794). L'un des auteurs de la Déclaration des droits de l'homme et du citoyen de 1793, il mourra sur l'échafaud pour s'être opposé aux partisans de Robespierre.

district to the south-west of Paris, on the banks of the Seine. L'Epinay had been informed that a large meeting of Freemasons was imminent. At around half past nine in the evening, he spotted around fifty people wearing white aprons and blue silk cords around their necks. None of those present was arrested, but on 14 September the following day, le tribunal parisien du Châtelet passed a sentence fining the caterer, closing his house for six months, and forbidding lodges to meet.[5]

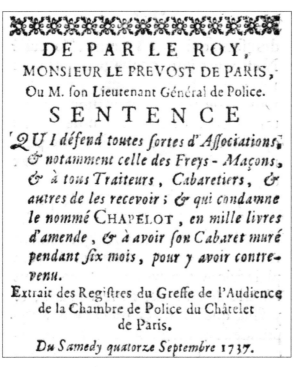

Copy of sentence passed upon Chapelot[6]

But an even tougher ordeal awaited the brothers, who were somewhat shaken by these police harassments. And a few weeks later, all their secrets were on sale in the streets of Paris.

The circumstances of the publication

It was in this turbulent context, after years of a discreet and peaceful life, that the Parisian Freemasons discovered in December 1737 that their secrets, now reproduced over and over again, could be bought for a few pennies!

5   Luquet, *op. cit.,* pp. 40-42.

6   Copy of the sentence passed on Chapelot and reproduced in Le Nouveau Catechisme, Pieces Melees. (1749) p. 98.

The story, which may seem like a gallant fable, is nevertheless supported by numerous documents: the singular truth is that for a few weeks the secrets of the Freemasons were a secret of the alcove!

It soon became clear who was responsible for this desecration. The culprit was Marie-Armande Carton d'Ancourt, daughter of the actor and playwright who had made a name for himself under the name of Dancourt. Her eldest daughter was known to all as "la Carton."

Born in 1685, she began her career at the Théâtre Français at the age of fourteen. Untalented and confined to minor roles, she joined the Opéra in 1730, where she was also a mediocre chorister and received only a modest salary. But that was not the main thing, for despite her marriage in 1702—at the age of 17—to the Sieur de Fontaine, controller of the navy and wars in Flanders and Picardy, Carton, like almost all the young ladies at the Opéra in her time, led a 'gallant' life, trading in her charms and collecting lovers, preferably influential and wealthy. One of them, the famous financier Samuel Bernard, gave her three daughters. In 1730, she was the mistress of Maurice de Saxe, the future victor of the Battle of Fontenoy (1745) against the English—who, many years later, would aspire to the title of Grand Master of the Lodges of the Kingdom of France.

All sources agree that she was the one who obtained a detailed account of an initiation ceremony from a brother's weakness. Opinions differ, however, as to the identity of the culprit and Carton's motives.

An initial account is given in a publication of 1738:[7]

> "The famous Carton of the Opéra came to the end [of the Freemasons' secret]. It was a year ago [i.e., late 1736, early 1737] that the fantasy had occurred to her to discover this secret at whatever price. Just in time for her, a Freemason appeared and asked for her good graces. She in turn asked him what the mysteries of his order consisted of. For a long time he refused to satisfy her on that point, and she likewise refused to satisfy him on the other. The poor lover found himself in the same situation as Samson, and he gave in in the same way. The victorious Carton communicated her discovery to M. Hérault, Lieutenant General of Police, and she now boasts of having done more than Queen Elizabeth, who was never able to obtain such a confidence from the Earl of Essex."

---

7   *Amusements littéraires ou correspondance politique, historique, philosophique, critique ou galante* par M. de la Barre de Beaumarchais. A la Haye, chez Jean van Duren, 1740. Amusements littéraires pour l'année 1738. Lettre première, p. 6/7. Luquet, *op. cit.*, p. 156.

It is not clear whether Carton had obtained this revelation at the request of René Hérault—for whom, according to another of their habits, the girls of the Opéra willingly worked—or whether it had been pure curiosity on her part, some reason having then given her the idea of disclosing everything, by selling it to the police.

As for the unfortunate divulger, some sources identify him as Le Noir de Cindré, a farmer-general with an interest in food supplies for the German army, and one of her suitors, of whom she had said, not without a certain cynicism: "I've thrown myself into food supplies, but I'll make him eat a lot of rations!" Others, perhaps more likely, think it was Lord Kingston, who had been initiated in Paris in September 1735 at a meeting that had caused a stir in Parisian circles. The latter, perhaps a lover of La Carton, had abandoned her in favour of her daughter! The spite of the abandoned lover or betrayed mother would have convinced her to reveal the secret, already written down, to the Lieutenant of Police.

Whatever Carton's debatable and, as we can see, still partly obscure motives, Hérault's ambition in widely circulating this text, which was thrown open to public scrutiny, was to make a mockery of the Freemasons' privacy and to affect the curiosity which was leading young men from the best society towards it.

The secret had already been out for a long time. If we are to believe the Duc de Luynes, in April 1737, he reported having been told by his son—who was not a Freemason—that at Versailles a jeweller's merchant he had met had given him the words ("Goaz" and "Zaquine") of all the grades, including, interestingly, that of Master, which he believed to be "Magueby."[8] But the disclosure orchestrated by the police was on an altogether different scale and could have led to fears for the worst. Judge by the lamentations, in January 1738, of President du Rocheret, a brother in Epernay, Champagne:

> "Oh! what a scandal! most venerable Brother; what a horror! what a profanation! The Brothers are hissed at, booed, sung at and I hear from Parnassus that our mysteries are going to be taken to the theatre. May the miserable joker who undertook it be crushed, pulverised, annihilated, he and the author of such a cowardly defection.
>
> The same fury has spread to the provinces; our town [Epernay] is inundated with copies of the report [Hérault's disclosure]. The people, holding hands and putting their thumbs to their knuckles, now only greet each other with these words: Bonjour Monsieur Jackin; Servant Monsieur Bouesse. A lady has just christened a dog and a bitch born to her with these two names. But these so-called insults,

---

8 *Mémoires du duc de Luynes sous le règne de Louis XV*, Paris, 1860, I, p. 227.

which only fall upon those who make them, would affect me little if part of our ceremonies were not revealed."[9]

However, things did not turn out as Hérault had perhaps imagined. In December 1737—the month of all dangers for French Freemasons—the King had declared that if a new Grand Master was appointed, he would find him a lodge in the Bastille prison. Probably in June 1738, Louis Antoine Gondrin de Pardaillan, Duke of Antin, who was close to the King, well-connected and had good relations with Fleury, was elected. Given his rank, he was not sent to the Bastille.

In April 1740, a police newslwtter noted that lodges "continued to assemble in various parts of Paris." Feydeau de Marville, the new Lieutenant of Police, had to take up his father-in-law's work again, but without any further success.

We still have, for the historian's pleasure, the disclosure obtained by the latter.

Reception of a Franc-Macon 1737

Hérault's exposure was circulated in mid-December 1737—Hérault had given notice of it on 5 December, at a police assembly held under the aegis of the Parlement de Paris. The text would be reprinted several times, with minor variations, in French as well as in English and German, over the following weeks,[10] giving it a truly European audience.

Concise, factual and hardly literary, Hérault's text describes a simple ceremony for the first two grades in less than 1,500 words. It is also noteworthy for its brevity—it takes just a few minutes to complete.

First of all, here is the text—that of the oldest French Masonic ritual known to date:

Reception of a Frey-Mason

> It is necessary, first of all, to be proposed at the Lodge as a suitable Candidate *[bon Sujet]* by one of the Brethren. Upon his reply *[sur sa reponse]*, one is allowed to present oneself. The Candidate is conducted by his Proposer, who becomes his Sponsor, into one of the Rooms of the Lodge, where there is no light, and where he is asked if he has a calling to be received. He answers yes, then he is asked

---

9 Luquet, *op. cit.*, p. 180.

10 Sur le détail de ces éditions, *cf.* A. J. B. Milborne, « The Early Continental Exposures and their Relationship to Contemporary English Texts - Parti I. The Réception d'un frey-Maçon », *AQC* 17 (1965), 172-200. Voir aussi G. Pasquier, « La Réception d'un frey-Masson (1737) », *Travaux de la Loge nationale de recherches Villard de Honnecourt*, 12 (1986), 85-90. R. Dachez, P. Mollier, « Divulgations et catéchismes maçonniques en France, de 1737 à 1751 », *RT* n° 147-148, juillet-octobre 2006, 166-183.

(1)

RECEPTION

D'UN

FREY=MACON.

L faut d'abord être proposé à la Loge comme un bon Sujet, par un des Freres, fur fa réponfe, l'on eft admis à fe prefenter, le Recipiendaire eft conduit par le Propofant, qui devient fon Parain, dans une dês Chambres de la Loge, où il n'y a pas dé lumiere, & où on lui demande

his name, surname, & status, he is deprived of all Metals & Jewels that he may have about him, such as Buckles, Buttons, Rings, Boxes, &c. His right knee is made bare, he is made to wear his left Shoe as a Slipper, his eyes are bandaged, & he is kept in that condition for about an hour delivered up to his own reflexions, after which the Sponsor goes and knocks three times at the door of the Reception Chamber, where the Worshipful Grand Master of the Lodge is, who replies from within by three other knocks, & orders the Door to be opened.

Then the Sponsor says, that a Gentleman presents himself, named so-and-so, who asks to be received: *(Note,* that there are Brother guardians *[surveillans]* outside and inside this Chamber, [with] naked sword in hand, to keep off the profane).

The Grand Master, who wears about his neck a blue ribbon cut in the form of a triangle, says, ask him if he has the calling, which the Sponsor goes to do; the Candidate having answered yes, the Grand Master orders him to be brought in. Then he is introduced, & he is made to take three turns in the Chamber, around a space marked on the Floor, where a kind of representation has been drawn in crayon, upon two columns, of the ruins of the Temple of Solomon; at the two sides of this space they have also drawn in crayon a great J. & a great B. of which the explanation is not given until after the Reception; & in the middle there are three lighted Candles arranged in a triangle, on which, at the arrival of the Candidate *[Novice]* they throw either [gun-]Powder or Powdered Resin, to frighten him by the effect which that produces. The three turns being made the Candidate is led to the middle of the marked-out space, as described above, in three movements *[en trois temps]* face to face with the Grand Master, who is at the upper end, behind an Armchair, on which the Gospel of St. John has been placed. He [i.e., the Grand Master] asks him, do you feel the calling; upon his replying, yes, the Grand Master says, let him see the light *[le jour*], he has been deprived of it long enough; at that moment his eyes are unbandaged, all the Brethren assembled in a circle take Sword in hand, the Candidate is made to advance in three movements up to a Stool, which is at the foot of the Armchair; the Brother Orator says to him, you are about to embrace a respectable Order, which is more serious than you imagine; there is nothing in it against the Law, against Religion, against the King, nor against Manners; the Worshipful Grand Master will tell you the rest. At the same time, he [the Candidate] is made to kneel on his right knee, which is bared, on the Stool, & to hold the left foot lifted in the air; then the Grand Master says to him, you promise never to draw, write, or reveal the secrets of the Free-Masons, & of Freemasonry, except to a Brother in Lodge, & in the presence of the Worshipful Grand Master. Next, his breast is uncovered, to see that he is not a woman, & a [pair of] compasses, which he holds himself, is put on his left breast; he lays his right hand on the Gospel, & thus pronounces his oath; I consent that my tongue may be torn out, my heart lacerated, my body burnt & reduced to ashes, to be thrown to the winds, so that there may be no further mention of it [? me] amongst men; so help me God.

After which he is made to kiss the Gospel. The Grand Master then has him brought to his side, he is given the apron of a Free-Mason, which is of a white Skin, a pair of men's Gloves for himself, and another [pair of] ladies' Gloves, for her whom he esteems the most, & they give him the explanation of the **J.** & the **B.** written in the circle, which are the symbol of their signs, for recognizing each other, the **J.** signifies *Jakhin,* & the **B.** *Boaier* [sic],* which are two English words, that they represent among themselves in their signs, by carrying the right hand to the left of the chin, & drawing it at the same level *[sur la meme ligne]* to the right side, & then striking the skirt of the coat, also on the right side; after which they shake hands, [each] placing the right thumb on the first & large knuckle of the index [finger] of his comrade's hand, while pronouncing the word *Jakhin;* after which each strikes himself on the breast with the right hand; then they clasp hands again, touching each other reciprocally with the right thumb on the large joint of the middle finger, while pronouncing the word *Boaies,* or *Boesse;* this ceremony ended, & this explanation given, the Candidate is called Brother, & they seat themselves at Table, where they drink, with the permission of the Worshipful Grand Master, to the health of the new Brother. Each has his Bottle before him; when they want to drink, they say, give the Powder, everyone rises, the Grand Master says, *charge;* the Powder, which is the Wine, is poured into the glass; the Grand Master says, lay your hands to your firelocks *[armes],* and they drink to the health of the Brother, carrying the glass to the mouth in three movements; after which, & before replacing the glass on the Table, it is carried to the left breast, then to the right, & then forwards, all in three movements, & in three other movements it is set down perpendicularly on the Table, they clap their hands three times & each of them cries three times *Vivat.*

It is customary to have three Candles on the Table, arranged in a triangle. If by chance they perceive or suspect that someone suspicious has introduced himself [amongst them], they make it known by saying, *it Rains,* which signifies that nothing may be spoken. As it might happen that some profane had discovered the signs which denote the terms *Jackhin [sic]* & *Boaies,* to avoid all surprise, they say, wh.en clasping hands as described above, J. to which the other must reply A, the first **K.** the second answers H. the other **J.** *[sic]* and the last **N.** which makes the word *Jakhin.* It is the same with regard to *Boaies* in pronouncing alternately & consecutively all the letters of that word, & that is the true hall-mark *[le vrai coin]* by which the genuine Brothers recognize each other.

* This word is pronounced as though it were written Boesse, [to rhyme with, Ed.] the name of Monsieur Haisse, written Hayes in English.[11]

If we refer to earlier British exposures, whether the earliest, which are Scottish—the manuscripts of the Haughfoot group, written between about 1696 and 1715—or the most recent, Prichard's English disclosure, Masonry Dissected, published in London in 1730, the consistency is immediately perceptible.

The three loud knocks on the door of the lodge by the blindfolded candidate, the oath taken on the Gospel and the text of the oath itself are all in line with Prichard, but constitute a more elaborate version, in terms of the variety of punishments, than the Scottish one.

The three great candlesticks are mentioned, as in Prichard, although their location is not specified —but contemporary iconography will make up for this, in particular the printed disclosures of 1744 and the very fine engravings attributed to Lebas in 1745. It should be noted from the outset that this the typical English layout i.e., with two candelabra to the east and one to the south-west —the oldest documented and the only one known at the time.

The same applies to the board drawn on the floor in the centre of the lodge, which would be considered a distinctive feature of Modern masonry compared with Ancient masonry, which always ignored it. But the very first description of this table is provided by this French text. It can be compared with the graphic elements found as early as 1742 in an English engraving depicting a London procession of Mock Masonry, where the emblems of the first three grades already appear on panels (in particular the Letter G, but also the Letters MB). It is also easy to recognise the elements that would appear on the first illustrations printed in France from 1744 onwards.

It is also worth noting the sobriety of the journeys, simple tours of the lodge that are not accompanied by any test or commentary—apart from a few pranks with "resin pitch" to frighten the candidate, reminiscent of the "ridiculous attitudes and grimaces" stipulated in the old Scottish texts.

Finally, this ritual is that of an apprentice-companion reception, without the "journeys of the companion" being in the least individualised—what H. Carr has called "a two-pillar degree." The recipient is solemnly asked "if he has the vocation" and informed that there is nothing "against the law, against religion, against the king, or against morals." At the end of the ceremony, having taken

---

11 Une traduction anglaise a été publiée par H. Carr en 1971 dans *Early French Exposures*. And that translation is used here for consistency. Courtesy of Quatuor Coronati Lodge No. 2076.

the oath, the candidate is successively and in the same movement given the words, signs and touches of the first two grades. It is clear that in Paris in 1737, the ambiguities of Prichard's text—which gave Boaz and Jachin in the 1ˢᵗ grade, and curiously Jachin again in the second—were removed: the two words were clearly separated and clearly attributed, Jakhin in the 1ˢᵗ grade and Boaies or Boesse in the 2ⁿᵈ. This is the so-called "Modern" order of words, the only one known to French Masonry throughout the eighteenth century. We can see that it was already being practised in Paris well before the alleged "inversion," supposedly carried out in 1739 by the Grand Lodge of London. The said "inversion" was no longer of any importance, since the first two grades were then given on the same evening, during the same ceremony—the second being reduced to its simplest expression, i.e., the communication of secrets. This custom, which was fairly widespread at the time, lasted quite a long time in some French lodges in the eighteenth century. In the Parisian lodges of Coustos-Villeroy and Bussy-Aumont, in particular, the third grade ceremony took place on average a fortnight after that of the first two grades.

Note the use of the sword, which gave rise to some controversy in Paris. Some Brethren were upset by the "innovations" introduced in the Grand Master's lodge—i.e., in Derwentwater's lodge—in particular the use of the sword, which was supposedly unknown previously, and which was intended to turn Masonry into "an Order of Chivalry!" This concern and fear must be emphasised because it was expressed in France, as early as 1737, at the very moment when, in his Discourse, Ramsay affirmed the chivalric origin of Freemasonry, perhaps laying the foundations for the future rank of Knight of the Sword, as we have seen. So did the reproach concern Derwentwater alone, or did it already betray a wider movement that was being talked about at the time in the Parisian Masonic world, and which was to give rise, in a very few years, to the first high grades? We can see that at the very moment when its existence was publicly revealed, Parisian masonry was already in the throes of change.

Note also the first description of Masonic table manners, which immediately borrowed from a military vocabulary. Similarly, the first use of the expression "It's raining" to indicate the presence of non-Masons—this was to become one of the most widespread usages in French Masonic circles.

As for the final mention of the white gloves, although it refers to an ancient custom for all members of the lodge—it is in fact attested to in Scottish documents from the end of the seventeenth century—it seems that the new custom of also giving them to the woman "whom one esteems most" is due to France: could it be that one of the first innovations of French Masonry was the homage paid to women? The betrayal of Carton—or one of her kind—would then be all the more unjust.

If the purpose of uncovering the Masonic ritual, at the instigation of the Lieutenant of Police of Paris, had been to discover extraordinary secrets or to unearth some plot, the disappointment would have been great for him; but if the ambition of the disclosure was to ridicule the Masonic order, despite the understandable emotion of the brothers, then the effect was totally unsuccessful. Better still, masonry suddenly became fashionable!

Le Discours de Ramsay (1736-1737) & the words 'Dites de Ramsay' (1738-1776)

This is not the place to go into detail about this Discours, both illustrious and misunderstood, which over time has become one of the founding texts of the French Masonic tradition. Nor will we dwell on the circumstances and reasons for its writing, nor on the reasons why we should rather speak of "the" Discourses, since at least two major versions are discernible and differ on several points.[1] We shall confine ourselves here to recalling the key facts of Ramsay's biography that shed light on the scope of the text,[2] and then mention and comment only on those passages that are of interest to us from the particular perspective of this book, namely the history of the grades in France between 1735 and 1745.

Andrew Michael Ramsay was born in 1686 in Ayr, Scotland, of so-called Scottish nobility, which was recognised after the fact by James III Stuart, following his reception into the Order of Saint Lazarus in France in 1723, in order to receive the pension. Presbyterian on his father's side but repelled by the austere doctrine of predestination, he leaned very early towards the mysticism of his mother, an Episcopalian. After a solid education in Glasgow and then Edinburgh, and a mastery of French, he took an interest in the work of Fénelon, becoming his disciple in Cambrai, which led him to Catholicism. Above all, between 1714 and 1717, he lived with Madame Guyon, the Quietist mystic condemned by Rome. Her imprint on Ramsay would be indelible. A Jacobite and supporter of the Stuarts, he was briefly the tutor of the young Charles-Édouard in Rome. Finally, in 1717, his book The Travels of Cyrus, a novel of learning translated into several languages, made him famous throughout Europe.

In March 1730, this Jacobite was admitted as a Mason in London, in the very Hanoverian Horn Lodge, where many aristocrats and intellectuals were members of the Royal Society. In April 1730, he also became an honorary doctor of civil law at Oxford University. When he returned to France in 1735, he was the subject of a satirical pamphlet, La Ramsaÿde, which says enough about his fame, and he married the same year. We know nothing of his possible but elusive

---

1 La question est en fait encore plus complexe. *Cf.* A. Bernheim, *Ramsay et les deux discours*, Paris, 2011.

2 Cyril N Batham, Chevalier Ramsay, a New Appreciation AQC vol.91 (1968) and L Kahler 'Andrew Ramsay and his Masonic Orations. Heredom vol.1 (1992) and Alain Bernheim, Ramsay and his 'Discours Revisited,' www.freemasons-freemmasonry.com/bernheim01.html

Masonic activity between 1730 and 1736. In 1736, assuming the title of "Orator of the Grand Lodge" in Paris, he wrote his famous *Discours*.

Forced to renounce Freemasonry in March 1737 by Cardinal Fleury, who was then ruling France under the distant aegis of the young Louis XV, he continued to correspond with well-known Freemasons, but devoted most of his time to what he considered to be his great work, which was never completed: The Philosophical Principles of Natural and Revealed Religion. Interested in the Jesuits' accounts of Chinese thought, he finally recognised Christianity as the "true universal religion of the heart." He died in 1743, leaving behind a Masonic text that would become a veritable literary myth.

For our purposes here, we will concentrate on three passages.

In the version dated 16 April 1737,[3] we find the following information—

We have three kinds of members in our society: novices or apprentices; companions or professed members; masters or adepts. Our allegorical symbols, our more ancient hieroglyphs, and our sacred mysteries teach three kinds of duties to these three different degrees of our Initiates. To the first the moral and philanthropic virtues; to the second the heroic and intellectual virtues; to the last the superhuman and divine virtues.

In the version printed in 1742[4] by La Tierce, there is a slight variation:

> We explain to the first [i.e. to the apprentices] the moral virtues; to the second the heroic virtues; and to the last the Christian virtues; so that our institute contains all the Philosophy of sentiments, & all the Theology of the heart.

A few comments are in order. The first is the apparently banal nature of the division into three grades of the secrets of Masonic initiation, in Paris in 1736. Secondly, it should be noted that Ramsay says nothing about the content of these three grades and that the subdivision of the "secrets" of the latter into "moral virtues," "heroic virtues" and "divine virtues"—borrowing from a vocabulary that belongs to the moral theology of classical Christianity—appears to be an editorial device, a rhetorical flourish, but clearly corresponds to nothing we know of the extremely succinct content, as we shall see, of these same grades, as they were known in Paris at the same time.[5]

On the other hand, if the 1742 paraphrase is still faithful to Ramsay's intention

---

3   *Cf.* A. Bernheim, *op. cit.*, p. 70.

4   *Histoire, Obligations et Statuts de la Très Vénérable Confraternité des Francs-Maçons*, 1742 & 1745. *Cf.* A. Bernheim, *op. cit.*, p. 71.

5   *Cf. infra*, « La divulgation des deux premiers grades ».

—and everything suggests that it is—the inspiration of Freemasonry is, according to him, explicitly Christian, which is consistent with the version of Title Ier of the Constitutions, as translated in 1735 and 1736[6], in the documents signed by Maclean and Derwentwater.

Le second passage qui nous intéresse est présent dès la version la plus ancienne, celle du 27 décembre 1736[1] :

> Moyse, inspired by the Most High, had a mobile temple erected in the desert in accordance with the model he had seen in a celestial vision on the summit of the holy mountain, clear proof that the laws of our art are observed in the invisible world where everything is harmony, order and proportion. This travelling tabernacle, a copy of the Invisible Palace of the Most High, which is the Upper World, then became the model for the famous Temple of Solomon, the wisest of kings and mortals. This superb edifice supported by fifteen hundred columns of marble from Paros, pierced by more than two thousand windows, capable of containing four hundred thousand people, was beaten in seven years by more than three thousand princes or master masons whose leader was hiram-abif grand master of the lodge of Tyre, to whom Solomon entrusted all our mysteries. He was the first martyr of our Order [...][7] faithfulness to guard [...] part of our lives [...].[8]

> his illustrious sacrifice after his death the king Salomon wrote in hieroglyphic figures our Statutes, our maxims and our mysteries and this ancient book is the original Code of our Order. after the Destruction of the first temple and the captivity of the favorite nation, the anointed of the Lord, the Great Cyrus who was Initiated in all our mysteries Constituted Zorobabel, Grand Master of the Lodge of Jerusalem, and ordered him to lay the foundations of the second temple, where the mysterious Book of Salomon was deposited. this Book was preserved during twelve centuries in the temple of Israelites, but after the Destruction of this Second temple under the emperor Tite, this ancient book was lost until the time of the Crusades that it was found in part after the capture of Jerusalem.

---

6   First French translation of the *Constitutions*, signed by the Jacobite Hector Maclean, then Grand Master in Paris, in 1735 and the following year: *Devoirs enjoints aux Maçons libres* (Duties imposed on Free Masons). The "religion on which all men agree" becomes "the religion on which all Christians agree." See also chapter "La Franc-Maconnerie arrives in France."

7   Ici figure une lacune du manuscrit qui peut sans doute s'interpréter par une formule comme « en raison de sa... »

8   Deux nouvelles lacunes plus délicates à combler, mais on saisit bien le sens global que la suite du texte confirme.

This Sacred Code was torn up and without penetrating the Sublime spirit of all the hieroglyphic figures found therein, our ancient order was renewed, of which Noah, Abraham, the Patriarchs, Moses, Solomon and Cyrus had been the first great masters.

This passage, which will not be repeated in the other known versions of the Discours, and therefore remains the property of a manuscript version and, we would say, almost confidential, calls for several remarks, not only because of the date and place of its writing, but also because of what is revealed.

We are told here that Solomon, following the death of Hiram Abif, whose "illustrious sacrifice" is praised, had recorded the essential secrets—which he no doubt shared with Hiram—in a "Code" which was later hidden by Zorobabel in "the foundations of the second temple." This Code was found "at the time of the Crusades" and its deciphering was to enable the Order of Masons to be "renewed."

It's easy to recognise the central theme of what, years later, would give rise to the Royal Arch: a secret hidden under the ancient Temple and found after its destruction. But here, the chronological context changes entirely: the secrets, the "Sacred Code," are buried in the foundations of the second Temple—the one erected by Zorobabel and considerably enlarged under Herod the Great, between 20-18 BCE—and it was during the destruction of the latter by the Roman armies of Titus, in 70 AD, that they were rediscovered!

Of course, nothing of the sort appears in the two editions of Anderson's Constitutions—in 1723, he simply describes Zorobabel as "General Master-Mason of the Jews" at the time of the rebuilding of the Temple, following the edict of Cyrus, and he makes no mention of any discoveries during the Crusades. Similarly, in the 1738 version, he specifies that Zorobabel, having completed the Temple, "celebrated its Capstone" (Cap-Stone), an obviously suggestive mention, but without any further development.

We know that Ramsay did not invent this legendary development. Its source is known and has long been reported. It is the account of Philostorge, a Greek historian active at the beginning of the fourth century. In his *Ecclesiastical History*, Book VII, chapter 14, he recalls the time when Julian the Apostate (331–363), Constantine's successor, who wanted to return to paganism, wished to contradict the prophecy of the Jewish people, which proclaimed that the destroyed Temple would never be rebuilt, by rebuilding it to his own glory! In the course of this work, according to Philostorge, a stone was loosened from the foundations of the ancient Temple and a cubic crypt, partly filled with water, was discovered. At its centre was a column on which, after descending to explore the crypt, a book was found that turned out to be the Gospel of Saint John—proof that "the word of the Lord could never be revoked."

Here we need to ask two questions and make a statement.

How had Ramsay come to know of this text? Certainly, as Bernheim states, this account, directly borrowed from Philostorgius, appeared in the *Histoire ecclésiastique* published between 1690 and 1720 and written by Claude Fleury, a priest and friend of Fénelon—with whom Ramsay, as we have seen, had stayed for a long time. Ramsay could obviously have drawn on this source. However, as B. E. Jones also pointed out in 1956, a version of this legend already appeared in Samuel Lee's *Orbis Miraculum*, published in 1659. The book is adorned with a frontispiece featuring Solomon and Zadok, his High Priest, in a garb that strongly evokes the decor of the Principals of a Chapter of the Royal Arch in bygone days! Jones points out that it is hard not to think that those who designed the ceremonial of the Royal Arch did not have access to this work. Where did Ramsay get this account? From simply reading Claude Fleury, or from a British—and perhaps Masonic—channel, of which he was merely the intermediary? Secondly, why did this passage then disappear? That's the first question.

The second point concerns two changes Ramsay makes to Philostorgius's account: firstly, the Gospel of Saint John is replaced by the "Sacred Code" in which Solomon is said to have recorded "our Statutes, our maxims and our mysteries." Why did Ramsay, so deeply Christian, make this change, or perhaps it was not Ramsay who made the change? Secondly, and this change is even more considerable, it is no longer in biblical times—as in the Royal Arch as we have known it since the end of the eighteenth century—nor in the time of Julian the Apostate as Philostorge reports, that the rediscovery in question takes place. It was at the time of the Crusades. Here again, the question is the same: did Ramsay make this change out of pure whim[9] or because a Masonic source known to him had inspired him to do so, or again, we must ask ourselves if it is not another author?

Finally, the point is this: whatever we may think of Ramsay's sources and the reasons why he introduced this modified version of Philostorge's story into a Masonic context, the fact remains that in Paris, in 1736, there was a *Discours* recounting a legend to be compared with the oldest "Ecossais" grades, and in particular with those that came more or less directly from between 1733 and 1735. Although their content is not directly known, if it could be surmised, or even reconstructed from other grades, available in French in particular, from the same period—and we shall see that this is possible, particularly from Berlin—would

---

9   A. Bernheim suggère (*op. cit.*, p. 26) qu'en évoquant l'époque de Godefroy de Bouillon comme celle du relèvement de l'Ordre, Ramsay agissait par flatterie envers la famille du duc de Bouillon dont les enfants, entre 1730 et 1741, avaient pour tuteur Ramsay lui-même. Rien n'est impossible mais la raison semble un peu futile. Ramsay l'était-il à ce point ?

we not be disturbed by the strange resemblance of their main theme to the story in Ramsay's Discourse, or would we not have to wonder whether it was written by another author?

Let us be clear that it is not a question of making Ramsay the author of these grades—or of any other, for that matter, as we shall see—but of questioning the degree of knowledge that a man like him, straddling the border between France on the one hand and Scotland & England on the other, having frequented the English Masonic elite in London from 1730 onwards, could have had about the developments that Masonry had undergone in England since then. Let us remember that we know absolutely nothing about Ramsay's actual Masonic activity between 1730 and 1736. His writings could possibly bear witness to these developments.

While the passage we have just studied did not in fact attract much attention from French authors, there was another that did. This passage appears in practically all versions of the Discours, with a few variations. However it does appear in all printed versions after 1738.

The quotation below is taken from the printed version of 1738, which has been lengthened compared to the manuscript version of 1736.[10] At the time of the holy wars in Palestine, several Princes, Lords and & Citoïens, entered into a Society, vowed to re-establish the temples of the Christians in the Holy Land, & undertook by oath to use their talents and their goods to bring architecture back to the primitive institution. They agreed on a number of ancient signs and symbolic words drawn from the depths of the religion,[11] to distinguish themselves from the infidels and to distinguish themselves from the Saracens.

> These signs and words were only communicated to those who solemnly promised, often even at the foot of the altar, never to reveal them. This sacred promise was therefore no longer an execrable oath, as is often said, but a respectable bond, uniting men of all nations in the same brotherhood.
>
> Some time later our Order joined the Knights of St John of Jerusalem. From then on our Lodges bore the name of Lodges of Saint John in all countries. This union was made in imitation of the Israelites, when they rebuilt the second temple; while they handled with one hand the trowel and the mortar,[12] they carried with the other the Sword and the Shield. (Ezra Chap. IV, v. 16)

---

10 A. Bernheim, *op. cit.,* p. 87.

11 Le manuscrit de 1736 porte ici : « tous les signes anciens et les paroles mysterieuses de Salomon ».

12 Dans le manuscrit de 1736 : « la truelle et le Compas ».

This passage from the Discourse has obviously fuelled many fragile theories, in particular that of Ramsay as the creator of the rank of Knight of the East or of the Sword, known in France probably a little before 1745, as we shall see later, and even more, as the founder of a system of high ranks—one of the first of its kind. It is certain that this last hypothesis is completely unfounded. There never was a Ramsay Rite. The author of the *Discours* ceased all Masonic activity in March 1737, after Cardinal Fleury, his protector, had made it known that he disliked assemblies of Freemasons. We now know that this fable originated in the early 19th century, the French historian Claude-Antoine Thory having given it a publicity[13] and, after him, a posterity that it did not deserve.

The fact remains that this connection between the presumed "refoundation" of masonry in Palestine "at the time of the Crusades" and the passage of Ezra irresistibly evokes the grade of Chevalier de l'Orient or of the Sword, which remained in France, for some ten years, the practically undisputed ne plus ultra of the masonic grades. The coincidence is too clear not to raise questions: here again, did the author make it all up, unaware that he was laying the seeds of a future Masonic grade—assuming that he could even have imagined that new grades would appear one day—or was he aware of a legendary theme, as in the case of the one taken from Philostorge, which was already making headway in certain Masonic circles, both French and British?

It has been said that Ramsay severed all active links with Freemasonry in 1737. This does not mean that his interest in Masonic matters had disappeared. We know that he discussed them in letters with his friend Gueusau.[14] Commenting on the correspondence between the two men, P. Mollier, who has extensively studied the sources of the knightly imagination in early French masonry, writes as follows:

> In the intimacy of a conversation with his friend Gueusau, Ramsay confided that he had tried to "re-establish the ceremonies as they had been in ancient times." In his view, these ceremonies dated back "to the time of the Crusades." Ramsay's plan was therefore to return Masonry to its supposed origins, i.e., to the practices of the Knighthood. We know that Fleury's ban was only an epiphenomenon and that, although it delayed a Grand Lodge meeting, it in no way prevented Masonry from prospering [in France]. We have also seen that Ramsay, although he subsequently avoided overly ostentatious responsibilities, nonetheless remained linked to the fraternity. It would therefore not be impossible that the "postponement of this

---

13 C. Thory, *Histoire de la fondation du Grand Orient de France*, 1812, I, p. 23 ; *Acta Latomorum*, 1815, II, p. 320.

14 P. Chevallier, *Les Ducs sous l'acacia*, reprint 1994, pp. 302-305.

meeting"[15] merely delayed by a few months the plan to "re-establish the ceremonies as they had been in ancient times." It has to be said that the ritual for the rank of Knight of the Orient fits in well with such a project.

If Ramsay can indeed be credited with the creation of the Knights of the East, one problem remains. Ramsay died in 1743 and the first mention of the rank was in 1748. It is quite conceivable that this new rank was established in the early 1740s and remained secret for several years. After all, Masonry was established in France in the mid-1720s and the first documented evidence of it dates back no further than 1736.[16]

We will even see that a text from 1745 suggests that this knightly rank already existed in France. We will also see that what we know for certain about the state of the ranks in Paris around 1745 makes Mollier's hypothesis perfectly conceivable.

One point needs to be emphasised in order to establish a new point between the two sides of the Channel at this seminal period. The poem relating to Sanaballat and the attacks upon Jerusalem when the walls were being rebuilt by Nehemiah first appears in a masonic connection in BookM published in the north of England in 1736. Neither the symbology nor the words were new and had come from the days of Elizabeth I (see earlier chapter).

To find it also appearing in Paris in the same year however, and some, is worthy of comment. The very format of Ramsay's Discourses, with its long orations, its emphasis on masonic moral values, and the tale of the "sword in one hand and the trowel in the other" very much had the feel of the Northern English Harodim, and of the Harodim of Kilwinning which focus upon moral values in the attributes given to each of its members. This makes one suspect that further research might well prove rewarding.

It is perhaps yet another example of how, in the eighteenth century world without instant communication or fast transport that ideas flowed across Europe without much delay or hindrance.

The printed words 'dites de Ramsay' are probably those of who?

There is no doubt that the Discours de Ramsay was an influential document, even if exactly what that influence was is still a much-debated matter and the

---

15 C'est l'expression employée par Gueusau dans son journal pour qualifier l'interdiction faite par Fleury aux francs-maçons de s'assembler.

16 P. Mollier, *La Chevalerie maçonnique – Franc-maçonnerie, imaginaire chevaleresque et légende templière au Siècle des Lumières*, 2005, pp. 98-99.

best book on the subject is *Ramsay et ses deux Discours* by Alain Bernheim. And in it there are two chapters entitled:

La Version Manuscrite et ses Sources
Les Versions Imprimees, Modifications et Additions

And he starts the second chapter with the words "The general plan of the Discours is identical but the respective lengths of the threeparts is considerably differenr and each contains numerous modifications."[17] The table of the word-counts produced by Bernhim is worth examining in a bit more detail:

Plan of Ramsay's *Discours*	MS Version	Printed Versions
1. Qualities required in the Order	ca. 1,000 words	ca. 1,800 words
2. Ancient traditions of the Order's history	ca. 840 words	ca. 65 words
3. True history of the Order	ca. 400 words	ca. 850 words
APPPROXIMATE TOTAL LENGTH	2,240 words	2,715 words

Table ex Bernheim 'Ramsay and his Discours Revisited' &at Pietre Stones website

Of the original wordcount of ca. 2240 words in ms 775 were removed and then 1250 words were added. Which means that 72% of the words in the printed version were different to those in the original ms version. This was 'radical major surgery' and the English author is amazed to find that no previous authors have even asked the question whether there changes were made by Ramsay or by some other person. It is also noting that the revised Discourses from 1738 onwards all (that have been read) have identical wording, and this might point to one person alone arranging the reprints

The most valuable asset on the book is a complete tabulation of four version of the Discours. The Epernay ms (1736) and Caumont ms (1737)—and of the printed versions of 1744 Lettre de M. de V*** and 1745 de la Tierce Histoires. It is unfortunate that Bernheim chose these two editions because neither were the first of their kind. And exact chronology is always to be recommended but in this case it was crucial.

·   the earliest Lettre printed in 1737 with the final changed text. This was of course very soon after the intervention of Herault and Ramsay's correspondence with Geseau

·   the first edition of the de la Tierce Histoire was 1742 which also hap-

17   A Bernheim, Ramsay et ses deux Discours, p. 28.

pens the be the year of the coronation Karl VII, and its associated celebrations.

· Sadly, Bernheim does not ask himself the question of why such radical changes were made to the Discours and was it likely that they were made by Ramsay or why identical version continued to be printed after Ramsay's death in 1743?

But the words of the various 'Discours' are simply accepted as those of Ramsay (who died 6 May 1743) himself and that may not be the case. If one looks through the excellent book *Ramsay et ses deux Discours* by Alain Bernheim and examine the 'Tableau Comparatif' one finds both manuscript versions of the Discours and then the text of the 1744 version of Letter de M de V*** and the 1754 extract from de la Tierce's Histoire. Sadly, Bernheim is totally silent upon the matter of who made the amendments; but then in all fairness so are others.

The Coronation of Charles VII (Karl VII) in Frankurt in 1742

Sometimes it is pure chance that events happen. It might have been pure chance that de la Tierce and Steinheil both arrived in Frankfurt in 1741, and de la Tierce forming a lodge, and also that Joseph Uriot arrived in a theatrical capacity and became a member of the lodge.

However, the War of Austrian Succession has resulted in Charles Abrecht becoming Duke of Bavaria in 1726, and also being one of the Prince Electors of the Holy Roman Empire. During the War of Austrian Succession Charles ended up being crowned King of Bohemia in Prague, elected King of Germany in 1741 and then crowned Holy Roman Emperor on 12 February 1742. It was this event that brought many to Francfort.

The Coronation itself does not seem to have affected freemasonry, but one must conclude that the meeting of Uriot with the members on Union Lodge provided friendship and encouragement to de la Tierce and Uriot.

The Versions of the Discours

This was clearly set out by Alain Bernheim and the changes that took place between 1737 mss and the 1738 and later print editions are significant, and his word count makes it clear how much the content changes.

There is a huge variance between the original manuscript Ramsay texts of 1736 and 1737 and the considerably revised printed text in the Lettre de M de V*** of 1738 and 1739. And looking in detail at the excellent comparator chart made by Bernheim in his *Ramsay et ses deux discours* the authors felt it worth investigating further. It is perhaps sad the Bernheim did not use the 1738 version as his standard 'extended text' and uses the later edition 1745 edition of de la *Tierce's Histoire, obligations* ... rather that the earlier 1742 one.

One is perhaps beguiled into considering that the key dates for printed editions are 1744 and 1745, but in reality they are 1738 and 1742. Alas, Bernheim did not ask himself why these significant changes in wordcount and content took place or state exactly when, and one is beguiled into thinking they were all changes made by Ramsay.

Joseph Uriot the Freemason

Beaurepaire describes him as a pioneer of European Freemasonry.[18] He was a theatre actor and taught French. He was a member of the prestigious Frankfurt lodge Zur Einigkeit (The Union), founded by La Tierce; Frankfurt was then a European centre for Masonic publishing thanks to the publisher Varrentrapp, and in 1742 the Union published his Lettre d'un franc-maçon à M. de Vaux (Letter from a Freemason to M. de Vaux), a work intended for lay people as well as Masons and the first public presentation of Masonry in Germany. He returned to Bayreuth in 1750, where he founded a French lodge, the Uriotino, which was badly received by the local community for social reasons. In some of his works (probably published in the Netherlands), he is mentioned as a member of a Brussels Lodge, the Egalité. A Wikipedia page on Brussels masonry lists him as a visitor to this lodge in 1743, when he spent a short period in Brussels working at the Théâtre de la Monnaie.[19]

There seems to be some distinct connection between the printed editions and one Joseph Uriot,[20] and the authors have explored these and the details are below.

Beaurepaire[21] notes that in 1742, a 24-page edition of the *Lettre d'un Franc-Macon a Mr de Vaux* was published at the expense of the Loge de l'Union in Francfort, and that the following year, 1743, there was a second edition. This seems like proof positive that these and subsequent editions which also all include the Discours de Ramsay were all using the same text as amended by Uriot.

The authors have not examined all the available editions in great detail to see

---

18 Pierre-Yves Beaurepaire. Libraires, francs-macons et Huguenots (2019). The letter to M. de V*** referred to the Beaurepaire was actually first published in 1738 using the same text.

19 The details from the informative website seem to tell what there is to say. http://mvmm.org/m/docs/uriot.html

20 Francois Labbe, *Cupidon en Loge: Joseph Uriot et sa letter d'un franc-macon*, is excellent background to Uriot. https://www.cairn.info/revue-chroniques-d-histoire-maconnique-2017-1-page-41.htm

21 Pierre-Yves Beaurepaire. Libraires, francs-macons et huguenots pp. 255-275. https://books.opennedition.org/pur/175961 The lodge paid for an edition of 500 copies.

whether there were any subsequent changes to the text. There might well be further surprises to be found.

But it is interesting to look at the 1744 edition of *Le Secret des Francs-Macons mis en evidence, Par Mr Uriot, Members des Loges de L'Union & de l'Egalite* and published in Francfort and available from J Antione Barrau at La Haye. Here he clearly is strutting the stage and proud of his membership of the Loge de l'Union in Frankfurt. But it is worth printing part of the introduction below:

LES LIBRAIRES AU LECTEUR

For several years there has been such a strong desire to know what Freemasonry is, that we thought we would please the public by providing two letters which may help them to discover at least some of the secrets of this Society.

Without mentioning the first of which four or five editions have been published, and two or three translations in less than six weeks, we will say that judicious and penetrating people to whom Mr. Uriot communicated the secondé, found it so measured, so singular and even so bizarre, that they judged that this letter was full of disguised mysteries which they do not believe to be impenetrable.

As a consequence of this judgement, we have done our utmost to obtain from the Author a copy of this mysterious piece, and permission to leave it to the conjectures of the curious *(bold by author)*.

We were advised to put at the head of these two Letters, a speech which is found in the Correspondence des Savans printed in Cologne N°. VII. &

VIII. & que Mr. Uriot prononça dans la Loge de Francfort, quand il y reçoitait la qualite de Maitre-Maçon. In addition the title of this brochure does not impose, because several Freemasons that we have consulted, have assured us word of honor—that it was not possible to better fill.[22]

So we have to leave the decision in the mind of the reader, but the wording 'we have done our utmost' indicates that they tried to obtain approval. The cleverly chosen words are trying to say that they tried to get the permission of the author but failed (or did not try very hard).

But it also indicates that the 1738 and 1739 editions probably did not have the approval of Ramsay. If this is correct then all the alterations, which of course then appeared in every other edition were NOT those of Ramsay. The multiple cities in which they were published also indicates that the author was well acquainted with the European publishing milieu of the 1740s.

Fortunately, we also found some useful notes in the *Annalan der Loge Einigkeit* produced by Georg Kloss in 1842. His words on Uriot seem to indicate that while he might have tried to obtain permission from Ramsay, that he had not succeeded in this—and simply published a heavily revised version. So not only did Uriot explain, but the Loge de l'Union also had doubts.

It is curious to note that de la Tierce placed the responsibility for the words upon the Grand Master in Paris speaking them in 1740. And in the 1742 edition of Histoires de la Tierce wrote:

DISCOURS
PRELIMINAIRE.

NOus n'avons rien trouvé qui fut plus propre à servir d'introduction aux Obligations, aux Statuts, & aux Réglemens de la vénérable confraternité que le Discours suivant: il a été prononcé par le Grand-Maitre des Francs-Maçons de France, dans la Grande Loge assemblée solemnellement à Paris l'an de la Franche-Maçonnerie cinq mille sept cent quarante.

„La noble ardeur que vous montrez, „Messieurs, pour entrer dans le très noble „& très illustre Ordre desFrancs-Maçons, „est une preuve certaine que vous possé-„dez déja toutes les qualitez nécéssaires „pour en devenir les membres, c'est à „dire, *l'humanité, la morale pure, le secret* „*inviolable & le goût des beaux arts.*

---

22 Joseph Uriot, Le Secret des Francs-Macons Mis en Evidence Par Mr. Uriot, Member des Loges de l'Union & de l'Egalite. A Francfort & se trouve A La Haye. (1744). This does not include the Discours de Ramsay, and is surely self justification.

It was spoken by the Grand Master of Free-Masons of France, in the Grand Lodge solemly assembled in Paris in the masonic year of 5740 (i.e., 1740). The reader should note that de la Tierce was also very careful to ensure that the whoe 'Discours' was contained within inverted commas—and then he could not be accused of theft of the words. But returning to Uriot and the records in Kloss's lodge history:

§ 9. Uriot's speech.

No less important was an acquisition which the Lodge made on 11 July 1742 to Br. Joseph Uriot. He read as a visiting Brother of the Lodge a : Lettre d'un francmaçon à un de ses amis, adressée à Mr. de Vaux which so that he was immediately affiliated free of charge, and received a small honorary trowel from the Lodge, to which he placed his lecture at its disposal. The lecture was immediately in French and subsequently in German; and the very numerous French and the very numerous French and German copies both under the above, as well as under modified individually or in collections, have certainly contributed in no small measure to the Freymacon's entrance into Germany, and to convince the non-masons of the purity and harmlessness of the Masonic League. The Loge de l'Union may boast, both by means of this epistle, an official declaration of its purpose, as well as with the above-mentioned speech of Br. Steinheil ... to give information about the purposes and the essence of Freemasonry.

Br. Uriot received the 3rd degree on 8 October, and left a few days later, supported with 150 fl. One still finds the report that he was working on another work on Freemasonry, which he wanted to send from Mons. This treatise of 1769 under his *Lettres sur la Franche Maçonnerie*, and that is to be with the approbation of the Lodge l'Egalité in Brussels; attached is his salutation when he was elevated to Master Mason. If, according to the protocols in the Union Lodge, the following passage in this speech is striking: "Why is it that I have not received this. Why am I not permitted here to extol the merits and virtues of our most honourable and virtues of our most honourable Master, our honourable Warden. Our honourable overseers, as well as the brothers de Deux Ponts, de La Tour Taris, de Tavannes, de Beaujeu, de Groflier, de Montperour and several others, of whom Freemasonry has cause to boast, etc." In our directories, only the brothers Taris and Beaujeu are known. Probably the others belonged to a temporary lodge. After a variety of fates, he died in 1788 as professor of history and ducal librarian in Stuttgart.[23]

The alternative 'Discours' proposition

Uriot was a comedian, an actor, and also clearly a writer, and from his later success also a librarian. A quick search indicates that he authored more than a dozen books, plus his masonic work, and a joint authorship of a German French dictionary. So by Uriot's admissions, by the words of Kloss and by his bibliography we strongly suggest that the 1738 and 1739 versions of the Discours were due to the efforts of Joseph Uriot, and had been undertaken after the 16 April 1737 *Lettre de Ramsay a Caumont* and before the publication of the *Letter de M de V**** in 1738.

It also seems that the apparent friendship of de la Tierce and Uriot may well have been a catalyst in events. It is also likely that his use of Ramsay's modified *Discours* in his Histoire indicates Uriot's involvement. It is this whole concurrence of events that seems to make the idea that it was Uriot who authored the changes to the Discours highly likely. Without travelling in time to ask the question better evidence seems unlikely to be found.

[47]	(37)
DISCOURS	**DISCOURS**
Prononcé à la Réception des Frée-Maçons.	*Prononcé à la Réception des Frée-Maçons.*
Par M. DE RAMSAY, grand Orateur de l'Ordre.	Par M. DE RAMSAY, grand Orateur de l'Ordre.
L A noble ardeur que vous montrez, Messieurs, pour	L A noble ardeur que vous montrez, Messieurs, pour entrer dans

| *1738 Discours title* | *1744 Discours title* |

This of course opens up the question of whether we should judge the outcome of Ramsay's Oration completely to Ramsay's efforts, or whether the influence of Uriot and his greater emphasis on Crusades and Chevaliers may also have had significant influence. We leave that idea for others to consider.

There were 12 replica editions of the *Lettre de M de V**** published between 1738 and 1766 in French, and across Europe. So it must have sold well enough to achieve those reprints, but how many copies were printed. The best view I can

---

23 Georg Kloss, Annalen der Loge zur Einigkeit 1742-1811 (1842) Frankfurt. Ch.1742 p. 6.

get is from a Professor of Typography[24] who could give me an approximation of 500-750 copies per edition. So we are talking of thousands of copies, and those thousands of copies will have been read by keen masonic minds. If so the spread of the word was by the hand of Uriot.

Beaurepaire also comments:

> The lodge decided to finance an initial print run of five hundred copies under the title Lettre d'un franc-maçon à Monsieur de Vaux, dedicated to Prince Alexander Ferdinand von Thurn und Taxis.

> Once printed, Uriot's speech was a great success. A pioneer of Masonic history in Germany, Georg Kloss even considered it to be "the first public presentation of Freemasonry in Germany [which] did much to facilitate the entry of Freemasonry into Germany, and to teach laymen of its purity and harmlessness."[25]

So there is further evidence that the most read words of the *'Discours'* were those of the Uriot version rather than the Ramsay text; although Ramsay must be credited for his original innovative words. Sadly, when Bernheim analyses the various versions, he fails to mention Uriot, nor does he seem to have been fully aware of the number of editions or number of copies printed. It is perhaps a heretical point of view to suggest that it was Uriot's words that shaped the future, and for that reason that perhaps this chronological list of the publications will result in the readers accepting this different conclusion.

Lief Eric Grutle clearly differentiates between the text of the manuscript and printed edition, noting that the printed versions all introduce the idea that:

---

24 Pers com. Prof Caroline Archer, Prof of Typography at Birmingham City University, England offered me the following comments on 20 September 2023 "In the eighteenth century, as today, the nature of the book and therefore the anticipated sales would have determined the number of copies; therefore, there is no 'norm' as such. The capacity of the printing house would also have had a bearing on production numbers – did the printer have a single press, or multiple presses which would have increased capacity and enabled a greater number of volumes; the number of compositors working on the job would also have had an impact on output. How much could the printing house afford to commit to the production of the book as income and profit were only accrued once the volume was on sale (unless it was printed on subscription?).

Between 1587 and 1637 the Stationers' Company put limits on editions of between 1,200-1,500 copies or up to 2,500-3,000 copies of certain smaller publications. But the regulations were often ignored. James Raven in *Publishing Business in Eighteenth-century England* states runs of 500 and 750 copies was common in bookwork of the period. However, Keith Maslen in *An Early London Printing House at work: studies in the Bower Ledgers* notes 20,000 copies of sheet A of *Poor Robin* and 2,000 copies of sheet A for Tillotson's *Sermons*. You see the wide discrepancies of possibilities!"

25 Pierre-Yves Beaurepaire, Libraires, francs-macons et Huguenots in https://books.openedition.org/pur/175961

The second version of Ramsays oration was printed for the first time in 1742. The main inspirational contribution in this version is of course the references to "Our ancestors, the Crusaders," the alleged union with the Knights of St. John, how the first Lodges were created by noblemen returning from crusade, and the special part Scotland was to play in preserving the traditions.[26]

It seems that confusion starts to creep in when authors cite dates for different printed editions. Grutle cites Batham who states that the first print was in 1742, while Bernheim notes the 1738 and 1739 prints but uses the 1744 edition in his comparative table of contents. So really it is only when one can provide a (much more) complete list of the editions that the chronological perspective becomes clear. And it was the interaction of de la Tierce and Uriot in Francfort sur Main that seemed to spark off the whole series of editions. There seems to be an obvious conclusion that the greatest influence on those contemplating creating degrees can only have come from the thousands of copies whose printing had been instigated by Joseph Uriot. The list below provides that perspective.

Les Discours 'dites de Ramsay'		
Note: All the printed documents below are available online (except the 1745 Histoire)		
Year	Title & details	Ramsay
1736	Discours de Mr le Cher de Ramsay Prononce a la loge de St Jean le 26 Xbre. Bibliotecque municipal d'Epernay ms124, tome xxxvi	
1737	La letter du 16 avril 1737 ay marquis de Caumont. Welcome Medical Library, London. MS 5744	
1738 La Haye	Lettres de M. DE V*** avec plusiers pieces de different auteurs Chez Pierre Poppy p. 178	pp.47-69
1738	ms of part of Lettres se M de V (at BnF)	
1739 La Haye	Lettres de M. DE V*** avec plusiers pieces de different auteurs Chez Pierre Poppy p. 178	pp.47-74
1742 Francfort	Lettre d'un Franc-Macon a Mr de Vaux Signed Uriot A Francfort le 15 Juillet 1742. Lu et approuve le 15 Juillet dans la Loge de l' Union p. 24 **The lodge funded a first print run of 500 copies**	
1742 Francfort	Histoire obligations et statuts de la tres venerable confraternité des Francs-Maçons tirez de leurs archives et conformes aux traditions les plus anciennes. By Louis-François de la Tierce.	pp.127-144

---

26 Leif Endre Grutle, Ramsay and the Higher Degrees – a Different Picture. And he references it to Cyril Bathsam, Chevalier Ramsay – A New Appreciation in AQC vol.81, p. 303.

1742 Constantinople	Almanac de Cocus. Discours (Prononce a la Reception des Free-Macons)	pp.30-45
1743 Francfort	Lettre d'un Franc-Macon a Mr de Vaux Nouvelle Edition	
1746 Francfort Leipzig	Le Franc-Macon dans la Republique ou Refletions Apologiques sur les persecutions des Francs-Macons. p. 110 *Reputed to be Steinheil and de la Tierce*	
1744	Discours Prononce au mois d'Octobre dans la Lodge d'Union a Francfort sur le Mein October 1742. Plus parts of Discours	(pp.9-12) pp.13-25
1744 Francfort La Haye	Le Secret des Francs-Macons mis en evidence par Mr Uriot, Membre des Loges de l'Union & de l'Egalite Aux depens. Read 'Les Libraires au Lecteur' p. 40	
1744 La Haye	Lettre de M. De V*** avec plusieurs pieces Galantes et Nouvelles. p. 238	pp.37-55
1745	Histoire des francs-maçons, contenant les obligations et statuts de la... maçonnerie. à l'Orient, chez G. de l'Etoille (Holland?)	p. n/a
1747 Paris	Lettre Philosophique par M de V*** avec plusieurs pieces Galantes et Nouvelles. aux depens p. 237	
1756 Paris	Lettre Philosophique par M de V*** avec plusieurs pieces Galantes et Nouvelles. Au depens. p. 237	pp.41-60
1757 London	Lettre Philosophique par M de V*** avec plusieurs pieces Galantes et Nouvelles. aux depens p. 288	pp.41-60
1760 Berlin	Lettre Philosophique par M de V*** avec plusieurs pieces Galantes et Nouvelles. (BnF) p. 238	pp.41-60
1762 Berlin	Lettre Philosophique par M de V*** avec plusieurs pieces Galantes et Nouvelles. Au depens. p. 192	pp.28-46
1769 Berlin	Lettre Philosophique par M de V*** avec plusieurs pieces Galantes et Nouvelles. p. 168	pp.28-41
1774 Berlin	Lettre Philosophique par M de V*** avec plusieurs pieces Galantes et Nouvelles (not scanned)	
1775 London	Lettre Philosophique par M de V*** avec plusieurs pieces Galantes et Nouvelles. aux depens p. 316	pp.42-61
1776 London	Lettre Philosophique par M de V*** avec plusieurs pieces Galantes et Nouvelles. (BnF) p. 254	pp.39-57
1797 London	Influence of Freemasonry on Society, in TheFreemasons Magazine, July 1797 pp. 35-37 (a poor short transcript) https://masonicperiodicals.org/periodicals/fmm/issues/fmm_01071797/page/44/articles/ar04401/	pp.35-37

Stuttgart	Discours pronounce a l'ouverture de la biblioteque publique ... de Wurwtemeberg et Teck par M J Uriot Professeur d'Histoire et Bibliotecaire de S.A.S. p. 26. (Not masonic but Uriot)	
1748 Jerusalem	L'Ecole de Francs-Macons p. 119 Frere de la T*** *Inc Lettre d'un Franc-Macon a un de ses Amis. Signed Votre fidele Ami U*** pp. 97-114*	

Une Amuse Bouche de Ramsay?

By chance the following was found in the 1739 volume 9 of the *Gentleman's Magazine* published in London and a source of much information. Curiously the entry for 'Rome' states that the author of the Relation Apologique of 1738[27] was none other than Ramsay. This is not normally attributed to Ramsay, but the author does declare himself to lecture to Lodges in Paris.

> *Rome.* There was lately burnt here with great Solemnity, by order of the Inquisition, a Piece in *French* wrote by the Chevalier *Ramsay* (Author of the *Travels of Cyrus*, &c.) entitled *an Apological and Historical Relation of the Secret of the Free Masons,* printed at *Dublin* by *Patric Odonoko.* This was published at *Paris,* in answer to a pretended Catechism printed there by Order of the Lieutenant *de Police,* (See Vol. VIII. p. 54.) much like *Pritchard's* in *English.*

A Final Thought by Ramsay himself

The very final page in Ramsay's Travels of Cyrus is like a dedication to rebuild the Temple in Jerusalem. How likely would it be that Ramsay would abandon that idealistic thought in favour of a band of Crusaders. Personally, I do not think he would have changed his mind.

> Ledg'd the God of *Israel* by this solemn Edict, for Rebuilding the Temple of *Jerusalem.*
>
>> Thus saith *Cyrus,* King of *Persia.* 'The Lord God of Heaven hath given me all the Kingdoms of the Earth; and he hath charged me to build him a House at *Jerusalem,* which is in *Judah.* Whoever among you is of his People, his God be with

---

27 Relation Apologique et Historique de la Societe des Francs-Macons, 'Dublin' 'Chez Patrice Odonoko 1738.

him: And let him go up to J*erufalem,* and build the Houfe of the Lord God of Is*rael.* HE IS THE GOD.

FINIS.[28]

---

186   *The* TRAVELS *of* CYRUS.

ledg'd the God of *Ifrael* by this folemn Edict, for Rebuilding the Temple of *Jerufalem.*

Thus faith **Cyrus**, King of **Perfia.** ' The Lord God of ' Heaven hath given me all ' the Kingdoms of the Earth; ' and he hath charg'd me to ' build him a Houfe at *Je-* ' *rufalem,* which is in *Judah.* ' Whoever among you is of ' his People, his God be with ' him: And let him go up to ' *Jerufalem,* and build the ' Houfe of the Lord God of ' *Ifrael.* HE IS THE GOD.

F I N I S.

---

28 Ramsay, Travels of Cyrus London (1727) p. 186.

Appendix: Joseph Oriot the man

The Bibliothèque de Nancy, in the town where Joseph Uriot was born has produced an excellent illustrated resume on the life of Joseph Uriot,[29] and it is quoted from below. His father was in the guard of Duc Leopold in Nancy, and they sent their son Joseph to the Jesuit College in Nancy. And it was in Nancy in 1729 that he first appeared on the stage:

> Les Pères accordaient une grande importance au théâtre dans la formation de leurs élèves, qui se produisaient en public. Le 23 février 1729 eut ainsi lieu la représentation d'une tragédie, *Thémistocle*, et d'une comédie, *Le Duelliste*, sur la scène de l'Opera, avec l'autorisation du duc Léopold, qui avait fait construire cette salle par un grand architecte italien, Francesco Galli. Uriot, qui allait avoir seize ans—il était né à Nancy le 17 mars 1713—, interpréta un rôle dans la tragédie et participa comme danseur aux intermèdes. On le sait grâce au programme imprimé qui fut remis aux spectateurs et dont la Bibliothèque Stanislas conserve deux exemplaires.

> The Fathers attached great importance to the theatre in the training of their pupils, who performed in public. On 23 February 1729, a tragedy, Thémistocle, and a comedy, Le Duelliste, were performed on the Opéra stage, with the permission of Duke Léopold, who had had the theatre built by a great Italian architect, Francesco Galli. Uriot, who was about to turn sixteen—he was born in Nancy on 17 March 1713—played a role in the tragedy and took part as a dancer in the interludes. We know this thanks to the printed programme given to the audience, two copies of which are held by the Bibliothèque Stanislas.

And it seems that he also danced on the stage during the intervals—and all at the age of 16. He was then a professor of history and librarianship at the Academy founded by Duke Leopold of Luneville, only leaving Lorraine in 1741. But it seems he remained in touch with his friends Mme de Graffigny et De Vaux. Perhaps here one might consider the ('Lettre d'un Franc Macon a Mr de Vaux, Conseilluer de sa maj Le Roy de Pologne, Duc de Lorraine...').

> He next appears in Francfort for theatrical presentations and where he became a member of the Loge de l'Union—but we already know that and that he left there in October 1742 when his theatre work ended. He then appeared in Brussels in 1743 when he also joined

---

29 Comedien, Bibliotecair, Professeur, Ecrivain: Joseph Uriot (1713–1788), un Lorrain au Service de Charles Eugene de Wurtemberg. https://epitome.hypotheses.org/1700

Loge l'Egalité.[30]

En 1744, Uriot entra comme comédien au service du margrave de Bayreuth et de son épouse Wilhelmine, une sœur de Frédéric II de Prusse ; ils lui confièrent aussi l'instruction de leur fille unique Frédérique, alors fiancée à Charles Eugène de Wurtemberg. Gardant des liens avec la Lorraine, où il revenait de temps en temps, il savait ce qui s'y passait. Il eut ainsi connaissance de l'établissement par Stanislas d'une bibliothèque publique et de la fondation de deux prix, l'un pour récompenser un ouvrage scientifique, l'autre une œuvre littéraire.

In 1744, Uriot entered the service of the Margrave of Bayreuth and his wife Wilhelmine, a sister of Frederick II of Prussia, as an actor; they also entrusted him with the education of their only daughter Frédérique, then engaged to Charles Eugène of Württemberg. Maintaining links with Lorraine, where he returned from time to time, he knew what was happening there. He was aware that Stanislas had set up a public library and that two prizes had been founded, one for a scientific work and the other for a literary work.

Au début de l'année 1759, il quitta le service du margrave et se rendit à Stuttgart. Le duc donnait chaque année en février, dans ses châteaux de Stuttgart et Ludwigsburg, des fêtes somptueuses pour son anniversaire. Renommées bien au-delà des frontières du Wurtemberg, elles attiraient de nombreux visiteurs. Uriot publia un bref récit de celles de 1762 que suivirent les relations beaucoup plus amples des réjouissances de 1763 et 1764.

At the beginning of 1759, he left the Margrave's service and moved to Stuttgart. Every February, the Duke held sumptuous birthday celebrations at his castles in Stuttgart and Ludwigsburg. Renowned far beyond the borders of Württemberg, they attracted many visitors. Uriot published a brief account of the celebrations in 1762, followed by much more extensive accounts of the festivities in 1763 and 1764.

Une lettre autographe d'Uriot conservée à la BnF l'atteste : c'est à son instigation que Charles Eugène fonda une bibliothèque publique à Ludwigsburg, sans doute sur le modèle de celle de Nancy. Il chargea Uriot de la former et le nomma bibliothécaire. Fondé officiellement le 11 février 1765—jour de l'anniversaire du duc—l'éta-

---

30 The details from the informative website seem to tell what there is to say. http://mvmm.org/m/docs/uriot.html Wikipedia page on Brussels masonry lists him as a visitor to this lodge in 1743, when he spent a short period in Brussels working at the Théâtre de la Monnaie.

blissement fut inauguré le 13, en présence de la cour et d'invités de marque. Uriot prononça un discours sur l'utilité des bibliothèques. Ce discours fut publié dans un recueil qui contenait aussi les autres textes relatifs à la fondation. Aspirant à devenir membre correspondant de la Société Royale de Nancy, le nouveau bibliothécaire envoya un exemplaire du volume avec sa lettre de candidature. Le texte du discours suscita l'admiration, mais son auteur ne fut pas admis, « parce qu'il avoit été comédien », note Durival dans son *Journal* à la date du 2 mai 1765. En 1776, Charles Eugène transféra la bibliothèque à Stuttgart.

An autograph letter from Uriot held by the BnF bears witness to this: it was at his instigation that Charles Eugène founded a public library in Ludwigsburg, probably modelled on the one in Nancy. He commissioned Uriot to train it and appointed him librarian. Officially founded on 11 February 1765—the Duke's birthday— the library was inaugurated on the 13th, in the presence of the court and distinguished guests. Uriot gave a speech on the usefulness of libraries. This speech was published in a collection that also contained the other texts relating to the foundation. Aspiring to become a corresponding member of the Société Royale de Nancy, the new librarian sent a copy of the volume with his letter of application. The text of the speech aroused admiration, but its author was not admitted, "because he had been an actor," notes Durival in his Journal of 2 May 1765. In 1776, Charles Eugène transferred the library to Stuttgart.

This short resume of Joseph Uriots's life demonstrates the diversity and determination of Uriot. We know that he was active masonically in both practical masonry and in publishing in Frankfurt in 1742 and that he also kept in touch with his brothers in Frankfurt. We must give serious consideration to Uriot having been the key person spreading (and maybe writing) an amended version of Le Discours de Ramsay. The final editions of 'Lettre a M. de V***' —under the title 'Lettre Philosophique par M de V***' were published in 1776—perhaps when Uriot moved to Stuttgart?

The Letter G and the Widow's Son

The period around the 1740s was a very active one in France when it came to the appearance of new degrees especially of the Ecossais variety. The result was a flood of new ideas. While what follows is not directly related to the work of Leonard Gabanon, it does perhaps relate to his choice of *nom de plume*.

It seems always to have been an assumption by British masonic researchers that the gap between Masonry Dissected in 1730 and Three Distinct Knocks in 1760 was filled by the masonic innovations in France. And our investigations hoped that we might find some early parts of the Installation ceremony of a Master of a Lodge being Installed. And we found one, but the majority of discoveries in the French craft exposures related instead to what in England is called the Traditional History of the Third degree—and which today comes as a separate part of the Master Mason's degree, and has remained into the 21st century within Emulation Ritual (for example).

But were the messages of the Maitre Anglois taken seriously by the brothers in France. So below we follow that letter G and the Children of the Widow. The traces remain today in the rituals and the texts below illustrate that thread.

However the dating of the manuscript resulted in a lively discussion between the authors. And the French point of view is below:

A FEW FRENCH THOUGHTS ON THE DEGREE OF "MAÎTRE ANGLAIS"

I have reread your text carefully and I do indeed find it interesting.

I do not dispute the existence or the interest of the degree of Maître Anglais, whose names have varied (Maître par curiosité, etc.) and from which other degrees have derived (Petit Maître anglais, etc.). Once again, the name of the degree, as we well know, does not always guarantee its content. Nor should it be confused with the Parfait Maître Anglais, which is a degree of purification and sanctification (by water, fire and anointing oil) in the Holy of Holies of the Temple of Jerusalem.[1] But this is a degree attested later (late 1750s, early 1760s).

---

1   In the famous correspondence between Willermoz (Lyon) and Meunier de Précourt (Metz), in
    1761 (Steel-Maret, Archives secrètes de la franc-maçonnerie, 1893, 73-74), Meunier de Précourt
    observes about the English Master, a degree then known in both cities under the same name
    (11th in the list in Lyon and 8th in Metz):
        "Two kinds of English Masters here. The 1st is about the complaint that Hyram, King of

The problem is the date of 1740 attributed to the Kloss Fund manuscript. No one knows where it comes from and it is not only uncertain: in my opinion, it is improbable.

There is no trace of this degree in Paris in the first known list of degrees in France, that of the Count of Clermont's lodge, in 1745: it lists only the Maître Parfait, the Maître irlandais, the Elu and the Ecossais (of the 3JJJ, or of Paris, or of Clermont).[2] At the same time, in 1745, correspondence between Paris and Bordeaux showed that only the Vray Maître et Ecossais was known in Bordeaux. However, in 1761, this degree, enriched (in particular with elements taken from the Parfait Maître anglais) was to be found in 14th position in Morin's list in 1761! Yet it was much older than several of the degrees that preceded it in the list. What happened in the meantime?

I agree with P. Mollier's account:

> Brother de Boulard (in Bordeaux) reported in a letter of 1750 "that it is necessary to be Elu Parfait to be a Chevalier de l'Orient, and that to be Elu Parfait, that is to say Ecossais, it is necessary to have passed through the nine degrees of Freemasonry."

At that time in Bordeaux, there was a family of rituals that gave access to the Ecossais de la Perfection in ten degrees: Apprenti, Compagnon, Maître, *Maître Secret*, Parfait maçon (?), *Maître par curiosité (i.e. Maître anglais),* Prévôt et Juge (i.e. Maître Irlandais), Intendant des Bâtiments (i.e. Ecossais des 3 JJJ), Elu, Grand and Vray Ecossais. At least, three new degrees were inserted (and added to the Parisian system attested in 1745): *Maître Secret, Maître par*

Tyre, made to Salomon about the poor quality of the land in Caboul. A guard listens, he is surprised and Hyram wants to immolate him, Solomon asks for mercy for him, obtains it and he is initiated into the mystery of the English Master; word: 3 times jehova, right knee to the ground.

The second one is a kind of Ecossism, it carries for attribute an equilateral triangle on which are written the words: 1st face Benchorin, Irachin, Aiad; on the 2nd face Juday Ka Jea. The painting depicts the Star of the Magi, the 7-branched Candelabra, a square pointed altar, 3 vessels for purification, the great brazen sea; the word Jiachin Jehova; 3 figures, surprise, admiration and pain."

In reality, the "second" one was none other than the degree that would become better known throughout France as the "Parfait Maître anglais"—in Metz, in 1761, they were still confused under the same name.

In the same letter, Meunier de Précourt also said that the Secret Master, known in Lyon, was "unknown in Metz under this name."

2   A. Le Bihan, *Francs-maçons et ateliers parisiens de la Grande Loge de France au XVIIIe siècle,* 1974, pp. 393-402. Bernheim, « Contribution à la connaissance de la genèse de la première Grande Loge de France », *Villard de Honnecourt,* n°17, 1988.

curiosité, Intendant des Bâtiments (which was not initially known in Bordeaux, but the traditional order was respected. *This new stage is more difficult to date, but must have taken place between 1745 and 1748.*[3]

In short, the appellation "Maître anglais" does not appear until 1750 at the earliest, in a list of degrees of the Mother Lodge of Bordeaux. It is therefore likely that this degree appeared between 1745 and 1750, perhaps in Bordeaux. In any case, no other source mentions it earlier.

In general, the position of the degrees in the lists, which became longer and longer as the eighteenth century progressed, especially before the early 1760s, gives a rough indication of the age of each degree: the "small numbers" are a priori the oldest—the degrees at the "top of the pile" always claimed to be the last word in Masonry, and were therefore the most recent.

But things are a little more complicated. For example, the grade of Secret Master certainly appeared after the four Parisian high degrees of 1745, as we have just seen. However, it is placed before them in all the lists known between 1750 and 1760 (and today it is the 4th in the REAA, whereas the Maître Parfait is the 5th). Why is this?

To understand this, you have to remember that from one city to the next (Paris, Bordeaux, Marseille, Lyon, etc.) the question at the time was who had the "best écossisme." This is what some authors have called "the rivalry of the ecossisms." If a Brother from Paris, for example, came to Lyon and said he had the B degree of a system of high degrees which, in Paris, was A, B, C, D, he would be told in Lyon: "That's very good, but you don't have the A' degree that we practise here (the system had by then become: A, A', B, C, D), so your B degree is incomplete!

The phenomenon has been repeated several times - generally, these 'barrage' degree are not very interesting and are more or less based on details borrowed from certain earlier degrees. Sometimes the process is rather crude: from an original single Ecossais, three are made (Scottish Apprentice, Scottish Fellow, Scottish Master)...

I think this is the case with the Maître anglais. The fact that in 1750 it was still ahead of the Ecossais des 3 JJJ, whose existence is certain from 1745 at the latest, probably shows that he was introduced later, perhaps to "block" the Ecossais des 3 JJJ from Paris, in Bordeaux—where all degrees were finally surmounted by the Vray Maître Ecossais - which would suggest quite clearly that the other Ecossais were false...

---

3   Le Chevalier du Soleil – *Contribution à l'étude d'un haut grade maçonnique en France au XVIIIe siècle,* Ecole pratique des hautes études, 1995, p. 10.

In my opinion, the most likely explanation is that the author of the catechism for the Maître anglais, being aware of the data relating to letter G published by Travenol as early as 1744, 'embroidered' on Gabaon, according to a technique customary in 'barrage degrees'.

This in no way detracts from the interest of this development on the meaning of Gabaon. There is no doubt that it existed. I simply think that it did not precede Travenol's text but that it came after it.

The English Authors Opinion

I have read the ms from the Kloss collection several times. And the introductory paragraph is worth reading:

> Ecossois Anglois
> ou le Parfait-Maître Anglois
>
> Ce Grade est à peu près conforme à l'apprentif Ecossois François, j'l'étoit peu connu en france avant la Guerre de 1740. quelques prisonniers Anglois en reconnoissance de l'urbanité avec laquelle j'ils avoient été traités, le Donnerent à ceux auxquels j'ils avoient des obligations. j'l y a plusieurs Loges en Angleterre dans les quelles on ne Donne pas d'autre maîtrise.

While the date cannot be substantiated, it also states it says that the text came from 'Several English prisoners'. When I read the totality of the text it did not feel like one complete degree, but rather a collection of different ideas often not in any particular order – in fact it felt to me like the ideas of several brothers recorded in an almost random manner. I note the suggestion that this was simply a 'blocking degree'; but I was unable to guess what it might be blocking. I have read the degree of the same name in Conversations Allegoriques of 1763 and I have another composite ms[4] with a version I have not yet read, and they do more closely resemble a degree.

What caught my attention was the number of different ideas that were present, and which then keep appearing again later, and clearly being like and adopted. So I have no evidence, just a 'gut feel' that this might just contain threads of some early 'higher masonry'. To add context there were by 1740 a dozen lodges

---

4   BnF Rituels FM4 (76)

with military warrants from the Grand Lodge of Ireland for Regiments that were variously Irish, Scottish or English.

So I choose to keep an open mind on the date of the ms, there is a possibility that the letter G either came to Travenol and he used it OR that his use of the word Gabanon was his 'creation' and was also used after 1745. Either way enjoy reading how Gabanon and the Widow's Sons has survived over 250 years in the masonic memory.

The Story of the Letter G and Hiram's widow

It starts with the need to give another understanding to the letter G because in England the letter G stood for God. But in the Anglois, which claims to come from England we are given this letter but with a French meaning which is completely different – but which has lasted until today. This chapter follows the development of those ideas from the Maitre Anglois to the 21ˢᵗ century. Being able to follow that trail is an example of what is possible by consulting old documents and manuscripts, across degrees and across countries.

The story starts with text from the Maitre Anglois:

p.35 Kloss Ms XXV

D. What means the letter G

A. G...which means God in English

D. So why do we call ourselves Gabaon?

A. It is the place where the Israelites deposited the arch in times of trouble and persecution, and which Salomon gave to the mother of Hiram, where she wept for her son for the rest of her life

[handwritten French text:]

D. que veut-dire Gabaon ?

R. c'est le nom d'un petit bourg que Salomon donna à la mere
d'hiram après la mort de son fils.

D. pour quoi dit on les Enfans de la veuve ?

R. parceque après la mort d'hiram, Sa mere adopta les maçons.

V.'. freres je vous exhorte à montrer vôtre zéle pour
les pauvres.

p.36. Kloss Ms XXV

> D. Why do we say Gabaon
>
> A. It is the name of a small town which Salomon gave to the mother
> of Hiram after the death of her son
>
> D. Why do we say the children of the widow ?
>
> A. Because after the death of Hiram, his mother adopted the masons
> Ven[erable]: . Brothers I urge you to maintain your zeal for the poor.

So here in the early 1740s we can read that after the death of Hiram his mother was accorded a special status by Solomon And we are told also that it is the name of the village given to Hiram's mother, and that she cared for the masons.

The Kloss ms for the Maitre Anglois does feel that it might have been compiled from the input of several brothers who sometimes had possibly slightly different rituals, but it does perhaps offer additional material that from parts of the English history behind the third degree.

But in 1744 the word Gabanon appears again in *Le catéchisme des francs-maçons*, by Léonard Gabanon - alias Louis Travenol. This consisted of around sixty pages and was unique in that it revealed for the first time the content and ritual of the Master's grade in French.

Clearly the authors name is a pseudonym as is the place of publication Jerusalem.

And on p.56 we can read:

> Q. Are you a Master?
>
> A. Examine me, approve me, & disapprove me if you are able, but the Acacia is known to me.
>
> Q. If one of your brothers were lost, where would you find him?

A. Between the Square & the Compasses

Q. What is the name of a Mason?

A. Gabanon

And in then 1745 in *Les Secretes des Francs-Macons* published in Amsterdam (1745) on p167. And here we can see for the first time that the widow is not Hiram mother, but indeed Hiram's wife.

> Q. When a Mason finds himself in danger, what should he say & do, to call his Brothers to his aid ?
>
> A. He must place his hands together on his head, his fingers interlaced, & say, To me, children (or sons) of the Widow.
>
> Q. What do these words signify?
>
> A. Just as Hiram's wife remained a widow when her husband was murdered; the Masons, who considered themselves as Descendants of Hiram, call themselves Sons (or children) of the Widow.

And in 1749 in Nouveau Catechisme by Travenol. In the First set of catechisms (p94-100) the whole issue regarding Hirams Widow is absent. However in the second part which is entitled 'Pieces Melees pour server a l'histoire de la Maconnerie' in a section headed 'Addition Aux Catechismes des Apprentifs, des Compagnonsm & des Maitre, tiree de l'Anti-Macon we can find (p.54) an almost complete story. There is the sign, the explanation, and that it is clearly 'la Femme d'Hiram' and the words 'sons of the widow'. So clearly Travenol ignores the theme of the widow in 1744, does not get the 1749 text reset, but does include the theme as per Les Secretes, but in his addendum we can read:

> D. Lorsqu'un Maçon se trouve en danger, que doit - il faire pour appeller ses Freres a son secours?
>
> R. Il doit mettre ses deux mains jointes sur la tête, les doitgs entrelaffés, & dire, *à moi les Enfans*, ou *fils de la Veuve*.
>
> D. Que fignifient ces mots ?
>
> R. Comme la femme d'*Hiram* fe, trouva veuve, quand fon mari fut maffacré. Les Maçons, qui fe regardent comme les defcendans d'*Hiram*, (1) s'appellent *fils*, ou *Enfans de la Veuve*.

Q. When a Masons finds himself in Danger, what should he do to call his Brothers to his aid?

A. He must place his hands joined on his head, the fingers interlinked, and say to me the children, or children of the Widow

Q. What do these words signify?

A. As the wife of Hiram found herself a widow, when her husband was massacred. The Mason, who regard themselves as the descendants of *Hiram*, called themselves children or *children of the widow*

Le Macon Demasque 1751

This exposure was published in London and in French, but notably it includes the words Adoniram Gabanon and Children of the Widow that keep appearing in various assortments.

> Le V. quel-eſt le nom d'un Maître.
> Le S. Gabanon.
> Le V. comment appelle-t-on ſon fils?
> Le S. Louffton?
> Le V. quel eſt ſon privilége?
> Le S. c'eſt d'être reçu avant touts ceux
>   qui ſe préſentent.
> Le V. quels font les mots de Paſſe?
> Le S. TUBALCAIN pour l'Apprentif, SCIB-
>   BOULETH pour le Compagnon, & GI-
>   BLIM pour le Maître.
> Le V. ſi vous vous trouviez en danger
>   que feriez vous?
> Le S. je mettrois les mains ſur la tête,
>   & je crierois, *à moi les enfants de la*
>   *veuve.*
> Le V. qu'eſt ce que cela ſignifie?
> Le S. c'eſt-à-dire, à moi mes freres.
> Le V pourquoi cela?
> Le S. c'eſt parcequ'Adoniram notre Pe-
>   re ayant été aſſaſſiné, touts les Ma-
>   çons qui ſont freres, ſont cenſés être
>   les enfants de ſa veuve.

So here in France, and in a 'French exposure published in London a couple of years later a theme which seems common in France (albeit with a confusion between mother and widow). But did it travel to England?

Three distinct Knocks (1760) and Jachin & Boaz (1762)

But this bring us to the 1760 start of a series of English exposures, of which the first was Three Distinct Knocks. What is most interesting is that while the French search for Hiram there is the search and then the return to burial of Hiram with honour and dignity, The English interest in 1760 seems to entirely on taking retribution upon the guilty three.

> ... One of those Parties travell'd down to the Sea of Joppa; one of them sat himself down to rest, by the Side of a Rock, he hearing a frightful Lamentation in a Clift of the Rock. Oh ! that I had had my Throat cut a-cross, and my Tongue torn out by the Root, and that buried in the Sands of the Sea at Low Water Mark , a Cable Length from Shore, where the Tide ebbs and flows in 24 Hours rather than I had been concerned in the Death of our Master Hiram. Says the other; Oh! that I had had my Heart torn from under my naked Left-Breast, and given to the Vultures of the Air as a Prey, rather than I had been concerned in the Death of so good a Master. But Oh! says *Jubelum,* I struck him more hard than you both , for I killed him ; Oh ! that I had had my body fevered in two, one Part carried to the South, and the other to the North ; my Bowels burnt to Ashes in the South, and the Ashes scattered before the Four Winds of the Earth, rather than I had been concerned in the Death of our Master *Hiram,*

> This Brother hearing this sorrowful Lamentation, hailed the other Two, and they went into the Clift of the Rock, and took them and bound them, and brought them before King Solomon, and they owned what had pass'd , and what they had done , and did not desire to live; therefore Solomon order'd their own Sentences to be laid upon them : Says he, they have sign'd their own Death, and let it be upon them as they have said.

> Jubela was taken out, and his throat cut across, &c. Jubelo's heart was torn from under his naked Left-breas, &c, Jubelum's Body was severed in two, and one part carry'd to the South and the other to the North, &c.

> After this King Solomon sent those 12 Crafts to raise their Master Hiram, in order that he might be interred in Sanctum Sanctorum . And Solomon told them, that if they could not find a Key-word in him or about him, it was lost for there were but Three in the World that knew it, and it can never be deliver'd without we Three are together ; but now One is dead, therefore it is lost. But for the future,

the first occasion'd Sign and Word that is spoke at his raising, shall be his ever after. So they went to raise him ; and when they had clear'd the Rubbish , they saw their Master lie dead, in a bruised Condition ; for he having already lain 15 Days, they lifted up both their Hands above their Heads in a great Surprize, and said, O Lord my God, (which is the grand Sign of a Master-Mason .)

So in England by 1760 the details of the search had vanished, the acacia gone and the body not unearthed, and perhaps even stranger there was no ceremonial burial. Instead the emphasis has become one solely of retribution and revenge.

In the section entitled 'The Master's Clap' the sign has moved into the Temple and to the time when Solomon dedicates it. And also any association with the widow of Hiram has vanished.! But the Masters Clap has survived:

The *MASTER's* Clap.

IS by holding both Hands above your Head, and ſtriking upon your Apron, and both Feet going at the ſame Time ready to ſhake the Floor down: this they call the Grand Sign of a Maſter Maſon. They give two Reaſons for this Sign, *viz.* When they ſaw their Maſter *Hiram* lye dead, they lifted up their Hands in a Surprize, and ſaid, O Lord, my God! *Second.* When *Solomon* dedicated the Temple to the Lord, he ſtood up, and lifting up both his Hands, ſaid, O Lord my God, 'Great art Thou above all Gods; for in this Hour will I adore thy Name.

1766 Solomon in all his Glory pub in English and being a translation of the 1751 Macon Demasque also published in London but in French (they are identical). Sadly the connection to the widow has disappeared although the word Gabanon remains.

M. What is a mafter's name?

W. Gabanon.

M. What is his fon called?

W. Louffton.

M. What privileges has he?

W. To be received before any others who prefent themfelves.

M. What are the watch words?

W. TUBALKAIN for the apprentice, SHIBOLETH for the fellow-craft, and GIBLIM for the mafter.

M. If you were in any danger, what would you do?

W. I would put my hand upon my head, and cry out, *The widow's children are mine.*

M. What does that fignify?

W. My brothers are mine.

M. Why fo?

W. Becaufe Adoniram, our father, having been affaffinated, all brother-mafons are looked upon as his wife's children.

Solomon in all His Glory, London 1766 p.50

The Sign of Grief and Distress

It is curious to note that the common practice in Europe and the USA was not accepted in Britain in the 1760s and neither was it accepted in 1876 - nor today. But it demonstrates how over time an exact meaning can change, and words and meaning disappear. It seems a long journey from the introduction of a word that began with a G in the 1740s; but it tends to be typical of what can happen as rituals move countries and ritual stories develop.

Should you ever travel on the Continent, the S. of G. and D. is there given in another way, by i...g the f...s and raising the h...s to the f...d, exclaiming, " Come to my assistance, ye children of the widow," on the supposition that all M. Ms. are Brn. to H. A., who was the son of a widow of the Tribe of N.

The surviving part of the 'Come to my assistance, ye children of the widow' and written in The Lectures of the Three Degrees in Craft Masonry. pub A.Lewis, London. (1876)

Another Curiosity – why the French Ecossais colour is red?

On page 29 of the Kloss ms, of the Maitre Anglois, the following question and answer appear. Whether these words appear elsewhere is not known. We leave the readers to consider the words.

D. what does the red collar we wear signify?

A. It is a commemoration of the blood which our Master shed for Masonry & which we always recall whenever re-enact that event.

And probably it is the same event and same memory that is invoked when in some third degree ceremonies a brother is laid on the floor and his face covered with a 'bloodstained' cloth so as to represent Hiram.

The Catechisms of Gabanon and the appearance of the grade of Master Mason in France

Between the first exposure and 1744

It is commonplace to observe that the decade 1740–1751 was a difficult one for English Freemasonry—culminating in the creation of the Grand Lodge of the Ancients. Conversely, it could well be said that, for French Freemasonry, it was a prodigious decade. One of the most striking manifestations of this profound dynamism was the emergence of the first high grades.

It would take seven years for this maturation to be completed. When new revelations were made in the mid-1740s, French masonry, as we shall soon see, would have taken on a new face, emerging stronger than ever from the trials that the royal authorities had inflicted on it—trials that were, incidentally, fairly benign.

After the Sentence against masonic activity in Paris[1]

After Hérault's disclosure of masonic principles in 1737, and with the exception of a very strange French translation of *La Maçonnerie Disséquée*, obviously inspired by an intermediate Dutch translation (*La réception mystérieuse* published in 1738), the first printed text following Hérault's revelation in 1737 was seven years later when *Le secret des francs-maçons* was published 'anonymously' by Abbé Pérau in 1744. This work of around a hundred pages covered the first two grades and was immediately a great success, with several editions. It provided little new information compared with Hérault's revelation, but commented extensively on the world and spirit of young French Freemasonry.

In the same year, but following on from Secret, *Le catéchisme des francs-maçons*, by Louis Travenol alias Léonard Gabanon—consisted of around sixty pages and was unique in that it revealed for the first time the content and ritual of the Master's grade in French.

Also in 1744, we should mention two very different texts, both anonymous: *La franche-maçonne ou révélation des mystères des francs-maçons*, and *Les véritables secrets des quatres grades d'Apprentis, Compagnons, maîtres ordinaires & Ecossais de la franche-maçonnerie*. We will consider them separately because they are part of the series of disclosures intended to mislead the public by revealing false secrets presented as the "real" ones. However, these texts, whose authors—and

---

1   Ex Louis Travenol, Noveau Catechisme (1749) on p. 98 of Part 2 'Pieces Melees'.

their intentions—remain unknown to us to this day, nevertheless provide us with interesting information on the problems already posed by the first high-grades and, on the other hand, very early on point to a possible source of the rituals of Adoption masonry—or reflect an influence coming from them. We will come back to this in detail later.

In 1745, two texts shared the limelight: *L'Ordre des francs-maçons trahi* (The Order of Betrayed Freemasons) —the exact title and content of which vary— contained very little that was new, since it essentially compiled data from Pérau and Gabanon, with only minor alterations. The second work, barely 70 pages long, highly original and often overlooked, but which seems to have been much less widely distributed, is *Le sceau rompu ou la loge ouverte aux profânes par un franc-maçon*. In contrast to the previous disclosures, the influence of Prichard's disclosure is quite obvious and we know nothing about its author, who claims to be a Freemason and a Frenchman.

In 1747, *Les francs-maçons écrasés*—a work attributed since Thory to Abbé Larudan, who is not otherwise known—is a large volume of around 480 pages which appears as a sequel to L'Ordre des francs-maçons trahis but adds polemical notes and iconographic and ritual elements relating to an Ecossais grade. It, too, must be regarded as largely fanciful or deliberately written to mislead the public, but what it says about the "Scots" needs to be examined more closely. In the same year, *La désolation des entrepreneurs modernes du Temple de Jérusalem* (The Desolation of the Modern Entrepreneurs of the Temple of Jerusalem) was presented as Léonard Gabanon's second opus, extending and developing his catechism published three years earlier. A different version, with significant additions was published in 1749 under the title *Nouveau catéchisme des francs-maçons.*[2]

In 1748, *L'anti-maçon*, a volume of around a hundred pages, contained few new features but gave an interesting account of Masonic practices ten years after they had first been revealed.

As for the last title in this series*, Le maçon démasqué* (The Mason Unmasked), which appeared in 1751, it has the immense interest of presenting itself as a disclosure of the practices observed in a French lodge in London and provides an opportunity to take stock of the differences that may have existed, at that time, between the two masonries now well established on both sides of the Channel.

This venerable and imposing corpus has one singular feature: it fills an almost complete documentary void in English sources between 1730 and 1760.[3] This

---

2   C'était du reste le deuxième titre de la première édition.

3   On peut consulter un important travail de synthèse sur ces divulgations françaises : H. Amblaine

point is far from insignificant. After the success of Prichard's text, nothing more was published on the subject in Great Britain before 1760.

But it is perhaps the works by Gabanon that are worth examining in more detail.

In the context of this chapter, the aim of which is to follow step by step the construction of the grade system in early French masonry, the second text on which we will focus is *Le Catechisme des francs-maçons*, published in 1744.

While the author of Le Catechisme states he is Leonard Gabanon, the agreed reality is that he was Louis Antione Travenol (b. ca.1683 or 1708 – d.1768). He was the son of a Dance teacher, and gained employment before 1735 as first violoin and master of music of the King of Poland at Luneville. In 1737 he joined the orchestra of the Royal Academy (The Opera in Paris). He is mostly known for his polemic debates against Voltaire, Rousseau or Mondonville, and on one occasion during his legal debates with Voltaire his eighty year old father was arrested in error. Illness caused him to leave the Opera in 1758, but it seems he received a pension from 1761.[4]

His main published masonic texts are:

> Le Catchisme des Francs-Macons 1744 (74pp)
>
> La désolation des entrepreneurs modernes du Temple de Jérusalem 1747 (156 pp)
>
> Le Nouveau Catechisme des Francs-Maçons 1749 (119pp plus Pieces Melees 109pp)

Unfortunately both Carr[5] and Snoek[6] considered that the 1749 edition was just a reprint, and this is actually not the case. Looking at the argumentative life of Travenol in the outside world, it would be not surprising to find him engaging with the authors of other masonic publications. And this is precisely what he does. The 1749 edition he adds a second section entitled *Pieces Melees pour server a l'Histoire de la Maconnerie*, which runs to 109 pages and seems to have escaped the attention of others. He takes exception to various other publications including the 1748 L'Anti Macon. The "Piece Melees" might well have been an

---

[A. Bernheim], « Masonic Catechisms and Exposures », *AQC* 106 (1993), pp. 141-153. Il n'existe malheureusement pas encore d'édition critique de l'ensemble de ces textes en français. Pour mémoire, *cf.* aussi H. Carr, *Early French Exposures*,

4 Sourced from https://www.musicologie.org/Biographies/t/travenol_louis.html

5 Harry Carr, *Early French Masonic Exposures* (1971).

6 Jan Snoek, *The Evolution of the Hiramic Legend in England and France, Heredom* (2003) pp. 11-53. These works of Carr and Snoek as invaluable because they approach the subject from different angles, and of course they were both cutting edge research when they were written. They are commended to the curious.

after thought because some of his text on the Third Degree is also changed.

This work followed on from the *Le Secret des francs-maçons*, published at the beginning of 1744, and from which the Catechism took much of its text. The author introduces himself under the enigmatic name of Léonard Gabanon. This last word appears in the body of the work as being "the name of a Mason." All the authors seem to agree that it is the pseudonym of Louis Travenol, who was a violinist at the Paris Opera and may have been a Freemason, although the date and place of his eventual initiation are entirely unknown.[7]

This new publication is in two distinct parts.

The first is a critique of what little the *Secret des francs-maçons* had revealed about the rank of Master, to which it devoted only two and a half pages—out of more than a hundred. In it we read that, in this grade, we saw:

> a kind of representation of Hiram's tomb. The Freemasons make many ceremonial laments over the death of Hiram, who died nearly three thousand years ago.

The author of the Secret added:

> Hiram, whom the Freemasons refer to, was far from being the King of Tyre; he was an excellent worker for all kinds of metalwork, such as gold, silver and copper.

One gets the impression from this reading that the author of the *Secret* knew of the existence of the rank but had little to say about it. The *Catéchisme* denounces this ignorance and, to begin with, disputes the identity of the hero of the third grade. In a long passage, it denies that the Hiram of the Master Masons was "a metal worker," as *Le Secret* claimed:

> It seems to me that the quality they take of Masons, the Apron of White Skin, the Trowel they wear, & all the other allegorical instruments with which they decorate themselves in Lodge, have nothing in common with Goldsmiths, Locksmiths, Smelters, nor Boilermakers.

---

7   J.M. Quérard, dans son ouvrage *La France littéraire, ou dictionnaire bibliographique...*, 1838, IX, 534, semble avoir été le premier à publier cette identité dont on ne trouve pas de trace chez les historiens classiques du XIXe siècle avant lui. Il mentionne de façon erronée l'année 1740 comme date de publication : cela s'explique peut-être par la date portée sur l'édition originale « 1440 [*sic*]. Depuis le Déluge ». Mais les mentions qui se trouvent dans *L'Ordre des francs-maçons trahi* et *Le Sceau rompu*, deux ouvrages dont la date de publication en 1745 est certaine, nous assurent que le *Catéchisme* a bien été imprimé en 1744. Louis Travenol (1698–1780) avait été l'auteur de plusieurs brochures polémiques sur divers sujets, dont une fois contre Voltaire, mais également d'une *Histoire de l'Opéra*.

In this case, it was not a great discovery. While referring to the biblical passage that mentions him, the Scottish rituals of the late seventeenth century, like Prichard, had seen no difficulty, despite the obvious paradox, in making Hiram Abif the one whom the Constitutions of 1723 had named "the most accomplished Mason on Earth" and King Solomon's "Master of Works."[8] However, the author of the Catechism refuses to make King Solomon the hero of Freemasons:

> [...] how can anyone be mistaken, since Scripture tells us that the man who supervised the construction of Solomon's temple was called Adoniram?[9]

Concerning his legend, the basis of the ceremony of the third grade, he adds:

The Freemasons claim that it was taken from the Thalmud, which is a compilation of Judaic Laws mixed with many reveries, but I think it is very indifferent to know where it can be derived, I have not done much research to be sure. I base myself solely on the Tradition received among the Freemasons, & I report it faithfully, as they all tell it.

This is followed by an account of the legend of Hiram—or Adoniram—the very first known version of this legend in French, and then a fairly detailed description of the ceremony of the third grade, as it was supposed to have been practised in Paris at that time.

Before discussing them, let's make an observation—or rather, ask ourselves a question: why is Adoniram substituted for Hiram Abif here? Was it just a fanciful idea of Louis Travenol, who was the first to speak publicly about it in France?

It should be pointed out straight away that from 1745, in *L'Ordre des francs-maçons trahi*, which practically reproduces *Le Secret* to which it adds, with a few minor variations, the text of the *Catéchisme*, although Adoniram still appears in the exposition of the legend, in the middle of the text he is suddenly replaced by Hiram. Adoniram reappeared in a few later disclosures. Towards the end of the eighteenth century, a printed work, undoubtedly a literary device, entitled *Recueil précieux de la maçonnerie adonhiramite* (1785–1787), restored some lustre "on paper" to this Adoniram—or now "Adonhiram"—of the third grade, but this name in no way reflected universal Masonic practice in France where, for several decades, the tutelary figure of the Masters had been Hiram Abif.

The fact remains that in the first public disclosure of the grade of Master, in 1744—when the grade had undoubtedly been practised for at least a dozen years

---

8 *The Constitutions of the Free-Masons*, 1723, pp. 11, 14.

9 Travenol mentionne aussi la forme « Adoram », qu'il tire de Flavius Josèphe.

in France—we see the appearance of Adoniram, until then apparently unknown in the Masonic world. Why did this happen? Was there at the same time, in Paris in particular, a new grade in which this character played an important role, giving him a particular lustre and leading a more or less well-informed author— we do not know Travenol's sources—to give him precedence over Hiram Abif? Let us confine ourselves for the moment to highlighting this curious point and asking the question. We shall return to it later.

The French form of the legend of Hiram 'or Adoniram'

Prichard's text of the legendary tale contained around 500 words: in the *Catéchisme* the volume has doubled and the story is told with much greater precision and detail. It was to become canonical in France, where it underwent only minor alterations and a few embellishments.

Here is the full text:

SUMMARY OF THE HISTORY OF ADONIRAM[10]
ARCHITECT OF THE TEMPLE OF SOLOMON

Adoniram, to whom Solomon had given the Stewardship and direction of the work on his Temple, had so many Workmen to pay that he could not know them all; and in order not to risk paying the Apprentice as the Journeyman, and the Journeyman as the Master, he agreed with each of them in particular words, signs and different touches to distinguish them. The Apprentice's word was Jachin, the name of one of the Brazen Columns at the gate of the Temple, by which they assembled to receive their Wages. Their sign was to bring the right hand to the left shoulder, withdraw it to the same line on the right side, and let it fall back onto the thigh: all in three times. Their touch was to press the right thumb on the first and thick joint of the index finger of the right hand of the person they wanted to make themselves known to.

The word for companion was Boz: this was the name given to the other Brazen Column at the gate of the Temple, where they also assembled to receive their Wages. Their sign was to place the right hand on the left breast, with the four fingers clasped and extended, and the thumb spread out. Their touching was the same as that of the apprentices, except that they touched on the second finger and the apprentices on the first.

The Master had only one word to distinguish himself from those

---

10 Leonard Gabanon, Catechisme des Francs-Macons, 1744, 'A Jerusalem et a Limoges.' pp. 27-33.

I have just mentioned, which was Jehova, but it was changed after Adoniram's death.

Three Companions, in an attempt to obtain the Master's pay, resolved to ask Adoniram for the word Master when they could meet him alone, or to murder him if he would not tell them. To this end, they hid in the Temple where they knew Adoniram went alone every evening to make his rounds. They positioned themselves, one to the south, another to the north and the third to the east. When Adoniram, who had entered through the western gate, passed in front of the southern gate, one of the three Companions asked him for the word Master, while washing a stick over him. Adoniram told him that he had not received the word Master like that. The Companion immediately struck him on the head with his stick. The blow was not so severe as to throw Adoniram to the ground, so he fled towards the Septentrion gate, where he found the second who did the same to him; however, not having yet been struck down by this second blow, he went to leave by the East gate: but there he found the last, who, after making the same request of him as the first two, murdered him without mercy. When he was buried, they cut off a branch from an Acacia tree that was near them and planted it on him so that they could see where he was when they saw fit. Solomon having gone seven days without seeing Adoniram, on the seventh ordered nine Masters to look for him and, to this end, to first go and stand three at each Gate of the Temple, to try and find out what had become of him. These nine Masters faithfully carried out Solomon's orders; and after searching for a long time without hearing anything about Adoniram, three of them, who found themselves a little tired, went just to rest near the place where he was buried, and one of the three, in order to sit down more easily, took the branch of Acacia, which remained in his hand; This made them realise that the earth had recently been disturbed, and wanting to know the cause, they began to dig until they found Adoniram's body. Then they beckoned to the others to come towards them, and having all recognised their Master, they suspected that it might have been some of the Companions who had done this, wanting to force him to give them the word Master, and fearing that they might have taken it from him, they resolved first to change it, and to take the first word that one of them could say when digging up the Body. One of them took him by the finger, and this finger remained in his hand: he immediately took him by another who did the same, and taking him by the wrist, which separated from the arm, as the two fingers had done from the hand, he said Macbenac, which means, according to the Freemasons, the flesh leaves the bones. They immediately agreed that this would henceforth be the word of a Master; they reported this to Solomon, who was very touched; and to show the esteem he had for the memory of Adoniram, he had him buried with great ceremony in his Temple.

Curiously an examination of the Abrege de Histoire in the 1749 *Nouveau Catechisme* shows the addition of the following words:

And had a golden triangular Medallion placed on his Tomb, with JEHOVAH engraved on it.

While the whole of the 1749 Abrege has been re-edited it is the final sentence that was added that indicates that a significant change in masonic thinking took place between 1744 and 1749.

Specific features and implications of the French legend

In the texts made public in the course of 1744–1745, but which a priori reflect a practice that had been in place for several years, we find all the characteristic elements of the legend of the third grade, as it was constantly transmitted throughout the eighteenth century in France. However, this version differs from the English version, which was to become the standard in Great Britain, on a number of points that are important from the point of view of the emergence of grades "beyond the rank of Master."

Apart from a few differences of detail which we will not go into here—because our subject is not the evolution of the Master's grade but the circumstances of the appearance of the high grades in France—the most remarkable divergence between the French and English versions concerns the fate of the "Word of Master" entrusted to Hiram's care.

The word Master was not lost in 1744, but by 1749, it is clear that attitudes or ritual practices changed. We cannot say exactly why or when.

The most important point is that in the French version, the Word was never lost! Not only is it still known, but throughout the eighteenth century it would appear on the table (or carpet) of the Master's grade, inscribed on the coffin, either in full ("JEHOVA") or by its initials ("J.A."). It is only said that its use is renounced for fear that the bad companions might have finally obtained it from their master before he breathed his last. There is an interesting variation on this in France.

The whole moral lesson of the legend is based on Hiram's firmness in refusing to communicate the Word, even at the cost of his life. It must have seemed

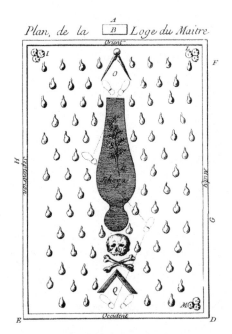

Tableau de Maitre
ex Le Catechisme 1744

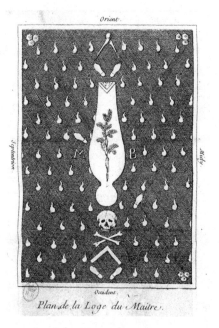

Tableau de Maitre
ex Le Catechisme 1749

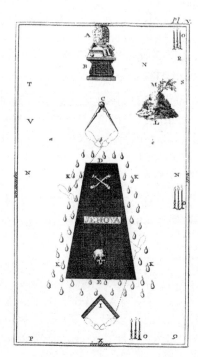

Tableau du grade de Maitre
ex L'Ordre des francs-maçons trahi (1745)

somewhat contradictory—and even disrespectful to the memory of the revered master—to suppose that this Word could, in the end, still have been snatched away by the three bad companions. Perhaps for this reason, there will be an enrichment of the French legend that only appears later. It is said that Hiram carried the Word with him at all times, having engraved it on a triangular gold blade that he wore around his neck. After the master's death, his assassins could therefore have learned of it, without Hiram being held responsible: his honour was safe.

Be that as it may, these developments are justified for only one reason: the Word is known, and has never been lost. All that has been done is to abandon its use and replace it with another—in French, "MACBENAC." An important consequence immediately follows.

If the Word has never been lost, if its pronunciation is always known, then there is no need to "find" it. The legend of the three Great Masters, and that of a crypt—wherever it may be, at whatever time it may have been discovered— where the "original secrets" are said to have been buried, are in no way necessary and are even meaningless and of no use in the French version.

The only facts that remain, at the end of the master's grade in France, around 1740, are as follows: the master has been killed, so his work is interrupted—who will replace him? His killers were still at large—would they be found and what would be their fate? Finally, if the Word, still present on the grade chart, in full or in the form of its initial letters, is no longer the subject of any symbolic or moral teaching during the Master's ceremony, where will the new Masters learn all that the Sacred Word means?

These are the only questions that the first known high grades in France attempt to answer.

As we shall see, they were already being practised before 1745 in the lodge of the Grand Master, Louis de Clermont.

A Chronology of the Appearance
of the Oldest High Grades in France

May 1733 to October 1735

The seed(s) of all the higher grades appear when, just after May 1733, Scotts Masons Lodge No.115 appears on the Engraved List of Lodges. We have no idea what type of degree (if any) they worked, but there appears to have been one grade of which only one mention before 1740 has been found. This was at Bath, a spa and elegant holiday town for the upper classes, in October 1735, when 10 candidates received the degree.

It is likely that this was the spring from which the higher grades originated and the earliest record of which is probably that of Coustos.

December 1736 and summer 1737

John Coustos, initiated in London in 1730, was Master of the Coustos-Villeroy Lodge in Paris.

Arrested in Lisbon following a denunciation and brought before the Portuguese Inquisition in March 1743, he testified to his Masonic knowledge:

> When the famous Temple of Solomon was destroyed, a bronze tablet was found under the First Stone[1] on which was engraved the following word, JEHOVAH, which means GOD, thus making it possible to understand that this Temple building had been instituted and erected in the name of the very God to whom it was dedicated, this same Lord being the beginning and the end of this magnificent world; and as in the Gospel of St. John are found the same words and the same doctrine, for this reason they are the cause of the Oath being taken upon it, thus showing that the whole institution of the Fraternity is founded upon the same doctrine, that which Solomon observed in his sumptuous work; and the reason why he said this was because he had heard it said by some French and English Masters, though he did not know whence they held this doctrine.[2]

---

1   C'est ici à une Pierre de Fondation davantage qu'à une Clé de Voûte que l'on parait faire allusion.

2   S. Vachter, "John Coustos and the Portuguese Inquisition," *AQC* 81 (1968), p. 52.

December 1736 to 1737

André Michel Ramsay prepared a *Discours* as "Orator of the Grand Lodge." In the "original" manuscript version of 27 December 1736, it reads:

> the king Solomon wrote in hieroglyphic figures our Statutes, our maxims and our mysteries and this ancient book is the original Code of our Order. after the Destruction of the first temple and the captivity of the favorite nation, the anointed of the Lord, the Great Cyrus who was Initiated in all our mysteries Constituted Zorobabel, Grand Master of the Lodge of Jerusalem, and ordered him to lay the foundations of the second temple, where the mysterious Book of Solomon was deposited. this Book was preserved during twelve centuries in the temple of Israelites, but after the Destruction of this Second temple under the emperor Tite, this ancient book was lost until the time of the Crusades that it was found in part after the capture of Jerusalem. This Sacred Code was torn up and, without penetrating the sublime spirit of all the hieroglyphic figures found therein, our ancient order was renewed, of which Noah, Abraham, the Patriarchs, Moses, Solomon and Cyrus had been the first great masters.

1738 onwards

In all later printed versions of the *Discours de Ramsay* we read:

> At the time of the holy wars in Palestine, several Princes, Lords and & Citizens, entered into Society, vowed to re-establish the temples of the Christians in the Holy Land, & undertook by oath to employ their talents and their goods to restore architecture to the primitive institution. They agreed on a number of ancient signs and symbolic words drawn from the depths of the religion,[3] to distinguish themselves from the infidels and to distinguish themselves from the Saracens.
>
> These signs and words were only communicated to those who solemnly promised, often even at the foot of the altar, never to reveal them. This sacred promise was therefore no longer an execrable oath, as is often said, but a respectable bond, uniting men of all nations in the same brotherhood.
>
> Some time later our Order joined the Knights of St John of Jeru-

---

3   Le manuscrit Ramsay de 1736 porte ici : « tous les signes anciens et les paroles mysterieuses de Salomon ».

salem. From then on our Lodges bore the name of Lodges of Saint
John in all countries. This union was made in imitation of the
Israelites, when they rebuilt the second temple; while they handled
with one hand the trowel and the mortar,[4] they carried with the
other the Sword and the Shield. *(Esdras Chap. IV, v. 16)*

11th December 1743

Règlemens généraux, adopted on the occasion of the election of the Count of
Clermont, an "article 20"—the last—already stipulates:

> [...] we learn that recently some brothers announce themselves un-
> der the name of *maîtres Ecossois* and form in the particular Lodges
> pretensions and demand prerogatives of which we find no trace in
> the old archives and customs of the Lodges spread on the surface of
> the earth.[5]

1744

La Franc-Maçonne, an innovative disclosure in terms of its content, contains this
information:

> Ignorance is so general that most Masters & Supervisors do not
> yet know that Masonry is composed of seven grades, & even the
> General Lodge[6] decided blindly, December 11, 1743,[7] it would
> not consider the Masons of the fourth, that is to say the Scottish
> Masters, as mere Apprentices and Companions.

1744

Le Parfait Macon, a exposure also different from others published at the same
time, reveals:

Secret of the Scottish Masons

> It is said among Masons that there are still several degrees above the
> Masters of which I have just spoken; some count six in all, others
> go as high as seven. Those called *Maçons Ecossois*, claim to compose
> the fourth grade. As this Masonry, different from the other in many
> respects, is beginning to gain acceptance in France, the public will

---

4   Le manuscrit Ramsay de 1736 porte ici : « La Truelle et le Compas ».

5   A. Bernheim, « Contribution à la connaissance de la première Grande Loge de France,» *Villard de Honnecourt*, 17 (1988), p. 129.

6   C'est-à-dire la Grande Loge.

7   Jour de l'élection de Clermont et de l'adoption des Règlements cités plus haut.

not be upset if I communicate what I read in the same manuscript,[8] which indeed seems to grant the *Ecossois* the degree of superiority over the apprentices, journeymen and ordinary Masters.

Instead of mourning, as their colleagues do, over the debris of Solomon's Temple, the *Ecossois* are busy rebuilding it.*

No one is unaware that after seventy and ten years of captivity in Babilona, the Great Cirus allowed the Israelites to rebuild the Temple and the City of Jerusalem; that Zorobabel, of the race of David, was appointed by him the leader and conductor of this people on his return to the Holy City; that the first stone of the Temple was laid during the reign of Cirus, but that it was not completed until the sixth year of the reign of Darius, monarch of the Persians.

It is from this great event that the *Ecossois* derive the time of their institution, and although they are later than other Masons by several centuries, they claim to be superior in rank: Here is what they base their pre-eminence.

When it came to rebuilding the Temple of the Lord, Zorobabel chose from the three states of Masonry the most capable workers, but as the Israelites had many obstacles and & crossroads to suffer during the course of their work, from the Samaritans and other neighbouring nations, the work would never have been completed, if this Prince had not taken the precaution of creating a fourth grade of Masons, whose number he set at 753. These were chosen from among the *most excellent artists*,[9] not only did they have the right of inspection over all the others, but they were also responsible for ensuring the safety of the workers; every night they made the rounds, both to advance the work and to recognise ambushes or prevent attacks by their enemies.

As their work was much more arduous than that of the other Masons, they were also paid more, and in order to recognise them, Zorobabel gave them a sign and special words.

1745

In *L'Ordre des francs-maçons trahi et leur secret révélé,* the author announces, in the preface to the book:

> [...] there is a vague rumour among Freemasons, concerning a cer-

---

8   Author's italics.

9   Author's italics.

tain order they call the Scots, superior to what is claimed to be the ordinary Freemasons, and who have their ceremonies and their secrets apart.

24th June 1745

Statutes of the Saint-Jean de Jérusalem, lodge of the Grand Master the Count of Clermont, in Paris

> Article XXxxe:[10]
> The Ordinary Masters will assemble with the Masters the Perfects and the Irish three months after St. John, the Elected Masters six months after, the Scots nine months after, and those provided with grade [sic] superiors when they deem it apropos.

> Article XLIVe:
> The Scots [i.e., the holders of the higher grades] will be the superintendents of the work, they will have freedom of speech, and will be among the first to give their vote, will place themselves where they wish, and when they are at fault, they can only be rectified by Scots.[11]

2nd April 1748

Certain indication of the rank of Knight of the East in the *Constitutions et Règlements de l'Ordre des Grands Ecossais* (BnF FM4 76), substantially contemporary with the *Règlements et Statuts des Chevaliers de l'Orient ou de l'Epée* (BnF, FM4 15).

10th March 1751

First record of the practice of the grade of Knight of the Sun in the Parfaite Loge d'Ecosse in Bordeaux (Sharp Documents, n°30).

1760

Plausible date of the oldest ritual of the grade of Knight of the Eagle, Pelican, Rosicrucian; Mason of Heredom, Knight of Saint Andrew, Perfect Mason (G.O. of the Netherlands, Kloss Fonds, 240C53).

---

10 A. Le Bihan, *Francs-maçons et ateliers parisiens de la Loge de France au XVIIIe siècle*, 1973, pp. 393-402.

11 Les articles Xxxe et XXxxe seront supprimés dans la version de 1755, mais le XLIVe persistera sans changement notable. On y précise en outre que les Écossais peuvent en loge « être toujours armés et couverts ».

June 1761

Correspondence between Jean-Baptiste Willermoz, of Lyon, and Meunier de Précourt, of Metz, compares the Masonic knowledge of the two cities:[12]

LYON	METZ
1. Apprenti	1. Apprenti
2. Compagnon	2. Compagnon
3. Maître	3. Maître
4. Fendeur (Cleaver)	
4. Master Elu	
	5. Me Parfit Irlandais
	6. Maitre Elu or Petit Elu
5. Second grade of Elu	
6. Elu des 15	
7. Maitre Illustre	7. Me Illustre
8. M^{tre} Parfait	
9. M^{tre} Irlandais ou Provost and Judge	
10. M^{tre} Secret Master	
11. M^{tre} Anglais	8. Me Anglais
	(two versions, one of which seems to be the Parfait Maitre Anglais)
12. M^e favory	
13. Apprentif Ecossais	9. Apprentif Ecossais
14. Compagnon Ecossais	10. Compagnon Ecossais
15. Maître Ecossais	11. Maître Ecossais
16. Ecossais des 3 J or Ecossais de Paris	12. Ecossais of Clermont
17. Ecossais Trinitaire d'Edimbourg	13. Ecossais de Prusse
18. Petit Architecte	14. Apprentif Architecte
19. Grand Architect	15. Compagnon Architecte
	16. Me Architecte
20. Ecossais des 3 lettres	

---

12 Steel-Maret, *Les archives secrètes de la franc-maçonnerie*, 1893, pp. 72-78.

21. Sublime Ecossais	17. Sublime Ecossais
22. Elu Supreme	
23. Chev^{er} de l'Orient	18. Chev^{er} de l'Orient
24. Chevalier du Soleil et des Adeptes	
25. Chevalier de l'Aigle, du pélican, Chev^{er} de St André ou maçon d'Heredon	
	19. Chevalier d'Occident
	20. Royal Arche
	21. Chevalier Grand Inspecteur Grand Elu d^{er} grade

27th August 1761

The grades of the Morin patent:

- Maître secret
- Maître parfait
- Secrétaire intime
- Intendant des bâtiments
- Prévôt et juge
- Maître Elu des Neuf
- Illustre Elu des 15
- Sublime Chevalier Elu
- Grand Maître Architecte
- Chevalier Royale Arche
- Perfection ultime de la maçonnerie symbolique
- Chevalier de l'Orient
- Prince de Jérusalem
- Chevalier d'Orient et d'Occident
- Chevalier de l'Aigle blanc ou du Pélican
- Grand Pontife
- Souverain Prince de la Maçonnerie ou maître ad vitam
- Chevalier Prussien ou Noachite

- Chevalier de Royale Hache
- Chevalier du Soleil Prince adepte Clé de la Maçonnerie
- Chevalier Kadosh nec plus ultra de la maçonnerie
- Royal Secret.

June 1761 (continued)

In the above-mentioned correspondence between the Lyon mason Jean-Baptiste Willermoz and masons in Metz, in eastern France. We learn of the existence in the latter city of a "Royal *(sic)* Arche" grade. Its characteristics are as follows:

> Salomon Roy, Hiram Roy and Hyram Architecte held their Council alone, which is what is meant by the initial letters [which will be revealed later]; the last [i.e., Hyram Architecte] having been murdered, Salomon, despite repeated requests from the Masters, refused to admit any of them to this eminent grade, telling them that they were working and that one day they would deserve to be invested with it. Gibellum, the word in the centre [of a "crowned triangular hyeroglyph" specific to this grade], discovered the mystery by three different repetitions on the reverse of the medal, the Emblem of the Sun, which revealed the words traced on the frontispiece of the Temple where the secret lodge was held. Word: 1° Ja. 2° Bu. 3° lum: Jabulum pronounced under the 3 raised arms of the brothers who pronounce it in their ears.[13]

1763–1766

Conversations allégoriques organisées par la sagesse, à Londres

This set of thirteen degrees was first printed in 1763 and then in 1766 and published by Erasme Pincemaille in Metz.[14] This set of degrees makes a fascinating comparison with the much longer set of degrees listed by Willermoz only a few years earlier (see above).

Maître Parfait

Maître irlandais

Maître Anglais

Maître Elu de l'Inconnu

---

13 *Cf.* Steel-Maret, *op. cit.*, p. 76.

14 Published in translation in English as Conversations Allegoriques by the Scottish Research Society in 2012. The Introduction provided a full explanation of the troubles its publication caused in Metz for the masons there.

Maître Elu des Quinze

Maître Illustre

Ecossais

Sublime Ecossais

Parfait Maître Anglais

12th December 1764

Jérôme Dulong, a Freemason from Beaucaire, claims to have been admitted to the "Royal Arch."[15]

Two other lists can be added for the end of the 1760s, the period at the end of our investigation: they were published in printed works and it cannot be said that they correspond to complete systems, made up of grades practised in their entirety, actually and in this exact order, in specific places. These works are a bit like "grade collections," published for amateurs or the curious.[16] But they do have the advantage of offering an overview of the main grades in use towards the end of the 1760s, at a time when the "creativity" of French masonic authors seemed to be waning and certain grades appeared to be more popular than others.[17]

1766

Les plus secrets mystères des hauts grades de la maçonnerie dévoilés, « A Jérusalem »

This was the first printed book to offer a set of seven degrees and was edited by M. de Berage. The place of publication is described as Jerusalem, but was probably in France or nearby.

Parfait Maître Elu

Elu de Pérignan

Elu des 15

Petit Architecte

Grand Architecte

Chevalier de l'épée et de Rose-Croix

Noachite ou Chevalier prussien

---

15 R. Désaguliers, « Le registre maçonnique de messire Jérôme Dulong », *Renaissance Traditionnelle* n°46, p. 84.

16 On peut en rapprocher un ouvrage qui sera publié une vingtaine d'années plus tard : *Recueil précieux de la maçonnerie adonhiramite* de Guillemain de Saint-Victor, en 1788, qui enrichit peu la liste des *Plus secrets mystères*, avec treize grades au total dont neuf hauts grades.

17 Manquent notamment un grade de Royale Arche, de Rose-Croix et de Grand Inspecteur Grand Elu ou Chevalier Kadosh, tous promis à un grand avenir en France.

1768

The last manuscript collection from this period is the 33-degree Rite of the Earl of Clairmont[18] (the collection is incomplete—some grades are missing or are only cited):

Apprentif maçon

Compagnon

Maître

Petit Elu

Elu de l'Incoinnu

Elu des Quinze

Chevalier de l'ancre (non strictement maçonnique)

Illustre Chevalier du Lion (*id.*)

Petit maître anglais

Sublime Ecossais

Sublime Ecossais d'Angleterre

Chevalier d'Orient ou Sublime grade de la Maçonnere

Chevalier d'Occident

Chevalier du Soleil ou des Adeptes

Chevalier du Phénix

Vénérable Grand Maître de Loge

Royale Arche

Souverain Prince et chevalier Rose-Croix

Grand Inspecteur

In summary, we can see that in France most of the high grades were produced between 1735 and 1760, corresponding to around ten main grades, of which variants or developments produced minor grades but which, towards the end of the century, increased the theoretical number of grades.

When, between 1783 and 1786, a synthesis of the high grades was produced for the Grand Orient de France, founded in 1773, a list of 81 grades remained.[19]

---

18 Publié par Jean-Bernard Lévy, Editions de la Hutte, 2012.

19 C. Léger, *Les 81 grades qui fondèrent au Siècle des Lumières le Rite Français*, 2017.

The "Maîtres Ecossais" enters the scene (1743-1745)

According to a tradition dating back to the astronomer Lalande, author in 1773 of the aforementioned *Mémoire historique*, it was during a Paris assembly held in December 1743 that Louis de Bourbon-Condé, Count of Clermont-en-Argonne, Prince of the Blood, succeeded the Duke of Antin, Grand Master in France since 1738. Lalande's account of this event some thirty years later deserves to be reproduced here, as it contains some very interesting information:

> On 11 December 1743, the Count of Clermont, Prince of the Blood, was elected perpetual Grand Master at an assembly of sixteen Masters, in place of the Duke of Antin who had just died; The act[1] was signed by all the Masters & Supervisors of all the regular Lodges of Paris & accepted by the provincial Lodges; Mr Prince de Conti & Mr Marshal de Saxe had several votes in this election, but Mr Count de Clermont had the plurality, & he fulfilled this function until his death.[2]

Clermont was not the first Grand Master to arrive: but from 1743 and for nearly thirty years, the French Freemasons had given themselves a leading protector. Born in 1709, this scion of the Condé family, a prince of the blood, was at once a high aristocrat, a military man of questionable talents and an academician. Appointed commendatory abbot at the age of nine, and in 1724 knight of the Order of the Holy Spirit, whose azure-blue cordon is said to be that of French Masonic decorations,[3] he received above all, in August 1737, the abbey of Saint-Germain-des-Prés, the embellishment of which he entrusted to a grandson of François Mansart. Despite his ecclesiastical status—which was very theoretical, as the prince, who was close to the Pompadour, was never really devout and lived with Mlle Leduc, a boarder at the Opéra—in 1733 he was granted the right to bear arms by Pope Clement XII. By 1735 he had become a lieutenant general—approximately a major general in the modern armies—but despite a promising

---

1 Lequel, à ce jour, n'a jamais été retrouvé.

2 *Mémoire historique...*, 1773.

3 En 1744, dans *Le Secret des francs-maçons*, l'auteur, l'abbé Pérau le dit expressément : « Les jours de réception le Vénérable, les deux Surveillans, le Secrétaire & le Thrésorier de l'Ordre portent au col un cordon bleu taillé en triangle, tel à peu près que le portent les Commandeurs de l'Ordre du S. Esprit qui sont ou d'Église ou de Robe. » (pp. 45-46). Ce nouveau rapprochement entre la franc-maçonnerie et les ordres de chevalerie, dès 1744, n'est peut-être pas indifférent.

start he made a pitiful showing at Krefeld in 1758, one of the saddest French defeats of the Seven Years' War.[4] Ironically, his victor was Duke Ferdinand of Brunswick-Lünebourg, a passionate Mason who, twenty years later, was to become the supreme dignitary of the Templar Strict Observance. Clermont was relieved of his command and devoted himself to Mlle Leduc, for whom he organised sumptuous parties in his château at Berny, and whom he ended up secretly marrying in 1765 despite her antics and frivolity, and above all to Freemasonry, of which he was the nominal sovereign until his death in 1771. It is likely that without Freemasonry, history would have forgotten him.

Clermont's rise to power marked a new stage in the daily lives of the several hundred Freemasons in France at the time.[5] In 1744, a witness described the Grand Master's supposed intentions as follows:

> It is said that the Count of Clermont is very unhappy not to have a command. It is believed that he will not be serving this campaign and that he has sent half of his staff home.[6] This will give him time to develop the order of frimasons [sic] of which he is Grand Master. He has planned new constitutions both for the brothers and for the Masters of Lodges. He must remove anything that is not a gentleman or good bourgeois. It is said that on his advice the police had several arrested who demanded money from the recipients. From now on, everything will be done with nobility and dignity:[7]

From the moment of his enthronement, the new Grand Master had to deal with a new dignity, claimed by certain Freemasons.

In the first *Règlemens généraux*, adopted on the occasion of the election of the Count of Clermont on 11 December 1743, an "article 20"—the last—already stipulated:

> [...] we learn that recently some brothers announce themselves under the name of Scottish Masters and form in the particular Lodges of the pretensions and require prerogatives of which one does not find any trace in the old files and customs of the Lodges spread on the surface of the earth.[8]

---

4 On fit alors sur son compte ce quatrain assassin : « Moitié plumet, moitié rabat/ Aussi propre à l'un comme à l'autre, / Clermont se bat comme un apôtre/ Et sert son Dieu comme il se bat. »

5 Une source de l'époque nous affirme que Paris comptait alors 22 loges et qu'il y en avait autant dans les provinces, soit une quarantaine en tout.

6 C'est-à-dire la moitié de ses troupes. L'année 1744 voit le début de la Guerre de Succession d'Autriche où la France va s'engager.

7 BHVP, ms. 624, f° 157 v°.

8 A. Bernheim, « Contribution à la connaissance de la première Grande Loge de France,» *Villard*

The expression "recently" is very vague: a few months? One or two years? More than that? We shall see later what hypotheses can be put forward. But there were now officially one or more grades higher than that of Master Mason in France.

In 1745, in *L'Ordre des francs-maçons trahi et leur secret révélé* (The Order of Freemasons Betrayed and Their Secret Revealed), the author announced, in the preface to the book:

> [...] there is a vague rumour among Freemasons, concerning a certain order they call the 'les Ecossois', superior to what is claimed to be the ordinary Freemasons, and who have their own ceremonies and secrets.[9]

Note the phrase "a vague rumour," suggesting to the reader at the time that the information was not certain, that not everyone was sure, that it was something fairly new.

Better still, a document strictly contemporary with what we have just mentioned, this time from a source of prime importance since it is the lodge of the Count of Clermont himself, confirms it unequivocally, barely eighteen months later: the statutes of the Saint-Jean de Jérusalem lodge, "drawn up on 24 June 1745." Article XXxxe reads as follows

> The ordinary masters will assemble with the masters the perfects and the Irish three months after the St jean, the elected masters six months afterwards, the Scots nine months afterwards, and those provided with grade [sic] superiors when they judge it apropos.[10]

Article "Xxxe" went even further:

> As masonry grants distinctive graces to those who have deserved them, if the master [of the lodge] who has just been replaced lacks any grade, they will be given to him this very day without making him languish, the same attention will be paid to the officers.[11]

And to make everything clear, article XLIV prefixed:

> The Scots [i.e., the holders of the higher ranks] will be the superintendents of the work, they will have freedom of speech, and will be among the first to give their vote, will place themselves where

---

de Honnecourt, 17 (1988), p. 129.

9   Ordre de Francs-Macons Trahis p.12

10 A. Bernheim, p. 119.

11 A. Bernheim, p. 117.

they wish, and when they are at fault, they can only be rectified by Scots.[12]

The new "Grand Master of all the regular L\ of France," as he is called in these statutes, therefore recognised and even regulated the practice of these new grades, which had been held in suspicion two years earlier by the General Regulations of his own Grand Lodge.

Where did these Parisian innovations come from? How long had they been circulating in the lodges? Can we really imagine that at least four grades—not counting the "higher grades," the number and names of which are not specified—could have appeared spontaneously in the space of a year and a half? We have little documentary evidence to answer these questions precisely. We can at least draw on two independent sources for some information.

The Coustos Case

John Coustos is well known to historians of Freemasonry.

Born in Switzerland in 1703 to a Protestant family, he lived in France in his early childhood before moving to England with his parents because of the persecution of his fellow Protestants in France. Married to an Englishwoman, he returned to Paris, where he worked as a jeweller between 1735 and 1740. Coustos was a founder member in 1732 of the lodge that later became known as the French Union Lodge No. 98, whose members are largely included in this book.

His masonic activity in Paris is well known between December 1736 and the summer of 1737. He was then Worshipful Master of the lodge founded in honour of the Duc de Villeroy—a close friend of King Louis XV—known as "Coustos-Villeroy," which was to suffer the vicissitudes of the police after the ban on Masonic meetings by the minister Fleury in March 1737. The lodge's register, which is still in our possession, was seized in the summer of 1737 and its work came to a definitive halt.

With a hypothetical plan to establish a lodge in Brazil in mind, Coustos moved to Lisbon in 1740. Having made the acquaintance of Freemasons there and taken charge of a lodge in a country where the Papal Bull of 1738, excommunicating Freemasons, applied (which was not the case in France), he was arrested following a denunciation and brought before the Portuguese Inquisition in March 1743. After several interrogations and a fairly lengthy detention, he was sentenced to the galleys, before finally being released on the intervention of the

---

12 A. Bernheim, p. 120. Les articles Xxxe et XXXxe seront supprimés dans la version de 1755, mais le XLIVe persistera sans changement notable. On y précise en outre que les Écossais peuvent en loge « être toujours armés et couverts ».

English ambassador in Lisbon in December 1744. It has often been said that his own account of his "sufferings"[13] is partly romanticised and does not tell the whole truth. However, we do have original documents that tell us what information he actually entrusted to the Portuguese Inquisition.

Our attention is drawn here to a passage from his testimony before the Inquisition on the secrets and practices of the Masons of his time. He reported that:

> That the reason and foundation that the Masters of this Fraternity have for causing those who newly join to take the Oath upon a Bible, or Book of the Gospels, at the place of that of St. John, is the following :-that when the destruction of the famous Temple of Solomon took place there was found below the First Stone[14] a tablet of bronze upon which was engraved the

> following word, JEHOVAH, which means GOD, giving thereby to understand that that fabric and Temple was instituted and erected in the name of the same God to whom it was dedicated, that same Lord being the beginning and end of such a magnificent work; and as in the Gospel of St. John there are found the same words and doctrine they, for this reason,

> cause the Oath to be taken at that place, thus to show that the whole institution of this Fraternity is founded on the same doctrine which Solomon observed in his sumptuous work; and the reason he has for saying this is that he had heard it so declared by some of the French and English Masters, though he does not know from whence they obtained this doctrine for its propounding.[15]

This statement is obviously of the utmost importance. None of this is found in Prichard—neither the word "Jehova,"[16] nor especially the fact that this word was found in Solomon's Temple "after its destruction." What's more, we're not told which destruction we're talking about: that of the first temple by Nebuchadnezzar in 586 BC, or that of 70 AD by the Roman armies of Titus? Did the rediscovery of the word take place between the two temples—as in the English legend of the Royal Arch—at the time of Julian the Apostate—as Philostorgius says—or at the time of the Crusades, as Ramsay might have suggested?

In a word—if we can put it that way—the idea that the word Master, which is

---

13 *The Sufferings of John Coustos*, 1746.

14 C'est ici à une Pierre de Fondation davantage qu'à une Clé de Voûte que l'on parait faire allusion.

15 S. Vachter, « John Coustos and the Portuguese Inquisition, *AQC* 81 (1968), p. 52.

16 Il n'est présent, avant 1730, que dans *The Whole Institutions of Free-Masons Opened*, 1724 – C'est le « Mot Primitif ».

none other than a name of God, had become unpronounceable and therefore definitively lost, according to the English legend of Masonry Dissected, could finally have been found in the Temple of Jerusalem—at a time as yet undetermined —is a new fact of major interest. He testified to the Inquisition that this was known to him in London before he left for Paris in 1736 and known to him in Paris while he was living there.

Whatever the source of Coustos's information, and even if he obtained it in England—and therefore before 1735! —the fact remains that during his stay in Paris, the Coustos-Villeroy lodge, which had a dozen or so French members and up to forty foreigners—and it was there that Baron Scheffer, the founder of Swedish Freemasonry, was initiated—provided him with an environment where Masonic discussions must have been going well. How can it be imagined that Coustos was the only person, not only of his own nation but also of the French people he met there, to possess the precious secrets he said he had received from "a few French and English Masters?" It is therefore reasonable to assume that shortly before and around 1736 and before 1740, the date on which Coustos left Paris, certain French Masons, like Coustos, must already have been aware of a special relationship between the "Word," namely "Jehova," and the Temple of Solomon where this word may have been preserved after Hiram's death. We should also note the reference to a 'First Stone' on which this name was engraved, and the direct relationship established between this same word and the Gospel of St John. This is obviously not enough to assume that they were aware, from that time, of one or more grades exploiting this theme, but it at least helps to explain the presence of the Word on the table of the grade of Master in Paris in *Le Catechisme* of 1744. It could also shed some light on the content of one of the oldest high grades, if not the first, known and practised in Grand Master Clermont's lodge, probably before 1745, namely the grade of Maître Parfait, to which we shall return in detail later.

Finally, it should be noted that none of the fairly numerous documents that have come down to us, correspondence between freemasons or the few lodge registers dating from 1737–1743, reveal the slightest hint of a "higher grade" in a Parisian masonic milieu that was nevertheless very active. On this subject, a rather enigmatic indication has sometimes been noted, recorded by R. F. Gould in his *Concise History of Freemasonry*. He states that the aforementioned Baron (later Count) Scheffer, a Swedish diplomat posted in Paris, who in 1737, as we have seen, received a patent from Derwentwater authorising him to create lodges in Sweden, received in Paris at that time the "grades of St John and two Scottish grades."[17] No precise source is mentioned by Gould. Does this mean

17 *A Concise History of Freemasonry*, 1904, p. 474. *Histoire abrégée de la franc-maçonnerie*, 1910, p. 287.

that as early as 1737 two grades were known in Paris beyond Master? However, there is nothing in the current documentation to confirm this: Gould either says too much or not enough. In fact, Scheffer had close ties with Jacobite circles in the French capital, with Derwentwater as well as with Maclean, with whom he maintained not only Masonic but also political links for many years. The key to the enigma is probably provided by A. Önnnefors, a very good connoisseur of Swedish Masonic history, who tells us that "in 1743 Scheffer returned to Paris as a diplomat, and it was probably at this time that he was initiated into the first Ecossais high grades."[18]

The very beginning of the 1740s therefore seems to be the period when the first high grades were introduced in Paris. Two other disclosures from this period provide further confirmation.

Atypical disclosures: *La Franc-Maçonne, Le Parfait Maçon* (1744)

Two disclosures printed in 1744 stand in stark contrast to those that preceded them and those that followed: we will call them "atypical disclosures." Their publication date and chronology are certain.[19] In fact, *Le Sceau rompu* (The Broken Seal) in 1745, after reporting the publication of *Le Secret* and *Le Catéchisme*, mentions that *La Franc-Maçonne* and *Le Parfait Maçon* had succeeded them— 1744 is therefore a confirmed date.

From that time onwards, these texts were denounced as absurd and of no use in learning about and understanding masonry—particularly in *Le Sceau rompu* (1747) and *Les Francs-maçons écrasés* (1747). Modern analysis does not contradict this judgement: the revelations made therein about the content of the first three grades are highly fanciful, and one might even wonder about the authors' intention: Either it was pure literary amusement, to distract readers then overwhelmed by Masonic publications, or it came from Masons anxious to "muddy the waters" in order to try, as far as possible, to minimise the effect of the revelations contained in the previous disclosures—which, as we know, are trustworthy. But that's not what we're interested in here. The two atypical disclosures also contain, for the first time, more curious indications about grades higher than Master. In Paris in 1744, such information should be considered carefully.

La Franc-Maçonne tells us nothing useful about the state of the first grades around 1745: all the information given in the corresponding catechisms is fanciful. However, it should be noted that many of the elements found there would find their way, a little later, into the rituals of the Adoption, i.e., into

---

18 A. Önnefors, U. Lindgren, « Suède », in *Dictionnaire de la franc-maçonnerie* (dir. D. Ligou – 2ᵉ éd. C. Porset, D. Morillon), 1987-2006, p. 1155.

19 *La Franc-Maçonne* porte sur sa page de titre : « MDCCLXIV – A Bruxelles » ; sur *Le Parfait Maçon* on peut simplement lire : « Imprimé cette année ».

the "androgynous" masonry that would see real development in France in the eighteenth century. The only interesting element, from our perspective here, is a statement attributed to a "dark and taciturn mason" whose words the author of the disclosure is supposed to report. This stern Brother makes various criticisms of the Freemasons of his time. In particular, he deplored:

> Ignorance is so general that most Masters & Overseers do not yet know that Masonry is composed of seven grades, & even the General Lodge[20] has decided blindly, December 11, 1743,[21] it would not consider the Masons of the fourth, that is to say the Scottish Masters, as mere Apprentices and Companions.

This statement calls for a number of comments and questions. Firstly, it confirms that the debate had been going on for some time within Parisian masonry on the subject of Maîtres écossais, and also shows that the author of the disclosure is well informed about the internal affairs of the Order and is on the side of the "new masons" of the higher grades. We have seen that the new Grand Master, who was elected on the very day that these disputed regulations were adopted, had himself put into practice a few months later, in his own lodge, this system which culminated, as we shall see, in a grade described as "Scottish." The ambiguity here concerns the composition of the four grades above the Master grade: the grade of Scottish Master is described as "fourth," but is it the fourth in a series of seven, or the fourth of the high grades—which would make it the seventh and last? We shall see that the system adopted in Paris at least a few months later raises this question.

Let us also underline the "ignorance" of the masons denounced by our "taciturn mason." The system seems both new and semi-secret, in any case reserved for a small number. One thinks here of the situation described in 1730 in London, shortly after Prichard's public revelation of the existence and content of the Master's degree—in *The Mystery of Free-Masonry*, published the same year, it is said:

> Note: There is not a Mason in an Hundred that will be at the Expense to pass the Master's Part, except it be for Interest.

One is led to wonder whether the Scottish grades, which were not officially regulated in the Count de Clermont's lodge until June 1745, were not already in force in a restricted and select milieu in December 1743, when the Grand Lodge, which Clermont discovered when he took the helm, decided "blindly" to condemn them in advance.

---

20 C'est-à-dire la Grande Loge.

21 Jour de l'élection de Clermont et de l'adoption des Règlements cités plus haut.

The full title of *Le Parfait Maçon* is immediately more explicit: *Le Parfait Maçon, ou les véritables secrets des quatre grades d'apprentis, de Compagnons, de Maîtres ordinaires et de Maîtres Écossais*. We note in passing the same terminology as in the Regulations of the Count of Clermont's lodge: "maîtres ordinaires" et "maîtres écossais."

Here again, we can pass over without insisting on the deliberately fanciful content of the first three grades, which is much the same as formulaic comments as those made on the subject in the *Franc-Maçonne*.[22] The most interesting is a small one-page chapter entitled "Secret des maçons écossais." It is the very first known text in French Masonic history to inform us of the content—true or supposed—of this new and mysterious grade. Here is the text:

> *Le parfait Maçon.* 97
> neuf différens temps ou mouve-
> mens : & la folemnité fe termine
> par un battement de mains unifor-
> me fuivi d'un *vivat*.
>
> ---
>
> # SECRET
> ### DES
> ## MAÇONS ECOSSOIS.
>
> ON débite parmi les Maçons, qu'il y a encore plufieurs de-
> grés au-deffus des maîtres dont je viens de parler ; les uns en comp-
> tent fix en tout , & d'autres vont jufqu'à fept. Ceux qu'on appelle
> *Maçons Ecoffois* , prétendent com-
> pofer le quatriéme grade. Comme cette Maçonnerie , différente de
> l'autre en bien des points , com-
> mence à s'accréditer en France , le
> I   public

---

22 B. Dat, « Le *Parfait Maçon* (1744). Une source méconnue des hauts grades, » *Renaissance traditionnelle* n° 161 (2011), pp. 4-83.

SECRET OF THE ECOSSOIS MASONS[23]

It is said among the Masons, that there are still several degrees above that of the masters, of which I have just spoken; some say there are six in all, & others go up to seven. Those called *Ecossois Masons* claim that they form the fourth grade. As this Masonry, different from the others in many ways, *is beginning to become known in France*,[24] the Public will not be annoyed if I relate what I have read about it in the same manuscript, which seems to give the *Ecossois* a degree of superiority above the Apprentices, Fellows, & ordinary Masters.

Instead of weeping over the ruins of the Temple of Solomon, as their brethren do, the *Ecossois* are concerned with rebuilding it.*

* My manuscript makes no mention of the *Ecossais* Lodge, but I assume that one may envisage various subjects analogous to the reconstruction of the Temple, for which these Masons are supposed to be meeting (Carr).

Everyone knows that after seventy years of captivity in Babylon, the Great Cyrus permitted the Israelites to rebuild the Temple & the City of Jerusalem; that Zorobabel, of the House of David, was appointed by him [Cyrus) the Chief & leader of that People for their return to the Holy City; that the first stone of the Temple was laid during the reign of Cyrus, but that it was not completed until the sixth year of that of Darius, *King* of the Persians.

It is from this great event that the *Ecossois* derive the epoch of their institution, & although they are later than the other Masons by several centuries, they consider themselves of a superior grade. The following is the basis on which their pre-eminence is founded.

When the question arose of rebuilding the Temple of the Lord, Zorobabel chose from the three grades of Masonry the most capable workmen; but as the Israelites had to suffer many obstacles & reverses during the course of their labours, at the hands of the Samaritans & of other neighbouring nations, the work would never have been completed, had not this Prince taken the precaution of creating a fourth grade of Masons, whose number he limited to 753, chosen from among the most *excellent artists*; these not only supervised all the others, but they were also charged with watching

---

23 Le Parfait Macon pp. 97-104. The English text shown here is that of Harry Carr in Early French Masonic Exposures (1737-1751) pp. 195-197 and the intention is to keep one single translation. With permission of QC Lodge No.2076.

24 Les italiques sont de nous.

the security of the workmen; they made their rounds every night, as much to forward the work, as to reconnoitre against ambushes, or forestall the attacks of their enemies.

Their work being much more arduous than that of the other Masons, they were also awarded a more favourable rate of pay: & to be able to recognize them, Zorobabel gave them a sign & particular words.

The sign of the *Ecossois* is made by placing the *index* finger of the right hand on the mouth, & the second finger of the left hand on the heart.

And their words are, *Scilo, Shelomeh abif:* The first of these words is no different from the *Schilo*[25] of ordinary Masters, except in the omission of the letter *h,* & it means the same thing: the other two words *Shelomeh abif,* mean, in French, *Solomon my father.*

Finally, the *Ecossois* Masters have a language & some questions peculiar to them; I have even heard some of them say, that these questions are very numerous, but unfortunately my brother's manuscript only gives eight,[26] which are:

Q. Are you an *Ecossois* Master?

A. I was brought out of the captivity of Babylon.

Q. Who honoured you with the degree of *Ecossois?*

A. Prince Zorobabel, of the line of David & of Solomon.

Q. When?

A. Seventy years after the destruction of the holy City.

Q. In what are the *Ecossois* Masons occupied?

A. In rebuilding the Temple of God.

Q. Why that?

A. To accomplish what was foretold.

Q. Why do the *Ecossois* Masons carry the sword & the buckler?*

A. In memory of the order given by Nehemiah to all the

---

25 Selon le catéchisme du grade de maître, qui précède ce texte, tel est en effet le « mot du maître ». Il est précisé que ce mot signifie « son fils, ou celui à qui il est réservé »...

26 Toutes les informations contenues dans *Le Parfait Maçon* sont supposées provenir d'un manuscrit détenu par la sœur de son possesseur, après la mort de ce dernier. Une fiction habituelle dans les divulgations littéraires.

workmen at the time of the rebuilding of the Temple, to
have swords always at their sides, & their bucklers near
at hand during work, for use in case of attack by their
enemies.

Q. How was the new Temple built?

A. On the foundations of that of Solomon, & according to his
plans.

Q. What time is it?

A. The Sun is rising

Or

The Sun is set.

It is with this last question that the *Ecossois* Masons open &
close their Lodges.

*My manuscript makes no mention [of the decor] of the Scottish Lodge, but I
presume that it must draw some subjects similar to the rebuilding of the Temple,
for which these Masons assume to be assembled.

**The Scottish Masons all wear a large red cord, from which hangs a form of
shield.

The theme presented here is of undeniable interest. It continues what Ramsay
was talking about in Paris as early as 1736, but:

- it is not set in the time of the Crusades;
- it does not mention a word lost and then found on the outskirts of the
  Temple.

He spoke of only one thing: the rebuilding of the Temple by Zorobabel and
the battles that the workers had to fight with "swords at their sides" and "their
shields close to them as they worked." The trowel and compass have even been
forgotten.

What is foreshadowed here, then, is *not* the theme offered by Coustos (a bronze
tablet under a stone), nor that taken from Philostorgius (a crypt containing a
book), but only that of the battles that the workers had to fight to rebuild the
Temple. This is essentially the theme of what will soon become the Knights of
the East or of the Sword. These fighting workers are called "Ecossois"[27]—the
term "Chevalier" does not appear. Finally, it should be noted that "the Scots are

---

27 Ce qui souligne à nouveau le caractère très polysémique et générique de ce mot en français, à
cette époque. On ne doit jamais perdre de vue cette notion.

beginning to gain recognition in France," further confirming the novelty of this "superior" masonry in 1744. Admittedly, we must not lose sight of the highly atypical nature of the disclosure Le Parfait Maçon, and therefore view its content with great caution, but this particular section concerning the Scots takes on, unlike the rest of the work, a certain air of truth. In any case, it is an important piece of evidence.

All the accounts of the period converge, as we can see—in 1744, there were probably at least four grades above the rank of master in Paris. In particular, the existence of "Scottish Masters" is asserted everywhere, with the clarification that they were interested in preserving the ancient word for Master, the name of God, mysteriously found on the outskirts of the destroyed Temple of Solomon. Others, who are also known as Ecossois, but who are more like knight builders, are only interested in reconstruction. No one can imagine that all these new ranks were established in just a few months. However, it is fair to say, based on the sources of the time, that they had only been known for a "short time."

On the other hand, we have indisputable evidence of their precise nature and content, as we have rituals that correspond exactly to the grades then mentioned in the regulations of the Grand Master's lodge. These are undoubtedly the very first high grades in French Masonic history.

We must now examine them.

Known grades in Paris around 1745

Between around 1740 and 1750, several, and sometimes rival, 'ecossismes' emerged and developed in France. Here again, we must abandon any thought that what was happening in Paris at the time was also happening in Lyon, Bordeaux or Marseille. Over the years, of course, exchanges multiplied and practices tended towards a certain degree of standardisation. As a result, the great Masonic Rites known at the end of the eighteenth century were born, through successive additions and reworking. But in early French Masonry—by which we mean the period before 1750—developments were mainly local. In the case of the first or "higher" Scottish grades, the best documented case is that of Paris.

In the lodge of the Count of Clermont, in 1745, at least four grades were practised above the grade of Master, and we have the names and sequence of these grades:

1. Maitre Parfait

2. Maitre Irelandois

3. Elu

4. Ecossais ("des JJJ" or "Ecossais de Clermont")[1]

Can more be discovered about these degrees? Before answering that question, some preliminary remarks need to be made.

The first concerns the precise identification of the content of the grades, according to their name. An overview of the very many rituals known in France, especially from the period 1740–1770—the "thirty glorious years" of eighteenth-century French masonry—teaches us that nothing is more misleading than the name of a grade: Sometimes, under the same name, or under very similar names, we can discover rituals that are in reality very different, with no real link between them; it also sometimes happens that two rituals that are more or less identical, or where one is a slight evolution of the other, bear completely different names! The difficulty is compounded by the fact that, in most cases, the documents bear no mention of origin or date. The work required of the ritual historian then consists of accumulating series of texts, classifying them into families according to their main characteristics, watching for the appearance of

---

1 Statuts de la loge Saint-Jean de Jérusalem, « dressés le 24 juin 1745 », article XXxxᵉ, A. Bernheim, « Contribution à la connaissance de la première Grande Loge de France, » *Villard de Honnecourt*, 17 (1988), p. 129.

new elements in the ritual of a given grade, and then trying to find in dated data concerning Masonic institutions, in lists of grades, in correspondence between Freemasons where some information is sometimes noted, as much as possible of an approximate dating. To classify chronologically the different versions of a grade, which sometimes lives its own life for years, changing more or less over time, we can also use a simple and useful— but not infallible—rule: the simplest version is a priori the oldest.

Another issue, partly related to the previous one, is the hierarchy of grades. As soon as a new grade appears, it spontaneously presents itself as "more interesting" than all those that preceded it: it is therefore "superior" to them. One of the consequences of this process is that when a series of grades, or degrees, is practised in a given place, its hierarchical order, the sequence in which these grades, or degrees, are conferred, reproduces a priori their order of appearance: the "most modest" grade, the one at the start of the sequence, is usually the oldest. But here again, there are exceptions to this general rule. Sometimes new grades are inserted into a pre-existing sequence, without claiming to be at the top. More often than not, it is a case of a grade which simply develops a previous grade, or duplicates—or even divides into three—the latter, without making any genuinely new contribution; it may also be a case of a grade which serves as a barrier to systems competing for Masonic supremacy and having certain steps in common: in this case, the new grade is deemed essential to obtain the next one—if you do not have this prerequisite, possession of the common grade is not deemed valid or, at least, is not complete. Generally speaking, these 'interleafed' grades exploit themes that have no necessary link with what precedes or follows them, or deal with a minor or anecdotal element; they are never fundamental and do not usually contain content of exceptional interest.[2]

To date, we have no rituals that we can say with certainty were those used in Paris before 1745 in the Count of Clermont's lodge, but on the basis of the principles set out above and certain earlier works, we can reasonably assume that the earliest versions of grades bearing the same name as those in the 1745 series must have been very close to the state in which the latter were in Paris at that time. This is what we propose to examine. The first of these is most probably the Maître parfait.

MAITRE PARFAIT

This is the first grade set out in article 40 of the Parisian Regulations of 1745 mentioned above. We can therefore assume that it was probably the one

---

2   Il est également parfois arrivé que des grades soient ajoutés, malgré leur faiblesse évidente et leur peu d'intérêt, pour parvenir à un nombre total « intéressant » : 12, 33, etc.

introduced earliest in the Parisian milieu. We shall see later what other elements confirm this working hypothesis.

The unpublished work of R. Désaguliers[3] focused on the evolution of this grade—which over time, after many developments and alterations, became a "low number" grade, in this case the fifth in a system of an eventual 33 grades! However, it is remarkable that this grade continued to be practised in France for several decades, while many others, which had appeared later, had obtained higher ranks in the Masonic hierarchy. One example is the Scottish Mother Lodge of Marseilles, which in the early 1780s practised this grade as the fourth in its hierarchy,[4] on a par with the Scottish Lodge of the Social Contract in Paris—at a time when there were dozens of grades in France, as shown, for example, by the list of the Sovereign Metropolitan Chapter, created in 1787, which counted up to 81[5]!

For the time being, the grade of Perfect Master, one of the very first high grades to appear in France, was also one of the longest practised, even though it had often been integrated and even drowned out by other grades where it now occupied only a marginal place. Could this surprising longevity be a sign that its content found an ancient memory and suggested its once fundamental nature?

The version we publish below,[6] of which several examples can be found in Masonic archives in France, expresses the simplest structure of this grade, and therefore a priori the oldest, undoubtedly the closest to its source.

[p1] Grade de Maitre parfait [p2] Grade of perfect master   Sine virtute nihil

****

> The lodge of the perfect master must be dressed in green it must be illuminated with 16 lights placed at the four cardinal corners the T. R. placed at the east it must ÿ have only one warden who is placed at the west The master who is called T. R. [Très Respectable] and the très-vénérable warden, when there is a reception to be made the T. R. orders the brother introducer to go and prepare the recipient and brought to the door of the lodge in the usual way, the brother

---

3   Archives privées de la revue *Renaissance Traditionnelle*. C'est à partir de ces travaux que nous avons élaboré certaines des hypothèses proposées dans ce chapitre.

4   Et qui adoptera plus tard un système décalqué sur celui des quatre ordres capitulaires du Rite Français.

5   C Leger, *Les 81 grades qui fonderent au siècle des Lumieres le Rite Francais*, p. 201.

6   Manuscrit de la Bibliothèque André Doré – Grand collège des Rites Ecossais, Paris. Document transmis par P. Paoloni qui en a assuré la transcription. L'orthographe, dans l'ensemble très fantaisiste, a été parfois modifiée pour une meilleure compréhension du texte.

introducer must knock 4 knocks at the door to which responds the supervisor and successively the T. R. to which the supervisor says that we knock in perfect master T. R. having told the supervisor to go see who it is, he comes to say that it is brother xxx who asks to be received perfect master.

The T. R. ordered him to be asked his name his age if he had worked if his masters were happy with him and at the same time he ordered him to examine him on the different grades to which he had been admitted, this having been done the supervisor came to report to the T. R. who ordered him to be admitted.

every time the overseer comes to the door he must take care to knock 4 times which must be repeated by the Q. R., the brother introducer before introducing the recipient into the lodge must disarm him, take off his wig if he has one and pass him a rope around his neck, the overseer who receives him at the door must lead him to the south of the lodge facing the tableau, having arrived the T. R. demands from him for the sign of the lodge. T. R. demands the sign the word and the grip apprentif mason companion, and definitively that of master and orders to make him travel four times from west to east, the tour done the T. R. orders him to cross the tomb and to make him pass by three [**p3**] steps of apprentice on the column J. Then to make him pass to the column B. by three steps of companion And to present him by three steps of master that being done the T. R. makes him put his right hand on the Gospel and in this attitude he makes him take his obligation.

Promise

****

I promise before the great architect of the universe and before this honourable assembly to keep and observe faithfully the grade of perfect master which has just been given and not to reveal either directly or indirectly under any pretext whatsoever under no less penalty of being dishonoured and undergo the penalties to which I submitted when I was received mason, so God may sustain me in righteousness and truthfulness, and after he has taken the obligation the T. R. removes the rope he has on the collar by telling him I release you from the bond of vice by the power I have received from the T. R. Lodge here assembled and I raise you to the very high and sublime grade of maitre parfait that under the conditions that you do not communicate this grade to anyone whatsoever without the consent of this your Mother lodge, the T. R. makes him rise and gives him the sign which is done by advancing the point of the foot towards the one you want to recognize to which he responds in the same way, until the two points touch, Then we touch each other with the right knee and this is what makes point against point and putting the right hand on the heart and withdrawing it from the [p4] right side always square the token is just like that of Master Macon with the only difference that we turn the hand alternately, that is to say that one of the two has it alternately both above and below and it is in this attitude that we must give each other the word of perfect master which is *Jehova*.

To open the lodge

The T. R. is placed in the east on a throne strikes 4 blows with his mallet to which the supervisor replies the T. R. asks him if the lodge is covered the supervisor having replied yes he asks him what time it is the supervisor replies 4 o'clock the T. R. says since it is 4 o'clock it is time for the workmen to go to work, he strikes 4 blows with his mallet and says the lodge is open.

To close the lodge

The T.R. asks what time it is the overseer replies it is five o'clock, the T. R. replies since it is five o'clock it is time to send the workmen away he strikes his mallet 4 times and says the lodge is closed.

The maitre parfait wears a green Ribbon at the bottom hangs a jewel which is a compass on a quarter circle the apron should be white and lined and bordered in green and have embroidered three circles in yellow silk. and a small black square where the letter J is embroidered. The Jewel is embroidered on the bib.

Catechism of the Perfect Master

[p5] My very dear brother, after King Solomon knew that the body of our respectable Master Hiram had been found, as you know from the rank of Master that you have already received, he had it embalmed and had a monument erected in the sanctuary where he had his entire body placed with the exception of his heart which he had placed privately, and which you will know in another grade,[7] whenever you become attached to your Lodge and continue to merit the

---

7   Ce sera l'objet du grade suivant, de Maître irlandais.

friendship of our respectable brethren.

after that the body was buried and that the temple had remained 9 days closed salomon wanted that the works continued and to effect this he choose 9 most learned masters so that they had to take care to take care of the works and named them perfect to distinguish them from the other Masters.

why did he name them perfect because as hiram was perfect in science he wanted that those there which had a superior dye to the others became then completely in accord with him and you will see in new grades the Recompense which they had after the definition of the works. May God grant that by the attachment you should have for your respectable Lodge you will attract from the first the grades which the continuation of this history leaves you to desire, may the master of heaven and earth fill you with his blessings and give you the strength and wisdom necessary to reach the end of masonry which although long will only seem easy to you being supported by its beauties.

[p6] The sixteen lights that you see in the lodge represent the four grades that you have received, they are placed at the four corners of the lodge to show you that you must remember in what part of the world you find your four grades, the catechism that I will make to the venerable supervisor will instruct you further.

So help you God

Catechism of the Perfect Master

D. Are you a perfect master?
R. the maitres parfaits recognise me as such

D. Are you a companion?
R. yes I am

D. Are you a master
R. approve me or disapprove me if you can

D. are you perfect
R. I have seen the circle and the quadratures in the holy of holies

D. where are they placed
R. on the place where was put the body of our T. R. R. father hiram

D. what do the accompanying doves represent?

R. the colomns jakin and Boos by which I passed to reach the grade of master and perfect master

D. what did you learn in the different grades where you passed
R. I learned to regulate my morals to purify my heart to put me in a state to deserve perfection

D. what does the sacred stone in the midst of the saints of the saints mean?
R. it teaches us that our building must have as its foundation the living stone from which we are all hewn or built

[p7] D. why the 3 circles
R. they represent to us the emblem of the divinity which has neither beginning nor end

D. what do they represent together
R. the creation of the universe which was accomplished by the will of god and the action which he gave to the primitive qualities

D. what do you mean by this
R. I have felt the cold, the heat, the fire, the wet of the mixture of which were formed the four elements

D. why are they placed in this place
R. to teach us that God is all, is perfect and that without his help we cannot build peacefully

D. what does the letter J. in the middle of the quarried stone mean?
R. it is the sacred word of the perfect master

D. pronounce it
R. jehova

D. what does it signify
R. is the name of the great architect of the universe

D. how were you received perfect master
R. by entering the holy of holies

D. how did you enter
R. the point on the heart, and the rope on the collar

D. why the noose
R. to teach me by this humiliation not to take pride in the progress I can make in virtue

D. why the point on the heart
R. to remind me that it would be torn from me if I revealed the secret

D. how many signs do you have
R. one by four

[p8] D. pourquoÿ un par quatre
R. to make me remember the grades where I passed

D. do you have the grips
R. yes T. R.

D. how many of them do you have
R. one by five

D. why one by five
R. to remind me of the five points of my Entrance

D. what do they mean
R. the four turns and the entrance to the sanctuary

D. what does the tomb mean that you crossed to enter the sanctuary
R. it is the representation of the grave of our T. R. R. father hiram in the valley

D. why is it situated to the south of the sanctuary?
R. to teach us that it is necessary to strip the man of the of the outside world to make him worthy to enter the holy of holies

D. what is the meaning of the rope that hangs from the coffin and ends up in the sanctuary?
R. it represents the rope the brothers used to pull hiram's corpse down into the coffin

D. does it mean anything more
R. it means that we have broken the bonds of sin

D. what did you do when you came in?
R. I arrived at the altar as a merchant as an apprentice as a companion and as a master to cross the two columns

D. why this
R. to remind me that it was only by passing through the first grades that I was able to reach perfection

[p9] D. are not there any misteries hidden under this meaning?
R. it tells us that one can only reach the holy of holies by purity of morals the uprightness of the heart and secrecy in the first grade are ecossois

D. why did you enter by the side of the sanctuary
R. to teach me to leave the ordinary Route

D. why have you your place in the middle of the lodge
R. to teach me that the middle is the seat of virtue

D. what colour are you
R. green

D. why so
R. to remind us that, having died to vice, we Hope to live again by virtue, to rise to the highest grades and reach the sublime sciences.

D. who can communicate it to you
R. God alone to whom it belongs to know everything

D. what do the two pyramids on your tableau mean?
R. they represent egypt where sciences took their beginning

D. what does your Jewel signify
R. that a perfect master must only act with moderation and must be attentive to everything

D. how old are you
R. Sixteen

D. give me the password
R. Cabul

End

Comments

Without going into a detailed analysis of the grade, a number of comments need to be made.

The first point simply concerns the very name of the grade: Maître parfait.. What does this mean? In 1745, in the regulations of Grand Master Louis de Clermont's lodge, it followed the "ordinary master," i.e., the classical third grade. From this vocabulary, which seems rather disparaging of the "ordinary" third grade, we can no doubt deduce that, for the initiators of the grade of Perfect Master, it completed and completed the grade of "ordinary" Master, which was therefore both imperfect and incomplete.[8] In any case, in Paris in 1745, it was considered that the grade of Master, as it was then commonly practised, had a flaw, a shortcoming, a gap, and that the essential function of the Perfect Master was to fill this gap, to repair this flaw.

The other intellectual approach is to see that there is a commonality with the requirement of the Royal Arch in Dublin Ireland in 1744 that to achieve that superiority one must have been not only a Master Mason but also a Master Passed the Chair to be entitled to obtain the superior degree. Or perhaps even the Harodim degree in both the North East of England and in London where the very word Harodim implied being a superior master (see Anderson 1723). When one puts that together with the fact that there was no proper ceremony, nor an higher knowledge given by being simply an ordinary Master Mason just sitting in the chair of a lodge.

The second point is graphic: it concerns the very interesting table of the grade—here again, we are considering one of its simplest and therefore most primitive versions.

This tableau immediately calls for an obvious remark: it bears a striking resemblance to the tables published for the Ecossois grade in Berlin, whose link with the Scots Masters in London, which itself appeared around 1733, is infinitely probable. A significant number of elements are found in common in these two paintings:

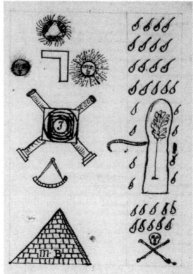

Tableau Maitre Parfait (BnFFM4 76)

---

8 La 3ᵉᵐᵉ édition du *Dictionnaire de l'Académie française*, publiée en 1740, définissait ainsi l'adjectif *parfait* : « A qui il ne manque rien pour être accompli dans son genre. »

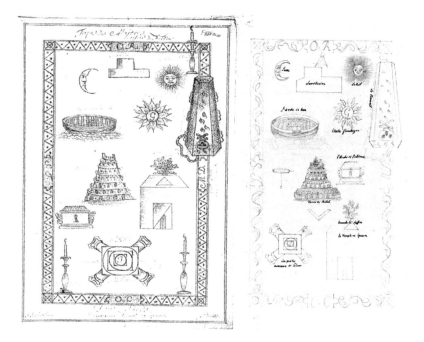

Tableaux Ecossois Berlin 1747

The most original symbol is that of two columns in saltire or sometimes of broken parts of four columns, arranged in a saltire and surmounted by a cubic stone bearing at its centre the letter J surrounded by several interlocking circles and squares. This can clearly be seen on both tableau. We will come back later to the idea, suggested by the Berlin painting, of columns in "pieces."

A second common feature concerns the coffin of Master Hiram, with its emblems of mortality, placed outside the layout of the "Temple," on the south side, but connected to the interior by a rope. It should be noted here that, contrary to French custom, as we have seen, the letter J does not appear on the coffin. It has been moved to the cubic stone

- The tableau for the Maître Parfait shows a sort of mausoleum in the form of a triangular pyramid with the letters MB, while the Berlin Ecossois depicts a simplified representation of the Temple surmounted by a triangle with an acacia branch, no doubt alluding to Hiram's death. There is a formal link between these two figures, but one doubt remains: is this mausoleum a real tomb, and what exactly does it contain?

- The sun, moon, compass and square, and a blazing star (with or without the letter G) are also found in both cases, but they are less specific; in addition, the German painting shows a plumb line instead of a square.

At this point, we can simply note that the Berlin Scots painting is a slightly more sophisticated perfect Master painting: it contains virtually all the emblems of the previous one, at least the major and specific emblems, with the addition of a few new symbols, such as Noah's Ark, the Ark of the Covenant and the Tower of Babel—these symbols appeared as early as 1744 in atypical printed disclosures, notably in La Franc-Maçonne and Le Parfait Maçon, but also in 1766 with the grade of Noachite published in Les plus secrets mystères, by Berage. It could be said that, from a strictly graphic point of view, the Scottish Master of Berlin is an "enriched" Perfect Master—although this point of view alone obviously does not allow any definitive conclusion.

The reception ritual is extremely simple: the candidate goes around the lodge four times, then is admitted to the Holy of Holies and passes over the cubic stone bearing the letter J. All that remains is for him to swear his obligation, receive the secrets—the 'sacred word' is Jehovah—and put on his apron, which is edged in green. This is followed by a very interesting question-and-answer instruction.

It was pointed out above that the very name Perfect Master implied that the grade of 'ordinary' Master was imperfect, and therefore incomplete. But we saw straight away that what was missing from the Master grade in France, and what the Perfect Master grade was supposed to bring, was not the word Master, which had been lost with Hiram's death. In France, as we have said, this name had never been lost in the French form of the legend, and its initial (or the letters J.A.) will always appear on the tableau of the third grade. The grade of Perfect Master therefore provided no new information on this point. On the other hand, it did reveal the scope and meaning of the word. It was in this that his 'perfection' consisted. This is shown in this significant passage from the instruction by questions and answers that follows the reception ceremony:

> D. What does *the letter J in the middle of the square stone mean?*[9]
> R. It is the sacred word for Master Perfect.
>
> D. Say it.
> R. Jehovah!
>
> D. What does it mean?
> R. It is the Hebrew name of the Great Architect of the Universe who is God and *the true Word of the Master Masons which has never been lost.*[10]

---

9 Les italiques sont de nous.

10 *Id.* La partie en italiques ne figure pas dans le manuscrit que nous avons transcrit mais dans plusieurs autres de la même époque (notamment Bristol).

In short, the essence of this grade was to find the name of God on a stone located in the Holy of Holies, which was placed on two columns in saltire, whose graphic representation is absolutely identical to that of the Scotsman of Berlin who sees "pieces" of these columns, as if they were debris from the temple—which is not said openly in the French grade of Perfect Master.

This last point should be emphasised. It should be noted that while the Perfect Master makes no allusion to the destroyed Temple either in the course of the ritual, or in the instruction, or in the speech, the notion of "debris of the temple" had already been present for years in the ritual corpus of French Masonry. If we go back to Hérault's disclosure, examined earlier, which describes an "Apprentice-Compagnon" initiation ceremony, we note this singular passage:

> [The candidate] is introduced, and made to make three turns in the Chamber, around a space written On the Floor, *where we have pencilled a kind of representation, On two columns, the remains of the Temple of Solomon [...].*[11]

The notion of the "destroyed Temple" had therefore been at the heart of French Masonic practice since at least 1736!

Finally, another detail catches the eye—the surprising idea that the Master Hiram was buried in the Holy of Holies—a blasphemous notion so contrary to the thinking of Israel. Could this be to suggest, in passing, a Christian allusion in the character of Hiram—he would then belong in the most sacred place in the temple?

Another passage from the ancient instruction of the grade may help us to understand this:

> D. What did you see at the bottom of the Perfect Master's Lodge?
> R. *The cornerstone*[12] on which all Masons must base their buildings.

> D. What do you mean by edifice?
> R. Our actions must be guided by these two precepts: *you must love your Creator above all things and your neighbour as yourself.*[13]

---

11 Les italiques sont de nous. The cornerstone is described in French as 'la pierre angulaire.'

12 *Id.*

13 *Id.* Marc, 12, pp. 29-31 : « Et Jésus lui répondit : le premier de tous les Commandements est : écoute Israël, le Seigneur notre Dieu est le seul Seigneur;/ Et tu aimeras le Seigneur, ton Dieu, de tout ton cœur, de toute ton âme, de toute ta pensée, et de toute ta force. / Voici le second : Tu aimeras ton prochain comme toi-même. Il n'y a pas d'autre commandement plus grand que ceux-là. »

The reference to the cornerstone, which is so important in Masonic rituals,[14] directly alluding to Christ, and to a passage from the New Testament referring to Jesus,[15] are not without significance at a time when it was written in Paris that the religion to which all Masons were bound was that "of which all Christians agree."[16]

As we can see, the Perfect Master, so long held in high esteem in eighteenth-century French Masonry, holds many surprises in store for us.

The next two grades of the system then practised in the lodge of the Count of Clermont, namely the Irish Master and the Chosen, will not keep us long in the perspective which is that of our present work. We will confine ourselves to a few remarks about them.

Maitre Irlandois

An exhaustive work has been devoted to the grade of Irish Master, and the interested reader may wish to refer to it.[17] The originality of this grade, devoted to a funeral tribute to Hiram, lies in its borrowing of certain elements from Chinese funeral rites, in particular with the words 'Givi' and 'Ki' and the term 'Xincheu' which appear in the ritual. It has been convincingly shown that these expressions derive from the ceremonial in which the ancient Chinese knelt and then stood (in Chinese: Ci Vi = "Kneel"; Ki = "Stand") before a tablet on which the name of the deceased was inscribed and which was considered to be the temporary seat of his or her soul (Xing Cheu = "Seat of the Soul"). We don't know why Chinese customs, documented in particular by the accounts of Jesuit missionaries returning from China, were introduced into a Masonic ritual! Let's just remember that at the beginning of the 18th century "chinoiseries" (painted decorations, fans, earthenware) were in fashion, and that Ramsay himself had shown a keen interest in Chinese culture and religion—his master Fénelon, Bishop of Cambrai, His master Fénelon, Bishop of Cambrai, had been consulted on the occasion of what was known as the "quarrel over Chinese rites," when Jesuits had adapted the ritual of the Mass in China in order to "acclimatise" it by introducing elements taken from Chinese ceremonies—to the great displeasure of the Vatican, which had condemned these mixtures. Did Ramsay[18] exert his influence in some

---

14 En particulier, mais pas seulement, dans le grade de la Marque.

15 Ephésiens, 2, pp. 19-21 ; 1Pierre, pp. 2, 6.

16 *Devoirs enjoints aux Maçons Libres* (1735).

17 R. Désaguliers, R. Dachez, « La pensée chinoise et la franc-maçonnerie au XVIIIe siècle : le grade de Maître Irlandais, Prévôt et Juge », *Renaissance Traditionnelle* n° 96, octobre 1993, 238-258 ; *English version* : « Chinese Thought and Freemasonry in the Eighteenth Century: The Degree of Irish Master, Provost and Judge," *Freemasonry in context, History, Ritual, Controversy*, Ed. A. de Hoyos, B. Morris, 2003, pp. 145-162.

18   A moins qu'il ne s'agisse de francs-maçons de son entourage.

way, perhaps in memory of his master, who had been unjustly punished by the Roman authorities, and to whom he had remained unfailingly loyal?

It should also be remembered that during the Gormogons' public demonstrations in London, in Wharton's entourage, a Chinese-style decoration was used. Was this a precedent that the Irish Master grade would have used? And why?

The question remains open, but it is nevertheless an anecdotal rank degree.

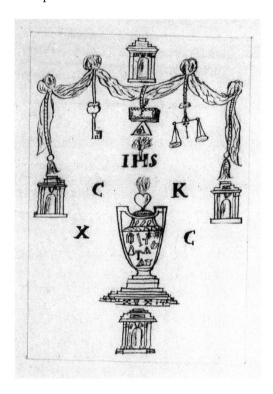

Maitre Elu

The rank of Chosen had a completely different destiny to that of the Irish Master, which was soon abandoned. The "Chosen One" traversed the entire history of eighteenth-century French masonry, from around 1745 until the middle of the nineteenth century, giving rise to various controversies. Dedicated, as we know, to avenging the murder of Hiram, its earliest versions, from the 1740s at any rate, featured the killing of the murderers—sometimes with macabre refinement. Of rather dubious initiatory significance, it was violently rejected by certain Masonic Rites in France in the 18th century—such as the Rectified Scottish Rite, established from 1773 onwards in Strasbourg and then the following year in Lyon, which formally banned decorations of an Elected rank degree being worn in its lodges! In any case, in France, it undoubtedly appeared to be a logical, or at any rate inevitable, conclusion to the "hiramique" chapter, while English Masonry chose the simpler, more discreet and less dangerous solution of devoting only a very brief allusion to it towards the end of the Master's grade. The first documented mention of the punishment of the guilty, in England, is found in the 'Master's Share' of the Three Distinct Knocks, published in 1760[19]—but this does not exclude, of course, that it had already been known for many years. In France, its presence in third position in the list of high ranks in Paris suggests its appearance in the early 1740s, at the latest.

---

19 « Jubela was taken out, and his Throat cut across &c. Jubelo's Heart was torn from under his naked Left-Breast &c. Jubelum's Body was severed in two and one Part carry'd to the South and the other to the North, &c.

L'Ecossais des JJJ ou Ecossais de Clermont, ou Ecossais de Paris (1745) – and the question of the Installation of Master of a Lodge

It is well known that between 1730, the date of publication of Prichard's Masonry Dissected, and 1760, the year of publication of Three Distinct Knocks, that practically nothing changed in England regarding the ritual practice of the first three grades. It has also often been pointed out that this gap in the documentation was partly filled, between 1737 and 1751, by all the disclosures printed in France—it is indeed likely that English and French Masonic practice, apart from a few local variations, did not differ fundamentally at that time. It was for this reason that Harry Carr, in 1967, published an almost complete English translation of the eighteenth-century French disclosures—but such an equivalent has not yet been produced in France.

The same applies to another subject, which was also very poorly documented before 1760: the Installation of the Master of the Lodge and the "secrets reserved for the Chair." However, in Paris, before 1745, such a grade existed among the hierarchy of the grades then practised, whose symbolic and ritual content had substantial similarities to what would be revealed, only about fifteen years later in England; in respect of the Installation of a Master of a Lodge: this was the *Ecossais des 3 JJJ*.

The existence of this grade was noted, at least in Paris, in a document that is certainly dated, as early as 1745—so it must have been introduced into French Masonic practice sometime before that date. We have already seen that in the French capital, and more precisely in the personal lodge of its new Grand Master, the Count of Clermont, elected to the position in December 1743, that a primitive system of at least four grades existed beyond the grade of Master. The last of these grades was called *Ecossais de Paris*, or *Ecossais de Clermont*, or *Ecossais des "3JJJ."*

It should be noted that this was the first grade in Paris to bear the name 'Ecossais.' We have already mentioned the fact that an early declaration, in December 1743, precisely at the time of the election of the Count of Clermont, tells us that: "some brethren have recently been announcing themselves under the name of Scottish Masters and are making claims and demanding prerogatives in the particular Lodges of which no trace is found in the ancient archives and customs of the Lodges spread across the face of the earth." (*Règlements généraux*, December 1743, art. 20)

There would seem to be little doubt that the "Ecossois" referred to in the new regulations of the Grand Lodge were the holders of the grade of Ecossais de Paris as practised in the Grand Master's lodge. This is also the place to point out that the names given to the grades at this early stage in French, and British, Masonic history can be misleading. We have seen that the grade of *Maître parfait*, given in Paris just after the grade of Master, was possibly similar to the mysterious "Scots Master" known in London since 1733; the Parisian grade of *Ecossais des 3 JJJ*, on the other hand, although literally translating the English expression "Scots Master," explores a very different theme: that of Hiram's replacement.

Let's look first at the main points of one of the oldest rituals of this grade:[1]

> The Lodge is lit by 45 red candles, namely to the right of the 'Most Excellent,' who presides over the Lodge, a three-branched candlestick, a five-branched candlestick and a seven-branched candlestick. On three small tables covered with a red carpet and placed to the right and left of the Most Excellent and at the back of the Lodge, will be placed three times fifteen lights in three lines: a line of three to the east, a line of five in the middle and a line of seven to the west.

> The table in front of the Most Excellent is covered with a red carpet on which is embroidered a triangle carried by a compass. On this table is a square, a compass and the new plan of Solomon's Temple. The hangings and all the carpets are red.

> The Tableau is visible in the Lodge [to the west, facing the Most Excellent:

---

1   Original ms in the Biblioteque National Francaise ref BNF FM4 112. *See also.* P. Paoloni, « Le rituel de Royal Arch du Chapitre Dovre n°40 (c.1784) », Renaissance Traditionnelle n°199-200 (juillet-décembre 2020), pp. 188-204.

There is only one Warden. The President represents Salomon and the Warden represents Adoniram. Adoniram occupies a chair identical to that of Solomon.

As soon as the candidate enters, he is covered with a sheet and the chair of the Warden, who has risen, is placed behind him. Facing the candidate, the Warden strikes him on the forehead with a mallet, thus seating him in Adoniram's chair. The sole Warden then takes his place to the left of the Most Excellent. After a moment, the Most Excellent addresses the Candidate as follows:

Discours

The body of our Respectable Master hiram having been brought back to jerusalem, salomon had it put in the Holy of the Holies and to replace this great man he appointed 7. experts to the head of which he put adoniram son of abda of the tribe of nephtali. it should be observed that the word of master was never lost as one believed it, because when titus took jerusalem and that he demolished the temple, one found it under the column jakin. where hiram had made it engraved on a gold plate; this word was jehova and jakin, which mean to you only eternal. they are the 2. sacred words the consecrated words are giblin and gabaon,[2] giblin is the word of the 7. experts and signifies excellent, gabaon is the name that salomon gave to the chamber of the third because it was the most elevated place of the temple, and that he wanted to preserve that of the highest mountain of jerusalem on which david his father offered sacrifices to the j.j.j.

When the story was over, the cover was taken from him and the Most Excellent gave him the ecossais without saying anything to him, leads him to the altar where he makes him kneel and after having made him take his obligation in which one obliges oneself to have ones belly severed if one has ever had an Affair with the wife of a Scotsman the Most Excellent makes him dress as an Ecossais and this clothing is to have a white apron bordered with red which the Most Excellent ties on him, on this apron is placed in the middle a . . .

---

2   Ordre des mots très légèrement modifié pour atténuer l'invraisemblance.

Catechism Ecossais

D. are you Ecossais?   R. yes, the 3 letters are known to me.

D. what do you mean by this?   R. 2. sacred hebrew words.

D. how did you get to the door of the chapter?   R. by 7 degrees.

D. how did you announce yourself to the chapter? R. by 3. 5. and 7. blows.

D. what does this number mean? R. the 15. Experts who raised the body of our Respectable Master.

D. give me the explain of each number   R. the number 3. signifies that 3. that govern the chamber of the 3rd.

D. why?   R. masonry being the emblem of the Holy Scripture, is governed as the G. M. of the universe governs the grand lodge; the number of 3. is the index of the triple society and the divine and eternal ownership of all power and all science.

D. why the number of 5.   R. because of the 5. orders of architecture which were employed with the temple.

D. why the number 7?   R. because 7 were substituted for one.

D. what path did you take to become an Ecossais?
R. I started from the middle chamber.

D. where did you go?   R. To that of the 3rd.

D. what do you call this room?   R. gabaon.

D. why?   R. because gabaon was a high place in the Holy City on which david and solomon offered sacrifices to the Lord before the construction of the temple, and it was to preserve the memory of this that Solomon gave this name to the highest place in the temple.

D. what did you see in this room?   R. a great light which the eye could hardly sustain.

D. where did this light come from?   R. from the flaming star.

D. what does this star mean?   R. it is the one that led the magi and stopped where the divinity rested.

D. why the 5. rays of this star?   R. because of the architectural orders with which the masons decorated the temple.

D. what does the circle in the middle signify?   R. that God has neither beginning nor end.

D. why the 3.j.j.j. inside?   R. to teach us that god is the source of all light, that he enlightens our spirit to learn everything, and that our soul is his sign.

D. what else did you see in the 3rd chamber?   R. the true sign, the true touch and the true word of the master which has never been lost.

D. how many signs are there?   R. three.

D. what do you call the first one?   R. a sign of astonishment.

D. the second one?   R. sign of character.

D. why?   R. because it is peculiar only to the ecossais.

D. the third?   R. a sign of appeal.

D. why?   R. because this sign must be used in case of need, but at the last extremity, to call the f'[rere]s to your aid.

D. how many grips?   R. one and 3. times.

D. give them to me?   R. (gives them)

D. how many words? R. two sacred. et 2. for the degree.

D. what are the first 2. words?   R. jehova and jakin.

D. what do these words mean? R. to you alone eternal.

D. what are the second 2.   R. gabaon and giblin.

D. what does the first mean?   R. it is the name of the 3rd chamber and means an elevated place.

D. what does the second one mean?   R. excellent maitre which is the name of a ecossais.

D. on what is your building founded?   R. on the cornerstone.

D. why?   To teach us that the house of the Lord and of wisdom had no other foundation than the living stone from which we are built, which is nothing other than the emblem of virtue.

D. who taught you all these things?   R. king solomon.

D. at what time?   R. after the death of the [T.R.] Most Respectable Master hiram.

D. how do you name the first of the 7. who were substituted for one?   R. adoniram son of dabda of the tribe of nephtali, he was clerk of the tribe and had inspection on the workmen who laboures in lebanon.for the cutting of wood which was to be used for the construction of the temple.

D. why is your lodge called the universal lodge of St. John? R. because St. John raised it.

D. who formed the first lodge?   R. the Great Architect of the Universe.

D. who held it?   R. St. John the Baptist in the desert on the banks of the Jordan.

D. why did he hold it?   R. to spread light.

D. what time is it?   R. opening in the morning and closing the lodge at midday and later.

D. how old are you?   R. eighty-one.

D. why?   R. because it was at this age that our Respectable master hiram was assassinated.

D. what is your ecossais password?   R. jordan.

It must be observed that in opening and closing the lodge the excellent masters strike 3. times 27. Knocks by hand.

End of the grade of Scottish Master

This grade is obviously of considerable interest from three points of view: first its very early date, second its content, and third its association with the function of Master of the Lodge.

We can only note here the association in one and the same grade, of Adoniram, the word Ghiblim and a touching on the elbow! Any connoisseur of the British rituals for the installation of the Lodge Master—first printed in Three Distinct

Knocks in 1760—cannot but be struck by the fact that in Paris, some fifteen years before the first documented mention of the secrets of the Installation of a Master in England, that such secrets were widely known and transmitted in Parisian lodges and reserved for Brethren whom we know, in the lodges of the first three grades, "claimed the superintendence of the work."

The origins and sources of this singular grade are unknown to this day, but while the exact origins of the secret Installation of the Master of the Lodge in England before 1760 are still open to question, it must be remembered that its essential ritual content was contained in the grade which, in Paris from the early 1740s, and made the candidate Adoniram's replacement and qualified him to preside over a lodge. Were these practices and secrets English or French in origin? The question remains unanswered to this day, but it does serve to underline the extent to which, between 1735 and 1745, the fundamental grades of Freemasonry were co-developed on both sides of the Channel.

THREE DISTINCT KNOCKS & ENGLISH EXPOSURES

Three Distinct Knocks and Jachin & Boaz are the two best known exposures that appeared in England after 1760. This was after a period in which freemasonry had fallen out of fashion and which had been managed by Grand Masters who were often indifferent to the management of the Craft. As a topic for research exposures have received little attention and there is not even a list of those that were printed published. That is unusual because there are lists of Constitutions and lists of Pocket Companions.

> Then the late Master takes off his Jewel and puts it upon him, and takes him by the Master's Gripe, and raifes him off his Knees, and whifpers in his Ear the Word, which is CHIBBILUM, or, an excellent Mafon; then he flips his Hand from the Master's Gripe to his Elbow, and ftrikes his Nails in as you do in the other Gripe at the Wrift. This is the Word and Gripe belonging to the Chair.
>
> N. B. The fenior and junior Warden, and Secretary, receive the fame Obligation as he in the Chair, only with this Difference, they have neither Gripe nor Word. Therefore I have no Occafion to infert it over again, as it is the fame, and the fame Penalties.

Here in TDK Hiram dies and it is Chibbilum who is described as an 'excellent mason' who is raised In J&B (1774) p.36 as a 'worthy Mason'—see quote below.

* CHIBBELUM fignifies a worthy Mafon. The Origin of the Words and Signs among Free Mafons was on this Account: *Hiram*, the chief Architect of the Temple, had fo great a Number of Workmen to pay, that he could not poffibly know them all; he therefore gave each Degree, or Clafs, a particular Sign and Word, by which he could diftinguifh them more readily, in order to pay them their different Salaries.

Quote from Three Distinct Knocks (1774) p.62

Solomon in all His Glory (London 1766)

This was not one of the more popular exposures but it did run to three editions. And is a *translation from the French Le Macon Demasque*—so we have Jehovah engraved on the tomb of Hiram in an English exposure (p.49).

M. What do thefe three knocks fignify?
W. The word Adoniram, our refpectable mafter.
M. How was he affaffinated?
W. By three fellow-craft, who wanted to force the mafters word from him, in order to receive their wages.
M. How was the body of Adoniram found?
W. By a branch of acacia, which the fellow-craft had planted upon the fpot where they had buried him, which is the reafon that it is engraven upon his tomb.
M. Is there nothing elfe engraved upon it?
W. Solomon caufed alfo the ancient word to be infcribed.
M. What word is it?
W. *Jehovah*, that is, *God* in Hebrew.
M. Why is it not ufed now?
W. Becaufe it was apprehended the fellow-craft had forced it from Adoniram's lips by torturing him.

"OTHER GRADES" IN PARIS AND BORDEAUX : THE 'GRADES ÉCOSSAIS DE LA VOÛTE' (1745-1760)

It was around 1745 that the expression "grade écossais" became highly confused in France. It meant both "a particular form of the Scottish grade"—the archetype of which, or at least the starting point, was the mythical *Scots Master* of London—and any kind of high grade, with the number of grades growing impressively to reach at least twenty-five or more by the beginning of the 1760s.[1] This is not the place to retrace the genesis of all these grades or to examine their details, as that is not the purpose of this book. Rather, it is a question of tracking the appearance in France, between 1745 and 1760, of grades that seem to embroider upon themes that were earlier to have formed the Royal Arch in England in the probable wake of the Scots Master of ca. 1733.

The questions that then arise are: how did the ideas behind this grade reach France? And in what form? At what date? What were their sources? What became of them?

It is not yet possible to provide precise answers to all these questions, but only then, armed with these historical and ritual elements, will we be able to consider, in the next chapter, the question of the Royal Arch in eighteenth-century France.

To shed some light on this context, we will confine ourselves here to a grade that was very popular at the time and represents the origin of what French Masonic historiography calls the "deuxième écossisme," which probably appeared in Bordeaux[2] shortly before 1745: *le Vray Maître et Ecossais*.

We know that, according to Morin himself, in 1744 he had received a grade of "la perfection écossaise"[3] from Admiral Mathews. William Matthews had become Provincial Grand Master in the English West Indies in 1737 and the sources of the rank he conferred on Morin a few years later are unknown. However, Morin

---

1   En témoignent notamment la célèbre patente Morin, de 1761 et, la même année, la très intéressante correspondance échangée entre le Lyonnais Jean-Baptiste Willermoz et le maçon de Metz Meunier de Précourt (*cf.* notamment, Steel-Maret, *Archives secrètes de la franc-maçonnerie*, 1893, rep. 1985, pp. 72-78).

2   Le "premier écossisme" est celui qui naquit à Paris au début des années 1740 – et sans doute dès la fin des années 1730.

3   A. Bernheim, "Notes on Early Freemasonry in Bordeaux (1732-1769)," *AQC* 101 (1988), pp. 96-97.

took advantage of the "Constitutions given by the Respectable Parfaite lodge of London dated the 25th of June 1745" to create a "Parfaite Loge d'Ecosse." Finally, around 1748, Etienne Morin created a lodge in Bordeaux called "des Elus Parfaits ou Anciens maçons dits Ecossais."[4] Moreover, the news soon reached Paris and caused quite a stir. In less than three years, what had been passed on in Bordeaux was revealed in the capital.[5] In the famous Patente Morin, issued in Paris in 1761, the grade of "*Grand Elu parfait et Sublime maçon*" was included.

Although the Vray Maître and Ecossais rituals that have come down to us and allow a plausible dating are from the early 1770s, and originating in the south of France, it is quite easy to offer an earlier date by at least a good fifteen years and to find traces of them elsewhere in France. It is clearly a "Vault" grade—a theme absent, as we have seen, from the oldest documented forms of the *Scots Master* grade in the form of its continental descendants, in Berlin as in Paris.

Several versions, all in accord, of the grade of Vrai Maître et Ecossais[6] thus provide us with another piece of the conceptual jigsaw that enables us to reflect on the constituent elements of the final grade of the Royal Arch.

It will suffice here to recall the main teachings of the legend of the grade, the account of which forms the essential part of the reception ceremony, itself very brief and very simple. Here is the essential part of this 'History' of the grade (Ms 3080, Avignon):

> You have seen by the grades you received, the revenge of our R.M. Hiram, and as the true word of Master was lost, here is how it was found; One can judge of the great value that our Ancients made of their mysteries, since the Galbanons (sic) testified to their zeal 400 years after the destruction of the temple under Nebuchadnezzar. This king having resolved to destroy it to the foundations, the Parfaits had no greater eagerness, after the troops had withdrawn, than to go to the ruins of the temple; They also found the body of

---

4 Bernheim, pp. 96-97.

5 Sur le détail des événements, *cf.* A. Bernheim, « Contribution à la genèse de la première Grande Loge de France, *Villard de Honnecourt*, 17, pp. 96-97.

6 *Cf.* R. Désaguliers, « Rituel du Vray Maître et Ecossais », *Renaissance Traditionnelle*, 9, pp. 68-74; 10, pp. 138-145 (ce rituel est issu d'une collection privée); *id.*, « Un second rituel de Vray Maître et Ecossais et trois tableaux du grade », *Renaissance Traditionnelle*, 83, pp. 203-224 (Ms FM$_4$ 232, Bibliothèque nationale de France); *id.*, « Deux rituels de Vrai Maître de 1769 (Aix-en-Provence) et 1774 (Avignon) », *Renaissance Traditionnelle*, 84, pp. 283-300 (l'un de ces rituels est issu de la Collection Alphandéry, à Avignon, Ms 3080 ; l'autre est le Ms Arbaud 127, Aix-en-Provence). On connait notamment un diplôme maçonnique établi à Marseille en 1766, reprenant intégralement l'image d'un tableau du grade de Vray Maître tel qu'il existe dans les manuscrits qui nous sont parvenus, ce qui suggère était pratiqué dans cette région au moins depuis le début des années 1760.

Gilead, son of Sophroni, a considerable man of the Galbanons and chief of the Levites under Sarojas the Great Master (sic). Gilead was on guard in the sacred vault to maintain the burning lamps that burned incessantly, and to worship the word innominable; like another Hiram, who 400 years earlier preferred to lose his life than reveal the secret of the Masters. Gilead preferred to be entombed under the ruins of the temple, and did not want to leave lest the sacred vault entrusted to his care to be discovered. The Gabalons erased the ineffable word, and stripped Gilead, whom they found with 3 fingers over his mouth; this is why the Gabalons have always kept this sign. They stripped him of the garments he wore as Chief of the Levites, consisting of a thiara, and a linen robe, and covered the pedestal with them, so that nothing would become known to the Gentiles; it was their greatest treasure; they were soon relieved of the trouble they had taken to search with ardour, and after they had erased the word, they were content to communicate it to each other. After the destruction of the temple, a number of skilled Perfect Workers dispersed to neighbouring nations whom they instructed in the royal art, but they taught this royal art only to children born to free and eminent people, and communicated their secret only to those who proved worthy. It was not until the end of time that they spread throughout the world, their number increased greatly, but their science, and their secret having become more common, became less valuable, only the zealous always made much of it, and to preserve the memory of those who had perfected the royal art, and respected its mysteries, they communicated in the future, under symbolic ceremonies to ordinary Masons.

Compared to the Maître Parfait or the grade of Ecossois of Berlin, previously mentioned, we can see that new and major themes have been introduced:

- The existence of a subterranean place, or "Sacred Vault," built by Solomon, Hiram of Tyre and Hiram Abif, during the construction of the first Temple, to preserve "the word which is the foundation and perfection of Masonry," "engraved on a pedestal";

- This word is "Gabalon" or "Gabulon"—replaced by "Mac Benac" for the "Ordinary Masters" after Hiram Abif's death;

- The holders of this secret are the "Gabalons," or "Parfaits Maçons", and they alone know its pronunciation, revealed to "Moses in the Burning Bush" - which establishes a direct link between this word and the Divine Name;

- It was the Gabalons who, immediately after the destruction of the Temple by Nebuchadnezzar, entered the Sacred Vault, which had miraculously remained inviolate, where they discovered the corpse of the Vault Keeper, Gilead—presented as "another Hiram" but also as the "chief of the Levites," who appear for the first time in a Masonic text. They buried him under the pedestal, erased the "ineffable word" engraved on it and decided to communicate it only to certain of their descendants;

- Since then, only the 'Vrais Maîtres' have held the authentic word, while the High Priests, after the Temple was rebuilt, ignored the pronunciation of the Divine Name, not knowing how to vocalise the four letters 'job, he, vau, hea' and substituting the name 'Adonai.'

- On all the tables of the grade, the name JEHOVA appears in full, placed under a vault.

It is also easy to see what is missing from the later classical forms of the Royal Arch, and in particular the fact that no chance discoveries have been made, or are yet to be made, in the Vault, all the secrets of which have been deliberately erased, neither in the first Temple nor in the second—the theme of the legend of Philostorgius is therefore in no way called upon here. We know, however, that this theme was present in Masonic texts from the late 1730s in France.

It is also worth noting the prominence of the word "Gabalon" in this grade, whereas the word "Jehova," which is central to the grade of Maître Parfait, for example, is relegated to the background, even though it is actually present in the grade. By consonance and phonetic proximity, the word "Gabalon" is obviously reminiscent of certain others, such as "Ghibbulum" or "Ghiblim."

This grade was destined for greatness. Enriched with the legend of Enoch, it was the direct ancestor of the grade of "Grand Élu Parfait et Sublime maçon ou Grand Élu de la Voûte Sacrée," 14th in the Ancient and Accepted Scottish Rite, whose themes are well known. Suffice it to say that many of the French rituals of this Ecossais de la Voûte are known, the earliest copies of which, undoubtedly dated, date back to the early 1760s.

At the provisional end of this wandering between two categories of grades (Maître Parfait, Ecossais de la Voûte), between 1740 and 1760 approximately, it is clear that all the constituent elements of the Royal Arch were then present in France, but in distinct and separate grades, with no immediate link.

We could then give in to the temptation to reconstitute a history of the Royal Arch in France, simply by imagining a "fusion" of the main elements of these grades, which would be an easy alternative to the hypothesis of a direct transmission from Great Britain. Some French Masonic writers have ventured this on occasion.

But the documented history of the Royal Arch in France tells a rather different story.

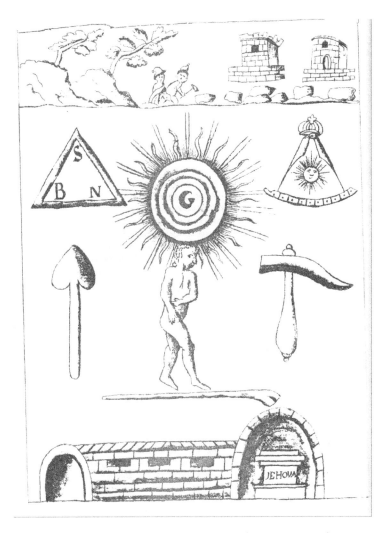

Tableau de Vray Maitre et Ecossais (BnF FM4 232)

The Arche Royal Arche in France (1760-1765)

There is a record in France of the Royal Arch. One of the most interesting facts to emerge from this file—and for English-speaking readers, which may be a little confusing—is that the oldest rituals of this grade in French pre-date the oldest manuscript English rituals of the Royal Arch!

This is not the only example in the history of Freemasonry since, as we have already mentioned,[1] the only rituals available for the first three grades, between 1730 and 1760, are French[2] and, in the absence of English sources from the same period, give us information on the practices of the First Grand Lodge between 1737 and 1751. However, as far as the Royal Arch is concerned, the fact has also been known for a long time.

The first French researcher to take an interest in the subject was undoubtedly Paul Naudon, in 1970, who published an early French ritual of the "Royal Arch,"[3] but the question was taken up in greater depth by René Désaguliers in 1981, in a seminal article containing four rituals.[4]

An Early Dated Ritual

Before examining the actual content of these texts, it is most interesting to know when the grade to which they correspond first appeared in France.

The antiquity of the Royal Arch in France was already well known to Bernard E. Jones, who, in his famous Freemasons's Book of the Royal Arch (1957), mentioned that

> The earliest Royal Arch ritual ever discovered dates from about 1760 and is to be found in an illustrated French manuscript in the Heaton-Card Collection, Freemasons' Hall Library, London [5] (Jones p.158).

---

1 *Cf.* pp. xx.

2 Nous mettons à part les rituels écossais du groupe Haughfoot (1696–1715).

3 *La franc-maçonnerie chrétienne*, 1970, pp. 218-220.

4 R. Désaguliers, « Quatre rituels français anciens de l'Arc royal (1760-1764) », *Renaissance Traditionnelle*, 48, pp. 241-257.

5 *Precis des huits premier Grades, ornes de discours et d'Histoires allegoriques, relatifs au respectable Orde de la Franc-Maconnerie,* Library & Museum of Freemasonry, London, A180PRE. The total ms is 304 pages.

The earliest R.A. ritual yet discovered dates from about 1760, and is contained a French illuminated manuscript included in the Heaton-Card collection housed in the library at Freemasons Hall in London (Jones p. 158).

Jones did not specify the arguments for his dating, but it is entirely plausible and can be based on indisputable documentary data.

The first element is to be found in correspondence exchanged in June 1761 between the Lyon mason Jean-Baptiste Willermoz and masons in Metz, in eastern France. By comparing their respective Masonic knowledge, the Brothers from Metz apparently taught the Masons from Lyon about the existence of a "Royal *(sic)* Arch" grade. The characteristics they gave were as follows:

> Salomon Roy, Hiram Roy and Hyram Architecte held their Council alone, which is what is meant by the initial letters [which will be revealed later]; the last [i.e., Hyram Architecte] having been murdered, Salomon, despite repeated requests from the Masters, refused to admit any of them to this eminent grade, telling them that they were working and that one day they would deserve to be invested with it. *Gibellum*, the word in the centre [of a "crowned triangular hyeroglyph" specific to this grade], discovered the mystery by three different repetitions on the reverse of the medal, the Emblem of the Sun, which revealed the words traced on the frontispiece of the Temple where the secret lodge was held. Word: *1° Ja. 2° Bu. 3° lum: Jabulum* pronounced under the 3 raised arms of the brothers who pronounce it in their ears.[6]

This very brief mention of a grade that was apparently not yet known by this name in Lyon already provided some very valuable information:

- after the death of Hiram Abif, no one was admitted to the rank of Master by King Solomon;

- a person called *Gibellum*, by attempting it three times, had discovered "the mystery," i.e., the true Word of Master? It should be noted that at the same time, and for at least twenty years, the word Gibblim was revealed in the Scottish grade of the 3 JJJ, reputed to be a Lodge Master grade;[7]

- this mystery was "traced on the frontispiece of the Temple where the secret lodge was held"; we are not told that the Temple had been

---

6   *Cf.* Steel-Maret, *op. cit.*, p. 76.

7   *Cf.* pp. xx-XX.

destroyed when this discovery was made; nor is there any mention of a scroll of parchment or a sacred Book;

- The word is *Jabulum* and is transmitted in the ear "under the 3 raised arms": this is clearly a ritual sequence that is easily recognisable and has become characteristic of the grade of the Royal Arch.

Another element of dating lies in the correspondence of a Provençal mason, Jérôme Dulong, who claims to have been received into the "Royal Arch" on 12 December 1764 in Beaucaire.[8] These points, and a few others,[9] are sufficient to confirm that the grade of Royal Arch, in an early form, was well known from the early 1760s in several regions of France, even if it had not yet become widespread.

To illustrate these early rituals of the Royal Arch in France, we first chose ms 5931 (301), currently held by the Bibliothèque municipale de Lyon. Certain elements suggest[10] that it could be the ritual that the Brothers of Metz, mentioned above, intended to communicate to the people of Lyon in June 1761. It would therefore be one of the earliest French versions of the grade, probably dating from around 1760 at the latest.[11] We will then describe the main variants—which are generally minor—found in a few other versions from the same period (1760–1765).

The French 'Royale Arche' Ritual – around 1760–1765

History and details of the grade

The true secret of the Royal Order having been conferred by Solomon only to Hiram King of Tyre, with whom he had contracted the closest alliance and Hyram abif, Grand Architect of the Temple. The latter having been assassinated, as is well known, the secret remained between these two, who had sworn not to confer it on anyone without an event forcing them to do so. The afflicted masters begged Solomon for a long time to grant them the grace to confer this sublime degree and to elect 39 among them so that this beautiful secret would not be destroyed: But

---

8 R. Désaguliers, « Le registre maçonnique de messire Jérôme Dulong », *Renaissance Traditionnelle*, 46, p. 84.

9 On connait au moins deux rituels de ce grade portant une date vraisemblable de 1764 et 1765. *Cf.* P. Mollier, « Le grade de 'Royale Arche' en France au XVIIIe siècle », *Renaissance Traditionnelle*, 198, pp. 74-140. Une contribution majeure sur ce sujet, la plus récente et la plus documentée à ce jour.

10 R. Désaguliers, *art. cit.*, p. 256.

11 L'orthographe française a été légèrement harmonisée et la ponctuation rétablie chaque fois que nécessaire.

this prince always said to them as if by inspiration (giving them the first sign they did not know and which will be explained below), go: work and the great Architect will grant it to you some day. As the work on the Temple was nearing perfection and they were working outside on the east side where they had often seen Solomon with the other two Directors of the Lord's work, the place where Solomon went to form the plans of the Temple building in the underground tunnels, the origins of which he alone knew, one of the masters named Gibellum + (+letter from the centre of the Triangular plate of the f. of Lyon) who often put his hand to the most difficult works, having engaged his pickaxe in an iron ring hidden under the ground he called all the other masters to make them observe it, they came to see that this ring was attached to a kind of trapdoor which closed the entrance to a subterranean passage; they all reunited, and managed to remove the piece which closed this place, but they were not much further ahead, for they only discovered the entrance to a subterranean passage where there was perfect darkness: But the ardent Gibellum, full of the desire to learn and to penetrate this immense depth, had a rope tied round the middle of his body and he agreed with the other Masters that they would withdraw him as soon as he shook the rope 3 times in this way***: his companions having asked him if he had discovered anything he replied the deep darkness and the lack of light prevented me from discovering anything, He then took two torches and having bound them as he had done the first time he agreed that if he had to emerge from the subterranean he would twist the rope 6 times in this way ***/*** Having already gone a long way he discovered large arcades one on top of the other, such as the Phoenicians and Tyrians made and which they had learnt from the Egyptians; No sooner had he reached the centre or the 6th row of arcades than his torches were extinguished by the damp. He withdrew, and his companions asked him what he had seen, to which he replied: a frightful and impenetrable vault, which man will never be able to know without the help of the Almighty; let us invoke his holy name, he will assist us and bring us there. Then, having asked if anyone wanted to accompany him, no one did. This courageous mason more than ever determined to push his adventure to the end, having recommended himself to the great Architect he made himself come back down and having agreed that he would strike the rope 5 times in this way ***/*/**/**/* if he found something favourable;

his zeal was rewarded this time, because while he was touching the Ninth Arcade a section of the wall had become detached: he saw the luminous sun beaming its rays perpendi-cularly and he saw the frontispiece of a Temple gilded with the Initial Letters which taught him that this was the place where the 3 chiefs of Masonry gathered to hold their secret Lodge. It was then that delighted with admiration he made the second sign, which will be explained below and having given the signal to the rope in the manner indicated on arrival he expressed his joy which was communicated to all the Masters who surrounding him exclaimed: Gibellum is yet a very good Mason.[12]

A simple reading of this early version of the legend of the grade clearly shows that almost all the fundamental elements of the grade are already in place, and in particular, in addition to those mentioned in the summary of the Brothers of Metz given above, the fact that the "discovery of the mystery" does indeed take place in an underground chamber, thanks to a stone accidentally loosened which allows the sun's rays to pass through, revealing the letters "S.R. H.R. H.A." on the "pediment" or "frontispiece" of the secret lodge. However, this last point remains partly obscure, or at least ambiguous: strictly speaking, it is not a word that is revealed, but the initials of the three Grand Masters do appear on an important underground monument. We are also told that the hero of the story, Gibbellum, is a "good mason."

But other versions from the same period provide additional details on points not covered in the Lyon manuscript.

For example, the version published by Paul Naudon, which also appears to be one of the earliest forms of the grade, provides the following information at the end of the narrative:

> (...) with a lighted torch in his hand, Gibillum reached the 9th arch, where a section of wall was detached at the time, the sun penetrated through the opening and shone its ray on a triangular stone under which was written the sacred word Royal Arch.

> (...) Gibillum told his comrades of his discovery, which finally determined them all three to descend with the help of a rope ladder. When they reached the 9th arch they gave thanks to God; then they lifted the triangular stone under which was engraved the sacred word Jabulum.

---

12 Cf. R. Désaguliers, « Quatre rituels français anciens de l'Arc royal (1760-1764) », *Renaissance Traditionnelle*, 48, pp. 241-257.

(...) They asked Gibillum what movement he had made when the wall came down: he replied that he had made a movement of admiration, with both hands raised towards the sky, and that he had then prostrated himself with his right knee on the ground, one hand behind his back and the other in front of his eyes to protect himself from the sun's rays. They agreed to take the same gesture as a sign; that the response would be to put a right knee on the ground, one hand behind the back and the other over the eyes, that the touching would be to take a brother by the arm as if to pull him out of a hole saying Gibillum is a good Mason ... that for password we say I am what I am ... they then decided that the sacred word would never be pronounced in Lodge saying Ja ... bu ... lum.

They put their right hands together over their heads, forming arches, and said the password under their elbows. To give each other the sacred word one said Ja. the other said bu and the 3rd said lum; this word is given by forming the arch below the elbow, only in Lodge and is repeated 9 times.[13]

In a very thorough study of known documentary resources, Pierre Mollier has noted these general characteristics in a dozen manuscripts dating from around 1765.[14] This suggests the relative stability of this ancient form of the grade and the legendary, symbolic and ritual elements it contained.

Note the importance of the information contained in the most complete versions from this period, in particular:

- a word was found on a "triangular stone";

- This "sacred word" is *Jabulum*;

- there is a 'password': 'I am that I am';

- One of the signs is to shield your eyes from the sun with your right hand;

- The sacred word is passed on in three parts, between three Brothers who form arches with their right hand "above the head" and pass on the word "below the elbow."

---

13 P. Naudon, *La franc-maçonnerie chrétienne – la tradition opérative, l'Arche Rpyale de Jérusalem, le Rite écossais rectifié*, 1970, pp. 217-220.

14 *art. cit.*, 85-87.

The sources of the Royal Arch in France?

As the purpose of this chapter is not to study the development of the Royal Arch in France up to the end of the eighteenth century, but only to consider the circumstances of its appearance in the context of the first 'Ecossais grades' on the Continent, we shall confine ourselves here to a few general considerations.

As we suggested at the end of the previous chapter, a purely theoretical view of Masonic history might lead one to envisage a French origin for the oldest rituals of the Royal Arch in France. Indeed, we have seen that many of the major elements of the grade had already been present since the early 1740s, scattered throughout various other grades, and in particular the fundamental idea that an essential Word —in this case a Divine Name—had been found in the ruins of the Temple of Solomon, and that a crypt, a "sacred vault," had been built in the base of the Temple to preserve the essential secret. Finally, with the Chevalier d'Orient, recorded no later than around 1745, the theme of the return to Jerusalem to rebuild a new Temple on the ruins of the first appeared. The Royal Arch in France, the first evidence of which is reported ten to fifteen years later than the preceding grades, would have been a synthesis of these, carried out in situ. In the previous chapter, we saw that a version of the Chevaliers de l'Orient grade, dated 1760 in Lyon, included the discovery by Zorobabel himself, in the ruins of the first temple, of a word in G. engraved on a triangular gold blade, near an "overturned altar"...

But such a view, once put forward by certain French authors at a time when very little was known about the history of the early Masonic grades in the British Isles, is completely unsupportable.

The first argument is obviously the date of the earliest accounts of the Royal Arch in Ireland, England or Scotland. These are 1743 in Youghall and 1744 in Dublin (both in Ireland), and 1752 in the Antients Grand Lodge in London.

However, there is no serious evidence of the existence of a Royal Arch degree in France before the end of the 1750s.

Secondly, the almost constant use of the term "Royale Arche" to designate this grade in France immediately attracts attention. While certain stylistic effects can be used in French to precede a noun with a qualifying adjective, the usual word order in this language naturally leads to writing and saying "Arche Royale." The form "Royale Arche," which is immediately found in the oldest forms of the grade, suggests a rather quick and clumsy translation of the expression "Royal Arch," betraying a recent English origin. Incidentally, the same phenomenon was to occur at the beginning of the nineteenth century, with the introduction of the Ancient and Accepted Scottish Rite from America in 1804: we would then see the appearance in France of a "Suprême Conseil"—a simple translation of "Supreme Council"—and not a "Conseil Suprême."

Consequently, while the British or Irish origin of the Royal Arch in eighteenth-century France no longer seems open to question, the objective content of the grade in its early French forms is of great interest insofar as the rituals available predate the first known English-language rituals by some twenty or more years! It is therefore reasonable to assume, as in the case of the Perfect Master, an indirect witness in Paris in the 1740s, to the Scots Master of London in the 1730s, that the first French rituals of the Royal Arch give us information about one of the earliest states of the grade, in the British Isles.

At least two constant features of these early French rituals can be highlighted:

- The first is that they all take place in the first temple, and never in the Temple of Zorobabel. The Lyon ritual even tells us that the discovery was made when "the Temple was nearing perfection"—and was therefore not yet complete. Other rituals place this event "a long time later," but with no further precision. This point is all the more remarkable given that the theme of reconstruction under Zorobabel's leadership had been known since the mid-1745s through the rank of Knight of the East—and especially since 1736 in the Ramsay Discourse.

- The question of the dating of the events in the grade is, however, more complex than it might appear. Indeed, the continental variants of the Maitre Ecossais (Paris, Berlin) place the action "at the time of the Crusades," while the Vray Maître et Ecossais places the discovery of the crypt immediately after the destruction of the first Temple by Nebuchadnezzar, "when the troops had withdrawn"—but let us stress that, in both cases, what is discovered, namely the word Jehova, differs from what we find in the oldest French rituals of the Royal Arch. This is a second remarkable point.

- In fact, the word Jehova was well known in France from 1744 in connection with the grade of Master and appeared as such on the tables of this grade. The same word was used in degree rituals—as Coustos clearly suggested in Lisbon in 1743 and as the Paris and Berlin rituals show at around the same time. In the same way, it is Jehova who is buried in the 'sacred vault' of the *Vray Master and Ecossais*—even if the candidate is taught that it is the word 'Gabalon' that is used to 'cover' it. However, Jehova does not appear as such in the oldest French rituals of the Royal Arch. On the other hand, it is strongly suggested that the "sacred word" revealed to the candidate (Jabulum), introduced by the password "je suis ce que je suis" (I am that I am), is very close to the Divine Name. The use of these words has persisted until this day.

. There is another detail that could be mentioned in passing: in these ancient rituals, the discovery of the Word is not linked to the detachment of a Bow Key: this latter theme is totally absent. In all the rituals of the period 1760-1765, we are told that Solomon had a subterranean passage dug, which was accessed by a 'trap door' fitted with an iron ring—it was by hooking his pickaxe to this ring that Gibillum discovered the subterranean passage. As for the revelation of the Word itself, it occurred because a "section of wall" had accidentally become detached, and the opening thus created allowed the sun's rays to illuminate the underground passage. The lifting of a simple stone slab still features in the ritual of the Royal Arch in Ireland:[15] this fact alone is probably not enough to found a theory, but is it an effect of chance or a clue?

The channel through which the Royal Arch was transmitted to France in the 1750s has yet to be identified. In any case, the characteristics just mentioned may also have been those of the earliest British rituals of the Royal Arch, at a time when they are not yet documented. This is a point that future research may be able to clarify.

The fact remains that these characteristics differ in many details from the oldest rituals available in English in the early 1780s (Sheffield, Dover), which reveal a much more elaborate stage of development and the use of other sources.

As for the French rituals of the Royal Arch, it was only towards the end of the 1760s, and until the end of the eighteenth century, that they gradually incorporated elements borrowed from other ranks that had appeared in France. While retaining the fundamental features of the original rank, they then moved further and further away from the models developed across the Channel until the beginning of the nineteenth century.

---

15 Pierre Mollier est le premier à avoir signalé ce point. *Cf. art. cit.*, p. 140.

Other Masonic Themes

Three themes are explored here, the Chevalier de l'Orient, the Rite of Adoption and Masonic Music. They are not explored in great detail, but they do deserve to be seen as part of the masonic panorama of the mid eighteenth century in Europe.

While time has not allowed the authors to explore every nook and cranny in detail it would be inappropriate not to mention other masonic themes. This is simply because they all occurred close together in time and are often linked, and they also add to the rich pattern of diversity. The one that has been almost completely forgotten is the role played by masonic song, and yet we found in the masonic records that everywhere that masonry went, that masonic songs followed. And they do of course provide a much clearer picture of the society of those times.

Chevalier de l'Orient & Knight of the Sword

Although the idea of an ancient relationship between chivalry and masonry is not absent from the historical account of the Constitutions of 1723,[1] it is Ramsay, as mentioned above, who is generally credited with having definitively established this theme in the Masonic world, through his *Discours* of 1736, which was to be widely disseminated in an amended and printed form. It is from this famous text that we learn, among other things, that the "Military and Religious Orders of Chivalry" borrowed "many solemn customs" from the "Ancient Fraternity" of Masons.

In Paris itself, this idea was initially considered by several Freemasons to be a worrying innovation. In March 1737, in response to the initiatives of Grand Master Charles Radcliffe, Earl of Derwenwater, who had introduced the use of swords in lodges, they pointed out that Freemasonry was in no way an Order of Chivalry!

The fact remains that as early as 1743 in Berlin, Germany, as we have also seen, a "Knight of Saint Andrew" rank was awarded and, during the reception ceremony for this rank, the candidate's shoulders were dubbed with the blade of a sword, in a chivalric manner![2]

---

1 *The Constitutions of the Free-Masons*, 1723, pp. 45-46. Passage repris en France dans La Tierce, *Histoire, Obligations et Statuts de la Très Vénérable Confraternité des Francs-Maçons*, 1742, pp. 229-230. Selon ses propres dires, La Tierce aurait effectué la traduction dès 1733 et il est probable qu'elle ait circulé dans les milieux maçonniques parisiens avant sa publication.

2 BnF, collection Joly de Fleury, vol. 184, f° p. 138.

In France, in Paris to be precise, in 1748 at the latest, and probably for some time previously, the grade of Chevalier d'Orient finally appeared, which was to remain, for at least a decade, the supreme grade of Freemasonry in France only competing with a few others.[3]

The ritual of the grade, in one of its oldest forms,[4] essentially consists of the candidate, named Zorobabel, crossing a bridge representing "the passage of the Euphrates which separated Syria from Judea." The grade comprises two scenes: the first is located in Babylon, at the Court of King Cyrus; the second in Jerusalem, on the "ruins of the ancient temple."

The manuscript begins with a "Précis du grade" that perfectly summarises the theme and the legend. We learn that following a dream, Cyrus, King of Persia, decided to set free the Jews who had been held captive in Babylon since the ruin of the first temple.

One of them, Zorobabel, came to ask him for permission to lead his brothers and Cyrus gave him the right to do so, arming him with a sword and a trowel. When the candidate has symbolically crossed the Euphrates on the bridge that separates Babylon from Jerusalem, he arrives at the site of the ancient Temple. The story then continues:

> Armed with his sword and shovel in hand, he cleared away the rubble at the entrance to the Temple, and began to uncover the Mosaic Pavement and other parts of the Old Temple.
>
> When he reached the altar, which had been overturned, he set about raising it; he was sent to fetch some water from the bottom of a well, and had it poured onto the altar in a vase in the middle. Resuming his first task as he advanced to the vault, he discovered the triangular gold plate on which was written the word G. precious token of Hiram's fidelity, and of the triple alliance of the three founders of the Royal Art that Solomon had had inlaid in a kind of altar raised in his memory near his tomb with the ring and the three keys.
>
> At this discovery the joy becomes general, and the Master (*of the lodge*) makes Zorobabel pronounce the word written on the golden blade, the sacred word which is the greatest of the names that the Patriarchs gave to the Supreme Being.

---

3   Notamment le Chevalier du Soleil, apparu vers 1750, qui exploitait des thématiques entièrement différentes.

4   Nous avons notamment retenu un manuscrit de la Bibliothèque municipale de Chambéry, en raison de sa parfaite rédaction et de sa datation certaine : certifié « conforme à l'original » par Jean-Baptiste Willermoz, maçon français de grand renom, à Lyon, le 5 juillet 1760.

In this ancient version of the grade, the theme of reconstruction - previously absent from Masonic degrees—is joined by that of an "altar" near a triangular golden plate on which a G-word has been engraved. However, the location of this altar is not clearly indicated, especially as it is said to have been erected "in memory" of Solomon and "near his tomb!"

The theme of the discovery of the Word is far from present in most of the other versions of the Knight of the East. But the fact that it appears in an early version shows the 'porosity' of all the elements revolving around what would later become the Royal Arch, which would reunite them all. In France, however, these themes were for a long time divided into separate and distinct grades.

It is, however, clearly demonstrated that from 1745 at the latest, in all probability, a French grade explicitly included the theme of the reconstruction of the Temple by Zorobabel. On the other hand, the theme of the Vault, i.e., a crypt established in the foundations of Solomon's Temple and containing essential secrets, although present in Ramsay's *Discours* some ten years earlier, was barely sketched out: as in the oldest ecossais grade, that of *Maitre Ecossois?*, there was only mention of the discovery of secrets—and in particular of the letter G—in the 'ruins' of the first Temple. However, the ritual described above, practised in the 1750s, indicated that the word had been discovered in a 'vault,' but without giving any further details.

I am not talking here about the first 'Ecossais' degree(s) in France, but about the Scots Master that started in London. But it was in another family of degrees that the essential details of this adventure, both legendary and initiatory, were revealed.

Disambiguation

The Chevalier de l'Orient as portrayed here is part of the French series of degrees associated with the 'return from Babylon' and the rebuilding of the temple. But even in France by 1763 in Les Plus Secretes Mysteres we can find among a 'rite of seven degrees' the Chevalier de l'Epee as the sixth in a series (and this was only one part of the series of three).

The current series has its place in the A&ASR series, but of course in Europe that develop differently. In Britain it perhaps took its place around the Royal Arch degree, in the end settling in between it and the Knights Templars degrees. By the early nineteenth century it had adopted a form of Knight of the Sword, Knight of the East and Knight of the East and West; and that is the form in which it is practiced today in both Ireland and in Scotland.

These degrees did fall into general disuse during the nineteenth century, but they maintained a following that refused to let them die. The result was that around 1923 they were brought alive again by the creation in Ireland of a Grand Council of Knight Masons after the degrees were liberated from the Knights Templars. In Scotland the degrees had been in storage with the Supreme Grand Chapter, and they were brought to life as a sub-organisation called 'Lodge & Council.'

However the journey taken by these ideas of the return to Jerusalem to rebuild the Temple of Solomon and the walls of Jerusalem remains, so far, without any clear idea of how it happened.

Rite of Adoption

The initiation of Elizabeth St Leger,[5] at around the age of 17, is well known but is probably as much initiation 'by accident' rather than 'by adoption.' Even so there is a hint that in the eighteenth century among the more prosperous part of society, where women were often educated, and given responsibility. Indeed they often managed large houses and their contents, no mean feat. Europe was an Enlightenment society in development.

The first thing to say is that anyone with a serious interest in the Masonry of Adoption needs a copy of Jan Snoek's *Initiating Women in Freemasonry*: The Adoption Rite.[6] He comments that he was able to answer many questions that could not before be answered just by the process of collecting as many adoption rituals as possible. This chapter simply serves to ensure that one of the threads of masonic development was the rite of adoption.

Mention has already been made elsewhere of the 'Loge de Juste' in La Haye in 1751. Snoek also names two lodges founded by Wilhelm Mathias Neergaard,[7] the first (from 3/10/1748 onwards) in Jena (Germany), the second (from 16/4/1750 onwards) in Copenhagen. This is interesting because it was the same Neergard who obtained a patent in 1749 for an Ecossois Lodge in Copenhagen from the Berlin Union Lodge. So Neergard just like Mitchell was not just interested in higher degrees but also those of Adoption.

Snoek also offers the thought that 'Adoption Lodges were in fact part of the Harodim tradition,' and we are not aware of any evidence of that. All we do know is that Mitchell came to London for a patent for the HRDM of Kilwinning to be a higher degree for the Loge de Juste. But by the time he returned to the Netherlands the lodge members had changed their mind and decided to use an Ecossais degree instead of the Harodim ones that Mitchell had crossed the

---

5   Edward Conder, The Hon. Miss St. Leger and Freemasonry, *AQC* vol.8, pp. 16-23.

6   Jan Snoek, *Initiating Women in Freemasonry*: *The Adoption Rite*, pub Brill 2012. All the quotes from Snoek and used with his express agreement and our thanks.

7   Snoek, *Initiating Women in Freemasonry*: *The Adoption Rite*, 2012, p. 3.

North Sea to obtain. But first it may be best to look at what was happening in France in 1744.

La Franc-Maconne & Le Parfait Macon – 1744

There were other exposures in 1744 but they were perhaps more masonically typical than these two. Indeed it is common in France to use the adjective 'atypique' to describe them; and perhaps it might be better to simply see them as representing another developing thread of freemasonry (in 1744 nothing was really typical anyway). Carr describes *La Franc-Maconne* as being 'highly artificial and contrived' and of the engravings that 'the intention was to mislead rather than to enlighten.'[8] When it comes to 'Le Parfait Macon' his words are no kinder, and no more illuminating. Typical are phrases like 'the whole piece is highly contrived,' or was 'deliberately designed to put people off the scent.' But 50 years after the publication of Early French Exposures there is perhaps new light to be shed.

It is worth looking at two images from each exposure and to note the startling similarity (the order in which these exposures were published is not known).

---

8   Carr in his book *Early French Masonic Exposures* only copies the text of *La Franc-Maconne* published 'A Bruxelles' in 1744; and he offers two images which he categorically states to be from this booklet. Sadly, whoever copied these images for Carr did not use the 1744 exposure (which has NO illustrations at all) and instead used the illustrations from the 1775 *L'adoption ou la Maconneries des Femmes*. The author uses the images anyway because they demonstrate a continuity of style over some 30 years (and are delightful pictures as well).

The similarities of these texts have generally been considered in much the same light as expressed by Carr—but others such as Bernard Dat, Andre Dore, Jean Marie Ragon and Kloss have noted the similarities between Le Parfait Macon and Adoption rituals.

Snoek offers us the alternative thought where the similarities between these exposures and Adoption rituals do in fact mark a formal start to an alternative

237

ritual theme. And he expresses it thus:

> One of the most brilliant articles about the history of freemason-
> ry remains, no doubt, Lionel Vibert's 'Prestonian Lecture' for the
> year 1925: "The Development of the Trigradal System," in which
> he develops his – until today unchallenged – theory about the
> transformation of the two degree system described in Anderson's
> *Constitutions* of 1723, into the three degree system, documented
> for the first time in Prichard's *Masonry Dissected* of 1730. His theo-
> ry is that in 1725 both the contents and the names of the two pre-
> vious degrees were redistributed over three degrees, such that the
> contents of the old 'Entered Apprentice' was divided between the
> new 'Entered Apprentice' and 'Fellow Craft' degrees, while the old
> 'Fellow Craft or Master Mason' was renamed into the new 'Master
> Mason' degree. When we look back at our previous section, it may
> seem at first glance that we are dealing with something similar: the
> materials of the first two degrees of the masonic Rite described in
> *Le Parfait Maçon* seem to have been redistributed over the three
> degrees of the Adoption Rite. There can indeed be little doubt that
> this is what happened, but there are also significant differences be-
> tween the two systems. Besides, the question arises as to why this
> action was taken in the first place.[9]

There seems no point in inventing another theory, but best simply to accept, as
it stands, the logic of Snoek. His description is below:

Le Parfait Maçon 1744

The first part of this booklet (pp. 3–37) tells the obligatory story
of how the author would have found the rituals disclosed here in
the inheritance of a deceased friend, in this case actually his older
brother. Then follow the rituals for four degrees: Apprentice (38–
57), Companion (57–72), Master (72–92), Table Lodge (93–97),
and Scots Mason (97–104), after which still follows a Conclusion
(104–108). The first remarkable thing about these rituals are the
themes of the degrees: in the first degree the Tracing Board shows
the story of the seduction of Eve by the snake (fig. 4); the second
degree mentions the stories about the Ark of Noah and the Tower
of Babel (fig. 5); the third degree is built up around the themes of
the Tabernacle and the Temple of Solomon, while the last degree
is an early form of the degree of the Knight of the Sword and of
the East ('*Chevalier de l'épée et de l'Orient*') which centres around

---

9   Snoek, *Initiating Women in Freemasonry: The Adoption Rite* (2012,) p. 78.

the rebuilding of the Temple under Zerubabel. The first degree has furthermore: the garter, the arch [*voute*] of iron and steel, and the 'seal of discretion' with the trowel on the mouth of the Candidate, while the second degree has the rite with the stone. In other words, while the third and fourth degree presented here correspond at least thematically with degrees practised in the male lodges, the first and second have a striking thematic relation to the Adoption Rite. Let us therefore have a closer look at these first two degrees. [10]

Snoek offers his proof that the Adoption ritual came from Le Parfait Macon by comparative quotes from the 1744 ritual and compares them with those of a later adoption ritual of 1770.[11] The samples given are only part of what Snoek presents, so one really needs to read the full text; but what is offered does demonstrate the point.

(p. 65)

Le Parfait Maçon 1744	Adoption Rite rituals
... he must remove the garter from his right knee ... that done, he puts a bandage over the Candidate's eyes ...	[In the second degree] A Brother ... blindfolds her, takes her left garter (which should be a blue ribbon which one gives the Candidate) ...

(p. 68)

Le Parfait Maçon 1744	Adoption Rite rituals
... under the penalty of being deemed infamous, & *being pierced by the avenging sword, and thrown into an abyss*, so that there will never be any mention of me in the fraternity of Masons.	... on the penalty of *being struck by the sword of the exterminating angel and of being swallowed up by the deepest abyss*; this in order to guarantee that a portion of the sacred fire which resides in the highest region of the sky may set fire to my soul and, cleansing it, enlighten me in the course of virtue.

---

10 Snoek, *Initiating Women in Freemasonry: The Adoption Rite* (2012), p. 63.

11 MS *Maçonerie des Dames ou Ordre d'Adoption. Pour le Frére d'Anieres Lieutenant d'Infanterie au Service de Brunswic 1770* (UGLE YFR.828.Mac). The translation of *Le Parfait Macon* is that of Harry Carr, and of the Brunswick ms by Snoek. (Snoek ref Ad1770).

(p. 68)

Le Parfait Maçon 1744	Adoption Rite rituals
As soon as the Candidate has repeated the obligation, the master has a *trough* brought to him in which he pretends to mix [mortar] with his trowel, which he passes lightly & with various movements over the mouth of the new initiate, [*nouveau reçu*], stopping a moment on his lips, saying to him: this is the seal of discretion that I apply to you.	[Second degree] He orders to bring him the hod ... and says to the Sister: The security of the [Lady] Masons still requires this precaution. Then he takes the trowel and passes it several times over her mouth, then halting it on her lips, saying to her: This is the seal of discretion which I apply to you.

(p. 69)

Le Parfait Maçon 1744	Adoption Rite rituals
The first sign is given by putting the second & third fingers of the left hand to the lips & placing the thumb under the chin: Any Free-Mason who sees this sign, must reply with another, by pinching the lobe of his right ear with the thumb & little finger of that hand.	[Second degree] The Sign is made by taking the right ear lobe between the thumb and the little finger of the right hand. The reply is to lay the second and third finger of the right hand on the mouth and the thumb on the chin.

It is perhaps both the difference of the ritual from that of the first three degrees and the similarity which supports his thesis soundly. Doubters probably need to read both version in the original side by side.

A final thought from Jan Snoek:

> In other words, I estimate that the Adoption Rite, though clearly rooted in the Rite described in *Le Parfait Maçon*, was, at least to some extent, a new creation. Even if in 1751 and 1767 (and in fact later), male Candidates were still initiated into it – no doubt a continuation of the older practice—the motive, which gave rise to its creation, was most likely the initiation of ladies from ca. 1744 onwards. One question which remains is: Which was the Rite, described in *Le Parfait Maçon*? The answer, I think, may be exposed in the first question of the catechism of its third degree:
>
> Q. Are you a master Mason?
>
> A. My name is *Harodim*.[12]

---

12 Snoek, *Initiating Women in Freemasonry: The Adoption Rite* (2012), p. 86.

The authors of the book view also use the same word *Harodim*, but sets the place more likely to be in the County of Durham, in the North-East of England, and in the early 1730s. But perhaps the embers which ignited all the other degrees lay in the descriptions of the distant past by Josephus, or more recently in 1736 inside BookM.

> 2. The Difference betwixt the Book of *Kings* and the Book of *Chronicles* concerning the Princes or Master Masons conducting the Works of the holy Temple according to *Solomon's* Directions, is thus reconciled by our learned Brother Dr. *Anderson*. In *1Kings v.16.* they are call'd *Harodim,* Rulers, or Provosts assisting King *Solomon,* who were set over the Work, and their Number is only 3,300. But, *2Chron.11.* 18. they are call'd *Menatzchim,* Overseers, and Comforters of the People in working, and in Number 3,600 because either 300 might be more curious Artists, and the Overseers of the said 3,300, or rather not so excellent, and only Deputy Masters, to supply their Places in case of Death or Absence, that so there might be always 3,300 acting Masters compleat; or else they might be the Overseers of the 70,000. *Ish Sabbal,* Men of Burden, or Labourers, who were not Masons, but serv'd the 80,000. *Ifh Chotzeb,* Men of Hewing, called also *Ghiblim,* Stonecutters and Sculpturers; also *Bonai,* Builders in Stone, Part of which belong'd to *Solomon,* and Part to *Hiram* King of Tyre, 1 Kings v. 18.[13]

The 'Rite' of Masonic Music

It is perhaps all too simple to rely upon Craft Ritual to explain how freemasonry developed during the 18th century, and it seemed appropriate to offer some comment on how these aspects developed; and in other chapters these things are mentioned. It is also true that Lodges met in taverns (or places with rooms for meetings and who provided food and drink and making merry with music, and what we see also reflects those social habits. And from 1734 in London and from there outwards and onwards travelled masonic books of songs.

The song have been little studied, with the exception of Malcolm Davies's *The Masonic Muse,*[14] which is the key published work on the subject.

---

13 William Smith, *BookM: Or Masonry Triumphant* (1736), Newcastle upon Tyne.

14 Malcolm Davies, *The Masonic Muse: Songs, Music and Musicians Associated with Dutch Freemasonry 1730*-1806 (2005).

Making Merry with Music and Song

We can of course start with the songs that appeared in in Andersons Constitutions, of which the music of the Fellow Crafts Song was written by Lewis Mercy (a member of Lodge No. 98).

The first book of masonic songs was edited by William Smith and titled '*Songs of Masons: To which is added Prologues and Epilogues spoken in the Theatres in London, for the Entertainment of Free-Masons.*' This contained the songs out of Anderson's Constitutions plus, 14 other songs, three Epilogues and Prologues, and a list of (English) Lodges. There is however no music, but perhaps it was thought that most of the songs were known to enough members for them to be sung.

And these were reprinted in French in 1735 in La Haye by Vincent la Chapelle, while de la Tierce found the Andersonian English words rather clashed with the European style and he re-wrote the words which were published in 1742, and again in 1745, in Francfort sur Main.

In the earlier chapter on the Union French Lodge No.98 several of the members were professional musicians or simply wrote or published songs (among them Lewis Mercy, Thomas Lansa, Louis-Francois de la Tierce) and in the Coustos-Villeroy Lodge in Paris, Jacques-Christophe Naudot was a founding member.

And it was Naudot who published who published *Chansons Notees* the first European in Paris in 1737—so soon after the foundation of the lodge in Paris, and his songs proved to be popular. Curiously the volume was republished in Berlin, without being dated, and under the (re)engraved title page the words 'chez A Fromery Berlin.'

So curiously, we find a Bro A Fromery who was a founder of the Union Ecossois Lodge in Berlin, and we know that this lodge worked closely with Drie Welt Kugeln lodge that was founded in 1737. Were these two 'Fromerys' one and the same? Probably—the picture on page 4 of the songbook which shows three globes proves they were one and the same. But it also demonstrated the point that all the key members of these early lodges in Europe were in correspondence with each other.

1749 Thomas Lansa and Song Management

Il est certainqu'il s'est trouve de tout tems des Francs Macons dispersez sur la
surface de la Terre;. rnais il eft egalement certain, que depuis
quelques Siecles on a point vu de Loges etablies dans .
les Pais Etrangers qu'aprez l'annee 1730. Depuis.
ce tems, certains Freres se sont hazardes d'en introduire.
en France, en Allemagne, & en Hollande,
ou ils ont affez bien reussi pour quelque tems ;
d'autres, qui ont voulu les etablir en Espagne, en,
Italie, & en Portugal, n'y ont pas trouves leur,
compte, & ont eu lieu de se repentir de l'enterprife.
Tous ces Freres sont sortit de Londres, & j'ai eu le
plaifir de les connoitre assez particulierement; je me
flatte rneme qu'ils ne trouveront pas mauvais que je
dise qu'aucuns d'eux n'etoient verses dans l' Art
de la Mufiqµe; & d'ailleurs les Chansons n'etant·
alors point encore gravees, ils furent contraint de les
introduire en les chantant eux-meme, & selon toute
apparence, d'une maniere que personne ne pouvoit
y prendre beaucoup de gout ; cela fit que chaque:
petit Musicien nouvellement initie.dans nos Mysteres,
a voulu donner un air de sa facon, sans s'embarrasser

(ou plutot sans savoir) que les Freres Etrangers qui
visitent les Loges ne doivent point trouver de nouveates
dans les. Chansons Originaires, non plus que
dans les Points principaux qui regardent notre Art
Divin. . Enfin,ces bons Freres n'ayant point eu
assez de talent pour travailler sur la Melodie primitive (qu'ils ne trouvoicnt pas
a leur gout) se font
avises de changer le tout. D'autres, un peu plus referves,
se sont contentes, pour leur commodite, de
changer seulement les nottes qui leur causoient de

la difficulte, ou qui ne convenoient point a leur
Chant; de la vint que tous les Livres de Chansons
Maconniques qui ont paru jusqu'a present ne s'accordent
point. Cette difference & ces changemens .
dans les Loges Francaises etant entierement contraires
aux Maximes, & reglemens des Loges Angloises,
d'ou nous tirons notre Origine, paroissent ici
fort ridicules, d'autant plus qu'Il n'y a pas une seule
notte de difference dans toutes les Loges qui se
trouvent aujourd'hui dans les trois Royaumes, ni
dans celles des Colonies de l' Amerique appartenantes a la Grande Bretagne,
dont le nombre est au moins dix fois plus grand que celui de toutes les
Loges qui se trouvent aujourd'hui dans l'Europe. Il est vrai que nos Choeurs,
ainsi que nos
Chansons, se chantoient autrefois a l'unison, & la
Loge ne repondoit que tres confusement a tout;
Ainsi, pour eviter cette confusion, on a juge qu'il
etoit mieux qu'un seul Frere chanta les Chanfons,
& que la Loge repondit en Choeur. Il ne s'agis- ·
foit done, pour rendre ces Choeurs plus agreables
que d'une seconde partie, qui foit en meme tem;
harmonieuse; facile, · & a la portee de tous les
Freres, & cela sans deranger la premiere Melodie.
Ceux qui ont le plaisir de connoitre le Frere. qui a
bien voulu preter sa main a les accommoder, favent
(comme toute l'Europe fait) qu'au lieu d'une seconde
partie sur le Chant primitif, il en auroit pu compofer
egalement (& peut-etre mieux que personne)
une demi douzaine ; mais ou se trouveront les Loges
pour les chanter ? Il est meme a craindre (quoiue
j'espere le contraire, que quelques-uns des Freres
ne voudront peut-etre pas se donner la peine d'apprendre
l'une ou l'autre Partie de ces Choeurs, tels
faciles qu'ils foient a prefent; c'efi cependant une
chose tres essentielle pour accomplir le divertissement
d'une Loge ; enfin il est desirable d'avoir toujours
un ou deux Freres qui foient Musiciens, ou qui entendent la Musique, tant
pour bien faire chanter les
Chansons que pour instruire les Freres qui ont l'inclination.
d'apprendre· l'une ou l'autre Partie des
Choeurs. Mais il efi ban d'avertir ceux qui a l'avenir

auront la demangeaison de travailler sur les Chanfons
Qriginaires, qu'ils ne sont point en droit de-changer
une feule notte de la premiere Partie, d'ailleurs s'ils
pretendent avoir plus de talent que celui qui a compose ces Secondes, le succes
en doit etre le temoignage.

On doit obferver que pendant la Loge ouverte, on.
ne doit point chanter de Chanfons Bachiques, ou autres;
& l'on ne doit point la fermer avant d'avoir
chante.la Chanson de. l'Apprentif. .

Aux Freres Lecteurs.-

But it is also certain that one can in all times find Free masons have
been dispersed across the surface of the Earth; but it is equally certain, that for some centuries no Lodges have been established until
after the year 1730. Since those times, certain Freres have taken the
risk and introduced them in France, Germany, & Holland, where
they have been well received for some time; others, who wanted
to establish lodges in Spain, in Italy, & in Portugal, have not found
their place, & have had reason to repent of the enterprise. All these
brothers came from London, and I have had the pleasure of knowing them particularly well; I even flatter myself that they will not
think it a bad thing if I say that none of them were versed in the
Art of the Music; & moreover the songs were not yet taken seriously, they were obliged to introduce them by singing themselves,
& according to all appearance, in such a way that no one could take
their flavour; this meant that each small Musician newly initiated
into our mysteries wanted to play an air of his style, without embarrassing himself (or rather without knowing) that the Foreign
Brothers who visited these Lodges should not find anything new in
the Chansons Originaires, no more than the main points concerning our Divine Art.

Finally, these good Brothers, not having had enough talent to work
on the original melody (which they found not to their taste), decided to change everything (which they did not find to their taste)
they decided to change the whole thing.

Others, a little more reserved, are content, for their own convenience, to change the notations which caused them difficulty, or
where did not suit their Song; hence all the Books of Masonic

Songs which have appeared until now do not agree.

This difference & these changes in the French Lodges being entirely contrary to the Maxims, & rules of the Anglo-French Lodges, from which we derive our Origin, appear here to be very ridiculous, the more so as there is not a single note of difference in all the Lodges now to be found today in the three Kingdoms, nor in those of the American Colonies belonging to Great Britain, the number of which is at least ten times greater than that of all the Lodges now to be found in Europe. It is true that our Chorus, as well as our Chants, were formerly sung in unison, & the Lodge only responded very confusingly to everything;

Therefore, to avoid this confusion, it was thought better for a brother to sing the songs, and for the Lodge to respond in chorus. To make these chorus's more agreeable, therefore, all that was needed was a second part that was at the same time harmonious, easy, and within the reach of all the brothers, without disturbing the first melody. Those who have the pleasure of knowing the brother, who has kindly lent his hand to accommodate them, know (as all Europe does) that instead of a second part on the primitive Song, he could have composed equally (and perhaps better than anyone) half a dozen; but where will the Lodges be to sing them? It is even to be feared (although I hope the opposite), that some of the Brothers will perhaps not want to take the trouble to learn one or other part of these Choruses, those easier ones as they prefer; it is however a very essential thing to accomplish the entertainment of a Lodge; finally it is desirable to always have one or two Brethren who are Musicians, or who hear Music, both to make the Chansons sing well and to instruct the Brethren who have the inclination to learn one or other Part of the Choirs. But it is good to warn those who in the future will have the desire to work on the Chansons Originaire, that they are not entitled to change a single note of the first Part, moreover if they claim to have more talent than the one who composed these Seconds, their success must be proof of this.

It must be observed that while the Lodge is open, no Bachic or other Songs must be sung; and it must not be closed until the Apprentice's Song has been sung.

TO THE VERY VENERABLE
Le Frere SCHOMBERG Master
ET LE
Brother KENNEDY I^{mier} Warden
DE LA
LOGE de ROTTERDAM;
Tres Venerables Freres,

I have deemed it impossible to present this second Edition des Chansons Originaires de la Venerable Societe des FRANCS MACONS, there's no one more worthy than you. I dare say, however, that it could be dedicated to a King, all the more so as it will be very difficult (unless one wishes to depart entirely from the Original & Primitive Chansons Originaires) to invent a work more suitable & easier for the entertainment of a Lodge than that which I have the honour of presenting to you. However, there is no doubt that it is possible to compose thousands of Chants on Masonry, but at the same time it cannot be denied that they become useless and superfluous, since the time of a single open Lodge is not sufficient to sing all those which are original and necessary to the Fraternity: moreover, it may be said with justice that our Chorus's [sic](which have been revised & corrected by the famous Brother, whose Name begins with the Letter G) leave nothing to be desired to form a most agreeable & harmonious Concert, provided that each Brother is willing to take the trouble to learn one of the two Parts. With the same Help of Music, I have added to this Edition an Air & a Chorus on the 'Apologie du Frere *Procope.*' I have changed the first Chorus (Buvons) to make it easier for the Lodge, & I have added a Chorus to the Air (Give us your vote). The whole thing did not go unapplauded among the intelligent Brothers here; but as only a very small part of their praise goes to me, I shall at least have the whole of it, for the choice I have made, (& which cannot fail to meet with a general approbation) to dedicate this Work to two Brothers, who, not only are at the head, but who make the most beautiful Ornamentation of a Lodge at least equal to all the most Illustrious, and the most Brilliant, which are to be found today in Foreign Countries.

Please accept this small tribute of my Fraternal & Masonic Affection, & believe that that no one can do this with more confidence & attachment than I do.

Tres Venerables FRERES,
Votre tres humble, & tres obeissant Serviteur,
le Frere Lansa.

a Londres, ce 1 Aoust, 1749.

The Ecossois Lodge Union at Berlin (1742-1749) and the sources of Maître Ecossois in France & Germany

On 29th November 1742, an 'ecossois' lodge, under the name L'Union, was created in Berlin. It had close relations with the Drei Welt Kugeln Lodge (formed in 1740 as the Kings Lodge). But freemasonry was still new in Germany, a lodge had been formed in Hamburg only in 1737, and then in Brunswick in 1739, Berlin in 1740 and then onwards to the Three White Eagles in Dresden, the Sun in Bayreuth and then to Leipzig, Altenburg, Brunswick, Hannover, Meinlingen, Frankfurt, Breslau, and Vienna. There were some lodges with English warrants after the mid 1740s, but quickly German freemasonry self-developed in a German style.

The whole issue of how the higher degrees developed in Europe is a complex one, and to better comprehend events in Germany there is nothing better than to quote from Eugen Lennhoff, because he sets the scene perfectly in both Germany and France at the time:

> The simple form of the English Lodges had undergone considerable change. The new ideas in England manifested itself in a ponderous, somewhat patriarchal, atmosphere, but in France it appeared in a scintillating and ever changing setting. Whereas in England the evening in the Lodge stood for personal meditation and sanctuary from the outsider world, in addition to the practice of friendly ceremony, The French Lodges were strongly affected by the yearnings and dissatisfactions of everyday life. The wider front of the attacks, the romance of the Knights, the mysticism which was again enjoying a new vogue, the maelstrom of philosophical ideas, the grudges and the fermenting influences of politics, all cast their disturbing and variegated reflections into the masonic Temples.

> Therefore, when Freemasonry made its entry into Germany it has already assimilated fragments from both these tendencies. Consequently, it could never be said that the development was of a uniform nature, especially as Freemasonry in Germany, more than anywhere else, was the subject of rumination., speculation, and investigation. First of all, this had adverse effects. Anything new was eagerly welcomed, however much it varied from the fundamental idea. But subsequently reaction set in, and whereas French

Freemasons were only the exponents of their philosophers, the German thinkers developed their own masonic philosophy.[1]

Two major sources provide information on the activities and ritual practices of the Union Scottish Lodge in Berlin:

- Firstly, a register of "the Most Respectable Society of Scottish Masters of the Most Venerable and Most Respectable Lodge of the Union," written in French and unearthed in 2002 in the archives returned from Russia and now housed at the Grand Orient de France in Paris.

- A German-language ritual (but presumably translated from a French original) dated October 1747, once belonging to the Berlin Union.[2]

Until 2002 any history of German freemasonry would hardly even have mentioned the 'Maitre Ecossois,' and indeed Lennhoff starts his higher degrees with the Strict Observance and then goes on to the Illuminati.

The seven founders held their first meeting on 30 November 1742.

---

1   Eugen Lennhoff, *The Freemasons* (Lewis, London) 1934, 1978, p. 89.

2   Actuellement conservé dans le fonds Kloss, à La Haye, Grand Orient des Pays-Bas. *Cf.* P. Noël, « Le plus ancien rituel connu de Maître Ecossais ? Le rituel de la loge écossaise de l'Union dans les années 1740, » *Renaissance Traditionnelle* n °170-171, mars-juin 2013, pp. 75-94.

But how did this Ecossois degree arrive in Germany?

It was only in 2000 that Russia returned part of the archives which had been looted by the Nazis during the occupation of France during World War II, and these French language document travelled to the Grand Orient de France.[3] One key document was a 150 page volume of a Lodge of Maitres Ecossois working in Berlin between 1742 and 1749. This Lodge was founded by an Italian Brother Jacob Fabris. Fabris, who was a self-declared member of Union French Lodge, is presumed to have received the Scot's Masters in London and took it to Berlin where he founded the Scot's Masters Lodge L'Union on St Andrews Day 1742.

> Fabris was an artist specialising in buildings and ruins in the landscape and an expert in perspective, and his paintings sell at auctions today at decent prices. His career took him across Europe and a summary of his life's travels is worth repeating. More important at the time, but more ephemeral, was probably his skills in scenery painting in theatres and opera houses. Information is ephemeral but it does illustrate that his moves around Europe were related to employment offered by the higher levels of society.
>
> Karlsruhe 1719-1721, Court Painter to the Margrave of Baden-Durlach in Karlsruhe
>
> Hamburg 1724-1730, theatre painter at the Opernhaus in Hamburg and designed the sets for Handel's 'Giulio Cesare' performed at Hamburg in 1725
>
> London 1730-1736, collaborated with Handel
>
> Mannheim 1736-1741,
>
> Berlin 1741-1747, Theatre Painter to Frederich the Great in Berlin
>
> Copenhagen 1747-1761, Theatre Painter to Frederich V in Copenhagen.[4]
>
> It is interesting to note that he did not go directly from London to Berlin, but worked in Mannheim from 1736 to 1741. There he would have worked with the famous stage designer Antonio Galli da Bibiena.
>
> However, the ground plan of the garden of the summer palace in Schwetzingen (near Mannheim) shows quite clearly the central iconography of the Scottish Master's "painting!" When Duke Carl

---

3   It is understood that the home of this valuable document is a matter of discussion, and that is not part of this research.

4   Source: wikidata.org and his occupations discovered from many sources.

Theodor took over as ruler here in 1742 and had this garden designed, Fabris had already left for Berlin. But his predecessor, Carl Philip, could also have been a Freemason. It is not unlikely that Count Albrecht Wolfgang von Schaumburg-Lippe founded a lodge in Mannheim in 1727. For political reasons, Carl Philip banned Freemasonry in 1737, which would have made no sense if it had not existed on his territory. However, he had appointed Franz Seedorff SJ as Carl Theodor's guardian, and Seedorf was an active member of the Mannheim lodge until his death in 1758. This Mannheim lodge, Zur Eintracht, was reactivated in 1745, and in 1756 transformed into the St. Charles Scottish Lodge of the Union with a seal that clearly shows the two broken columns that are so characteristic of the Scottish Master degree.[5]

It is assumed that he was 'recu Maitre Ecossois' while working in London and in, or in association with members of the Union French Lodge No.98. Because there are no records we only have his word that he was a member of Union Lodge in London and his references in the minutes to written communication with a lodge in London, and there is also no evidence of exactly what ritual arrived in Berlin in 1742. Until we recently discovered that he had in fact been in Mannhein for five years it was an easy assumption that he simply moved from London to Berlin taking the then current ritual with him. However because he spent five years in Mannheim and during those years there had been other changes, such as Ramsay's Oration, which could possibly have resulted in changes in the original 1733–1736 (unknown) ritual used in London. Neither should one assume that the 1737 Kloss ritual was the one adopted by the Lodge in 1742. And there is evidence that there were changes between 1742 and 1747.

There is however clear evidence that Fabris was still in touch with the Union Lodge in London, confirmed in the minutes of the Berlin Lodge for December 1743. Such evidence strengthens the position that the ritual came from London:

> He [Fabris] then proposed that he should write to the Union Lodge
> in London concerning Brother Maurern's Lottery... (p. 29)

But that work should bring him to London at the right time and then he should arrive in Berlin in the year following the formation of the Drei Welt Kugeln, and then presumably to find other brothers keen to discover a new degree has to a serendipitous piece of good fortune.

---

5   Jan Snoek, pers comm 2023.

Was the Maitre Ecossois also practiced in other cities in Germany?

Just one year after the first meeting the minutes of 18 November 1743 records two interesting notes:

> Brother Secretary has been instructed to write to the Semische brothers in Leipzig and to Brother Perad, inviting them to the celebration of the feast of St Andrew, as well as to the brothers here in Berlin. (p. 41)

> Tres Digne Frere Fromery proposed to the Tres Sublime Loge, that he thought it fitting, that on the feast of St Andre, it should make a present to the brothers Kockhan, Chambeau and Millinet of a silver Medal, to each, that the Lodge of Absolom de Hamburgh has struck.[6] (p. 41)

Or even on 2 Mars 1744 the following:

> ... concerning brother Soumiac, who states he is a Maitre Ecossois, and who he says was received in Dresden. (p. 40)

The implication of these notes is that there were other Ecossois Lodges working in Germany by 1744. Because otherwise why would L'Union be inviting brothers in Leipzig to joint them for a St Andre celebration? And would the Loge Absolom in Hamburg be sending silver medals to three members of Loge l'Union in Berlin? And the Minutes show that Berlin had not granted any patents in that first year.

Perhaps one needs to consider the possibility that by 1744 the Maitre Ecossois degree was much more widely spread across Germany than just with one lodge in Berlin as the 'Mother Lodge.' While records of Ecossois lodge may be scarce this might be worth investigating. Nothing however can detract from the high social and political position of many of the members of Loge de l'Union.

Contact with 'Freres Maitre Ecossois' in France

The Minutes of 16 February 1745 demonstrate that there was contact with France, and also that the French Ecossois required proof by production of a certificate by the visiting brother.

> Brother D'Allencon, who is at present in Paris, has written a letter to our Lodge, in which he asks it to send him a certificate of his re-

---

6   Pappenheim names the source of these medal in *Kleine Gesichte der Freimaurerei in Hamburg (2023)*: 'These medals were produced in 1741, by the well-known medallist Magnus Gustav Arbien who produced the first German masonic medal in 1742. In July 1743, the lodge adopted the name Absalom [Father of Peace].'

ception as a Scottish Master in our Lodge, signed by all the officers and stamped with the Seal of the Lodge. (p. 60)

Traces of ritual in the Berlin L'Union record books

One thing that does deserve great respect is the minute book of the Secretary Frere Roblau because there are many gems inside. And strangely they do not seem to have been previously found and rejected, but they are displayed below to be enjoyed.

1. Le Chevalier de l'Ordre de St Andre – created 1743

Being an Ecossois Lodge seems to have been associated, maybe almost automatically with the patron Saint of Scotland, St. Andrew (St. Andre), but the appearance but the degree of Chevalier de St Andre seemed to have come from nowhere.

Among those who have commented upon it there seems to be a generally held opinion that the use of the word 'et' (and) between a candidate receiving the Maitre Ecossois and the Order of St Andrew and was simply a form of words that was spoken after the conferral of the Maitre degree. And yet the degree remained in the Strict Observance and then the Illuminati, so perhaps there was more than just saying the words. But it appears that the evidence to contradict that opinion was always in plain sight, but not seen by readers.

At the meeting held on 10th June 1743 there is an interesting entry in the minutes:

> Brother Funster presented to the T[res] V[enerable] Lodge a Model of the Order of St Andrew which each brother Master Ecossois (should) receive in our Lodge from now on, the brothers then expressed their approval.

And if we move on to the meeting of 30 November 1743,[7] we can read of the Past Masters all receiving the same Chevalier Order.

---

7   Berlin Minutes, p. 42. Minutes of the meeting held 30 Nov 1743.

The Tres Venerable Past Master Brother Fabris created the new Master in the Chair Brother Roman Chevalier of the Order Ecossois by 3 strokes of the sword on the back[8] with these words. I create and make you Chevalier of the Order Ecossais by these Three strokes of which the first is for the King the second for the Patron and the third stroke for the Lodge, then >>>>> for the Ecossais Order. The Tres Venerable having taken possesion of the Chair created Chevalier of the said Order

The Brothers Past Masters Fabris

> Lamprecht
>
> De Gerresheim
>
> Fromery
>
> Roblau

---

8 The records are not explicit as to whether one sword was used or two. Given the white saltire cross, and the two crossed columns one might have expected two swords to be used simultaneously, thus simulating the 'saltire.'

Funster

Perard

Dalenuro

Rollet

De Often

A de Beilfeld in the same forms and cermonies mentioned below, then a small spoken discourse concerning the words which are associated with the said order to which the brother Secretary answers with a second discourse, in which one can see Concerning this Orders noble progress and its sublimity.

And then at the meeting of 8 December 1743,[9] the first one after the Celebration of St Andrews day we find the wording which used thereafter.

> A recu... ... Maitre Ecossois com toutes les forms due et re-gular, **puis** les a cree Chevaliers de L'ordre de St Andre selon les Ceremonies usites le jour de notre fete de St Andre,... (p. 43)

> Was received... ... Maitre Ecossois in all due and regular forms, **then** created Chevaliers of the Order of St Andre according to the Ceremonies used on the day of our feast of St. Andre... (p. 43)

> [ed because the use of the word 'puis' is crucial the quote in original French and in Translation are both shown]

So there it seems we have the exact date, the name of the originator, the first time the degree was delivered and subsequent workings as well. The fact that Roblau describes this as first being the conferral of the Maitre Ecossois, and then uses the word 'puis' (then) before the words 'Chevalier de l'Ordre' indicates clearly that this is something separate. (That is, first you do one thing and then after it do something else.) And afterwards Roblau always uses the same terminology. The only vagueness is how Roblau described the event on the 30th November, but we probably just have to excuse that.

---

9   Berlin Union minutes, p. 43, December 1743.

Obligation d'un Maitre Ecossois – 17 September 1744[10]

The Very Worthy Brother Lamprecht, having drawn up an obligation in conforming with our most Illustrious Ecossois Society, and having admitted him. Le Very Venerable who asked if he wanted to pronounce it, and him submitting to it, brother Lamprecht made him repeat it word for word, which being done, he signed it. This form of obligation is worded as follows.

The Most Worthy Brother Lamprecht, having drawn up an obligation in accordance with our most Illustrious Scottish Society, and having let him in. The Tres Venerable, having asked if he wished to pronounce, and he having complied, brother Lamprecht had him repeat it word for word, which being done, he signed it. This form of obligation is governed by these terms.

> I solemnly swear in the presence of the Great Architect of the Universe and of this Just and Perfect Lodge of Scottish Masters, that I have not been made a Scottish Master, either in Berlin or in the States of the King. Nor by a Scottish Master of this Lodge in the manner I have spoken and declared to the Brother Overseer without any deviation or reservation of any form. Moreover, I swear never to receive a Scottish Master in any manner whatsoever nor to take part in any clandestine reception but to declare to this Lodge all that I can learn and will be able to learn of these unworthy receptions which expose us to the contempt of the Maitres Ecossois who are legitimately so, so help me God.
>
> Berlin 17 September 1744.

---

10   Berlin Union minutes, p. 54, 17 September 1744.

1747 Ritual of the Berlin Lodge (ex Kloss Collection)[11]

It is worth starting this section with the exact manner in which the degree of the Chevalier de St. Andre as conferred in 1747, because it had changed from the 1743 version by the addition of a fourth blow. Given the fact that this was a degree after the Third degree, then this is perhaps understandable.

> My Brother,
> I dub you as a Knight of our Worshipful Scottish Order of St. Andrew through
> the following four blows.
> You therefore receive the first blow for the Great Architect of the Universe.
>
> > the second for the Patron of the Order.
> > the third for the Grandmaster.
> > the fourth for the Order.[12]

A summary study of the ritual practised in this lodge around 1747—and therefore probably for the most part since it was founded—highlights the following points:

---

11   Klaus Bettag Paul Ferguson & Josef Wages, Scottish Master and Knight of St Andrew of the Scottish Lodge l'Union in Berlin, 7th October 1747. *Ritual, Secrecy and Civil Society* vol.5 no2 (2017). There is an inconsistency between the dates.

12   Klaus Bettag Paul Ferguson & Josef Wages, Scottish Master and Knight of St Andrew of the Scottish Lodge l'Union in Berlin, 7th October 1747. *Ritual, Secrecy and Civil Society* vol.5 no2 (2017). p. 15.

- The tableau is surrounded by four candlesticks;

- A basin, depicting the Brazen Sea—not shown on the tableau—is probably used;

- The candidate is admitted into the Holy of Holies;

- Having taken the obligation, he is made a "Chevalier Ecossois de l'Ordre de [Saint-]André";

- The words of the grade are J. (in the Discourse of the grade, which we shall see later, confirms that it is JEHOVA) and G. (which here means GABANON, as specified in the Instruction of the grade);

- The grip is at the elbow;

- The colour of the aprons is not explicitly specified, but the Scottish Order's register for the same lodge clearly stipulated the colour green, and the Kloss Fund ritual adds that the officers' cords must be green and that the board must be covered with the same colour.

These are "ritual markers" that we will find in various "Scottish" grades of the period. The incomplete document does not describe the reception ceremony in detail. Moreover, there are some significant modifications in detail between the ritual in the Kloss collection and the lodge register from the Russian archives. We will come back to these variances later. Nevertheless, the Berlin ritual informs us that the ceremony ends mainly with a speech, of which the following extract deserves our full attention (sadly we do not have an earlier 'Explanation'):

The 1747 Explanation

In the following centuries the Master Masons noticed that the word M... B...N... had simply been foisted on them due to the absence of the earlier word, and they made every imaginable effort and spared no expense or travels to discover this valuable treasure. And it happened at the time of the Holy Wars in Palestine that they were fortunate enough to find it. The Scottish Knights, who had joined forces with the Knights of St. John, worked together on the rebuilding of the Temple of Holiness in Jerusalem, and when they removed the foundations of the old Temple, in the holy place which was called the Holy of Holies, they found buried in the middle of it three cubic and three round stones, which were the true foundation-stones. The Knights, who were Masons, were beside themselves in the greatest delight when they noticed, under the last stone, the word J... or A...., which was the true Master's Word. They removed this stone with the greatest care, and when they returned to Scotland from the Holy Land they took it with them. Back in Scotland they used the material in the foundation of the Scottish Lodges which were dedicated to St. Andrew, whose feast-day we are accustomed to celebrating every year on 30th November. In the Holy of Holies of the Temple they also noticed three plates of fine gold laid one on top of the other. On the lowest of these plates was a large ... J... made of silver, which stood for Geometry or the Fifth Science. They also found four pieces of a bronze column one cubit in length, from which has been derived the gesture of grasping the elbow. The cord with which you were led in is the likeness of that cord which the murderers tied around the neck of Hiram and which they used to drag him out of the Temple after they had killed him.[13]

What is absolutely clear is that the ritual used by the Union Lodge was modified between being received and then a later version copied in 1747. The appearance of Scottish Knights at the times of the Crusades tells us that in Berlin they had adopted some key parts of the printed version of the 'Discours de Ramsay'!

Finally it is worth displaying the tableau, which is also in the register, and which is fascinating:

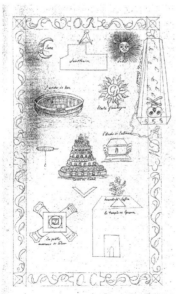

Tableau of Maitre Ecossois Berlin 1747

---

13   Klaus Bettag, Paul Ferguson & Josef Wäges. *Ritual, Secrecy, and Civil Society* vol.5 no.2 (2017), Scottish Master and Knight of St. Andrew of the Scottish Lodge l'Union in Berlin. p.15. (This section is a translation from the French by the authors of part of 190. E.27 in the Library of the Grand Orient of the Netherlands). It is reproduced here verbatim to avoid 'another translation.' I thank them for their work.

Tableau de la loge écossoise L'Union de Berlin (1747)

Without insisting for the moment on the details of this tableau, which will be compared later with that of the Maitre Parfait of Paris, we can provisionally distinguish two groups of symbols:

- A figure made up of squares and circles at the centre of which is the letter J; it is placed on what are describes as "the four pieces of column" arranged in the form of a St Andrew's cross. Nearby, we can see "a branch of cassia" and, further on, the coffin shown at the top margin of the tableau, and the top (the masonic East) a very simplistic architectural layout called "Sanctuary" (and in the East of course one cannot get any closer to God).

- The second, more central group includes an Ark of the Covenant, Noah's Ark and the Tower of Babel (but missing the Brazen Sea).

Un puzzle écossais – A Scottish puzzle.

This raises two questions:

1. Is this 1747 ritual a fairly faithful reflection of what had been practised in London for perhaps ten years? In other words, have we reached the Holy Grail of research into the Scottish first grades? The answer to that is categorically NOT. What arrived in Berlin in 1741 had the Ch de St Andre soon added and then by 1747 was now set in the days of Scottish Knights in the times of the Crusades.

2. What relationship can we establish between the Scottish Master of Berlin and the grades known in Paris at the same time—in the first place with the Perfect Master, known very early and then held in such high esteem in the French capital? Secondly, could this tell us something about the sources of the latter grade and the circumstances of its arrival in Paris?

Perhaps the nearest we can get to an answer to the first question is that it cannot be answered with any certainty. There is, however, another witness who reinforces our hypothesis of a very close relationship: John Coustos, at whose forced confession before the Inquisition in Lisbon, he revealed that " at the time of the destruction of the famous Temple of Solomon, a bronze tablet was found under the First Stone on which was engraved the following word, JEHOVAH, which means GOD." He added that he got this information from "some French and English Masters, although he did not know where they got this doctrine from."

The second question regarding interaction between Berlin and Paris there is currently no research published. The authors reflect that the colour of the Ecossias degree in Paris was always red, while that in Berlin is green.

A different approach allows us to answer our first question more fully and also to address the second. To do this, we need to turn to two other sources.

- The Copiales manuscripts, a series of encrypted texts whose decoding was published in 2011 and which provide us, in the Masonic section they contain, with additional information on the Scottish lodges in Germany at the time it was written, estimated between 1745 and 1751.[14]

- The ritual of Fredrik Horn, a Swedish Mason who was initiated, made a Companion and then raised to the rank of Master in Paris between 1743 and 1744, before returning to his country. A "Chosen and Scottish Master" ritual belonging to him is currently held by the library of the Swedish Masonic Order in Stockholm; it can reasonably be dated to 1744–1750.

We can see that all the sources used here are almost certainly dated between 1742 and 1750, a truly seminal period for the destiny of the Maître Ecossais on the Continent, starting with Germany and France, to which all the texts concerned are immediately linked. A number of observations can be drawn from their examination.

The Copiales manuscripts, apparently very well informed, indicate that the French rituals and the purely German rituals already differed in several respects, reflecting an early diversification of the original grade of Scotts Master (London) and its subsequent development(s).

Chapter 7 of Appendix A of the Copiales manuscripts, entitled "Histoire ancienne mais augmentée nouvelles observations dur le monde de la franc-maçonnerie," informs us that the "Maître Ecossais," was an "entirely new invention," was worked on by "the French lodge," "the other Scottish lodges in Germany" and "the lodges of Berlin and Brunswick." The document lists the similarities and differences between these early versions of the grade of Scottish Master.

Essentially:
- The version "from the Berlin and Brunswick lodges," described in more detail than in the ritual in the Kloss collection, is said to "conform to

---

14 Le texte allemand décrypté est disponible : http://stp.lingfil.uu.se/~bea/copiale/
Cf. C. Weiler, « Les manuscrits Copiales, une découverte singulière : présentation historique » et « Les manuscrits Copiales 1 et 2, traduction française, » *Renaissance Traditionnelle*, n°183, pp. 230-275.

general German practice," with a few rare variations. We learn that the candidate is put on a rope around his neck and walks around the lodge four times, then is purified "in the manner of the Levites by a few drops of water on his bare head," before being placed on his knees in the centre of the tableau, "on the ruins of the temple" (i.e., the four pieces of column arranged in a saltire and the stone bearing the letter J). Having taken the oath, he receives the words, signs and grips: it is specified that if the word is indeed "JEHOVA," "it is pronounced ADONAI out of respect for the divinity." Finally, it is confirmed that the apron has a green border. The only noticeable difference between Berlin and the "other German Scottish Lodges" is the presence of additional symbols on the board of the latter, in particular the Bronze Sea and the Tables of Moses.

·   On the other hand, what the Copiales manuscript calls "the French lodge" seemed to practise a grade substantially identical to that of the German rituals but differing from them on at least two points: "the lodge must be opened by three times twenty-seven strokes, and most of the operations are done three by three." —This is in contrast to the rule of four that prevails in the German forms of the grade.[15] In addition, the apron is edged in red. The other symbolic and ritual elements—"the ablutions of the Levites," the entry into the Holy of Holies, words, sign, and touching—remain unchanged. Finally, there is no mention of Saint Andrew in the rituals of the French lodge.

We can now compare the Berlin ritual with that of the Maître Parfait grade in Paris, examined elsewhere. The points in common between the two are very clear, but the shortcomings of the latter grade compared with its German cousin are also notable: no purification as for the Levites, no mention of Saint Andrew, no notion of chivalry for the candidate, no allusion to the discovery of the foundation stone in the ruins of the Temple of Jerusalem—as for the tableau, it does not contain the second group of symbols mentioned above, but only the first.

Finally, the grade of Maître Parfait known in Paris before 1745 appears to be a 'simplified' version of the one that prevailed in Berlin from 1742 to 1747. In particular, everything relating to the discovery of a secret in the foundations of the ancient Temple has disappeared, without the meaning and scope of the grade being really altered. The link between the two is obvious, but to this day no one can say under what circumstances the Parisian grade reached the capital: from Germany—in which case why would it have been 'simplified?'—Coustos and

---

15   Mais tout n'est pas si clair car le rituel de fonds Kloss prescrit bien d'ouvrir la loge écossaise de Berlin « par trois fois 27 coups »...

his companions might be good candidates, but nothing has yet been established.

We are therefore reduced to formulating a few provisional, more or less hypothetical conclusions:

1. It is very likely that the Scots Master grade, practised in London between 1733 and 1741, was passed on to Fabris in Germany. To date, this is the only form in which it is indirectly known to us.

2. This grade of Maître Ecossois in Germany, known from a ritual of 1747, was based on the discovery of the Name of God (JEHOVA), the "ancient Word of Master," engraved on a "foundation stone" of the Temple of Jerusalem and on the candidate's entry into the Holy of Holies; to this was added the notion of the candidate's consecration as a "Levite," hence the presence of the Brazen Sea and a ritual of "purification"—but not in all the versions known in Germany.

3. Once on the Continent, the original grade was rapidly modified and enriched in various ways, around a fundamental theme. Two components of the grade seem to have been dissociated fairly quickly: a) the central theme described in point 2, and b) the notion of "chivalry." The Parfait Macon, known in Paris before 1745, essentially comprises only the first part. The circumstances in which this separation was made, and the immediate sources of the Parisian grade (directly from England or through another channel) are not known to this day.

4. It should be noted that in the Berlin grade (1742–1747), in that of Fredrik Horn or in the Copiales manuscripts, a fortiori in the Paris Perfect Master (c. 1745), there is never any mention of a crypt or a discovery being made—this last theme, taken from Philostorgius, was nevertheless known in Paris as early as 1736, as shown by the Discours de Ramsay. It should be noted, however, that the theme of the reconstruction of the Temple was known in France at the same time and would be the subject of a grade considered to be major between 1745 and around 1760, that of Chevalier de l'Epée. We'll come back to this when we talk about the "other grades" known around 1745 and the circumstances surrounding the appearance of the Royal Arch in France.

Although "the French lodge," according to the Copiales manuscript, practised a "red Ecossais," the grades of this type known in France at the same time do not really correspond to the scheme of the Maitre Ecossois of Berlin—nor, consequently, to the probable initial content of the Scots Master of London. On the other hand, the various families of French Ecossais around 1745 hold many other surprises in store for us—beginning with the one in Paris.

Ecossois Warrants for Copenhagen

These do require some serious research because while two warrants came from the Berlin Union Lodge, while the third for an Ecossois Lodge is of unknown origin. It is just possible that such a warrant might have emanated from London, or even that Fabris has retained the original warrant for the Berlin Lodge and simple reused it again (such things have often been practiced in Freemasonry).

The first charter for an Ecossois Lodge in Copenhagen was a patent to Frere Dall dated October 1747

At the November 1746[16] meeting, the new Master was elected—the Tres Venerable Baron de Schwertz. The premier Surveillant Frere Pott declined to become Master (...qui a dabord declare a la loge, qu'il n'accepte pas La Chaire). And he remained as premier Surveillant. The words in the minutes are remarkably blunt, and clearly there were some problems within the lodge.

By the time of the 12th January (p. 74) meeting Baron de Schwertz had left for Silesia, and Passe Maitre Baron d'Often took his place 'ad interim.' For the April and July meetings Frere Pott took the chair 'ad interim.'

At the August meeting (p. 78), *Dall Gentilhomme Danois*, was proposed, balloted, and 'Recu le meme Jourdans toutes forms dues et (undecipherable) et Creer tout de suite Chevalier de l'Ordre de St Andre'. And the minutes record that he then requested a patent for Copenhagen and offering to pay 50 rC for it.

The patent was in Dall's name for an Ecossois lodge called '4 Colonnes' to meet in Copenhagen. And (for the record) he received his Ecossais degree at a meeting of the Lodge on 2nd August 1747 (p. 78) and received the patent itself on 5th October. It would appear that this would probably have been at an unrecorded meeting, or perhaps simply merely at a gathering at which some nominal act of handing over the patent took place.

---

16   Berlin Minutes, p. 74.

As far as the records of the General Old Scottish Lodge (the Ecossais Union Lodge) as recorded in the centenary proceedings they state (including a Danish Brother called von Dall, who immediately after his intitiation on 8th October 1747 received a patent for the founding of a Scottish Lodge in Copenhagen. Look above and it is clear that their date was incorrect on both accounts. The Protocols of the Hamburg Grand Lodge give the date as the 6th December and the membership list (p. 7) of the Abel Lodge in Oldenburg give the date as being 2nd October. Clearly some caution is needed regarding precise dates.[17]

The 'third' charter for an Ecossois Lodge in Copenhagen was a patent to Frere Neergard dated October 1749

The chronology of events relating to Neergard are interesting. At the meeting held on 12th January 1747 (p. 75), "Frere Roblau a propose le frere Neergard ... etre recu Maitre Ecossais." Neergard was present on that occasion, but did not appear in the lodge records again.

The patent was accorded to Fr Neergard under the name of "4 Etoiles Resplendantes" for Copenhagen but only issued on 11 January 1749 (p. 91).

Onnerfors provides an addition fascinating part of the picture when he writes:

> 'A prominent freemason Willhelm Mathias Neergard, formed irregular lodges working in Craft and higher degrees from 1750 onwards.'[18]

And he adds that Neergard also established the first Danish adoption lodge. So clearly by almost any criteria the situation in Denmark was in a state of flux.

The 'second' charter for an Ecossois Lodge in Copenhagen dated 30 November 1748

The travels of Fabris across Europe are well charted simply because he painted stage sets for the wealthy opera houses. When I discovered that he moved to

---

17 These dates are fully detailed in Bettag, Ferguson, and Wages.

18 Andreas Onnerfors, *Freemasonry in Denmark, in Western Esotericism in Scandinavia*, pp. 145-151 (2016).

Copenhagen in 1747, the first question was did he take his (beloved) Ecossois with him or not. The first clue came when there was an Ecossois Lodge founded in 1747, but the name of Fabris did not seem to be associated with it. The required evidence came in Jan Snoek's appendix to his book of German Rituals[19] and the other in a 2018 paper by Bettag, Ferguson, and Wages.[20]

There is an interesting statement by Snoek where he says:

> The Ecossaise Lodge *De la Gloire* was founded in Copenhagen on 30-11-1748 by the future Admiral Count Christian Conrad Danneskiold-Laurvig (1723–1783). He was also the Master of this lodge. Jacopo Fabris, founder of the Union Lodge in Berlin, was also a founding member (and treasurer). The MS Laurvig does not have the name "Saint Andrew of the Thistle" in the title of the ritual, but he does mention it, or "the Order of Saint Andrew or the Thistle," three times:

> "And so it is with the Scottish Order. At the time of the so-called Crusades, the Chevaliers de Saint-Andre du Chardon who were also Master Masons, would have travelled to Jerusalem to take part in its conquest, along with the Maltese Knights or the Knights of St John."

> The Chevaliers Écossais de l'Ordre d'André ou du *Chardon* then took what they had found to Scotland, sought out the most experienced and honest brethren among the large number of Masons, received them into the Order of Knights and at the same time taught them the secrets of the Maitres Ecossais; this is why the l'Ordre d'André ou du *Chardon* was constantly linked to the Maîtrise Écossaise.[21]

It answers the part of the question as to whether Fabris, who founded the Union Lodge in Berlin, also took it to Copenhagen. This would seem to indicate that he did, but the complication is that there is no mention of this Charter being granted in the minutes of the Berlin Union Lodge. This resulted in a search through the minutes of all those attending the meetings; and the result was that the last occasion the Fabris attend a Union Lodge meeting was on 16 September 1745.

---

19 Jan Snoek Appendix to his book in German, but in *Renaissance Traditionelle* No. 205, Jan-Jun 2023, pp. 4-33

20 Klaus Bettag, Paul Ferguson & Josef Wages, Scottish Master and Knight of St. Andrew of the Scottish Lodge 'Union in Berlin, 7th October 1747.

21 Snoek in German Rituals references this as le MS Laurvig: « Laurvig: Loge de Maîtres Écossais *De la gloire*, Copenhague 1748 » (GLD G III-1 a1-a11).

On the meeting of 12th July, the minutes show that Fromery demits from the post of Treasurer (and Geresheim was elected), and Fabris demits voluntarily from Senior Warden (and D'Often was elected). Then at the 6th September 1745 meeting the minutes state that Fromery 'demits voluntarily from the list of members having given commission to the tyler to notify the lodge.' This September meeting was the last one attended by Fabris.

Thus it is clear that Fabris was not involved in either of the patents later granted for Copenhagen. So when he arrived in Copenhagen he may have found that the existing Ecossais Lodge was somehow not 'regular in his eyes.' That might well have accounted for the decision to be associated with the Count Danneskiold-Laurvig and the Copenhagen Lodges with English warrants. Perhaps Fabris prefered to be within 'English' masonry without an Ecossais patent from Berlin, or with no patent, or a patent from elsewhere. Maybe some Danish researcher can provide the answer?

Suffice it to say that that there were considerable tensions between Denmark and Prussia as nations, and thus similar tensions between German and Danish Lodges. One might guess that Fabris supported the faction that were perhaps closest to the patrons who provided his employment.

It is worth noting that all patents are also recorded to the alphabetical section of the records and they are reproduced below (pp. 120-121).

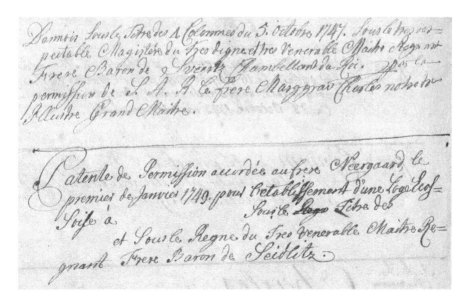

268

The Royal Arch in Ireland

An Introduction

Typically any book or article on the subject of the Royal Arch considers that the Royal Arch started at the same time, followed a similar evolution of structure and ritual, across the British Isles. This book will demonstrate that such an assumption is incorrect and that the paths followed in either Ireland, England, or Scotland are different both in time, content, and style.

What happens at the end of the 18th century is different in each of the nations of Britain and varies greatly, although the driving force was in each case a need of each Grand Lodge to endeavor to search for some way to being order into what had become, by the end of the century, a huge number and variety of degrees.

The original intention of the authors was simply just to follow the Royal Arch degrees, and only for the first fifty years of their existence. This proved to be a foolish objective and in the end in each nation the process of development is followed until it reaches a natural end. Thus largely the process might have been complete in the first couple of decades of the 19th century, but that did not happen. A separate Supreme Grand Chapter in England in 1817, in the same year as in Scotland (although it remained without a final resolution in Scotland until the 1860s). In Ireland an attempt to find order 1805 failed and the warfare that followed was not resolved for over two decades.

When the research started there was no intention at all to include the Knights Templar but events in Ireland were totally different and the Royal Arch was governed by the KT for around half a century.

Thus each British nation has its own chapter, with an additional one on the Arche Royale in France. This is particularly fascinating because there are no extant Royal Arch rituals in England before the very late 18th century, but they did exist in France from the 1760s.

On the Origins of the Royal Arch Legend

In the beginning was the Word ... The sources used for many of the huge number of degrees are generally thought to use the Old Testament legends as a primary source. But it seems appropriate to offer part of Book 7 Chapter 14 of the Ecclesiastical History of Philostorgius.[1]

---

1   E Walford (translator), The Ecclesiastical Histories of Sozomen and Philostorgius, London: 1855, https://archive.org/details/ecclesiasticalh00walfgoog p. 483.

CHAP. 14. When Julian bade the city of Jerusalem to be rebuilt in order to refute openly the predictions of our Lord, concerning it, he brought about exactly the opposite of what he intended. For his work was checked by many other prodigies from heaven; and especially, during the preparation of the foundations, one of the stones which was placed at the lowest part of the base, suddenly started from its place and opened the door of a certain cave hollowed out in the rock. Owing to its depth, it was difficult to see what was within this cave; so persons were appointed to investigate the matter, who, being anxious to find out the truth, let down one of their workmen by means of a rope. On being lowered down he found stagnant water reaching up to his knees; and, having gone round the place and felt the walls on every side, he found the cave to be a perfect square. Then, in his return, as he stood near about the middle, he struck his foot against a column which stood rising slightly above the water. As soon as he touched this pillar, he found lying upon it a book wrapped up in a very fine and thin linen cloth; and as soon as he had lifted it up just as he had found it, he gave a signal to his companions to draw him up again. As soon as he regained the light, he showed them the book, which struck them all with astonishment, especially because it appeared so new and fresh, considering the place where it had been found. This book, which appeared such a mighty prodigy in the eyes of both heathens and Jews, as soon as it was opened showed the following words in large letters: "In the beginning was the Word, and the Word was with God, and the Word was God."[2]

These are the translated words of Philostorgius' Ecclesiastical History written a few decades after the time of Julian the Apostate who was Emperor in Constantinople between 361–363 AD. Those words in a somewhat similar form also appear in Fleury's Ecclesiastical History, a twenty-volume work written between 1690–1720. Bernheim in his analysis of Ramsay's 1736 Oration concludes that he used Fleury's words rather than those of Philostorgius— with the key difference, and innovation. that the later Discours set the discovery to be made by Scottish Crusaders between 1099 and 1187; some 700 years later.

By comparison the masonic Royal Arch legend seems to have been unanimously dated to be connected with the rebuilding of the second Temple around 516 BC.

The structure of the Royal Arch Chapters

The Royal Arch almost certainly came out of the seething jungle of new degrees that surfaced in London in the 1730s, and was then visible when it was adopted in Ireland around 1744 while in England it only appeared in 1752 in the Antients and in 1766 with the Charter of Compact of 'Moderns Masons.' Then the story vanishes again only to appear after the Knights Templars arrive in Ireland in 1772; and both the Royal Arch and Knights Templars gather energy and life, first in both Ireland and later in Scotland.

Unfortunately a completely different saga of the Royal Arch in Ireland came from the pen of the renowned Irish masonic historian Philip Crossle in the form of 'The Irish Rite' published in the Transactions of the Manchester Association for Masonic Research and in the Transactions of the Lodge 200 the Irish Lodge of Research CC in 1929. Crossle's thoughts have beguiled Irish researchers ever since in a sadly unquestioning way. The Crossle 'Irish Rite' was challenged by John Heron Lepper in *AQC*, but alas his words failed to gain acceptance in Ireland. The matter is addressed in a subsequent chapter of the book.

However upon the earliest pieces of evidence there is almost complete agreement so we will requote them in full. All too often previous quotes have been only partial and thus one is not able to appreciate the full context; something we have corrected. And they all come from Ireland, and within a couple of years.

Faulkner's Dublin Journal, 14ᵗʰ January 1744

The celebrated Masonic historian and scholar, Bro. W.J. Chetwode Crawley discovered, and referred to, in Volume I of his work, *Caementaria Hibernica,* (published 1895), the earliest reference to the Royal Arch in Ireland which appeared in newspaper *Faulkner's Dublin Journal,* dated 14ᵗʰ January 1744. The Article in the Journal referred to the St. John's Day celebrations of 'Youghall' Lodge No. 21 on the 27th December, 1743, and described the public procession as follows:

> "St. John's Day, celebrated by the Lodge in Youghall, No. 21.
> - Firstly. The first Salutation on the Quay of Youghall, upon their coming out of their Lodge Chamber, was, the Ships firing their guns with their colours flying.
> - Secondly. The first appearance was, a Concert of Musick with two proper Centinels with their Swords drawn.
> - Thirdly. Two Apprentices, bare-headed, one with twenty-four Inch Gage, the other a Common Gavel.
> - Fourthly. The Royal Arch carried by two excellent Masons.
> - Fifthly. The Master with all his proper Instruments, his Rod gilt with Gold, his Deputy on his left with the Square and Compass.

- Sixthly. The two Wardens with their Truncheons gilt in like manner.
- Seventhly. The two Deacons with their Rods gilt after the same manner.
- Eightly. Two Excellent Masons, one bearing a Level, and the other a Plum Rule.
- Ninthly. Then appeared all the rest most gallantry dressed, following by Couples, each of them having a Square hanging about his Neck to a blue Ribbon. From the Quay, they took the whole length of the Town, the Streets being well lined, the Gentlemen and Ladies out of their Windows constantly saluting them, until they went to Church. The two Centinels stood at the Pues, holding the Doors open, until the Whole went in. And after Divine Service, came in the same Order, so their House of Entertainment, where, at the Approach of Evening, the Windows were illuminated with Candles, and the Street with Bonfires. They were greatly applauded, and allowed to be the finest and most magnificent Sight that ever was seen in this Country."

With their procession starting and finishing at 'the Quay of Youghall, upon their coming out of their Lodge Chamber,' their presence would be obvious to all the brothers arriving by sea. There is plenty of circumstantial evidence of transmission of degrees by sea, but sadly one never knows who the travellers were. It is quite probable that they took the opportunity of accosting Master Mariners as the boats docked and often of initiating (and very often passing and raising them the same evening) them with alacrity. This was common practice in many port towns and the Grand Lodges of England and Scotland worked hard to prevent this—for the lodge would charge its fee which went in the lodge box and sent off the papers to Grand Lodge with the required fee, and usually the certificate could be given to the mariner before the candidate's vessel left port with a full hold. The Grand Lodges only got one initial fee and never any annual renewals, and because it was the annual dues that financed the Grand Lodges they first restricted this practice and later stopped it.

The procession at Yougall is displayed in the advertisement as the Lodge proudly and publically 'strutting its stuff' in front of the town. One ought to take that into account when deciding its validity.

```
                        A
        S E R I O U S and I M P A R T I A L
    E N Q U I R Y
        Into the Caufe of the prefent Decay of
    F R E E - M A S O N R Y
                    I N   T H E
    Kingdom of I R E L A N D.
    Humbly Addrefs'd to all the B R E -
        T H R E N Accepted of before and
        fince the Conftitutions.
                To which are added,
    Such Inftructive Remarks as may be
        found ufeful to Revive the Honour of that A N-
        T I E N T  C R A F T.
    As likewife, by way of A P P E N D I X, will be inferted
        the O L D and N E W R E G U L A T I O N S of the London
        CONSTITUTIONS, by the Confent and Ap-
        probation of the GRAND-LODGE of Ireland,
        and Dedicated to the Right Worfhipful and Right
        Hon. the Lord Vifcount A L L E N, Grand-Mafter-
        of this Kingdom.
    The Whole adorned with a Curious Copper-Plate
        fuitable to the Order and Defign.
    _____
    By   Fifield Daffigny, M.D. Author of the Impartial
        Anfwer to the Enemies of F R E E-M A S O N S.
    _____
            D U B L I N :
    Printed by E D W A R D  B A T E  in George's-Lane next
            Dame-Street.   M,DCC,XLIV
```

Fifield Dassingny[2] *– Impartial Inquiry*

Little is known of Fifield d'Assigny[3] (1707–1745) except it seems that his grand-father was Pierre d'Assigny who was said to be a Walloon who was in London in 1636 and a convert to Protestantism. The letters after his name ASLLS indicate that he was probably an 'Apothecary Society Licentiate and Licentiate in Surgery.' He died in January 1745 and his funeral was attended by many brethren and six Sergeants of Foot. He wrote several masonic pamphlets and it is from his 1744 'A Serious and Impartial Enquiry into the Cause of the Present Decay of Freemasonry in the Kingdom of Ireland' that his comments on the Royal Arch are taken. Often just a snippet regarding the Royal Arch is quoted,

---

2   The entry in the records of the National Library of Ireland. *A serious and impartial enquiry into the cause of the present decay of Free-Masonry in the Kingdom of Ireland*, 1744; *An answer to the Pope's bull : with the character of a Free-Mason*, 1738 ; An impartial answer to the enemies of Free-Masonry, 1741 by Fifield D'Assigny. Together with *The general regulations of the free and accepted Masons in the Kingdom of Ireland*, 1744, and *A Pocket Companion for Free-Masons*, 1735 [by William Smith].

3   R E Parkinson, *An Answer to the Popes Bull 1738* and *An Impartial Answer to the Enemies of Freemasonry*, *AQC* vol.77 (1964), p. 148.

but d'Assigny does say more that is relevant, and we find it essential here to offer a more complete reprise.

REMARKS.

It is too well known that in this city lately hath appeared a number of mean and low spirited wretches, who, (if ever just) have turned rebels to our well formed Government, and artfully brought into their iniquitous net several unguarded men, who from me shall meet with pity instead of blame (because they knew not the truth) wherefore I shall beg leave to acquaint them, that the laws of our constitution are so agreeable to the d disposition of every good man, and so easily performed, that I dare say no one can have an excuse for not obeying ; but as these labourers work not to serve our worthy masters, they receive instead of the advantages accruing from our vineyard, the just reward of their actions, and in each honest breast are stigmatized with a name I here shall not mention.

These despicable traders or hucksters in pretended Masonry, every prudent

Brother ought carefully to avoid holding any converse with them;...[4]

And on the following page the paragraph usually quoted; sometime only partially, but here in full:

Now as the landmarks of the constitution of Free-Masonry are universally the same throughout all kingdoms, and are so well fixt that they will not admit of removal, how comes it to pass that some have been led away with ridiculous innovations, an example, of which, I shall prove by a certain propagator of a false system some few years ago in this city, who imposed upon several very worthy men under a pretence of being Master of the Royal Arch, which he asserted he had brought with him from the city of *York*; and that the beauties of the Craft did principally consist in the knowledge of this valuable piece of Masonry. However he carried on his scheme for several months, and many of the learned and wise were his followers, till at length his fallacious art was discovered by a Brother of probity and wisdom, who had some small space before attained that excellent part of Masonry in *London* and plainly proved that his doctrine was false; whereupon the Brethren justly despised him and ordered him to be excluded from all benefits of the Craft, and altho' some of the

---

4   WJ Hughan, in Memorials of the Masonic Union, "Dr Dassigny's Serious & Impartial Enquiry" pp.111-130(1913), p. 129.

fraternity have expressed an uneasiness at this matter being kept a secret from them (since they had already passed thro' the usual degrees of probation) I cannot help being of opinion that they have no right to any such benefit until they make a proper application, and are received with due formality, and as it is an organis'd body of men who have passed the chair, and given undeniable proofs of their skill in Architecture, it cannot be treated with too much reverence, and more especially since the characters of the present members of that particular Lodge are untainted, and their behaviour judicious and unexceptionable ; so that there cannot be the least hinge to hang a doubt on, but that they are most excellent Masons. (p. 127)

and in the subsequent, and almost never quoted, paragraph:

I cannot help informing the Brethren that there is lately arrived in this city a certain itinerant Mason, whose judgment (as he declares) is so far illumin'd, and whose optics are so strong that they can bear the view of the most lucid rays of the sun at noon day, and altho' we have contented ourselves with, three material steps to approach our Summum Bonum, the immortal God, yet he presumes to acquaint us that he can add three more, which when properly plac'd may advance us to the highest heavens. (p. 127)

The next two quotations relate only to the state of masonic standards and management, but they are fascinating because they do indicate a state of decay in Ireland in 1744. Curiously the Craft in England in the 1740s also seemed to be in a not dissimilar state of decay.

The by-laws and general regulations of the Lodges in this city are exceedingly well calculated for the good management of the Craft, but what avails the best contrived and most salutary laws if they are not put into form, and properly executed? To pass over indiscretions is in some measure granting a sanction or approbation of them, wherefore it highly concerns our worthy Masters to let no crime remain unremarked, but duly to admonish the offender, and if he repeats his transgression, to inflict such punishments as they and the Brethren shall judge necessary.

As my intention in taking notice of these transactions, is rather to reform than offend, ...(p. 128)

If our noble Grand Master and his deputy would make a general visitation throughout the Lodges of this city (as hath been a custom according to the constitutions at least once in the year) the Brethren would be more careful in preserving that due harmony, and just decorum, which ought to shine amongst them, for as they would not be sensible of the hour of their Lord's coming, they would always be upon the watch, and keep so strict a guard that irregularity or indiscretion would take no place amongst them, but on the contrary, the Craft would then appear in its pristine state, adorned with true and lasting glory, and its virtues conspicuously appear to all mankind. Having now described the cause of the present decay of Free-Masonry, together with some remarks, which I hope will be found useful to the Brethren shall give them the following friendly admonition, and then conclude. (p. 129)

D'Assigny complains of the 'hucksters in pretended Masonry (the Americans call them 'degree pedlars'), he tells us that the Royal Arch came from both York and London and that the London story was eventually preferred; that there were three more degrees to be had from 'an itinerant mason'; and that the governance of masonry in Dublin was poor.

And he was probably right that the Craft in Dublin was not being well governed, but then at the same time neither was it in London. We learn that brothers are always looking for another degree, but then that is as true today as it was in 1744. In particular he also says that the rules on masonry were not being enforced, that the writ of masonry did not run in the lodges, but one has to acknowledge that communication was not easy and was also expensive. Irish Lodges took the view that their warrant from the Grand Lodge allowed them to work all and any degrees they chose, and that remained unchanged right through the 18th century until 1805. At that point the Grand Lodge of Ireland unilaterally decided to create a Grand Chapter and a separate Grand Encampment; and a decade of revolt and schism ensued. It was the ability of Lodges to work any degree they chose and the proliferation of military lodges which was responsible firstly for enlivening the masonic scene by promoting the Royal Arch and Knights Templars—that is detailed in the following chapters of this book.

Vernon Lodge No. 123, Coleraine, Ulster

Vernon Lodge No. 123 was a preexisting lodge that obtained its warrant and was constituted on 8th May 1741. It is assumed that it did so in response to the instruction from the Grand Lodge of Ireland. These also appeared in Faulkner's Dublin Journal on 1st July 1740. While the lodge minutes of 16th April 1752 note that "At this Lodge Bro.r. Thos. Blair propos'd Samson Moore a Master & Royal Arch Mason to be admitted a member of our Lodge," but the real evidence is earlier and in solid silver.

The first Master of the Lodge was Bro Dominic Heyland and the minutes also record that he presented the jewels for the three senior officers of the lodge in 1747.[5] The front of the Senior Wardens jewel and the Mastrer's jewel all have Craft symbols, while the rear shows the Royal Arch symbols. There can be no doubt what degree the lodge was practicing!

There is a list in the lodge minutes, compiled in 1767, of those members who obtained the Royal Arch Degree and the dates of their exaltation to that Degree, the earliest being 11th March, 1745.

Laurence Dermott, Dublin 1746

Bernard E Jones on page 56 of his *Freemason's Book of the Royal Arch* says of Dermott 'He was born in Ireland in 1720, initiated in 1740 in Lodge No.20, Dublin, of which he became Master and Secretary, and came to England in 1747–1748' and 'he is thought to have become a Royal Arch Mason in his Irish Lodge in 1746.' And in the first Minute Book of the Antients,[6] in a roll of members that is the date given which confirms his being a Companion in 1746. While one cannot produce actual evidence the statements in the Minute Book seems to fit in with other statements. And because of Zerubbabel legend of England Royal Arch that it was what Dermott brought to London. If it had

---

5   irishfreemasonry.com/Vernon%20Lodge%20No%20123%20Coleraine.pdf

6   *Quatuor Coronati Antigrapha*, vol.11, p. 134. In a list complied later (after Dermott's death).

been otherwise traces of an alternative would have appeared somewhere in the history—they have not!

Ahiman Rezon, London 1756 and Dublin 1760 et seq.

We are all capable of seeing these works as merely books to refer to, and never to spare a thought for the writer. But Brother Dermott describes falling asleep at his desk and dreaming of being advised by an old man with a long white beard; and then of waking up. Such human touches are rare in serious writings—and we should all enjoy the moment of Laurence Dermott's dream of 1756.

> From whence he gave me to understand, that Such Histories were of no Use to the Society at present; and further added, that the Manner of constituting Lodges, the old and new Regulations, &c. were the only and most useful Things (concerning Free-Mafonry) that could be wrote: To which I beg'd to be informed, whether Songs were to be introduced: His Answer was * (* Eccles, xxxii. 1,2,3) : *If thou be made the Master, lift not thyself up ; but be among them as one of the rest: Take diligent Care for them, and so sit down. And when thou hast done all they Duty, sit down, that thou mayst be merry with them; and receive a Crown for thy good behaviour. Speak thou that art the elder, for it becometh thee; but with sound Judgement: And hinder not Music*
>
> While he was speaking these last Words, I was awaked by a young Puppy that (got into the Room while I slept, and, seizing my Papers, eat a great Part of them, and) was then (between my Legs) shaking and tearing the last Sheet of what I had wrote.
>
> I have not Words to express the Sorrow, Grief, Trouble, and Vexation I was in, upon feeing the Catastrophe of a Work which I expected would outlast the Teeth of Time.
>
> Like one distracted (as in Truth I was) I ran to the Owner of the Dog, and demanded immediate Satisfaction: He told me he would hang the Cur; but at the same Time he imagined I should be under more Obligation to him for so doing, than he was to me for what had happened.
>
> In short, I looked upon it as a bad Omen; and my late dream had made so great an Impression on my Mind, that Superstition got the better of me, and caused me to deviate from the general Custom of my worthy Predecessors; otherwise I would have published a History of Masonry: And as this is rather an accidental than a designed Fault,

I hope the Reader will look over it with a favourable Eye.[7]

There is yet another early reference to the Royal Arch, and is in the Ahiman Rezon of 1756. The famous quote (oft requoted) is that "the Royal Arch (which I firmly believe to be the Root, Heart, and Marrow of Free-Masonry)," but just underneath is another key quote which has been almost totally ignored, and which appears first in the London 1756 edition, then later in Dublin 1760 and in *all* later editions which states:

> This is the Case of all those who think themselves Royal Arch Masons, without passing the Chair in regular Form, according to the ancient Custom of the Craft: To this I will add the Opinion of our Worshipful Brother Doctor Fifield D'Affigny, printed in the Year 1744.

> "Some of the Fraternity (says he) have expressed an Uneasiness at this Matter being kept a Secret from them since they had already passed through the usual Degrees of Probation) I cannot help being of Opinion, that they have no Right to any such Benefit until they make a proper Application, and are received with due Formality: And as it is an Organized Body of Men who have passed the Chair, and given undeniable Proofs of their Skill in Architecture, it cannot be treated with too much Reverence; and more especially since the Characters of the present Members of that particular Lodge are untainted, and their Behaviour judicious and unexceptionable: So that there cannot be the least Hinge to hang a Doubt on, but that they are mot excellent Masons."[8]

Interesting that Dermott uses Dassigny to try and strengthen his case that the Royal Arch should only reached after having been through the chair. After all the It is perhaps significant that this was only TEN years after Dassigny wrote specifically that there was pressure from 'ordinary brothers' to gain the Royal Arch. But it is a significant statement of the growth of the Royal Arch, in both London and Dublin, and the pressure to join from ordinary brothers who were not yet 'passed the Chair' that the statement of Dassigny that only Past Masters were admitted, was the best evidence that Dermott could provide to try and reverse this trend. Although soon after that battle would be lost.

In the 'Editor to the Reader' section Dermott pleasingly recites his sources of reference for Ahiman Rezon and later how the task preyed on his mind by recounting a dream and how he awoke from it:

---

7   Laurence Dermott, Ahiman Rezon. 1756.

8   Laurence Dermott, Ahiman Rezon, London (1756), pp. 34-35.

My next Step was to furnish myself with a sufficient Quantity of Pens, Ink, and Paper: This being done, I immediately fancied myself an Historian, and intended to trace Masonry not only to *Adam*, in his sylvan Lodge in Paradise, but to give some Account of the Craft even before the Creation: And (as a Foundation) I placed the following Works round about me, so as to be convenient to have Recourse to them as Occasion should require, viz. Doctor *Anderson* and Mr. *Spratt* directly before me, Doctor *D'Assigny* and Mr. *Smith* on my Right-hand, Doctor *Desagulier* and Mr. *Pennell* on my Left-hand, and Mr. *Scott* and Mr. *Lyon* behind me: A Copy of (that often called) the Original Constitutions (said to be in the Possession of Mr. *John Clark*, in Paris), and another Copy of the same Magnitude handed about in *England*, together with the Pamphlet printed at *Frankfort* in Germany, I tied up in the *Public Advertiser* of Friday, October 19, 1753, and threw them under the Table.[9]

The list is fascinating because he refers both to Pennell's 1730 and Spratt's Constitutions 1751, which are respectively based on Andersons 1723 and 1738 Constitutions and Smith's 1735 and 1738, plus Scott's 1754 Pocket Companions. The German pamphlet is presumably Steinheill's 'Quintessence' of 1747. The references to Clark and to Lyon are yet to be resolved.

Floorcloth of General Blakeney's Regiment of Foot

---

9   Laurence Dermott, Ahiman Rezon, London (1756), p. vi.

This regiment was later more commonly known as the Iniskilling Fusiliers. They fought in Scotland at the Battle of Culloden (part of the Jacobite uprising of 1745) in 1746 and remained in Scotland for two years before being transferred to Belfast in 1748. They mostly stayed in Ulster until they were transferred abroad where they served until 1784 when the 205 warrant was transferred to the Royal Sussex Regiment.[10] The warrant was issued on 7 February 1749. Thus one could reasonably assume that the floorcloth was painted sometime between 1749 and the regiment going overseas in 1756.

The floorcloth gives a fascinating picture of both Craft and Royal Arch degrees and there can be no doubt at all of that from the dress and symbology. Sadly the date cannot be proved exact because it is the date the Lodge was consecrated.

Ahiman Rezon also became the standard constitution used in Ireland after the Spratt 1750 edition, and the same clause including the Dassigny quote, and accompanying text, appears in the following Irish editions, 1760 Dublin, 1764 Drogheda, 1782 Belfast, 1790 Dublin, and 1795 Belfast but was absent in the 1803 Belfast edition. The difference was that in Ireland the warrants given by Grand Lodge were taken by Lodges as permitting them to work any degree(s) they chose. This resulted in the eventual schism of 1805 and it took 20 years to resolve.

But the analysis of evidence makes it clear that that the degree of 'Passing the Chair' probably started in Dublin a few years after Dassigny and had rapidly spread widely—because it appeared in every Ahiman Rezon in both Ireland and London until around 1790. And by then Grand Bodies had virtually given up the insistence of reserving the Royal Arch for an 'elite.' Surprisingly these facts seem to have avoided the attention of researchers—but it has proved possible to shed more light on the 'Passing the Chair' degree being a precursor to the Royal Arch, and now being able to determine its limited life—from ca. 1750 to ca 1790 before fading rapidly away.

The five key Irish sources

Most of these Irish sources have been traditionally quoted in part, but rarely in full, so here we have given the fuller quotations, because it provides a broader perspective.

But when one reads the full entry in the newspaper describing the Youghal procession there is stronger evidence in this Irish sources than simply that a Royal Arch was paraded through the streets of Youghal. It is clearly a very formal

---

10 Keith Cochrane, Irish Masonic Records 4th Edition. Lodge Data extracted from Lodge 205 records. The whole digital package is available from the Library, Grand Lodge of Ireland, Molesworth St, Dublin.

procession, and done according to a set procedure and in public.

But Fifield Dassigny enlightens us considerably regarding masonic affairs in Dublin. True he offers the quote regarding the arrival of the Royal Arch in Dublin, first from York and then from London, but offering a different version. Almost as important he records the arrival of an 'itinerant Mason' who claimed to be able to offer a further three degrees to the existing three. Alas he gives no clue to the degrees, but it is an interesting comment upon a practice that was common in both 18th and 19th centuries, that of masons mingling and passing of degrees.

Finally and usefully he complains that the Grand Master and his deputy had not been taking their duties seriously by 'make a general visitation throughout the Lodges of this city (as hath been a custom according to the constitutions at least once in the year).' This is a fascinating comment because the exact same lack of attention was being exercised by the Grand Master in London, and the Craft suffering because of it (this is covered in detail elsewhere).

The last two quotes are supportive of a conclusion that the Royal Arch ritual worked in Ireland and then carried to England and practiced there by the Antients. The jewel dated 1747 gives visual, if not verbal, proof that the basic Royal Arch ceremony being worked in Ireland was the one brought over by Laurence Dermott in 1748. And indeed it would almost certainly have been the Zerubbabel tradition—for if not then there would have been arguments—but the records are totally silent upon that.

Josiah and the Grand Lodges of York and of Ireland

Ireland has always been unique in the Royal Arch in having *two* different Royal Arch legends, and especially so when in 1864 a committee sat in Dublin and determined that the only legend used would be that 'of the repair of the Temple by Josiah' rather than the 'rebuilding by Zerubbabel.' Dassigny tells us that even in 1744 there were two legends each of which had its own ritual, and that the first came from York and the second which supplanted the York form came from London.

But there is another 'traditional history,' an oration from York, and later printed in 1727, by Francis Drake the Junior Grand Warden of the Grand Lodge of York, and part of it is below:

> BUT I must not trespass too much on your Patience, and shall therefore, tho' unwillingly, pass over the Building of *Solomon's Temple*, a Building where God himself was the Architect, and which to all Masons is so very Particular, that 'tis almost unpardonable to neglect it.

BUT that with the Repairs of it by *Josiah*, rebuilding by *Zerubbabel* and *Herod*, to the final Destruction by *Titus Vespatian* together with the History of the *Grecian* and *Roman* Orders and

Architects, the *Gothick* Intrusion over all, and its late Resurection and present growing Greatness, may be Subjects sufficient for several Discourses; which, since I have ventur'd to break the Ice, I hope some abler Hand will carry on.[11]

Reading this one is obliged to consider the possibility that it was some 15 years after that it could well have been a Josiah legend that travelled from York to Dublin as a Royal Arch degree, and it also poses a nagging question that perhaps there was an alternative masonic tradition, an alternative social and religious ethos as well as a large physical distance between London and York. So perhaps there were alternative practices, in Durham before and after 1736, an extra part of traditional history in York in 1727, and by the late eighteenth century a huge predominance of Royal Arch being practiced in the counties of Yorkshire and Lancashire, both of which are distant from London.

We are not suggesting that York *was* the source of the 'Josiah Royal Arch Legend' as used in Ireland, but are merely pointing out that Drake in York was referring to the Second Temple as part of a 'Traditional History.' But *nowhere* else have we found Josiah mentioned masonically in relation to the temple at Jerusalem.

As a point of curiosity at Canterbury Cathedral there is a stained glass window which depicts Josiah holding up his 'laws.'

---

11 Francis Drake, "A Speech Deliver'd to the Worſhipful and Ancient Society of Free and Accepted Masons." St John's Day, December the 27th, 1726 and published in York 1727.

More Irish Chronology

1749 Among the warrants issued by the Grand Lodge of Ireland in the year 1749, were two to the city of Dublin, Nos. 190 and 198 both of which were soon to be known as "Royal Arch Lodge."[12] These two Lodges also had a significant Huguenot membership, and they will appear again later in the century promoting the Royal Arch degree.

1750 Exaltation of a future Grand Master in Lodge No.2 Dublin (the Earl of Lansborough GM in 1757).[13]

1752 This entry occurs in the Minute Book (No. 1) of Vernon Lodge No. 123,

Coleraine, County Derry, Ireland, and reads as follows:

> 1752) April 16th. At this Lodge Bro. Thos. Blair propos'd Samson Moore a Master & Royal Arch Mason to be admitted a member of our Lodge.

ca 1763 The symbolism of Sword and Trowel is undoubtedly ancient in the Craft, and these emblems are prominently displayed on the floor doth with which the brethren of Lodge 394, Lurgan, provided themselves shortly after the foundation of the Lodge in *1763*. (*Hist G L of I* vol.1, p.112.)

1764 1ˢᵗ September 1764 a certificate issued to a Bro Jean de Cluzeau and initially dated 15ᵗʰ March 1759 and attesting that he was a Master Mason which also had a later endorsement as follows:

"Attestons aussi qu'il a passe depuis Parle fameux Labarinte de l'Ecosisme: qu'il s'est desaltere a la fontaine de Maitre Elu et qu'il a vu de plus le grand Effroy des Cinq Epees ayant Combattu en Vray Chevallier de L'Orient, de La Loge francaise le 1 Septembre, 1764. De Court Secretaire de la Lodge Bleue de Dublin.[14]

There are other minor "references in Lodge minutes, but they add nothing new."

---

12 R E Wilkinson, *History of the Grand Lodge of Ireland*, vol 2., p. 322.

13 JH Lepper, "The Traditioners" in *AQC* 56, p. 163.

14 R E Parkinson, History of the Grand Lodge of Ireland, vol. 2 (1957), p. 324.

Passing the Chair Degree

The seminal work on this subject was done by Bro Bernard E Jones and published in AQC in 1958.[1] He treats it almost as a part of the Craft installation ceremonies, but he does also mention it in relation to the Royal Arch degrees. However he, and all other authors, fail to emphasise that it was the 'rule' that was applied in Ireland which required all aspirants for the Royal Arch to be 'Masters passed the Chair.' And more importantly, even in 1744 the Brethren's desire for the degree, and probably lodges and chapters to keep the fees paid by the candidates for the degree, that caused the Passing the Chair degree to arise. This chapter charts the beginning and end of this practice in the British Isles.

This is not a significant degree, but rather one of curiosity. During the research we chanced upon two pieces of information that gave a different shape to, and an understanding of this degree.

There seems to have been very little to it apart from giving the word and grip and allowing the recipient to sit briefly in the Masters Chair—and then become qualified to obtain the Royal Arch degree. But quite where or when this practice started was unclear.

Chronology is Crucial—An analysis of Eric Ward's Paper of 1975

The evidence in the early years of the Royal Arch is particularly interesting, and has been the subject of considerable debate among masonic scholars. It is perhaps worth examining one paper to serve as an example—and to demonstrate what this paper is aiming to avoid.

Sometimes the picture can get distorted by researchers who prefer another conclusion and one such case is that presented by Eric Ward publish his 1975 paper in AQC with the title "Dassigny, Youghal and All That."[2] In the opening section he writes "This paper is not intended to disparage Dassigny's undoubted qualities as a Mason, but since his name and that of the Lodge at Youghal have become inevitable tags on every occasion that the antiquity of the Royal Arch is mentioned, it seems timely that we should look at these sources in their proper perspective." He then proceeds to disparage each point in turn, uses some incorrect evidence, and failed to find all the evidence. One might also feel that he has absolutely no wish at all to credit Irish freemasons with having made

---

1   Bernard E Jones, Passing the Chair, *AQC* vol.70 (1958), pp. 33-53.

2   Eric Ward, 'Dassigny, Youghal and All That.' *AQC* vol.88 (1975), pp. 20-31.

any innovation into freemasonry. There is also the habit of English masonic researchers all believing that all the innovations in masonry occurred only in England. Ward's paper tends to adopt both those approaches.

It is well worth offering the chronological trail of evidence which runs as follows:

1. 1743. Youghal. Co. Cork. Faulkner's Journal (of Dublin) records that the masonic lodge paraded through the streets and that a Royal Arch was carried by two Excellent Masons.

2. 1744. Dassingy publishes his 'Serious and Impartial Enquiry...', and states that prior to writing his book, that is before 1744, a brother came from York with a new degree which was adopted in Dublin, and that later another brother came from London with a different version and that later the York version was discarded.

3. 1744. Dassigny also relates, for the very first time, the statement that the Royal Arch is "is an organised Body of Men who have passed the Chair."

4. Vernon Lodge No.123 (Coleraine, Co. Down) has a set of founders collar jewels inscribed with Dominic Hyland's name and on the rear is carved a vault and other working tools of the Royal Arch are also used. (Ward was unaware)

5. 1746. Laurence Dermott becomes Master of his Dublin Lodge. He later stated in the first Minute Book of the Antients that in 1746 he also became a Royal Arch mason (sadly we only have his later word for that) when he was Master of his lodge in Dublin.

6. ca. 1749. A painted floorcloth called the 'Eniskillen floorcloth' clearly demonstrated the presence of a Royal Arch degree. (not mentioned by Ward). The warrant was granted in 1749.[3] The regiment had been at the Battle of Culloden in the 1745 rebellion and moved to Ulster in 1748, remaining there till they were sent to America in 1756. So these images were probably painted between 1749 and 1756.

7. 1756. In the first edition of Ahiman Rezon where Dermott wrote that the Royal Arch was 'the root, heart and marrow of free masonry' further down the same paragraph he goes on to state that to be a genuine Royal Arch mason a Brother must be a 'Master passed the chair' and then proceeds to quote from Dassigny. (Ward also missed this).

8. Ward also states that the standard Irish Royal Arch legend used (at that time) was the Josiah alternative. It is believed that some lodges used it,

---

3   Keith Cochrane, Irish Masonic Records. Warrants 205. Available from the Library,, Grand Lodge of Ireland, Dublin.

but it did not become the only official ritual theme until the 1860s. (Ward just got this wrong).

But the alternative to consider probably should be that the Youghal Lodge presented a very professional listing of all the officers in the procession (they paraded in public so why risk saying something that did not happen), and that would surely have been written by a brother. Dr Fifield Dassigny also would have been taken to task if he made incorrect statements in his book which would have been read by his peers in Dublin. The Vernon lodge jewels with their engraved pictures on the officer's jewels give an image of a vault and tools that would be recognised today; we see no reason to doubt them.

Discovering that Dermott quotes Dassigny would indicate that he agreed with Dassigny's statement. And it also indicates that the requirement to be a Past Master was already a problem for the Antients a mere five years after the Grand Lodge was formed. Dermott wanted the Royal Arch to have a feeling of superiority above the Craft; and perhaps that made the Brethren desire it even more?

Ward tries to demolish each piece of evidence, and at the end is he left with nothing; even though the Royal Arch degree actually does appear and was worked in Ireland. The approach of these authors is to read widely and diligently, and then list the points of evidence and to make an assessment of them. In this case it seems to us that there is a clear series of events showing a widespread acceptance of the Royal Arch degree in Ireland.

Neither do we find any reason to doubt that the 'Passing the Chair' degree was the response of the Brethren because they were excluded from obtaining the Royal Arch degree for themselves.

Likewise there seems to be an expectation that only seeing something written in a lodge minute book is the only real proof; but the reality is that it does not prove exactly what was done on that day or what ritual was used. And actually, having a complete ritual ms in itself does not prove its words were the words used. Both are just small pieces of evidence which indicate the practice of those times.

It also reflects the mid eighteenth century practice of the members of any Craft lodge opening 'a Lodge' to work whatever degrees they chose. There was no requirement to explain anything to anyone. Indeed there were no bodies, nothing 'Grand' to report to—these were the days of the 'masonic wild west.' During the second half of the eighteenth century there was complete degree chaos; and Grand Lodges eventually determined to bring back order, and expel all other degrees to other places. This was resolved in Scotland between 1800 and 1817, in England from 1813 to 1830 and in Ireland from 1805 to circa 1835. Similar processes also took place in the United States.[4]

The situation in Ireland was that the Grand Lodge had even less control, and Lodges were adamant that their warrants allowed them to work any degrees they chose. That combined with the self creation of two Knights Templars bodies caused the Royal Arch and KT degrees to prosper, but the resulting crash of 1805 was all the greater because of that.

Dermott's Struggle to keep the Royal Arch 'Superior'

In Ireland the superiority of rank was clear, and we know that Dermott took the degree to England and that by 1756, a mere five years after the formation of the Antients Grand Lodge he was stating in the first edition of Ahiman Rezon that the Royal Arch was 'the root, heart and marrow of free-masonry.' So many have offered that quote but they failed to read to the end of the same paragraph, because Dermott makes it clear that the restriction of obtaining the Royal Arch is even by 1756 causing problems. Dermott's use of Dassigny's word is demonstrated below:

> This is the case of all those who think themselves Royal Arch Masons, without passing the chair in regular form, according to the ancient custom of the Craft.

> To this I will add the opinion of our worshipful brother, Doctor Fifield D'Assigney, printed in the year 1744:

> > "Some of the Fraternity, says he, have expressed an uneasiness at this matter being kept a secret from them (since they had already passed through the usual degrees of probation). I cannot help being of opinion, that they have no right to any such benefit until they make a proper application, and are received with due formality: and as it is an organized body of men who have passed the chair, and given undeniable proofs of their skill in architecture, it cannot be treated with too much reverence; and more especially since the characters of the present members of that particular Lodge are untainted, and their behaviour judicious and unexceptionable: so that there cannot be the least hinge to hang a doubt on, but that they are most excellent Masons."[5]

---

4   John Belton, Brother Just One More Degree. *Scottish Rite Journal* March/April 2013, pp. 7-9. This explains that Henry Fowle and William Smith Webb resolved the problem by creating in 1798 a General Grand Chapter Royal Arch Masons and later the Grand Encampment of Knights Templar of the USA.

5   Laurence Dermott, *Ahiman Rezon* London (1756 – the first edition!), pp. 48-49.

And that exact quote was used in every subsequent edition of Ahiman Rezon through to 1800, as well as the Irish editions of Ahiman Rezon. But that brings us back to some innate need or urge of human beings, including masons, to gain just another degree, another inner secret. So the brethren and the lodges found a way round the problem. They just created a simple degree in which a brother was placed in the chair for a minute or two after taking an obligation and learning the token and word—and he could then be given the Royal Arch degree. There would of course be a fee for that, and the money would go into the lodge's chest and nothing needed to be paid to a Grand Lodge.

The Moderns raise the stakes

The Grand Royal Arch Chapter of the Moderns has not been prospering for some decades and as part of their attempt to rekindle interest in 1782 they published a new set of Regulations informing the reader that these rules were "Done from our ancient Code, and now revived in our Grand and Royal Chapter, this 10th Day of My, A.L. 5786, A.D. 1782." The second clause sets out the requirements for joining and clause eleven the reduction of the fee for exaltation from five guineas to one.

> II. That to this exalted degree, none are to be admitted but men of the best character and Education: open, generous, liberal in sentiment, .and real Philanthropies; who have passed through the three probationary degrees of Craft Masonry; and have presided as Masters, and have been duly proposed and recommended by two or more Companions of the Chapter, balloted for, and approved of ; the recommendation to be (unless on particular occasions) at least one Chapter previous to the ballot: Each brother to be not less than twenty-three years of age at the time of initiation, except the son of a Companion of the Chapter, or that he has been two years of the Master's degree in the Craft; and then, under the above regulations, may be exalted at twenty-one; but none to be admitted if on the ballot there appears more than one negative.[6]

> XI. Although it is ordained by our Charter of Compact, that Ten Guineas shall be paid for every Constitution, and Five Guineas for every Exaltation fee; yet there existing in the Grand Chapter a power of dispensation, and it having been represented to us that the said sums of Ten and Five Guineas may restrain many Brethren of Merit and Character from entering into the Society ; which will counter-

---

6   *Abstract of Laws for the Society of Royal Arch Masons*, (Moderns) London 1786, pp. 14-15.

act those benevolent purposes intended by its institution, We have resolved, that for every Constitution, granted after the date hereof, until notice be given to the contrary, there shall be paid the sum of Three Guineas; and no Brother shall be exalted, in any Chapter constituted by us, for a less sum than One Guinea . . . .

And in truth the Grand Chapter (of Modern brothers) had decided to relax the rules, and to all practical intents and purposes removing any absolute requirement to be a Past Master by introducing alternative routes to become exalted. And had also felt the effect of the Antients and cut price for the same Exaltation to a MERE One Guinea.

The Antients response to the 'Moderns' Actions

In the 1800 edition of Ahiman Rezon the Antients Grand Lodge admit defeat because in their Grand Chapter they passed revised *Laws and Regulations for the Order of Royal Arch Masons* in 1794.[7] While this was the first published appearance of such a certificate as shown below; it does seem it was actually in earlier use. Such a certificate was issued on 11 February 1790 to Sir Watkin Lewes[8] and described him as a Geometrical Master Mason,

III. That no Brother fhall be admitted into the H. R. A. but he who has regularly and faithfully paffed through the three progreffive degrees, and has performed the duties in his Lodge to the fatisfaction of his Brethren; to afcertain which, they fhall deliver to him in open Lodge, held in the Mafter's degree, a certificate to the following purport:

" *To the prefiding Chiefs of the Chapter of Excellent Royal Arch Mafons, under the fanction of Lodge No. Whereas our trufty and well-beloved Brother a Geometric Mafter Mafon, and member of our Lodge, has folicited us to recommend him as a Mafter Mafon, every way qualified, fo far as we are judges of the neceffary qualifications, for paffing the Holy Arch: We do hereby certify, that the faid trufty and well-beloved Brother has obtained the unanimous confent of our Lodge, No. for the recommendation and figning this certificate.*

Given under our hands this day of 179

           W. M.
           S. W.
 Secretary   J. W.

---

7 Ahiman Rezon, 1800. Revised and corrected at a General Grand Chapter, held at the Crown and Anchor Tavern, in the Strand, London, October 1, 5794.—Confirmed in Grand Lodge, December 3, 1794, p. 29.

8 Roy A. Wells, *Freemasonry in London from 1785* (1984), p. 79. A large section of this book relates to the Royal Arch as worked by Domatic Lodge No.177 and provides an excellent background to masonry as worked in Antient Lodges and Chapters.

But there was a further, and significant, problem faced by both sides. The strict entry requirements meant that any Royal Arch Chapter was only able to function by taking the Past Masters of the lodge it worked nearby, and probably also needed several other lodges Past Masters as well. In short the system as defined by Dassigny (and supported by Dermott) hardly allowed a viable Chapter to be created—so the Chapters themselves were under real pressure to break the rules in order to get a numbers of members to make the lodge viable. And they did break the rules.

This difficulty was made even worse because very often lodges chose their master not by the members moving through all the offices once a year and then arriving at the chair; but instead they appointed and reappointed the same brother year after year. They habit used today of doing one office per year only seemed to become the norm from somewhere around the start of the twentieth century in England. Some brothers spent a number of year in the chair. That of course was another impediment to the prospering of the Royal Arch. The story of the Royal Arch in Ireland was also complicated by the arrival of the Knights Templars—they had their own independent Grand Encampment—so they overcame their shortage of candidates by including the Royal Arch within their encampments—and solved the problem. What is not clear whether they still used a 'Passing the Chair' option or whether they simply dispensed with that requirement (that is a challenge for others to resolve).

And new Supreme Grand Chapter (formed after the Union of Antients and Moderns Grand Lodges in 1813 in its 1823 Regulations[9] had carefully avoided upsetting brothers from either Antients or Moderns by combining both pre-existing clauses of each previous Grand bodies.

CANDIDATES, &c.

That to this order none ought to be admitted but men of the best character and education, open, generous, of liberal sentiment and real philanthropists, who have passed through the probationary degrees of masonry, have presided as masters, been duly proposed, recommended by two or more companions of the Chapter, balloted for and approved; the recommendation (unless on particular occasions) to be at least one Chapter previous to the ballot. The brother to be

---

9   Laws and Regulations for the order of Royal Arch Masons. London: 1823, p. 29.

And that really is the tale of the degree of 'Passing the Chair'—It was the British attempt to create higher ranks, but in the end authority was defeated by the desire of many ordinary brothers to also gain the same degrees.

Ireland 1773-1805: The Knights Templars
arrive in Dublin

The reader is going to ask why Ireland gets another whole chapter in this story, and before I started the detailed research that would have been my opinion. I cannot do better than quote the introductory words of Bro Stephen Forster:

> The Early Grand Encampments of Ireland and Scotland represent little more than a name to many Freemasons, while by others they are regarded as small unimportant chapters in the history of Freemasonry. To a few Masonic scholars of earlier times, they were the subjects of scathing criticism, A.E. Waite in particular, was extremely severe in his opinions concerning the Early Grand bodies. Possibly due to certain events in the first two decades of this century, many older Scottish Masons still hold the Early Grand Encampment of Scotland in particular disdain. The object of this paper is not to defend the Early Grand Encampments, but is certainly to illustrate that they had more than a little influence in the destiny of some contemporary Orders.[1]

The idea for this book was to take the story of the development of the 'masonic myth' from 1730 as far as the establishment of the Royal Arch degrees, but it did not take long to discover that Ireland embraced the (masonic) Knights Templars with great enthusiasm, and then spread it to Scotland, and probably around the world through the global travels of the Irish Military Lodges. So Ireland, and Dublin, far from being a poverty struck and cultural backwater actually seemed to lead the development of the degrees of the Royal Arch through to the Knights Templars and with strong connections to France. You will not find words like dissident or irregular in these chapters—but instead simply an acceptance of the facts according to the practices of those times, and as we have found them. The picture is a very different one to the normal story that is told, and it is one that links both RA and KT inextricably together. Again it was both circumstances and personalities, and in the case of Ireland that combination led

---

1   Stephen Forster, The Early Grand Encampments of Ireland and Scotland and in England, *Trans Lodge CC* vol.18 (1982–1984), p. 134. I was able to visit Stephen on 13th March 2020 on an opportunistic dashing visit to Scotland only a few days before Britain was locked down for the Covid-19 pandemic, and we spent a great day together. I pay tribute and thanks for his knowledge and writings and his generosity. Sadly he passed to the GLA in September 2020.

ultimately to a huge crisis that took a quarter of a century to bring back into a manageable format.

What remains an enigma, for others to explore, is how and when the Knights Templars arrived in Ireland.

Three things mark out Ireland as exceptional in the history of the adoption of non-Craft degrees, and the first is the large number of military lodges, not only military lodges with Irish officers and soldiers and Irish warrants but also English and Scottish regiments with Irish warrants, and after 1752 the rise of Scottish and Antient military Lodges and then Moderns Lodges. The first military lodge with an Irish warrant was created in 1732 and by 1773, when the KT was in Dublin there had been 88 military lodges with travelling Irish warrants created. Just as mingling of humans in 2020 spread the Covid-19 virus, so it is known that the movement of soldiers round the world fighting the battles of Empire was what contributed greatly to the spread of masonry, and spread a host of other degrees wherever they went.

The second contributing factor was the (perhaps) unique practice that started around 1773 in Dublin was that of the Knights Templars s advertising their activities in the press. They soon discovered that the major impediment in increasing the number of Knights Templars was the requirement to be a Royal Arch Mason to become a Knight. The solution they chose was to also confer the Royal Arch degrees themselves—but the advertisements show they were not without competition. Indeed it is possible to trace the outlines of this growth and developments through the newspaper advertisements, indeed over eighty such advertisements have been traced in the Dublin press between 1773 and ca 1789.

Ireland in the Eighteenth Century

While everyone is familiar with the '45 Uprising and Bonnie Prince Charlie in Scotland but most are much less familiar with events in Ireland. Since the Middle Ages Ireland had been under the control of England, first the King and later under Parliament in London. The purpose of this section is not to relate Irish history but simply to warn those unfamiliar with this background that Irish history and especially Irish Masonic history is different to that of England, and was driven by other factors and at different times. The 18th century in Ireland had been one of Protestant ascendancy, of a Protestant north with immigration from Scotland, and towards the end of the century of rising social tensions. This led to the rise of the United Irishmen and the 1798 Rebellion which was followed by the Union with Britain to create the 'United Kingdom of Great Britain and Ireland' in 1800. And it was partly the same United Irishmen's radical views which caused the Illegal Societies Act of 1799 which closed all organisations that required member to take an oath of secrecy in England and Scotland, and from which freemasonry only just escaped being banned. This law did not apply in Ireland, but the social tensions in Ireland; between Dublin and the rest of Ireland, and between Dublin and Ulster, around the turn of the century were going to play a significant role.

The Irish Famine of 1822, and the campaign for Catholic Emancipation led by Daniel O'Connell brought about the Unlawful Oaths (Ireland) Act 1823 (39 Geo III c79). This caused Irish lodges to close and they stayed closed until after 1825 when Irish masonry got its act together. But in that time the number of lodges that closed decimated the Craft, especially the number of lodges in more rural parts of Ireland where (like Scotland) even small villages would often have their own lodges.

Sadly the masonic chaos that started in 1805 left the Grand Lodge struggling to find a new way forward which it only achieved with the formation of a Supreme Grand Royal Arch Chapter of Ireland in 1829 and finally a Supreme Grand Encampment in 1837 (which renamed itself as the Grand Priory of Ireland in 1872). The wounds of the battles that started in 1805 took a long time to heal.

Back to the 1760s and 1770s

The third is the Irish practice of Lodges believing and insisting that under their warrants they were free to work all and any degrees under those warrants, and Grand Lodge failing to be able to control lodges. The same things also happened in both England and Scotland throughout the eighteenth century, with a similar disapproval by grand lodges; and it was a problem all the grand lodges failed to control. To be honest the technology and services simply did not exist at that time to allow flows of communication to take place in a dispersed organization of thousands of members.

The Royal Arch was quiet before the arrival of the KTs but it is worth noting the appearance of two lodges. Among the Warrants issued by the Grand Lodge of Ireland in 1749, were two in the city of Dublin, numbered 190 and 198, and both of which were soon to be known as "Royal Arch Lodge." And also feature in this chapter.[2]

---

2   The numbering of Irish Masonic Lodges can be confusing. First Irish lodge have always been primarily know by number rather than having a name of the place where they met. Lodges in Dublin had two numbers, one allocated by Grand Lodge and the second a local Dublin number. Lodge numbers were recycled, and lodges always preferred to have the lowest possible number. Keith Cochrane's *Irish Masonic Records* is available for a modest fee from the librarian at the Grand Lodge Library in Molesworth Street, Dublin.

> Laſt Sunday evening the remains of Mr. Robert Blake (an old Knight Templar) were carried from the aiſle of Chriſt Church to Cabbage-garden grave yard, attended by the maſters, wardens, and brethren of all the Freemaſon lodges in this city attired in all the regalia of the order, their aprons, jewels, &c. The proceſſion was grand and ſolemn, and exceeded any thing of the kind that has appeared here for theſe thirty years paſt, as upwards of eleven hundred of the fraternity attended on the occaſion, with ſeveral bands of muſic belonging to the regiments in garriſon.

Saunders Newsletter, Dublin, 15 June 1773

The first visible arrival of the Knights Templars came with three lodges, on the face of it ordinary Craft Lodges but in reality they were primarily vehicles for the promotion of the KT degrees.

> We have now to turn to the activities* of a group of Masons in Dublin who held in succession Warrants Nos. 506 (1773–75), 518 (1775–79) and 584 (1781–1813). The two former had short lives, and the loss of Grand Lodge Minutes leaves it doubtful precisely why. The brethren turned to "Mother Kilwinning" by whom they were constituted into a Lodge by the name of "High Knight Templars of Ireland, Kilwinning Lodge" the Warrant bearing date 8th October, 1779.
>
> No. 506 probably, and 518 certainly, took the title "Kilwinning High Knight[s] Templars Lodge," and there seems no doubt that the main purpose of the brethren holding these Warrants was the practice of the "Higher Degrees"; and a Warrant from Kilwinning, the traditional source of the higher degrees (though Mother Kilwinning herself solemnly declared that she had never practised more than the Three Steps of the Craft) was a palladium lending lustre to their working of such ceremonies. At any rate the members speedily established a regular succession of "Excellent, Superexcellent, Royal Arch, and Knight Templar." They made their peace with the Grand Lodge of Ireland, and obtained Warrant No. 584, dated 1st March 1781. From then on this was used for craft working, and as an approach to the higher degrees, which were worked exclusively under the Kilwinning Warrant.
>
> The activities of these brethren stimulated or revived an existing body of which unfommately little is known, the "Early Grand

296

Encampment of Ireland," which, in 1805, claimed to have existed in Dublin for over a century.[3]

Wilkinson's view that it was Lodge's 506 and 518 that revived the EGE, but it is probably more likely that part of their membership left to become the Kilwinning Grand Encampment but when we look at the earliest newspaper advertisement so far found it is for 1773 (but not found until recently) and shows the same multiple degree practices did predate the arrival of Lodge 506.

> 1765 "We have seen how the activities of the brethren of the "Kilwinning High Knight Templar Lodge" in Dublin stimulated the Early Grand Encampment; this latter body in 1788 published a small printed pamphlet, "The Rules of the High Knight Templar's of Ireland," which gave the names, with the respective dates when dubbed Knight, of the ninety-four brethren then comprising the Early Grand Encampment; first name on the list is
>
> "1765, March 24 Sir Edward Gilmore."[4]

And Edward Gilmore was a real person, because in the 1790 Fratrimonium Excelsum he was still an officer in the Early Grand Encampment.

The Dublin battle for the Higher Degrees

One of the strangest contests in masonic history is the practice in Dublin of advertising masonic meetings firstly of the 'Grand Knights Templars of Ireland.' These meetings were held on the traditional masonic feast days of St John. In total 89 adverts have been found between 1773 and 1793, and there will be more because the run of papers that have been scanned by the archives is incomplete. The rest of Ireland's newspapers around these dates was also searched and nothing like this was found in the cities of Belfast and Cork or elsewhere; so clearly it only applied in Dublin. The next advertisement for St Johns Day in June 1774 appeared in the *Hibernian Journal* but very rapidly it was *Saunders Newsletter* that became 'the newspaper for masons to buy.' There can only be one purpose for all this advertising, and that was to attract curious masons to the St John's Day meals and to seek to interest them to take other degrees. And one can see even from the early days that there were competing KT Encampments. And because one could only gain the KT degrees after the Royal Arch these degrees were all practiced together by Encampments right from the beginning.

---

3   R E Wilkinson, *History of the Grand Lodge of Ireland Vol. II*. Lodge of Research CC, Dublin (1957), p. 322.

4   R E Parkinson, *History of the Grand Lodge of Ireland*, vol. 2 (1957), p. 328.

1773

> The Grand Knights Templars of Ireland, Mark, Royal Arch Blue and Excellent Masons, No. 41[5], intend dining together at the Phoenix in Capel-street on Monday the 28th Day of June inst. to celebrate the Festival of St. John; all Members who purpose attending, are requested to leave their Name at the bar of said Tavern two days before, that dinner may be provided accordingly. The Conclave to be opened at Three. Dinner on the table at 4 o'Clock,   Signed by Order,
> M.O.R. Grand Secretary,
> EA—FC--MM--RA--PM--MM--KT

Saunders Newsletter, Dublin, 21 June 1773

This advertisement clearly shows that (at least) this lodge worked the full range of degrees and that they describe themselves as the 'Grand Knights Templars of Ireland,' and that tends to give an indication that they see themselves as an order in their own right. But things developed so that by 1774 we can find the following advertisement.

> The Knights Templars of Ireland, Royal Arch, Excellent, and Super-Excellent Free and Accepted Masons, Lodge, No.506, intend dining together at their Lodge-Room at the Thatched Cabin, in Castle-Street, on Friday the 24th Instant, to celebrate the Festival of St. John: Such of the Fraternity as chuse to dine with them, are requested to leave their Names at the Bar two Days before.
> Signed by Order
> J.O. E.G.S.
> Dinner to be on the Table at Four o'Clock

Hibernian Journal, Dublin 15 June 1774, repeated 17th June.

This practice greatly annoyed the GL of Ireland because they were using one of their lodge numbers under the name of the Knights Templars—and the warrant was withdrawn in February 1775. Interestingly the warrant of Lodge No. 518, in fact the replacement for No. 506, was issued on 2nd February 1775. The next advertisement under No. 518 was more tactfully worded.

> THE KNIGHTS TEMPLARS OF IRELAND
>
> Lodge No.518, intend dining together, at their Lodge Room, at the Phoenix, in Caple-street, on Saturday, the 24th Inst. To celebrate the Festival of St. John. Such of the FRATERNITY as chuse to dine with them are requested to leave their Names at the Bar, two days before.
> Signed by Order of the
> E.G.M.
> R.W.E.G.S.

Hibernian Journal, Dublin. 16th June 1775
Lodge No. 518 lasted until February 1779

1778 St John's Day in Summer. **The Royal Arch Lodge of Ireland** ... dining at the Kings Arms, Smock-Alley (the 1778 list in Free-Masons Calendar 1778 tells us that Lodge No. 198 was meeting there!). Lodge No. 198 was warranted in 1749 and had always made the Royal Arch its speciality. They must have realised that greater interest in the KT required all those master masons to take the Royal Arch before they could join the KT—and decided to take advantage of that. It would seem that the members of Lodge No. 198 were in direct competition with the group that met at the Eagle Tavern!

1779 Warrant from Mother Kilwinning for a **High Knights Templars of Ireland Kilwinning Lodge** issued 27th October 1779. This finally marks the break between the two parts of the Templars in Ireland. The granting, in 1779, of a warrant by Mother Kilwinning of Scotland to a group of Irish Templars, members of an Early Grand Encampment to establish a "High Knights Templars of Ireland, Kilwinning Lodge" in Dublin is a highly significant event. Those Knights remaining in the Early Grand Encampments galloped into action—and thus two separate and competing Knights Templars bodies were created. Mother Kilwinning was at this time its own Grand Lodge and it created a considerable minority of Lodges under its banners which to this day contain the word 'Kilwinning' in their title. The warrant should probably be classed as one of the most significant documents in masonic history, because of its role in spreading the Knights Templars degrees.

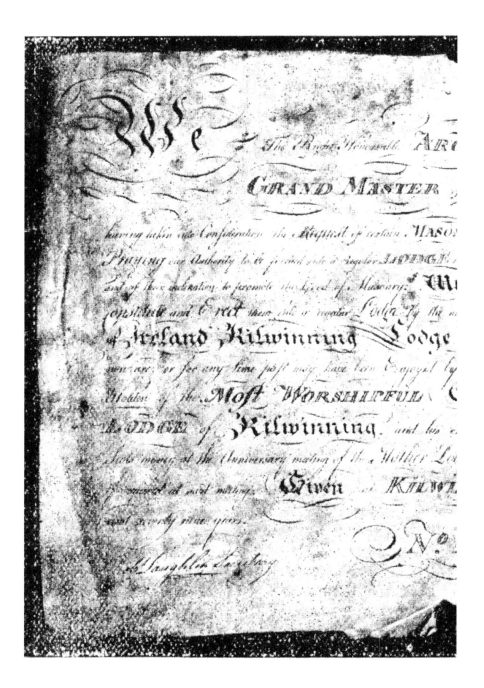

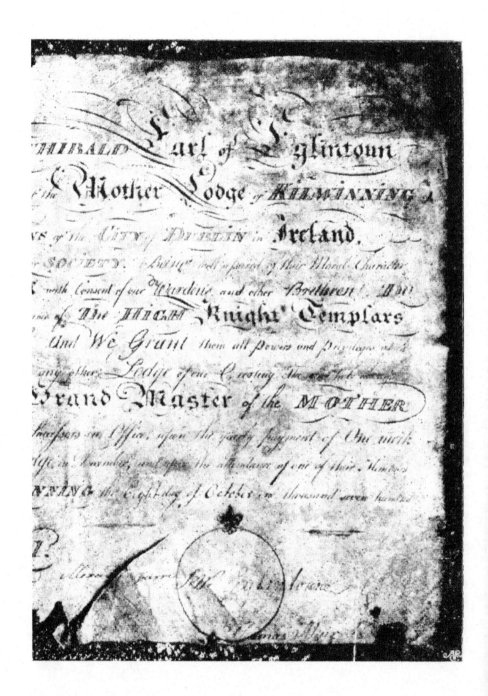

The warrant might only have been granted of 29th October 1779, but we can read of developments in the newspaper advertisements of December 1779 because they chose to use their new warrant to advantage and using the name of High Knights Templars (Kilwinning) Lodge of Ireland.

> The members of the High Knight Templar's (Kilwinning) Lodge of Ireland, Intend dining together on the 27th instant, at the Eagle in Eustace-Street, to celebrate St. John's day. Such Brethren as wish to dine with them, are requested to leave their names at the bar, some days before. – P.G.E.G.M.
>
> Signed by order,
>
> LEWIS ALLEY, Secretary
>
> N.B. The Lodge will sit as Blue Masons, in order to accommodate visitors

The advertisements go on for meetings to celebrate St. John's Days. Those for the 1780 St John's Day in Summer contain the curiosity that: "The Royal Arch Lodge of Ireland formerly No.28, now 18, of Dublin ... dining at the Kings Arms, Smock-Alley." The advert for the first time gives some information of the events of the day: "The Conclave meet at Half past two o'clock the Lodge opens to do Business precisely at three... ." The times do vary but *it is the use of the word Conclave that is puzzling.* It is usually associated with KT and not with Royal Arch. So were they conferring Templars degrees, or...?

The situation also gets more complicated because on St John's Day in Winter. **The Royal Arch Lodge of Ireland** ... dining at the Eagle, Eustace Street. Dinner on the table at Half past four. And this seems to be confirmation that they seemed to have moved from the Carterets Head to the Eagle in Smock Alley.

And for the same day **The High Knights Templars of Ireland, Kilwinning Lodge,** advertised that they intended dining at the Eagle, Eustace Street, but without giving a timing for dinner. Interesting that two competing groups would meet at the same place on the same day. One has to feel sorry for the cooks and the serving staff.

This seems that the competition was getting much closer, and it all broke out into the public domain

1783 St John's Day in Summer was to see the outbreak of further hostilities in Saunder's Newsletter between the two opposing sets of Knights. The series of advertisements are below:

KNIGHTS TEMPLARS OF IRELAND
LODGE, No.584, intend to dine at their Rooms, the Eagle, Eustace-street, this Day Tuesday 24th inst. to celebrate the Festival of St. John. Such of the Fraternity as will favour them with their Company, are requested to leave their Names at the Bar two Days before. Dinner to be on the Table at four o'Clock.
Signed by Order of the
E.G.M.
W.R.W.G.S
To accommodate Visitors the Lodge will sit as Apprentices.

This appeared in Saunders News-Letter on 19th June and 20th June 1783

A CARD.
Reading an advertisement in Saunder's Newspaper setting forth that a Set of Gentlemen, who style themselves Knights Templars of Ireland are to assemble and dine on the 24th instant. Now the E.G.M. and Brethren of the most noble Order of High Knights Templars, O.I.E. and S. do hereby inform the Publick, that those Gentlemen have no Sanction or Authority from the E.G.L., for assuming such Title, and that the Title they now unwarrantably assume is in no sort constituted by the E.G.L. 23rd June 1783.
Signed by Order
W. R. E. G. S.

The top two notices appeared immediately below the one above
on 21st June, 23rd June, and 24th June

The Gentlemen of the High Knights Templars of Ireland, Kilwinning Lodge, held at the Eagle, Eustace-street, having this day met with a very extraordinary Card, endeavouring to depreciate them, and to bring a dispute forward that is uninteresting to the Public, think it necessary to declare that in their Advertisement they offered NO OFFENCE to any one; and with Respect to the TITLE they are SAID improperly to assume, they are willing and able in proper Time and Place TO SUPPORT IT, and to show they have from the PUREST FOUNTAIN an AUTHORITY for it, not SELF CREATED, as their great and mighty Opponents are, who have often in private been told, as they are now publicly, that "They know not what they do". As the private differences of Societies no Way concern the Public, the Gentlemen of this Society will treat any other Publication of this Kind, with the contempt such unmeaning scurrility deserves.
Signed by Order of the
E.G.M.
W. R. E. G. S. E. S. R. A. H. K. T. O. I. K. L. P. M.

The third advertisement appeared immediately below with the other two in
Saunder's News-Letter on 25th June and again on 26th June.

From these advertisements it is clear that there were two competing groups of Knights Templars, each trying to make the case to be the most senior, or the most regular of origin. It is also interesting to note the usual 'signatures' used and the interpretation of this one is below:

W. R. E. G. S. E. S. R. A. H. K. T. O. I. K. L. P. M.

W.R. (Initials of the writer) Grand Secretary Excellent Super
Excellent Royal Arch High Knights Templars of Ireland
Kilwinning Lodge P.M. (probably the rank of the writer)

1786 Cameron notes (p. 68) that in 1786 Lodge No. 620 also worked under a dispensation from KHKT. This was in spite of the members of the lodge being staunch supporters of Grand Lodge. It was also closely related to Lodge No. 2 and they seemed to work or have members who worked a multiplicity of other 'higher Degrees.'

1787 On the 1st November, 1787, a Bro. John Rigby, Worshipful Master of Lodge No. 620 presented a memorial to the Grand Lodge of Ireland: *"...praying that the Higher Degrees of Masonry - .... shall or may be made subordinate to the Grand lodge of Ireland."* A committee was appointed but nothing came of it.

1788 The Early Grand Encampment published a small printed pamphlet, "The Rules of the High Knight Templars of Ireland."

1789 Richard Hely Hutchinson, 1st Earl of Donoughmore (29 January 1756 – 22 August 1825) was elected Grand Master of the Grand Lodge of Ireland (1789–1813). He supported Catholic Emancipation and voted for the 1800 Union with Britain. Probably a new Grand Master being in charge of both orders would want to see rather less public advertising of meetings. It is the most likely reason that this advertising episode drew to a close.

1790 The 1790 **Fratrimonium Excelsum**, A New Ahiman Rezon published in Dublin by Wilkinson, carries this page which clearly delineates the two competing Templar organisations. It would later turn out to be embarrassing for Donoughmore as GM of the Grand Lodge of Ireland to also be Grand Master of the Templars when it came to the crisis of 1805. It also contains toasts and songs for both Royal Arch and KT.

It is also important to note that in the title of the HKT is added the words "AND K.R.C No.1" —Knight of the Red Cross! It is also worth noting that Deuchar in Scotland also ended up with HRDM and KRC as part of his package KT package.

GRAND HIGH KNIGHTS TEMPLARS EN-
CAMPMENT of IRELAND, and K. R. C.
No. 1.

Right Worshipful and Right Hon. Sir RICHARD,
Lord Baron Donoughmore, Grand Master of the
Order.

Sir John Fowler, D. G. M.
Sir Oswald Edwards, G. Sec.
Sir Edward C. Keane, C. Gen.
Sir Thomas Molony, G. Mar.
Sir James Mills, D. G. Mar.
Sir Joseph Logee, G. S. B.

meet the second *Thursday* of every Month, at the
Old Bristol, Crane-lane.

EARLY GRAND KNIGHTS TEMPLARS
ENCAMPMENT.

Sir John Gamble, E. G. M.
Sir Andrew Kelly, D. G. M.
Sir John Kennedy, C. G.
Sir John Hunter, E. G. Mar.
Sir Edward Gilmore, D. E. G. M.
Sir Thomas Cuffe, E. G. S. B.

meet the last *Thursday* of every Month, at *Cassen's,
Kennedy's-lane.*

L O D G E, No. 2.

William Fleming, Master.
John Maddock, S. W.
Edward Clerke, J. W.

meet the first *Wednesday* of every Month, at *Shaw's,
Capel-street.*

L O D G E, No. $\frac{2}{6}$.

Edward C. Keane, Master.
Lawrence Tighe, S. W.
James Logee, J. W.

meet

It is worth noting that the Deputy Grand Master of the GHKTE was one John
Fowler. He is not to be confused with his son, also John Fowler who became the
Grand Secretary of the Grand Lodge of Ireland and was heavily involved in all
higher degrees in Ireland.

ca 1790 EGE begins issuing warrants, not only in Ireland, but also in England,
and especially in Scotland. Thus KT arrived in Scotland from Ireland and
around 30 warrants in total were issued to Scottish lodges.

Ireland 1805–1838 Masonic Revolution and eventual Reorganisation

It is impossible to end the story of events in Ireland without continuing to the
point where the battles had been fought, and then to discover when normality
was restored to freemasonry in Ireland.

The United Irishmen was founded in 1791 (and actually in the Eagle, in Eustace
Street, Dublin where the High Knights Templars met) and the dissatisfaction

grew through the decades culminating in the 1798 rebellion.

And of course Ireland itself was to a degree fractured with a mainly Protestant population in the North, a Catholic countryside, and a wealthy, cultured and cosmopolitan Dublin. First there was a problem in Dublin where there were competing lodges each offering both the Royal Arch and KT degrees who by the end of the century were both gaining some formal structure and both granting dispensations to lodges to work their other degrees. The events that follow have to be considered against the social unhappiness in Ireland at the time.

The masonic events that follow need to be understood, because they mark the end of an era, followed by 35 years of fractured freemasonry while matters were organisationally resolved. But the Irish eventual solution brought with it a much more controlled set of Orders all of which were under the leadership of the Duke of Leinster who ruled from 1813 until his death in 1874. Leinster would rule Irish masonry for a truly amazing 61 years.

But returning to 1800, because the Deputy Grand Secretary[5] (DGS) Thomas Corker died in 1800, having been DGS since 1767, and left behind him a short-fall in collection of the fees to be paid by lodges. It had become the practice for the DGS to both perform the active secretarial and dues collection work, leaving the GS as simply a masonic rank; and more to the point the DGS was paid a percentage of what he collected in order to get the dues in the bank account of Grand Lodge. It happened that the GS had changed in 1797 when Georges D'Arcy Irvine was elected, and he came from a family in the North and upon the death of Corker he appointed Alexander Seton a Barrister in Dublin, (who was also a northern man) as DGS (from 1891 until 1805).

The other player was John Boardman who became Grand Treasurer in 1791, a post he held until his death in 1814. Upon Corker's death Boardman took it upon himself in 1801 to appoint William Semple to a new post of Deputy Grand Treasurer (DGT) and when Semple resigned to appoint W F Graham. The position carried a salary of 50 guineas and a 10% commission on all dues collected. This commission would previously have been paid to the DGS, and Seton saw these potential payments he thought were his to vanish into another brother's pocket. This was a volcano waiting to erupt, and this is demonstrated by the events of 1806.[6]

This was especially true because at the 1st May 1806 meeting of Grand Lodge D'Arcy Irvine was defeated in the vote for Grand Secretary and Seton waited

---

5   In the GL of Ireland, the position of Grand Secretary was an honorific, and it was the Deputy GS who did all the work, including the collection of the annual dues.

6   A fuller account can be read in JL Belton, *The English Masonic Union of 1813*. Chapter 8. The horse-whipping is on page 68.

outside the room in which the meeting had been held and when Boardman emerged he proceeded to publicly horsewhip him in front of the Brethren.

So far we have dealt with the matter of the main players in Grand Lodge intensely disliking each other, but it was also a dispute between a Dubliner and two 'Northerners.' Next comes a set of proposals made by John Boardman at the Grand Lodge meeting in August 1805, Boardman proposed to Grand Lodge, that that body passed the following resolutions. And there was also a matching set of Royal Arch resolutions:

> I. - That in order to establish uniformity in the principles and ceremonies of the Knights Templars degree, and to avoid many irregularities which prevail and have unavoidably resulted from the want of a controlling power to regulate the proceeding of the numerous Knights Templars Encampments in this Kingdom, It is indispensably necessary that the Grand Lodge should take that Degree under its immediate sanction, and that warrants to hold Encampments should be granted to such brethren Knights Templars as shall make proper application; and no person is to be admitted or initiated a Knight Templar under such warrant except a Royal Arch Mason duly registered.

> II. - Until the 1st day of June next, the Grand Officers and Members of the Grand Lodge being Knights Templars, shall constitute the Grand Templars Encampment, and from the said first of June the Grand Knights Templars Encampment shall consist of such of the Grand Officers and members of the Grand Ledge as are Templars, and Members of Encampments held under warrants issued under the sanction of the Grand Lodge pursuant to the first resolution.

> III. - That the Grand Knights Templars Encampments shall be invested with as full power and authority over Encampments of Knights Templars and Masons of that degree as is exercised by the Grand Lodge of Ireland over the warranted Blue Lodges, and the members thereof, under its jurisdiction. The Grand Knights Templars Encampments at all times conforming in its proceedings, as much as possible, to the rules and regulations of the Grand Lodge.

> IV. - That a register of all warranted Encampments, and the members thereof, shall be kept – two guineas to be paid for each warrant; two shillings for registering a member; and three shillings for a Grand Knights Templars certificate. These sums to be applied to the general funds of the Order.

V. - The Sublime Commander, for the time being, of each Encampment held under warrants granted pursuant to the resolutions, shall be a member of the Grand Lodge, provided election had been approved of by the Grand Knights Templars Encampment, and notice of such approbation transmitted to the Grand Lodge.

VI. - That the Grand Treasurer to be appointed Treasurer and registrar of the Grand Knights Templars Encampment, and the Grand Secretary, Secretary thereto.[7]

John Boardman had managed to upset the Northerners from Ulster, and probably almost every brother who was either a Royal Arch Mason or a Knights Templar, and every brother who thought he was already paying enough to Grand Lodge, and a considerable proportion of the Dublin hierarchy. If one reads the proposals with care then perhaps it does seem that the intention was to bring both degrees under the (financial) control of the (Craft) Grand Lodge, and to ensure they obeyed the rules of Grand Lodge and that they had no control over their own funds. And actually in the letter written by John Boardman to Thomas Harper DepGM of the Antients in London it is clear that was precisely his intention.

Abstract of a letter from John Boardman to Thomas Harper,
DepGM of the Antients in London and dated 10 August 1805.

---

7   Stephen Forster, *The Early Grand Encampments of Ireland, Scotland, and England.* Transactions Lodge No.CC, Dublin (1982-1984), pp. 144-145. See also, WJ Hughan, "Freemasonry in Ireland" in *The Freemasons* 25 March 1871, p. 181.

Given the comment by Boardman at the bottom of the letter his intent was clearly as much financial as organisational or personal. The two bodies were created, but gained little acceptance and were soon abandoned. But this did not happen without creating further problems, and a breakaway Grand East of Ulster was created in 1808 and lasted till around 1812. This break was cataclysmic, with two grand lodges both appealing to the same Grand Master for his support. In the meantime both the Royal Arch and KT degrees continued to be performed by the previous organisations. It was only years later and with the passing of time that in December 1829 that the wounds had healed sufficiently for a Supreme Grand Chapter of Ireland to be formed. And it took thirty years before a Supreme Grand Encampment was eventually formed in 1838.

> As well as the Early Grand Encampment, "Kilwinning" Encampment had been issuing charters from 1805, and, apart from these bodies, the Degree was worked up and down Ireland by practically every Lodge under the wide powers conferred by the Grand Lodge Warrant. With the suppression of Masonic meetings in Ireland in 1823, the Early Grand Encampment lapsed into oblivion, and it was not until 25th August, 1836, that a Grand Convocation of High Knight Templars was held in the rooms of the Grand Lodge of Ireland. There was a strong representation from "Kilwinning"; Chapter Nos. 1, 5, 85, 284 and 888 were also represented, and Nos. 331 and 957 sent their adhesion to the decisions of the meeting. It was resolved to establish a Supreme Grand Encampment, with the Duke of Leinster as Illustrious Grand Commander, a title altered in 1838 to Grand Master, with John Fowler as Grand Registrar.[8]

It is a sad and complicated story and one often mistold (probably because it is embarrassing) and one suspects largely not understood. The usual way of portraying it is that of Pick and Knight in their Pocket History of Freemasonry:

> The story of this discreditable episode, which culminated in a violent struggle between two rival parties in Grand Lodge and eventually in the (temporary) formation of a separate Grand Lodge in Ulster, can be told quite simply.

> In 1801 D'Arcy Irvine, the Grand Secretary, had appointed as his deputy his friend, Alexander Seton, an able and energetic but dishonest barrister. This Seton was the villain of the piece. As soon as he was appointed, he went to the house of his predecessor and carried off a "hackney coach full" of books, MSS and other articles

---

8   RE Parkinson, *History of the Grand Lodge of Ireland*, Vol. 2, Lodge CC Dublin, p. 39.

belonging to Grand Lodge some of which have never since been recovered.[9]

As you have read it was far more complicated, but one is only able to understand Irish masonic history with a better and fuller picture. To aid understanding the chronology is continued.

And probably it was the fact that the Knights Templars formed an Early Grand Encampment, which in its turn took into its control the Royal Arch, and then in 1779 formed a splinter organisation, and they both used the newspapers in Dublin to promote their 'product.' Plus of course it was further spread by the military lodges as they travelled around the world. While NOT a 'rite of seven degrees' it is interesting to note that in Ireland they had found it convenient to bring a number of degrees all under the same organisation from about 1773.

1823–1824 All freemasonry was suppressed in Ireland for 10 months under the Unlawful Oaths Act of 1823 (an Irish version of the (British) Unlawful Societies Act of 1799). This caused a decimation of Irish freemasonry especially in the rural areas from which there never was a full recovery. Early Grand Encampment lapsed into oblivion.

1825 Ireland establishes its Supreme Council in 1725 with a charter from Charleston, South Carolina, and years ahead of either England or Scotland, and even before it had resolved its own internal Royal Arch and Knights Templars problems.

> There is a strong Irish connection with the founders of the Mother Supreme Council at Charleston. John Mitchell, the first Sovereign Grand Commander, was an Ulsterman, and is said to have been initiated in an Ulster Lodge before emigrating to America. Frederick Dalcho, first Lieutenant Grand Commander, was initiated in Philadelphia, which was in intimate Masonic communication with Ireland. He was an intimate correspondent of John Fowler, who induced him to allow his "Orations" to be printed in Dublin for the Original Chapter of Prince Masons, with the Metropolitan College of Heredom, in 1808. From these we learn that the "Dublin Royal Arch" was worked in Charleston as early as 1782, and was accepted by the Rite of Perfection as the equivalent of the 13°. Thomas Bartholomew Bowen, though born in Ireland, was initiated in Philadelphia in 1784, and finally, as we have seen, Israel de Licben,

---

9   F L Pick & G N Knight, *The Pocket History of Freemasonry*, (1992), pp. 163-164. Sadly this excellent paperback size book is out of print but second-hand copies can often be found at fair prices online.

first Grand Treasurer, claimed to have received the degrees in Dublin in 1770.

Negotiations in progress for the establishment of a Supreme Council 33° in Dublin, were interrupted by the War of 1812, and not resumed till 1822. Finally, the Supreme Council 33° for Ireland was patented 13th August, 1824, and constituted, 10th June, 1826, with the Duke of Leinster as Sovereign Grand Commander.[10]

1829 Grand Chapter formed through the Grand Lodge of Ireland—and which only becomes truly independent in 1834. Fifty-three Chapters attended the meeting which agreed the formation.

1836 Grand Convocation of High Knight Templars met in the rooms of the Grand Lodge of Ireland. There was a strong representation from 'Kilwinning,' Chapters 1, 5, 85, 284, and 888, and Chapters 331 & 957 sent their adhesion to any decisions.

1836 Grand Council of Rites formed. The intent was that it would be a home for the Knight of the Sword, Knight if the East and Knight of the East and West degrees but this did not happen and they remained with the Grand Encampment.

1838 Supreme Grand Encampment formed. The Early Grand Encampment did not survive the 1823 closure of masonry and it was only the Kilwinning Encampment that returned.

Addendum

The following relates to a Bro Cesar Gautier who had a legal battle with John Boardman which he ended up losing:

> Jean-Baptiste Hyacinthe César GAUTIER, arrived in Dublin in 1796, joined First Volunteer Lodge No. 620 (Dublin) in 1801— Worshipful Master in 1804, joined Lodge No. 205, Moy, Co. Tyrone in 1805.
>
> In 1805 Bro. Gautier was prominent in the secession movement in the North of Ireland. He wrote libellous letters to the two Grand Lodge Officers and after complaint to the Grand Committee Bro. Gautier was expelled from the Craft in March, 1806.
>
> Bro. Gautier then Memorialised the Grand Lodge as follows:
>
> "To the Right Worshipful the Grand Master, Grand Wardens & Members of the Grand Lodge of Ireland —Most humbly Sheweth

---

10 RE Parkinson, *History of the Grand Lodge of Ireland*, Vol. 2 (1957), p. 330.

That I Jno. Baptist Hyacinth Gautier, Past Master of Lodge 620, Honorary Member of 23 Lodges in the North of Ireland, an Elect of Nine, Elect of Paragon, Elect of Fifteen, a Noachite, an Architect, Grand Architect, Scots Master, an Knight of the Sword, Excellent super-excellent & Royal Arch Mason, Past Sublime Commander of the Only Legal & Warranted Chapter of High Knight Templars in the United Kingdom of Ireland, High Priest of Royal Arch Knight Templars, Knight of Malta, General of the Prussian Eagle, Knight of the Crescent, High Priest of the Indians, Most Wise & Most Powerful Sovereign of the Order of Rose Croix or Prince Masons, Grand Dadouque, Grand Epitome, the Only Grand Hierophante of the Gymnosophist Masons of Ireland &c., &c. In behalf of Myself & those I shall deem Prudent & safe to Initiate into the Grandest of all Degrees possibly to be Acquired in Masonry, beg to intreat the Grand Lodge to take into its serious Consideration what Great & Sublime Advantages it will require by taking under its Cognizance & High Protection the Order of Prince Masons & the Gymnosophists.

The Petitioner humbly & Most Submissively begs to suggest that the Fees arising from this Most Salutary Measure Might stand the Grand Lodge Sum proper, be appropriated to the support of the Orphan School Which it Appears has been unfortunately Obliged to Encroach Upon the Funds of the Order.

Therefore should the Grand Lodge yield to my Suggestion I pray a Warrant may be Granted to me, Enjoying for Myself & such Others as shall be Initiated under the said Warrant that I & they will in all things pay the most strict Obedience to the unlimited necessary & divine Authority of the Grand Lodge & conform to such Rules, Decrees, Statutes, Orders & Ordinances as it may in its Spotless Conception, Celestial Wisdom & lawful Authority seem requisite for the Government of Prince Masons & Gymnosophists in their theological polemical & Mystical Ceremonies.

Jno. Baptiste Hyacinthe César GAUTIER

The Freemasons' Quarterly Review of the 17th February 1837 discloses the fact that the Mark Master Masons Degree had been introduced into Dublin from the United States of America by John Fowler, then Deputy Grand Master, about six years anterior to the date of the newspaper notice. This would bring the suggested date to about, say 1830 or 1831, or only about one year after the formation of the Grand R.A.C. of Ireland in 1829. However, according to the Records of Chapter No. 2 Dublin the Degree was introduced by Bro. John

Fowler on the 13th December 1825 at a combined meeting of Lodges Nos. 2 and 620.

1 The following is a copy of a Minute of the first Mark Master Masons Lodge constituted in Ireland, so far as can be ascertained from any existing Irish Masonic Records:

Dublin December 13th, 1825.

The following members of Lodges No 2, and 620, being assembled, Brother John Fowler, late D.G.M., & *P.M.* of Lodge 620 on the throne.

> Present John Fowler, P.D.G.M. & P.M. 620.
> Trim, G.T. & P.M. 2 *& 620.*
> Tyndall.
> Grant, P.M. 2.
> Murphy, Senr.
> Warren.
> Murphy, Junr.
> Robinson.
> Allen, P.M. No. 2.

Opened a Mark Masons Lodge in full form.

Bros.	Robinson	S.W.
	Tyndall	J.W.
	Trim	*M.O*
	Warren	S.O.
	Allen	J.O
	Murphy, Senr.	S.D.
	Murphy, Jnr.	J.D

After which Brother .John Fowler, in his capacity of a Sovereign Inspector General for Ireland, constituted this meeting a lawful Lodge of Mark Master Masons. & having (by, & with the consent of the meeting) placed Brother Grant on the throne, he empowered him & them to assemble & perpetuate the said degree in like manner as all regularly constituted Lodges of Mark Masons do throughout the two Hemispheres.

Resolved, that each Brother who has here received this degree do pay the Sum of 10s/6d British, which shall form a separate fund for the use of this degree.

Resolved. that the dinner Bill of *this* day be paid out of this fund.

Resolved, the Brother Fowler be requested to provide what

furniture may be necessary.

Resolved, the Brother Grant be appointed Treasurer to this Mark Masons Lodge.

Lodge closed in Usual Peace, Lore, and Harmony.

J. FOWLsER

Geo. B. GRANT,

P.M. No. 2. (AQC 30. p. 22/3)

Some concluding thoughts

Typically this mid eighteenth century view of developments in freemasonry within Britain would have focussed on England, and with hardly a word about Ireland or Scotland. But taking a holistic view of the evidence it was clear that the key player in spreading both the Royal Arch and Knights Templars degrees was Ireland, and especially in Dublin. The tendency to consider masonic history only in a tight narrow focus of the three Craft degrees, or to write just about the Royal Arch offers little more than looking down a telescope while embracing the full panorama offers a very different picture.

The role played by the military lodges, the Irish warranted ones especially, in spreading the degrees requires further research. The conferral of the Royal Arch in Fredericksburg, Virginia, or the Knights Templar in Boston are often quoted; but one must wonder how many other examples there are hidden away inside other minutes.

Masonic historians need to stop considering everything that does not conform to twentieth century custom and practice as being irregular, clandestine or as generally being unworthy. The example of the KT in Ireland proves that point precisely. Both the EGE and the HKT simply allowed their degrees to be worked by dispensation. So far there no evidence has been found of this being done in writing, maybe even it was simply verbal. The EGE provided a charter for Aberdeen (in Scotland) in around 1794 and to Maybole in around 1796, but it was only after 1804 that most of the Scottish warrants were issued. With perhaps even greater clarity the High Knights Templars only issued their first written charter in 1805—seemingly because they had to demonstrate their right to do so when they were challenged by the Grand Lodge of Ireland's plan to take control of their degrees. The EGE went on to play a key role in Scotland by granting various warrants which enabled the Royal Arch and KT to comply with the Illegal Societies Act of 1799—another fascinating story, and in the next chapter.

But one of the key problems was that Craft (Blue) Grand Lodges in Britain found it difficult to work out how to deal with the rise of other degrees, with the fact that these degrees developed organisations and were often led by men with strong personalities. All this was seen as, and actually was, competition for grand lodges who were struggling to maintain control. The same situation applied in the United States and it was Henry Fowle and Thomas Smith Webb who brought order by creating the General Grand Chapter of Royal Arch Masons and later the Grand Encampment of Knights Templar of the USA.[11]

Appendix: Celebrating St John's Days in Dublin 1773–1793

aka Data-Mining the Masonic Advertisements in the Dublin Press

I have never discovered another occasion where repeated newspaper advertisements have been used to promote various degrees and in what was clearly a 'competitive marketing strategy.' The run of papers is not complete, so some years are missing, and of course some issues are also missing. But it was possible to gather about 90 such advertisements. Why this happened starting in 1773 is guesswork but the first issue of Saunders Newsletter was on 10th March 1773. The other problem is that the search does not always gather all the results because of the quality of the OCR. But the searching was done with multiple slightly different search terms to maximise success.

Dublin Newspapers & Saunders' Newsletter

Des Keenan offers a fascinating insight into the Saunders Newsletter in the start of his chapter on Dublin papers, Clearly as a newspaper its approach seemed to find favour the masonic community.

> From every point of view except appearance the best newspaper was *Saunders' Newsletter* (1753–1879). For the historian a single line of unadorned fact from *Saunders'* is worth more than whole columns of obscure diatribes from others. Its tone was moderate Tory, and a family named Potts owned it. These opposed the Union until 1829 and its rare editorials up to that date expressed this fact. After 1829 they supported the Union. Early in the century editorial comment was virtually non-existent, but later it adopted the valuable habit of reprinting editorial comment from the more judicious London papers. These were usually Tory papers but Whig papers were not excluded. The editor of *Saunders'* was scrupulous about his facts. His reports of events like the meetings of the Catholic Association were models of accuracy, conciseness, and fairness. On the reporting of happenings outside Dublin as late as the Forties *Saunders'* copied an editorial from the London *Times* complaining about the

---

11   JL Belton, "Brother Just One More Degree," *Scottish Rite Journal*, (March-April 2013), pp. 7-9.

difficulty of establishing what was actually happening in the worst famine-stricken areas. Two reporters, eyewitnesses, writing within a fortnight of each other about conditions in the same workhouse flatly contradicted each other. One said that the place was remarkably filthy, the other that it was remarkably clean. It was obvious that the reports were deliberately distorted for political reasons, and *Saunders'* wished to make this clear to its readers. Altogether an excellent newspaper.[12]

---

12 Des Keenan, Pre-Famine Ireland: Social Structure (2000). http://www.deskeenan.com/4Pr Chapter27.htm#Dublin

Royal Arch & Knights Templars in Scotland
1743-1817

Before 1800 the evidence for the Royal Arch in Scotland is sparse, and if Lodges wanted to work other degrees they simply did it within the lodge; this required no authorization from anyone or from anywhere. But the fear that the ideas of the French Revolution could spread to the mainland of Britain through the auspices of the United Irishmen forced the government to take action. The government plan was to pass legislation to declare any organisation which required its members to take an oath of secrecy an illegal organisation. This of course not only included the United Irishmen, and a number of other organisations, but Freemasonry as well. The Deputy Grand Master of the Moderns, the Earl of Moira together with the Duke of Atholl representing both the Antients and Scotland argued their case, and there was an exemption granted for the masons. Note that Ireland was not included in this legislation.

The history of the Royal Arch in Scotland does not go back as far as that of either England or Ireland, but for all that is equally fascinating. And the first few Chapters which joined the Supreme Grand Chapter in 1817 are listed below. All the others seemed to have started after 1779:

No.1 Edinburgh. First chartered under a warrant No.31 of Early Grand Encampment of Ireland in 1779.

No.2 Stirling Rock. Claimed to have first worked the degree on July 30ᵗʰ 1743 (details below). *Dormant 1844, Reponed 1862.*

No.3 Enoch. Montrose, Angus. First worked the degree January 18ᵗʰ 1765 *Dormant 1837, Reponed 1853.*

No.4 Operative. Banff, Banffshire. First worked the degree August 25ᵗʰ 1766.

No.5 Linlithgow. West Lothian. First worked the degree in Ancient Brazen No.17 (Craft) in 1768. *Dormant 1849, Reponed 1861; Dormant 1887 Reponed 1892.*

No.6 Union. Dundee. First worked the degree 18 February 1773. *Dormant 1837, Reponed 1853.*

No.7 Noah. Brechin, Angus. Earliest evidence. January 14ᵗʰ 1774. *Dormant 1821, Reponed 1875.*

No.8 Haran. Laurencekirk, Kincardine. Evidence September 1774. *Dormant 1821, Reponed 1896.*

The Early Records of Stirling Kilwinning Lodge

The evidence for the appearance of the Royal Arch in 1743 in Stirling lack accuracy, and I use the exact words of Draffen (which were carefully chosen). That is because there is another entry for 1745 of the same two men being admitted masons, and sadly there is no way to completely resolve matters.

> The evidence of the Royal Arch Degree having been worked in Stirling in 1743 rests upon a sworn declaration, duly attested as copied from the original record then existing, deposited in 1818 with the Grand Scribe E. The minute so attested is in the following terms:
>
>
>
> STIRLING
>
> July 30th 1743
>
>
>
> Which day the Lodge of Stirling Kilwinning being met in the Brother Hutchinson's house, and being petitioned by Mungo Nicol, shoemaker, and Brother James McEwan, Student of Divinity, at Stirling, and being found qualified, they were admitted Royal Arch Masons of this Lodge, having paid their dues to the Treasurer, John Callender, R.W.M.

The difficulty with the 1743 statement is that the records also contain a very similar statement, and the great similarity where the year and degree are almost all that changes but two years later. The problem is that both entries cannot be correct. But the 1745 entry is also worth reading and is below:

>
>
> STIRLING
>
> July 30th 1745
>
>
>
> The Which day the Lodge of Stirling Kilwinning having meet in the Brother Hickson's hous And being petitioned by Mr. Mungo Nicoll, Shoe Maker, & Mr Brother James McEuen, Student of Devenitie at Sterling, & they being found qualified, they were Admitted as prenticess and payed the accustomed dues accordingly to the trer:- Jo Callender M.

The next Chapter in the list only started its work in 1765. It is interesting that all these Chapters are on the east coast of Scotland, and also that Chapters 3, 6, 7, 8, 9, and 12 were all in the Counties of Angus and Mearns (an area around Dundee). And it is unusual to have found that half of the 12 'earliest' Chapters were situated in a close geographical area.

Ancient Superexcellent Royal Arch Lodge constituted
18th February 1773 in Dundee

What is below might not be the earliest mention of the Royal Arch degree, but its detail is truly fascinating, because it records a military lodge No.52 opening constituting the Ancient Super Excellent Royal Arch Lodge and conferring the degrees on the members of Lodge Ancient No.49 (chartered on 2 May 1745). The words are those of Lindsay and he describes his findings.

> In the "Ancient" Lodge Room, on 18th February, 1773, "The Ancient Superexcellent Royal Arch Lodge was duly constituted by Edward Brereton, Grand Master of the Superexcellent Royal Arch Lodge, No. 52, held in H.M. Thirty Seventh Regiment of Foot, with Richard Brodly belonging to same and Alex. Ross, Shipmaster in Dundee." It was worked according to the regulations received by Lodge No. 52, from the Grand Lodge of England. Bro. Brereton with the consent of the members of No. 52, sent "true copies of the original resolutions now in our Lodge" to the Ancient and through it to the other two Lodges in Town if they cared to accept them.

> The first of these is a resolution of Grand Lodge of England, on December 4th, 1771; and the next was made at a General Chapter held the 3rd January, 1772. These and others that follow are for the guidance and admission of Arch members under the jurisdiction of the Grand Lodges of England, Ireland, and Scotland, and are issued from the office of the Grand Lodge of England, Bow Street, Covent Garden, on 23rd January, 1773, by William Dickey, Grand Secretary. [*ed. Note that this was the Antients GL*]

> These articles or regulations seem to have been considered as a form or a sort of charter and were accepted and put in force by the "Ancient" in Dundee, the "Enoch" in Montrose, and probably by Arch Lodges in Aberdeen and the North of Scotland, where the 37th Regiment was quartered in 1773.

> Although the Arch, as well as the "Higher degrees," were worked by the Craft Lodges in Scotland long before that date—each according to its own rule—there can be no doubt that in issuing these regulations of the "Ancients" Grand Lodge of England, Bro. Brereton, and Lodge No. 52, gave Arch Masonry a lift in their march northward.

> In a letter before me, dated Montrose, 28th January, 1818, the writer, an enthusiastic Mason, states the "Arch was first established in Montrose by the Wool-Combers-Travellers from Ireland and also by

them in Aberdeen." This was previous to 1764, for the writer records a conversation he had with an old Mason who was exalted that year. "The order they then practised prior to 1769 was, as they termed it, modern—which modern order then was the same now authorized by the Grand Chapter of England and Scotland, and in 1769 the Ancient way was given them by Travellers, Shipmasters, and Soldiers."

It is worth looking at exactly what those two extracts produced by Brereton were because they shed light onto the Antients view of the Royal Arch. The books are rare, and the author has not previously seen these extracts in full:

I. GRAND LODGE OF ENGLAND (ANTIENTS).
"Dec 4th 1771, *Resolved,* THAT no Person for the future shall be made a R.A. Mason but a legal Master, OR Past Master, of the Lodge, except a Brother that is going Abroad, who hath been twelve Months a Registered Master Mason, and must have the unanimous Voice of his Lodge to receive such Qualification; and in order to render this Regulation more expedient, it is further ordered, That all Certificates, granted to the Brethren from their respective Lodges, shall have inserted the Day the Brother, or Brothers, joined, or was made in the said Lodge; and that this Regulation shall take Place on St. John's, the 27th day of December, 1771."

II. GENERAL GRAND CHAPTER (ANTIENTS).
"And at a General Grand Chapter, held the 3d of January, 1772. it was *Resolved,* That those Brethren, who have been introduced (contrary to ancient Custom) into the Mystery of the R.A. shall be made (gratis) upon producing a proper Recommendation from their respective Lodges, to the General Grand Chapter, which shall or may be convened for that Purpose; such Recommendation to be signed by the proper Officers of the Candidate's Lodge; and it is the Intent and meaning of this Chapter, that no Recommendation of that Sort shall be signed by the said Officers" without having first obtained the unanimous Consent of the Lodge, for that Purpose."

Throughout the research for this book, one comes across mentions of Chapters and Encampments meeting in ports, either naval or commercial, and all in my mind asking questions about the work done by military lodges in spreading the ritual. So in Dundee one can find good evidence of all aspects of how it actually happened. The 37th Regiment of Foot was founded in 1702 and received its warrant as Lodge No.52 in 1756 and was the Antients second military lodge. They fought in the Seven Years War from 1758 to 1763, and then spent a year in Minorca before being garrisoned in Scotland between 1769 and 1774. After that they went to Ireland and on to the American War of Independence. They were in Dundee while being garrisoned (i.e., resting), and they met up with the local lodges.

Alexander Lawrie and his 'new rules'

Alexander Lawrie (1768–1831) was bred as a stocking maker but became a printer and bookseller in Edinburgh. For his services he was appointed Bookseller and Stationer to the Grand Lodge of Scotland, a title he even used in the Edinburgh Trade Directories. Shortly after he published the *History of Free Masonry* in 1804 he was appointed Assistant Grand Secretary, then was Grand Secretary from 1814 till 1826. This was followed from 1826 to 1831 jointly with his son Wm Alex Lawrie until his death, and then his son took over till 1870. It is interesting to note that his controversial book of 1804 did his reputation no harm—and that he published it before he had any official position in Grand Lodge (this was also the same for both Pennell and Spratt in Ireland). Lawrie was responsible for two acts that changed masonry in Scotland.

1. Degrees that Lodges were permitted to work.

Since 1792 the Grand Lodge in Edinburgh had complained of the introduction of 'non-Masonic ceremonies' and at the Grand Lodge on 19 May 1800 Lawrie proposed

> "that the Grand Lodge of Scotland sanction the three orders of masonry and those alone of Apprentice, Fellow Craft and Master Mason being the ancient Order of St John but understanding that other descriptions of Masons under various titles had crept into this country borrowed from other nations which he conceived to be inconsistent with the purity and true principles of the order. He therefore moved that the Grand Lodge of Scotland should expressly prohibit and discharge all Lodges from holding any other meetings than that of the three orders above described under the certification that their charters shall be forfeited ipso facto in case of transgression."

The Grand Lodge approved the clause in June 1800 and letters were sent to all the Lodges. This was linked with compliance with the Unlawful Societies Act and lodges had to submit copies of their certificates from the Justices of the Peace (Civil Magistrate). This placed all the lodges working other degrees in a bind; if they failed to comply then they would have their warrants withdrawn and none wished that to happen. Grand Lodge then decided to change their rules and dele-gated the responsibility for doing this checking to the Provincial Grand Masters. And the new rules were specific about that as well:

REGULATIONS AND INSTRUCTIONS FOR THE GOVERNMENT OF PROVINCIAL GRAND MASTERS

II. That it is of the utmost consequence to be accurately informed, whether the lodges holding of the Grand Lodge have "literally complied with the requisites of the act of Parliament, the Provincial Grand Master is requested particularly to attend, that the lodges in his district have strictly and literally complied with the terms of the act of Parliament, and the resolutions of the Grand Lodge, a copy of which accompanies these instructions." (p. 316)

IX. That the Provincial Grand-Master shall make inquiry into the orders and degrees of Masonry practised in the respective lodges in his district, and shall strictly prohibit and discharge them from practising any other degrees than that of St John's Masonry, consist-ing of Apprentice, Fellow Craft, and Master Mason, the only three degrees sanctioned by the Grand Lodge of Scotland. (pp. 317-318)

The Grand Lodge of Scotland faced three issues. It had always had difficulty in getting its lodges to pay the annual 'test fees' (dues) for all members, and second-ly that often lodges did not declare (all) their new members to the Grand Lodge, but instead provided their own Certificates. And by the end of the 18th century the number of extra degrees being worked in lodges—for which they did not need any approval to work—was undermining the functioning of the Grand Lodge in Edinburgh.

They saw the Unlawful Societies Act as an answer to their problem. Unlike England where each lodge had to lodge the names of its members with the local magistrate; in Scotland the Grand Lodge obtained permission to collect all the date from the lodges and then make one submission. This meant that the annual dues would be paid for all members on time. Plus, because they now stated that only three degrees could be worked, they could solve the problem of 'other de-grees'—simply by having nothing to do with them.

Sadly, for Grand Lodge it was only a few years before the reporting of members became less urgent, and alas the Grand Lodge failed to be assiduous in keeping its records up to date. There are cases to be found where some lodges had failed to submit all the names of their members—and if caught they had to reach some agreement with the Grand Secretary and then paid a (sometimes large) agreed sum of money. It was only in 1860 when they started keeping large ledgers, and keeping them updated, that the problem was resolved.

The great success was firmly pushing all other degrees completely and totally outside the scope of Grand Lodge. The problem simply went away and was somebody else's responsibility.

Strangely Lawrie promotes the Knights Templars in his 1804 History. In the 350 pages of the book, 146 are devoted to the history of Freemasonry in general and 36 of those pages (some 25%) are devoted to the Knights Templar and their connection with Freemasonry. This seems strange because only four years earlier Lawrie was proposing to Grand Lodge that all other degrees be expunged from Scottish masonry—and here he is offering positive encouragement to masonic Knights Templars.

The response of Masonic brothers to these new Rules

Quite simply, the brothers decided to find a way round this problem. This took several different alternatives. Lodges in the Borders (with England) who wanted to work the Royal Arch applied to the English Grand Chapter in London, and they already had an example in the Land o' Cakes Chapter which got its warrant from London in 1787, and it was followed in the next fifteen years by another seven chapters.

The other response was to obtain a warrant from the Early Grand Encampment of Ireland (EGE). The earliest warrant they had issued to Scotland was to Aberdeen in 1794 and a further twenty-one up until 1822.

The advantage of an EGE charter was that it entitled the owner to work both the Royal Arch degree and the Knights Templars series as well. The Knights in Ireland, almost as soon as they started working had found themselves with a problem—a shortage of Master Masons wanting to obtain the KT degrees because they were not able to find a chapter willing to give them the essential Royal Arch degree which was required to qualify to become a Knight. The EGE found the simple answer to this, which was to also confer the Royal Arch degrees, and then the KT—and that was the pattern that was followed in Scotland as well.

The other option that was used both by the Early Grand Encampment in Ireland, but also it seems by the Grand Conclave of Scotland was to apply for dispensation instead of a warrant. This allowed the recipient to work those degrees and without all the expenses of obtaining a warrant. Interestingly Lindsay that "On 13th February 1811, they [the Union Encampment of Knights Templars No.16 in Dundee] received a letter of Dispensation from the Royal Grand Conclave of Scotland."

The actions of the Grand Lodge of Scotland did not achieve their objective of collecting all the annual dues; but it did force those who wanted to work other degrees to form their own Grand bodies. Thus it was in Scotland that the basic structure we all recognize today, of a multiplicity of separate organisations, was first created. In the case of Scotland, it was also the energy and initiative of Alexander Deuchar whose vision enabled him to that the rejection of all other degrees by the Grand Lodge offered him potential to create both Knights Templars and Royal Arch bodies in Scotland. He was able to do this quite quickly, and it seems with a minimum of aggravation.

The Lodge of Perth & Scoon visit St Stephens Lodge

The masonic events in England, Scotland, and Ireland in the final quarter of the eighteenth century are complicated and nothing demonstrates that complexity perfectly than the case below because it demonstrates how degrees delivered in Lodge St Stephens, consecrated on 15th September 1777, and produced the Royal Grand Conclave and then the Supreme Grand Chapter, and involved the driving personality of Alexander Deuchar.

The first two entries in the Minute Book of Lodge St Stephens, dated 2nd and 4th December 1778, read:

> "This day the compliment of six sundry steps in Masonry was offered to the Office-Bearers of St Stephen's Lodge by sundry of the Brethren from the Ancient Lodge of Perth and Scoon. Accordingly there was a Committee called, so there was then present: the Right Worshipful Master . . . who all of one voice accepted of the compliment of that degree of Masonry, viz., the 4th called Past the Chair."

> "This night 4th Dec. 1778 being set apart by the Brethren of Perth and Scoon Lodge in order to confer upon the Office-Bearers of St Stephen's Lodge the following Degrees of Masonry, viz.: Excellent and Super-Excellent Masons, Arch and Royal Arch Masons, and lastly Knights of Malta."

It is worth recording that at this time the Lodge of Perth and Scoon was not part of the Grand Lodge of Scotland, but independent of it, and therefore it was not obliged to stop visiting other lodges, nor stop conferring novel degrees.

> The next minute of 10th December (1778) records that "a Committee belonging to St Stephen's met and entered Donald M'Donald, an apprentice in the Mystery of Free Masonry, in our Lodge here in Canongate, and at the same time conferred the 4th degree of Masonry upon Br. James Robertson, viz., that of Master past the Chair." Similar Meetings were held on 12th December 1778, and 19th January 1779, and on 28th January a Meeting was held when

"Petitions presented for John Cleghorn, James Thomson, George Zeigler, junr., and James Robertson, to be admitted Members of the Royal Arch of St Stephen's."... (p.5)

This minute is significant because in 1817, at the formation of the Supreme Grand Royal Arch Chapter (of Scotland), this was the earliest mention that the descendants of this 'lodge working the Royal Arch' could produce as evidence of working the Royal Arch. It also demonstrated the sequence that the degree of 'Passing the Chair' always came before receiving the Royal Arch degrees.

On 29th July 1783, it was recorded that "This night, at a meeting of the Society of Royal Arch Masons of St Stephen's Lodge, Edinburgh, the following persons were admitted members thereof, they having gone through the several steps necessary thereto, viz.: Brs James Ramsay (afterward the Governor), James Kegie, Wm. Scott, George Anderson, John Cowan, Thomas Drummond, and made Knights of the Royal Order of St. John—after which the lodge was closed in due and regular form (p. 7). Unfortunately, the minute book is missing some pages but there is evidence that they were working the both the Knights of Malta and of St. John.

Alexander Deuchar and the EGE Warrant from Ireland

The story of the arrival of the Royal Arch and KT degrees at Lodge St Stephens in 1778 was recounted above, and it is appropriate to take up the story again in 1805 because in February of that year Deuchar joins Lodge St Stephens. It is also worth noting that this was after the Grand Lodge of Scotland had cast aside all higher degrees. In the eighteen months between Deuchar joining the Lodge he has managed to become Grand Master in the KT & High Priest in the Royal Arch. The history of the lodge however omits one thing—that during the year 1805 the Early Grand Encampment of Ireland had issued a warrant, No.31, presumed to be for a Grand Encampment in Edinburgh. That specific action is not in the lodge history but what is recorded would fit in entirely. One is drawn towards the conclusion the Deuchar had a plan which he executed will some speed and efficiency.

A Chronological Explanation

When the Early Grand Encampment warrant No.31 for Edinburgh was issued in 1805 included the right for the Encampment to work both Royal Arch degrees and Knights Templars Degrees. Not all the evidence is available for all orders; and this brief chronology perhaps explains the speed at which events happened.

1805 21st January 1805 Deuchar joins St Stephens Lodge
1805 Early Grand Encampment warrant No.31 issued
1806 23rd January Regalia etc designs agreed
1806 27th April Laws and Regulations agreed
Grand Assembly of Knights Templars in Edinburgh formed
1809 Royal Grand Conclave of Knights Templar of Scotland established
1810 10 July letter sent to all known Encampments announcing the Duke of Kent as Grand Patron
1810 27 July Foundation meeting of Grand Conclave

It was that warrant from the Early Grand Encampment of Ireland No.31 that marked the seminal moment in the organisation of both Knights Templars and Royal Arch in Scotland and is still reflected in the organisations of today. The recorded history from Lodge St. Stephen's is below:

> ...on 21st February 1805, succeeded William Stoddart as head of the Order, viz. : Captain General, being supported by William Kinnaird as High Priest and John Allan, Alex. Milne, and John Arnott, as 1st, 2nd, and 3rd "Grand Masters." Seven Brethren were Initiated including Alex. Deuchar, Member of St David's Lodge (a name which later figures largely in the history of this Chapter), and he is thereafter elected Treasurer. (Davis p.11)

> The first Meeting of 1806, held on 23rd January, records that "Alexander Deuchar presented several drawings, and forms for Seals, Vails, Jewels, Sashes, &c., which were all aprovan of and ordered to be laid in the chest as Paterns when the funds should be able to afford them, and a chest was ordered to be procured for the purpose. Br. Alex. Deuchar moved that the Committee of Office-Bearers should be allowed to order from time to time such articles as the funds shall be able to afford, which was unanimously agreed to."

> The question of domicile is referred to for the first time on 27th February 1806 when it was agreed to that the Lodge of St Stephen's should be rented for a twelve months. (Davis pp. 11-12)

There was a General Meeting held on 27th April 1806, when a new set of Laws and Regulations[1] much more extended and elaborate than those hitherto recorded are "read, considered, and agreed to." The Rules are interesting, as showing that whereas up to January 1805, the last recorded election of Office-Bearers, the head of the Chapter was the Captain "General" (evidently meant for Governor), and the second the High Priest, the new Rules reverse these offices, the full list now being:

1. High Priest.	8. Grand Treasurer.
2. Captain Governor.	9. Grand Secretary.
3. 1st Grand Master.	10. Grand Provisor General.
4. 2nd Grand Master.	11. Grand Cup Bearer.
5. 3rd Grand Master.	12. Assistant Stewards.
6. 1st Grand Standard Bearer.	13. Guards.
7. 2nd Grand Standard Bearer.[2]	

The Installation took place at the Meeting following on 18th September 1806, when the Most Worshipful and Reverend Brother William Charles Kinnaird, H.P., installed "Our Most Worthy Brother, Alexander Deuchar into the Most Holy and Sublime Office of H.P. of the Royal Arch Encampment of Edinburgh [which office agreeable to last Chapter falls to his lot to fill from having been chosen Grand Master of the K.T. Order]."[3]

What follows next has been concisely summed up by Bob Cooper, so it is best to quote him:

> In 1809, Deuchar who was then Commander of the Edinburgh Encampment No.31, chartered by the Early Grand Encampment of Ireland, convened a meeting of *The Grand Assembly of Knights Templar in Edinburgh*. He announced that Prince Edward, the Duke of Kent (1767–1820), who was Grand Master of the Order in England, has accepted the position of *Royal Grand Patron of the Order in Scotland*, and that he Deuchar, has been appointed *Provisional Grand Master*, The Duke provided a Charter of Dispensation for the new Scottish body, to be known as the *Royal Grand Conclave*.[4]

---

1   The use of the words 'Laws and Regulations' of 1806 relate solely to the Royal Arch and there is no hint of anything Templar.

2   William A Davis, *History of Edinburgh Royal Arch Chapter No.1 1778–1911*, Edinburgh (1911); these three quotes are from pages 11-13.

3   William A Davis, *History of Edinburgh Royal Arch Chapter No.1 1778–1911*, pp. 13-14.

4   Robert LD Cooper, *Freemasons, Templars & Gardeners*, ANZMRC Melbourne (2005), p. 183.

And the title of the 1810 Charter reads as follows:

HIS ROYAL HIGHNESS PRINCE EDWARD DUKE OF KENT
Knight of the Most Honorable and Illustrious Order of the Garter
St Patrick etc etc etc
To the Knights Companions of the Exalted Religious and Military
Orders of
the Temple and Sepulchure, and of Saint John of Jerusalem
H.R.D.M. + K.D.S.H.
HEALTH-PEACE-GOODWILL

It does seem strange that the Charter does not seem to state the Duke's membership of the Templars, and if Deuchar stated the Duke as being Grand Master then he was wrong, he was Grand Patron. But in reality, it is probably correct to state the 'Time Immemorial Masonic Custom' (which still occurs today) of the use of a patent obtained elsewhere for a somewhat different and intended purpose. It is also curious to see that the Charter also included the H.R.D.M. It does seem that another Charter was obtained from the Duke of Kent in 1815 similar to the above which named Deuchar as Grand Master for Life.

One would guess that Deuchar was firstly seeking legality with his EGE warrant, and then later respectability with a Charter from the Duke of Kent; and he met those objectives. But in doing so the Royal Arch degree was suddenly orphaned, and without any ruling body. Probably in practice this made little difference to the degrees being conferred and the Conclave Encampments probably just continued their business. But Deuchar still had another objective in mind—a Grand Royal Arch Chapter.

Progress towards a Grand Royal Arch Chapter of Scotland

In the interim the Chapter remained busy, and some mentions are worthwhile, for example those of 1st April 1815.

> What was the nature and extent of the Rituals used in working the Degrees in the period under review (and possibly of later date) it is impossible to say, but the Records show that the number of the Degrees conferred upon the Candidates were numerous. Thus we read in the Minute of 1st April 1815 that the Petitioners were "Initiated into and instructed in all the Mysteries of The Excellent, Super-Excellent, Arch and Royal Arch Masonry, and were afterwards Initiated into the Mysteries of the Ark, Mark and Link Masonry, the Jordon and Babylonian Passes, and the Royal Prussian Blue Order." It reads rather a heavy handful for one Meeting. One other point to which attention may be drawn is a continuance of

the large number of Military and Naval men who are Exalted in the Chapter during these years.[5]

... on 24th April 1816 the Committee held its first Meeting for the purpose of adopting Measures for establishing a Supreme Grand Chapter of the Order in Scotland, when it was agreed that in future the word "Committee" be dropped and the Meetings be henceforth designated "The Lodge of Intelligence." The Members who attended this Meeting were "Bros. Alexr. Deuchar the M.E. Principal, P. Deuchar the Chief of the Tribe of Ephraim, James Gilchrist the Chamberlain, Murray Pringle the Scribe, Wm.Brydon the Priest, Walter H.Blackie the Sojourner." It appears from a later Minute Bro. Patrick Cunningham, Treasurer, completed the original Committee of Seven. There is incorporated a lengthy correspondence with the Grand Lodge of England, having for its object the obtaining of information as to procedure, but which appears not to be forthcoming, the explanation being that Mr White, Secretary to the Grand Lodge of England, had handed the first letter to the Duke of Sussex, who had mislaid it, and he (the Duke) explained that "he would not be able to turn his attention to the Royal Arch Order sooner than eight or ten months hence, in consequence of the business relative to the union betwixt the Ancients and Moderns not being completed." It was therefore agreed that a letter be sent to the Substitute Master of the Grand Lodge of Scotland requesting to know if the Grand Lodge of Scotland had any intention of taking the Royal Arch Degree under her sanction, and failing an affirmative answer, "that the Lodge proceed forthwith to adopt measures for forwarding the business which had been intrusted to it." (Davis pp. 25-26)

The Lodge of Intelligence next met on 3rd July 1816, ... A -comprehensive Circular Letter prepared by the Secretary for issue to all the known Chapters in Scotland was read and "was unanimously approven of and ordered to be printed and circulated forthwith." It contained a series of Resolutions providing for the conduct of the Supreme Chapter when erected, and also a series of Resolutions For the guidance of the Lodge of Intelligence prior to the Establishment of Supreme Chapter. It also provides for proxy Commissions to be issued by those Chapters who cannot attend the Meeting to be held in October 1816 for the Erection of Supreme Chapter, such

---

5   William A Davis, *History of Edinburgh Royal Arch Chapter No.1 1778–1911*. Edinburgh (1911), pp. 21-22.

proxy-holders becoming Members of the Lodge of Intelligence. It finishes up with "Any further information you may desire by letter (post paid), addressed, &c., I shall be happy to afford you." The Circular Letter was sent to 51 Royal Arch Chapters and also to 25 "whom we presume to be Royal Arch Masons."[6] (Davis pp. 27-28)

While all this had been going on Deuchar had also been trying to get the Duke of Sussex to be Grand Patron of the Grand Chapter in a similar fashion to getting the Duke of Kent to be Grand Patron of the Scottish Conclave. However, he was clearly not aware of the complications in England regarding how the Royal Arches of both Moderns and Antients would be united, nor that the Duke needed to resolve the English Royal Arch difficulties before thinking about Scotland.

Subsequent to sending the letter of April 1816 from the Lodge of Intelligence, a reply by the Grand Secretary to UGLE was sent to 'M Excellent Companion' in September 1816. The position of the Duke of Sussex is explained quite clearly and diplomatically, and he does in effect decline to be a Grand Patron of the Grand Chapter in Scotland and goes on to say:

> Under these circumstances I am commanded to suggest that if you should feel that a delay of a few months would be injurious to the Order, and you should find it indispensable to proceed in the immediate formation of a National Grand Chapter then it should be done in such a way as not to impact any general arrangements which might be agreed upon by the two Grand Lodges.[7]

There was now nothing stopping the creation of the Grand Chapter, and Deuchar proceeded with his plan. It is however clear that Deuchar has a very clear purpose in mind, and he seemed to be able to execute his plans smartly and get others to join him in the work. But first he ensured that his new organisation would be legal.

> On 19th February 1817 the Principal and one of the Chiefs appeared before Sir Patrick Walker, one of His Majesty's Justice of the Peace for the County of Edinburgh, and took the Oath of Qualification prescribed by Act of Parliament and thereafter lodged the necessary documents with the Justice of Peace Clerk. (Davis p. 32)

A series of important motions were submitted at Chapter Meeting

---

6   William A Davis, *History of Edinburgh Royal Arch Chapter No.1 1778–1911*, pp. 27-28.

7   Letter from William H White, Grand Recorder to the Gd Chapter to Alexander Deuchar, Z Royal Arch Chapter, Edinburgh, dated 7th September 1816. Ref 15/C/11C Museum of Freemasonry, London.

of 21st February 18 17. (1) That the smaller Degrees connected with the Royal Arch Order be committed to the charge of Committees "who should have the Management of the Initiation into the respective Degrees so that the Ceremony may be conducted in a more orderly manner." (2) To call together those Brethren in possession of the Priestly Order to consider the best steps to be adopted for having it introduced into Edinburgh "that the Priests belonging to the Royal Arch Degree may be regularly admitted into it."[8] (Davis p. 32)

The Minute of the Lodge of Intelligence of 11th August 1817 is mainly concerned with appointments of Proxy representatives and communications from Chapters asking for information principally as to costs to be incurred. One Chapter (St Luke's, Aberdeen), writing in name of the six Chapters in that City concludes its list of questions by desiring to know "what is meant by First, Second, and Third Principals mentioned in the Copy Warrant, as no such terms arc used in the Aberdeen Chapters." (Davis p. 36) [Note: the EGE issued a warrant to Aberdeen number 6 or 7 in its register in 1794—and they were presumably still working the Irish style of Royal Arch.]

The Minutes of 28th August 1817, bear that "The Chapter having this evening met proceeded to St John's Chapel to witness the consecration of a Supreme Grand Royal Arch Chapter for Scotland. A general Chapter of the Order having been opened by the First Most Excellent Principal of the Edinburgh Chapter aided by the two Senior Principals present, Br. Deuchar stated to the Meeting in very appropriate speech the causes which gave rise to the propositions for the Erection of this Institution, and complimented the Meeting upon the numerous list of Chapters which had come forward in support of it, he then proceeded to Consecrate the Supreme Grand Chapter which having been done with Corn, Wine and Oil, according to Ancient Custom the Chapter was proclaimed in the East, North, South, and West to be the Supreme Grand Royal Arch Chapter of Scotland, the Senior Grand Scribe p.t. (pro tempore) having previously read the Minutes of the proceedings of the Lodge of Intelligence which were unanimously approven of."[9]

---

8   William A Davis, *History of Edinburgh Royal Arch Chapter No.1 1778–1911*, p. 32.

9   William A Davis, *History of Edinburgh Royal Arch Chapter No.1 1778–1911*, p. 38.

An Overview of Scotland

The occurrence of the Royal Arch was relatively infrequent in Scotland, much as it was in England, but it seemed to find better welcome in Ireland in the 1740s and clearly it was the role of Laurence Dermott that popularized it in England. But everywhere at the end of the eighteenth century, change began to be driven to try and bring better organization in the face of the appearance of a multitude of degrees, and the brothers willing to take them, and to pay the fees. I suppose the way in which Lodge St Stephens received the Royal Arch and Knights Templar from the Lodge of Perth and Scoon would have been typical or the Lodge in Montrose. But it was not until around 1800 that several events occurred close together and which cumulatively sparked change. Unusually these events, international, national, military, masonic and individual can all be linked together to define the end result.

It seems that other degrees were spread though contact with military and travelling brothers bringing with it a low level of degree innovation. But then by around 1792 the Grand Lodge of Scotland felt that it did not have any control over the 'foreign degrees' worked in its lodges, not could it collect its annual test fees (dues. The Unlawful Societies Act of 1799 gave the Grand Lodge the chance it needed, and they seized the opportunity. They sent out warning letters to all their daughter lodges to behave or pay the price. Perhaps what they could not have expected was the radical action taken by one individual, Alexander Lawrie (printer, bookseller, and activist brother), to publish a book in 1804. This history did something very novel—it devoted **25%** of the 'History of Masonry' section to demonstrating the Knights Templar of the Crusades to the masonic Knights Templar. And from the 1770s it was possible to find texts in newspapers on the (Crusading) Knights Templars—it was something of general interest then, and it is still so today.

And the (masonic) Knights Templar had already been active in Ireland around 1770, and word would have travelled across the Irish Sea to Ayrshire and Galloway in the south-west of Scotland. So while it was new to appear a masonic book it was really already 30 years old news. But applying for EGE warrants suddenly enabled both the Royal Arch and KT degrees to gain a rapid foothold in Scotland. Nothing can forecast the arrival of the scene of a single-minded activist on the scene and in this case, it was Alexander Deuchar. He joined Lodge St Stephens, who were working both Royal Arch and KT, in February 1805 with a plan. Within months he had an EGE warrant, and by 1806 he led a KT Grand Conclave, and by 1810 had gained the approbation of the Duke of Kent. It took him rather longer to create a Grand Chapter, probably because he kept rubbing up against post 1813 Union issues in London and the antipathy of the Grand

Lodge of Scotland to 'other degrees'—so the Grand Chapter was eventually consecrated in 1817.

Below is added an additional chronology, because this was not completely a deal to which all parties agreed. Some EGE Encampments joined the Royal Grand Conclave, but some in the west of Scotland did not, eventually creating an Early Grand Encampment of Scotland in 1822. And some issues were not finally resolved till the 20th century.

The Mark Degree in Scotland

The earliest known Scottish record of a Lodge working the Mark Degree is in the minutes of the Lodge St John Operative in Banff and dates 7th July 1778; and the earliest record in the Lodge of Journeyman Masons in Edinburgh is no earlier than around 1789. However, it and other degrees vanished from Craft Lodges following the Unlawful Societies Act of 1799. It appears again in 1817 when all the 'sundry degrees' worked around the Royal Arch and KT were divided up between the two orders when the SGRAC was formed. And there is stayed until around 1860 when there were several complaints from senior Lodges because the Grand Lodge wanted them to cease working the Mark degree. Two committees, one from Grand Lodge and the other from Grand Chapter met and produced a report, in which it was agreed the practice would be allowed to continue. The key part of the report is below:

> What is generally known as the Mark Master's Degree was wrought by Operative Lodges of St John's Masonry in connection with the Fellow Craft Degree before the institution of the Grand Lodge of Scotland. Since then it had continued to be wrought in the old Operative Lodges; but in what may be called the Speculative Lodges it never has been worked at all—or at all events only in a very few. With the exception of the old Operative Lodges above-mentioned, this degree having been entirely abandoned by the Lodges of St John's Masonry, the Supreme Grand Royal Arch Chapter assumed the management of it as the Fourth Degree of Masonry in order to complete the instruction of their candidates in the preliminary degrees before admitting them to the Royal Arch. The degree, however, whether viewed as a second part of the Fellow Craft Degree or as a separate degree, had never been recognised or worked in England, Ireland, or the Continent or in America, as a part of St John's Masonry. It, therefore, now being desirable that an arrangement may be made which would reconcile the differences between the Grand Lodge of Scotland and the Supreme Grand Royal Arch Chapter and admit of the first three Degrees of St John's Masonry

being worked in the Lodges in Scotland in a manner similar to that allowed by Sister Grand Lodges, resolve to recommend the Grand Lodge of Scotland and the Supreme Grand Royal Arch Chapter of Scotland to enact and declare as follows, viz.:

1. That all Lodges holding of the Grand Lodge of Scotland shall be allowed to work this degree in virtue of the charters which they already possess.

2. That to prevent confusion with Brethren belonging to Lodges out of this kingdom, or with Sister Grand Lodges, this Degree, although held by the Grand Lodge to be a second part of the Fellow Craft Degree, shall only be conferred on Master Masons, and the secrets shall only be communicated in presence of those who have taken it either from a Lodge or Chapter entitled to grant it.

3. That the Grand Lodge of Scotland and the Supreme Grand Royal Arch Chapter of Scotland shall adopt the same Ritual in conferring the Degree, being that now adjusted by their respective Committees.

4. That any candidate applying to be admitted to the Royal Arch Degree, if he has received the Mark Degree in a regular Lodge of St John's Masonry, shall not be required to take it a second time from the Chapter into which he seeks admission; but in the event of his not having received it, he shall be obliged to take it from that Chapter.

5. That as regards the Royal Arch Degrees, the Mark Degree shall be reckoned as the Fourth Degree in Masonry.

6. That nothing contained in these regulations shall interfere with the Superintendence which the Supreme Grand Royal Arch Chapter of Scotland claims over Mark Masonry out of Scotland, or with the Lodges holding of it in England or abroad.[10]

From 1800 when Grand Lodge stated that its only recognized the three degrees the official wording in the 1836 (first) Book of Constitutions was "*The Grand Lodge of Scotland practises no degrees of Masonry, but those of Apprentice, Fellow-Craft and Master Mason*" which *after 1860 became* "All Lodges holding of the Grand Lodge of Scotland are strictly prohibited and discharged from holding any other Meeting than those of the three Orders—viz., Apprentice, Fellow-Craft, and Master Mason—denominated St John's Masonry, the Mark forming part of the Second Degree."

---

10 R S Lindsay, History of the Mason Lodge of Holyrood House (St Lukes) (1935), p. 489, and also in GS Draffen, The Mark Degree, Grand Lodge of Scotland Yearbook (1954), pp. 82-92.

Clearly on this occasion the position of the members of the lodges was such that both Grand Lodge and Grand Chapter were forced to concede on their established positions. A lodge in Scotland would typically hold a Mark degree meeting once a year, and all recently qualified members would be invited to take the degree. The Mark degree is part of the Royal Arch in Ireland and in England it is a separate Grand Lodge.

Some Additional Scottish Chronology

1768 Linlithgow RAC No.5—John Belton's Chapter. First mention in the minute book of its parent Lodge Ancient Brazen No.17 in Linlithgow (itself founded before 1654).

1779 It is worth adding here the warrant from Mother Kilwinning Lodge in Scotland for the constitution in Dublin of a High Knights Templars of Ireland Kilwinning Lodge.

1792 GL of Scotland complains that lodges were not paying their annual test fees (dues).

1817 When the Grand Chapter was formed the two parties split all the degrees that had been worked, and each took those most relevant to them. The list is considerable.

Until 1817 the Royal Arch Degree, along with numerous others, was worked in the Templar Encampments in addition to being worked in many Lodges. The fact that the Craft Lodges had been prohibited in 1800, by the Grand Lodge of Scotland, from working any degrees other than the first three, made little difference to the country Lodges who continued to "gang their ain gait" [do what they chose to do] in this matter. When the Supreme Grand Chapter was founded, it became necessary to arrange with the Royal Grand Conclave as to the division of the degrees then under the supervision of that body. After negotiations the following division was agreed to[11]:

ROYAL ARCH DEGREES

1. Master Passed the Chair
2. Excellent Master
3. Super Excellent Master
4. Arch Degree
5. Royal Arch Degree
6. Mark Mason

---

11   George Draffen, *Triple Tau* (1955), p. 7.

7. Ark Mason

8. Link and Wrestle

9. Babylonian Pass or Red Cross of Daniel

10. Jordan Pass

11. Royal Order or Prussian Blue

12. High Priest

TEMPLAR DEGREES

1. Black Mark

2. Mediterranean Pass

3. Knight of Malta

4. Knight of the Holy Grave

5. Knight of Patmos

6. Knight of the Red Cross of Constantine

7. Knight Templar

1822 Four or five Conclaves with warrants from the Early Grand Encampment of Ireland petitioned 'praying that the Scottish Encampments be erected into a Sovereign Jurisdiction.'

> The Irish Chapters-there were but four or five-remained loyal to Ireland until 1822 when the Early Grand Encampment of Ireland granted them a Constitution to erect an Early Grand Encampment of Scotland.

This petition was granted by the Early Grand Encampment of Ireland on 22 June 1822.[12]

1836 The Grand Conclave was remodeled, becoming non-masonic and admitting non-Masons.

1858 The Grand Lodge of Scotland and SGRACS agree on joint control of the Mark Degree.

1863–1868 A General Grand Chapter for Scotland (or Early Grand Royal Arch Chapter) was formed after arguments between SGRACS and Walker Arnett.

1872–1895 A Convent General was planned to be created by merging the Convents of England, Ireland and Scotland. Scotland withdrew before its formation, but the joined body struggled on before dissolving back into its national parts. In 1873 the Albert Edward, Prince of Wales was elected as Grand Master

---

12 George Draffen, *Triple Tau*, p. 9 & Charles A Cameron, *On the Origin and Progress of Chivalric Freemasonry in the British Isles* (1900).

of the 'Convent General of England and Wales, and Ireland' (perhaps that was the motivation for the whole enterprise?)

1877 The Early Grand Encampment of Scotland remained small and insignificant (only four or five lodges) until the advent of the Mathew McBain Thomson as Grand Master in 1877. He remained at the head of the Order until 1881. During his term of office he revised the rituals of the various degrees and divided the Grand Encampment into three bodies:

> *(a)* The Early Grand Royal Arch Chapter of Scotland.
> *(b)* The Grand Encampment of the Temple and Malta in Scotland.
> *(c)* The Scottish Grand Council of Rites.

1877 Cryptic degrees imported from Illinois in 1877 and a Grand Council formed in 1880.

1895 Early Grand Royal Arch Chapter absorbed by the SGRACS, taking in some 9 Chapters situated in the southwest of Scotland..

1909 The two KT bodies eventually merge to become 'The Great Priory of the Religious and Military Order of the Temple in Scotland.'

1915 SGRAC takes the "Royal Ark Mariners Grand Body" (including RAM, Knights of the East, Knight of the Sword and Knight of the East and West) and the Grand Council (Cryptic Degrees of Royal Master, Select Master and Super Excellent Master) under its wing as 'Lodge and Council' and 'Cryptic Council.' Until then these degrees were simply worked in Royal Arch Chapters with a Chapter Warrant.

1923 The Red Cross Order refused to disappear, and it emerged again (with the Royal Ark Mariners) under the banner of the SGRAC as 'Lodge and Council.'

Appendix: Unlawful Societies Act 1799

The Unlawful Societies Act of 1799 seemed to fall out of being strictly complied with fairly early. And certainly in England, most of the returns were not retained and only a few reached the archives. In Scotland the GL of Scotland obtained agreement that it would provide all the data of all the lodges, and thus treat the law as a tool to enable them to collect all the test fees (Scots for annual dues) and to stop lodges practicing any degrees other than the three Craft degrees.

What had always remained unclear was how the many other degrees that were outside the Grand Lodges either complied with the 1799 law, or even if they complied at all. *This example demonstrates that there was both compliance by 'other degrees' and acceptance by the Civil Magistrate of other 'masonic organi-*

sations' other than the large Grand Lodges.[13] For interest the text of the statements is reproduced below. No other such example is known of such compliance with the 1799 Act by anybody other than a Craft Grand Lodge, and as such it is a rare curiosity.

> Affidavit made before a Justice of Peace Certifying the Political Respectability of the Chapter.[14]
>
> At Edinburgh 26 day of October one Thousand Eight hundred and Eight years.
> Before Peter Hill, Esqr., one of his Majesty's Justices of the Peace in Edinburgh.
> Appeared: Alexander Deuchar, Seal Engraver, Grand Master, and Samuel Cunningham, Dept. Grand Master of the Society of Royal Arch Masons and Knights Templars, in said City agreeable to the terms of an Act of Parliament passed in the year one thousand seven hundred and ninety-nine years.
> Entitled : an Act for the more Effectual suppression of societies Established for seditious purposes and for the Better preventing Treasonable and Seditious Practices—And made oath, That in the Society of Free Masons over which they preside as Office-Bearers, called the Royal Arch Masons and Knight Templars, nothing Prejudicial to Church or State is transacted, and that said Societies meet exclusively for the purposes of Free Masonry as of old practised among the Craft. That they meet on the fourth Wednesday of every month in the Room Belonging to the Lodge Edinburgh St Stephen in Advocates' Close. Also, that the list herewith Presented and attested by the above Alexander Deuchar, contains a complete Roll, to the Best of our knowledge and belief, of all the Members of the Lodge.
> All which is Truth they hereby Certify—as they shall answer to God.
>
> Signed   Alexr. Deuchar.
>   Peter Hill.

---

13 The Unlawful Societies Act of 1799 included England and Scotland but did NOT apply to Ireland. After the text of the bill was first made public and heard in Parliament there was a complaint by Mother Kilwinning via a member of Parliament that she and her daughter Lodges were also proper, regular, and indeed older than the Grand Lodge of Scotland. This point was accepted, and the terms of the Act were altered so that Kilwinning would be included. It is possible that this might have made it possible other lodges of other degrees also to make similar declarations either possible, or probably just simpler.

14 WA Davis, *History of the Edinburgh Royal Arch Chapter No.1*, Appendix 2, pp. 175-176.

Copy of Certificate of the Justice of Peace Clerk.

I, Robert Newbigging, Depute Clerk of the Peace for the Shire of Edinburgh, Do hereby Certify that there has been lodged with me a Certificate upon Oath, by two of the Members of the Royal Arch and Knights Templars Mason Lodge in Edinburgh attested by Alexander Deuchar, Seal Engraver, Master, and Samuel Cunningham, Writer, Past Master, in terms of an Act of Parliament passed in the year seventeen hundred and ninety-nine entitled "An Act for the more effectual suppression of Societies established for seditious and treasonable purposes and for better preventing Seditious and Treasonable Practices." Together with their denomination of said Lodge, its usual times and places of Meeting, and a list of the attending members to be recorded in terms of said Act.

As witness my hand at Edinburgh the Twenty-eighth day of October Eighteen Hundred and Eight Years.

(Signed) R. Newbigging (pp. 175-176)

Appendix: 1816 Letter from the Lodge of Intelligence to those believed to be working the Royal Arch

Lindsay in doing his research says that during his research he came across various circulars including one from the 'Lodge of Intelligence' created by Alexander Deuchar to help him create the Supreme Grand Chapter in 1817. On 24th April 1816, at Edinburgh, he sent out a letter identifying the various groups of chapters according to their origin who were working in Scotland:

1. Those Chapters in Scotland already holding warrants from the Grand Royal Arch Chapter of England.

2. Those Chapters who have for a long period of years been established in Scotland, and that prior to the year 1800.

3. Those Chapters which are attached to the Encampments of Knight Templars, who hold of the Royal Grand Conclave of Scotland.

4. Those Chapters, if any, which are held under authority from Ireland.

5. Those brethren who have assumed the right, within these few years, of holding Royal Arch Chapters.

The circular also included a full list of masonic bodies they believed were probably working the Royal Arch degree. The big surprise is that there were so many names on the list, but especially the number of KT Encampments also working the Royal Arch. And Deuchar was in a position to know exactly how many there were because he had previously created the Royal Grand Conclave in 1810. It is not generally understood that both in Ireland and (after 1800) in Scotland the Royal Arch and KT were totally interlinked. This list is positive proof of what was happening.

There were 14 warrants issued for Scotland by the Irish Early Grand Encampment. Two were before the 1799 Unlawful Societies Act and 11 were all for Encampments in the west of Scotland, in Ayrshire or Glasgow. Interestingly of the 11 Encampments in the west only three joined the Supreme Grand Royal Arch Chapter of Deuchar, and 8 did not. That was to be the source of later problems.

What must be noted from the list below is that there are 43 Chapters whose name included "Encampment KT," but only 14 warrants. That means that 29 of the 43 were working simply with a dispensation, or perhaps simply choosing to work the degree. That situation tells us that there was a high degree of informality; and that was what the Grand Lodge and Grand Chapter etc all sought to being into order around 1800.

This Circular sent to the following Royal Arch Chapters.

Edinburgh Royal Arch Chapter.
Encampment Knights Templars Kilmarnock.
St. John's Encampment K.T. Glasgow.
Union Encampment K.T. Ayr.
Duke of Kent's Encampment K.T. Glasgow.
Shetlestone St. John's Encampment K.T.
St. James' Encampment K.T. Aberdeen.
Caledonian Encampment K.T. Dunse.
St. John's Encampment K.T. Strathaven.
St. John's Encampment K.T. Castle Douglas.
Ayr Military Encampment K.T.
Grand Assembly K.T., Ayr.
Wallace Tower Encampment K.T. Ayr.
St. Cuthbert's Encampment K.T. Whitehom.
Prestwick Encampment K.T.
Union Encampment K.T. Dundee.
St. John's Encampment K.T. Haddington.
St. Cuthbert's Encampment K.T. Tweedmouth.
Union Encampment K.T. Maybole.

Greenock Encampment K.T.

Aboyne Encampment K.T. Aberdeen.

St. Paul's Encampment K.T. Lanark.

Paisley Encampment K.T.

Champaign Encampment K.T. Ochiltree.

St. John's Encampment K.T. Dundee.

St. Bryde's Encampment K.T. Douglas.

Grampian Encampment K.T. Perth.

Strathmore Encampment K.T. Glammis.

Port Spain Encampment of K.T. Trinidad.

Lomond Encampment of K.T. Cupar Fife.

St. Salem's Encampment K.T. Beith.

Girvan Encampment K.T.

Hamilton Encampment K.T.

Inverness Encampment K.T.

Creiff Encampment K.T.

Encampment of K.T. Bathgate.

St. Ninian's Encampment K.T. Brechin.

Dumfermline Encampment K.T.

Muirkirk Encampment of K.T.

Wigton Encampment of K.T.

Biggar Free Operatives K.T.

Annan St. Andrew's K.T,

Gatehouse of Fleet Encampment K.T.

Cree Bridge Encampment K.T.

St. Bryde's Encampment K.T. Kirkcaldy.

St. Luke's Lodge, Gilcolmscleugh, Aberdeen.

Dalkeith Lodge.

St. Andrew's Lodge, St. Andrew's.

Stirling Royal Arch Lodge.

Thistle Lodge, Stewarton.

Eymouth Lodge.

And also to the following, whom we presume to be Royal Arch Masons.

Dunbar Castle Lodge.
Falkirk Lodge.

Melrose Lodge.

Mother Kilwinning Lodge.

Langholm Lodge.

Old Lodge Peebles.

Gal stone St. Patrick, Kilmarnock.

St. Cuthbert's, Kirkcudbright.

Dunkeld Lodge.

Old Lodge Stirling.

Montrose Kilwinning Lodge.

Keith's Lodge Peterhead,

Glasgow St. Mungo.

Glasgow Royal Arch.

Glasgow St. Mungo Royal Arch.

Cambuslang Royal Arch.

Rutherglen Royal Arch.

Patrick St. Mary's.

Tarbolton St. David's Lodge.

Selkirk Lodge.

Jedburgh Lodge.

Paisley Royal Arch Lodge.

Royal Arch Lodge, Pollockshaws.

Linlithgow Lodge.

Scoon Lodge.[15]

This list is highly significant because it demonstrates the predominance of bodies working the Royal Arch and associated rituals used by the *Early Grand Encampment of Ireland* in the period from 1800 to 1817. It is clear proof of the strong Irish influence on the higher degrees in Scotland.

---

15   Thomas A Lindsay, *AQC* vol.8 (1895), pp. 7-11.

The Royal Arch and Templars in England

The earliest 'evidence' for the Royal Arch in England comes ironically from Ireland, and from the pen of Dassigny in 1744.

> Now as the landmarks of the constitution of Free-Masonry are universally the same throughout all kingdoms, and are so well fixt that they will not admit of removal, how comes it to pass that some have been led away with ridiculous innovations, an example, of which, I shall prove by a certain propagator of a false system some few years ago in this city, who imposed upon several very worthy men under a pretence of being **Master of the Royal Arch, which he asserted he had brought with him from the city of *York***; and that the beauties of the Craft did principally consist in the knowledge of this valuable piece of Masonry. However he carried on his scheme for several months, and many of the learned and wise were his followers, **till at length his fallacious art was discovered by a Brother of probity and wisdom, who had some small space before attained that excellent part of Masonry in *London*** and plainly proved that his doctrine was false ; whereupon the Brethren justly despised him and ordered him to be excluded from all benefits of the Craft, and altho' some of the fraternity have expressed an uneasiness at this matter being kept a secret from them (since they had already passed thro' the usual degrees of probation) I cannot help being of opinion that they have no right to any such benefit until they make a proper application, and are received with due formality, and as it is an organis'd body of men who have passed the chair, and given undeniable proofs of their skill in Architecture, it cannot be treated with too much reverence, and more especially since the characters of the present members of that particular Lodge are untainted, and their behaviour judicious and unexceptionable; so that there cannot be the least hinge to hang a doubt on, but that they are most excellent Masons.[1] (p. 127)

The Oration of Francis Drake in York

There is an interesting quotation that comes from York, spoken in 1726 and printed in 1727 and is entitled: *A Speech Deliver'd to the Worshipful and Ancient*

---

1 Fifield Dassigny, *Serious and Impartial Enquiry*, in WJ Hughan, *Memorials of the Masonic Union* (1919 reprint), p. 127. Bold in text by author.

Society of Free and Accepted Masons. At a Grand Lodge, Held at *Merchant's-Hall,* in the City of Y*ORK, on* St. *John's* Day, *December* the 27th, 1726. The RIGHT WORSHIPFUL Charles Bathurst, *Esq; Grand-Master.* By the Junior Grand Warden.

> BUT I must not trespass too much on your Patience, and shall therefore, tho' unwillingly, pass over the Building of *Solomon's Temple,* a Building where God himself was the Architect, and which to all Masons is so very Particular, that 'tis almost unpardonable to neglect it.

> BUT that with the Repairs of it by *Josiah,* rebuilding by *Zerubbabel* and *Herod,* to the final Destruction by *Titus Vespatian;* together with the History of the *Grecian* and *Roman* Orders and Architects, the *Gothick* Intrufion over all, and its late Resurection and present growing Greatness, may be Subjects sufficient for several Discourses; which, since I have ventur'd to break the Ice, I hope some abler Hand will carry on.[2]

This is the only time that the repairing of the Temple by Josiah is mentioned in any English masonic publication up to the 1740s. The statement by Fifield Dassigny that the Royal Arch arrived in Dublin first from York, and then later from London, and that it was the London version that was adopted in Ireland raises a question. Was it a Josiah version of the Royal Arch that came from York? It is an important thought because the Irish 'always' had two Royal Arch legends, a Zerubbabel one and a Josiah one that ran side by side. The matter was only finally resolved in 1864 when the Grand Chapter of Ireland formally adopted the Josiah legend for the Royal Arch in Ireland. There is no evidence known the support the thought that the York version of 1744 had been based upon a Josiah legend, but it remains a fascinating probability.

As further evidence of the Royal Arch we have little more than Thomas Dunkerley's own claim that he was exalted in a Portsmouth Lodge in 1754.

England 1751 – The Antients arrive in town

Laurence Dermott arrived from Dublin after serving as Worshipful Master of his Lodge in 1746 and in the same year, by his own claim, becoming a Royal Arch Mason. He must have brought with him the Zerubbabel legend, because whatever it was there did not seem to be any variance with what was (assuming Dassigny was correct) being worked in London.

---

2 Francis Drake, *A Speech Deliv'r'd to the Worshipful and Ancient Society of Free and Accepted Masons.* (1727) pub Thomas Gent, York, p. 11.

It is worth explaining here that at this time in England the Royal Arch had no status. There was no organisation responsible for the degree, and no certificates, and few records remain and those that do partly remain because they were mentioned in ordinary lodge minutes. Research has no choice but to use what little information is available. Similar situations appear for many of the multitude of degrees that appeared during the eighteenth century.

However the formation of the Antients Grand Lodge in 1751 brought with it the arrival of the Royal Arch. As the first (1756) edition of Ahiman Rezon tells us is:

> That part of Masonry commonly called the Royal Arch (which I firmly believe to be the Root, Heart and Marrow of Free-Masonry).[3]

But in 1752, only one year after the formation of the Antients Grand lodge, comes a mention of the Royal Arch in the Minutes of the Antients Grand Lodge. At a meeting of the Grand Committee of the 'Antients' on March 4, 1752, some Brethren made formal complaints that two individuals, Phealon and Mackey, "had initiated many persons for the mean consideration of a leg of mutton," and had pretended "to have made Royal-Archmen."

> Grand Committee at the Griffin Tavern Holborn
> March 4. 1752.
> Brother John Gaunt Master of No. 5. In the Chair

> The following Brethren viz Thomas Figg of No. 5. Laurence Folliot of the same Lodge, Samuel Quay of No. 2. Richard price of No. 3 & Henry Lewis of No. 4. made formal Complaints against Thomas Phealon and John Macky, better known by the name of the leg of Mutton Masons----

> In course of the examination it appear'd that Phealon and Mackey had initiated many persons for the mean consideration of a leg Mutton for dinner or supper. to the disgrace of the Ancient Craft. that it was deficult to discover who assisted them if any. as they seldom met twice in the same Alehouse. That Macky was an Empiric in phisic; and both impostors in Masonry. That upon examining some brothers whom they pretended to have made Royal-Archmen, The parties had not the least Idea of that secret. That Doctor Macky (for so he was called) pretended to teach a Masonical Art by which any man could (in a moment) render himself Invisible. That the Grand Secret[y] had examined Macky, at the house of Mr. James Duffy Tobacconist in East Smithfield who

---

3   Laurence Dermott, Ahiman Rezon, London (1756), p. 41.

was not a Mason and that Macky appear'd incapable of making an Apprentice with any degree of proprety. Nor had Mackey the least Idea or knowledge of Royal Arch masonry. But instead thereof he had told the people whom he deceived, a long story about 12 white Marble stones &c &c and that the Rain Bow was the Royal Arch, with many other absurdities equally foreign and Rediculous.

The Grand Committee Unanimously Agreed and Order'd that neither Thomas Phealon nor John Mackey be admitted into any Ancient Lodge during their natural lives.

And 6 months later the minutes record:

Grand Committee at Temple Eating house &c
Sep. 2nd 1752
Resolved that this Grand Committee shall be formed immediately into a Working Lodge of Master Masons in Order to hear a Lecture from the Grand Secretary Laurence Dermott
The Lodge was Opened in Ancient form of Grand Lodge and every part of Real freemasonry was traced and explained: except the Royal Arch.
The Lecture ended, and the Lodge was Closed with the most agreeable and harmonious humour. (*QCA* vol.11, p. 31)

7th March 1757
Order'd the Masters of the Royal Arch shall also be summon'd to meet in Order to regulate things relative to that most valuable branch of the Craft. (*QCA* vol.11, p. 37)

It is also important to note that it was in the first edition of Ahiman Rezon, in 1756, that Dermott first quotes Dassigny in support of his 'rule' that only those who had passed the Chair were able to gain the Royal Arch. Clearly the Royal Arch was more widely in demand among ordinary brothers than Dermott had expected. And in March 1757 the Antients Grand Lodge also took steps to provide some structure for the Royal Arch.

Whether Dermott was prompted to include the Royal Arch into the Antient's workings because of his liking for the degree or whether he saw it as part of his marketing strategy we shall never know. But clearly it was a success because the membership requirement to be a 'master past the chair' had become an immediate problem in England by 1756. But that decision was to influence and control the structure of English freemasonry for the next few centuries!

The Rise & Fall of the 'Passing the Chair' Degree.

From what Dassigny has to say about the Royal Arch in Dublin in 1744 then, it is absolutely clear from his text that the Royal Arch is intended to be a degree only for the select of the brotherhood, that is only for those who have served their lodges as Master. And that also gives it perhaps a similar imperative to the Scots Master degree; of being a degree for the "rulers in the free-masonry"!

We know that Dermott took the degree to England and that by 1756, only a mere five years after the formation of the Antients Grand Lodge he was stating in the first edition of Ahiman Rezon that the Royal Arch was 'the root, heart and marrow of free-masonry.' Many writers have offered that quote but sadly they failed to read to the end of the same paragraph, because Dermott words make it clear that the 'master past the chair' restriction of obtaining the Royal Arch was even by 1756 causing problems in England. Dermott's need to attempt keep control by requoting Dassigny's words is demonstrated below:

> This is the case of all those who think themselves Royal Arch Masons, without passing the chair in regular form, according to the ancient custom of the Craft.

> To this I will add the opinion of our worshipful brother, Doctor Fifield D'Affigney, printed in the year 1744:

>> "Some of the Fraternity, says he, have expressed an uneasiness at this matter being kept a secret from them (since they had already passed through the usual degrees of probation). I cannot help being of opinion, that they have no right to any such benefit until they make a proper application, and are received with due formality: and as it is an organized body of men who have passed the chair, and given undeniable proofs of their skill in architecture, it cannot be treated with too much reverence; and more especially since the characters of the present members of that particular Lodge are untainted, and their behaviour judicious and unexceptionable: so that there cannot be the least hinge to hang a doubt on, but that they are most excellent Masons."[4]

And that quote was used in every subsequent edition of Ahiman Rezon through to 1800, as well as the Irish editions of Ahiman Rezon. But that perhaps brings us back to some innate need or urge within human beings, including masons, to gain just another degree, another inner secret. So the brethren and the lodges found a way round the problem. They just created a simple degree in which a

---

4   Ahiman Rezon (1756), p. 48.

brother was placed in the chair for a minute or two after taking an obligation and learning the token and word—and he could then be given the Royal Arch degree. There would of course be a fee for that, and the money would go into the lodge's chest and nothing needed to be paid to a Grand Lodge. But in the 1800 edition of Ahiman Rezon the Antients Grand Lodge admit defeat because in their Grand Chapter they print the revised Rules and Regulations in approved in 1794.[5] It could also be the Antients response to the clear definition of the requirements to become a Royal Arch mason as set out by the (Moderns) Grand Chapter in 1786 (see previous chapter).

While this was the first published appearance of such a certificate; it does seem it was actually in earlier use. Such a certificate was issued on 11 February 1790 to Sir Watkin Lewes[6] and described him as a Geometrical Master Mason. But clearly and almost unnoticed the requirements to become a Companion had become the norm. But even today the more closely one looks at the qualifications need to become a member it is clear that a similar process is still required today.

But there was a further, and significant, practical problem faced by both sides. The strict entry requirements meant that any Royal Arch Chapter was only able to function by taking the Past Masters of the lodge which also worked nearby, and probably also needed several other lodges Past Masters as well to form a functioning Royal Arch Chapter. In short the system as defined by Dassigny (and supported by Dermott) hardly allowed a viable Chapter to be created—so the Chapters themselves were under real pressure to break the rules in order to get a numbers of members to ensure that a Chapter prospered. And they simply chose to break the 'rules.' Antients lodges typically installed new Worshipful Masters twice a year and that might have slightly reduced the recruitment issue for them.

1766 – The Moderns wake up

That is probably not quite correct because Thomas Dunkerley states that he was created a Royal Arch Mason in the naval port of Portsmouth in 1754, which was also (& curiously) the same year that he was initiated. So it is probable that there were some lodges working the Royal Arch degree around English naval ports on the south coast.

Bernard Jones states that on 13th August 1758 the earliest known English minute

---

5   Ahiman Rezon (1800). Revised and corrected at a General Grand Chapter, held at the Crown and Anchor Tavern, in the Strand, London, October 1, 1794.—Confirmed in Grand Lodge, December 3, 1794. Rule III, p. 119.

6   Roy A. Wells, Freemasonry in London from 1785 (1984), p. 79. A large section of this book relates to the Royal Arch as worked by Domatic Lodge No.177 and provides an excellent background to masonry as worked in Antient Lodges and Chapters.

of a brother becoming a Royal Arch Mason was in Lodge 220 meeting at Lord Blakeney's Head when a Brother William Gordon was 'raised to a Royal Arch and accepted.' The lodge in the next year held seven Royal Arch meetings and raised a total of thirteen brothers.[7] This was a Moderns lodge but worked an Antients ritual.

Perhaps the most fascinating record is from York in 1762 in which four members of a Moderns Lodge were made Royal Arch Masons and that meeting was recorded in a book entitled *Minute Book Belonging to the Most Sublime Degree or Order of Royal Arch appertaining to the Grand Lodge of ALL England*, in York! We cannot better Bernard Jones's explanation, so it is repeated below:

> On Sunday, February 7, 1762, a Royal Arch lodge was opened at the Punch Bowl Inn, in Stonegate in York, by members of the Punch Bowl Lodge, No. 259, founded in the preceding year (and expiring in its seventh). Four members, all of them actors and members of the York Company of Comedians, opened the Royal Arch lodge, so providing an early instance of a separate organization especially formed for the working of the Royal Arch ceremonial. Under the 'Antients,' and legally so, that ceremonial was worked in their Craft lodges, while under the 'Moderns' at that time the Royal Arch Degree was irregular and, if worked, quite unofficial. But this was not a 'Moderns' lodge! It was held under the authority of the Grand Lodge of ALL England, a Grand Lodge erected by an old City of York lodge in 1725 and holding sway actually in parts of Yorkshire, Cheshire, and Lancashire. The separate organization had a minute-book entitled *Minute Book Belonging to the Most Sublime Degree or Order of Royal Arch appertaining to the Grand Lodge of ALL England, held at the City of York, 1762*. (This lodge or chapter became in the course of time a Grand Chapter.) The first minute recorded relates to the meeting of Sunday, February 7, 1762, already mentioned, and states that "Brothers Burton, Palmes, Tasker and Dodgson petition'd to be raised to the Fourth Degree of Masonry, commonly call'd the Most Sublime or Royal Arch, were accepted and accordingly made."[8]

This example makes it clear that in the eighteenth century the formal rules and understandings of 'regularity' that we have today, did not apply, even did not exist. And looking at what Jones wrote in 1957 say that 'under the Moderns the

---

7 Bernard E Jones, *Freemason's Book of the Royal Arch*, pp. 50-51. The quote below is from the same page.

8 Bernard E Jones, p. 51.

Royal Arch degree was irregular,' it feels that it gives a false impression of events. We would take the view that in 1762 that any group of brethren were free to do whatever they chose to do. Quite simply it was a different age, and masonry was just starting to develop.

It must surely have been that because the Antients had made it part of their marketing strategy, and their success had been apparent, that prompted Grand Master Blayney to decide in 1766 to create the 'Excellent Grand & Royal Arch Chapter of Jerusalem'[9] in London. Blayney was an Irishman, a professional soldier and a believer in the old traditions of masonry while retaining his loyalty to the government in London. And it was probably the same for many of the preexisting lodges that joined the Grand Lodge of England from the 1720s onwards, who also sought social status, the respectability of the Hanoverian establishment; while firmly maintaining their old traditions and practices. As Lepper defines them, Blayney was a 'Traditioner.'

Blayney was exalted on 11 June 1766. The following next three meetings were all held in July 1766. At the first on 2 July James Heseltine (then a Grand Steward) and three others were exalted. On the 22 July 1766 the Charter of Compact was signed, but curiously the date on the Charter as seen today appears to be 1767. But careful examination shows that underneath the final '7'of the date had been a '6,' thus making it appear that the date of the signature was a year later. And also, where the name of Lord Blayney appears together with his title of Grand Master—a letter P has been added to make it seem that Blayney was signing only as a Past Grand Master. One cannot know who made the alterations but the culprit might have been the Grand Secretary, Samuel Spencer, who remembered mainly for his dislike of the Royal Arch.

The difficulties facing the Grand Chapter are probably exemplified by the fact that the first warrants (for existing Chapters) were only issued in 1769—after a delay of three years. And they were:

1. The Restauration Lodge or Chapter of the Rock Fountain Shilo (at Brother Brooks' House in London).

2. The Euphrates Lodge or Chapter of the Garden of Eden (at Manchester).

3. The Lodge of Tranquility or Chapter of Friendship (at Portsmouth).

4. The Bethlehem Lodge or the Chapter of the Nativity (at Burnley, Lancs.).

5. The Cana Lodge or Chapter of the First Miracle (at Colne, Lancs.).

6. The Most Sacred Lodge or Chapter of Universality (at London).

---

9   But by 1786 they were styling themselves "The Grand Lodge of Royal Arch Masons!" and later in 1801 "The Supreme Grand Chapter."

6.b. The Lodge of Intercourse or Chapter of Unanimity (at Bury, Lanes.).

7. The Lodge of Hospitality or Chapter of Charity (at Bristol).

A possible explanation seems to have been provided by Bro Dashwood in *AQC*.[10] It seems that the influence Spencer, Grand Secretary of the Moderns, who died in October 1768, can maybe found in the minutes of Grand Chapter of 14 October 1768 when the Chapter was summoned to meet in November "on very special business" (underlined in the minutes). The minutes do not explain why, but soon afterwards in January 1769 the first warrants were issued. While Spencer has often been stated to have signed the charter his signature is absent, and neither did he ever pay any dues.

For the next warrant for a Chapter was for Bengal (No.10) in 1773 (another three year gap!). Looking at the Minute Book of the Grand Chapter[11] it becomes clear that there was very little activity after the first 1769 warrants were issued. Alas the dates that warrants were issued remains vague (and needs more research) but No.47 was issued in February 1787; and of those thirty seven chapters in the next fifteen years around ten might have been due to the work of Dunkerley.

Thomas Dunkerley (1724–1795) – Freemason Extraordinaire

Dunkerley remains a respected figure in English freemasonry. His mother was a servant, and he had to make his own way in life. In 1742 he had joined the Royal Navy as an able-seaman, and in 1745 was appointed as schoolmaster (on his ship) and in 1746 also a gunner. He also served on a large ship, HMS Vanguard and was present at the siege of Quebec. He retired in 1764 and received a pension; and that was after 22 years of service. It seems that he was initiated in 1754 and also exalted in 1754. He also obtained a warrant for a lodge on his ship the HMS Vanguard.

The Vanguard went twice to Quebec. The first time it returned home to reprovision in January and then by May that year had arrived back in Quebec. By some means Dunkerley had managed, during that time in port, to obtain 'a roving commission from the Grand [Lodge] of England as "Acting Grand Master of all Warranted Lodges in Quebec." And quoting from Henry Sadler:

> "The 24th of June, 1760, Brother Simon Frasier, Colonel of the Highland Regiment, was elected to preside over the Lodges, and

---

10 J R Dashwood, "The Falsification of the Royal Arch Charter of Compact," *AQC* 64 (1951), pp. 136-137.

11 JR Dashwood, "Notes on the First minute Book of the Excellent Grand & Royal Arch Chapter," *AQC* 62 (1949), pp. 165-185.

Bro. Dunckerley, of His Majesty's ship the Vanguard, who was possessed with a power from the Grand [Lodge] of England to inspect into the state of the Craft wheresoever he might go, honoured them with his approbation of their conduct and installed Brother Frasier in his high office."[12]

This seems to indicate that Dunkerley was a man of special skills, and both educated and personable. That he had managed to obtain such a power from Grand Lodge while having been a brother either at sea or probably in port marks him out as being exceptional. Once retired from the Royal Navy in 1764 he managed by 1766 to become a signatory to the Charter of Compact, and in February 1767 to be made provincial Grand Master for Hampshire[13] (a southern county containing the naval town of Portsmouth). He was then able to establish that he was the illegitimate son of George II, and receive an annual pension of £100 (soon rising to £800) and an apartment in Hampton Court Palace. This meant that while he had a good income, he was not wealthy; but this did allow him to be very active masonically.

While his apartment in Hampton Court Palace might have been his residence, both he and his wife seemed happy to travel across Britain, and wherever he went the would usually hold a 'Provincial Grand Lodge' followed by a good dinner afterwards.

However 1768 saw other changes which it seems were also about to change the direction of Dunkerley's masonic life. In October 1768 the Grand Secretary of the Moderns, Samuel Spencer died, and his place was taken by Thomas French from October 1768 to May 1769 and then by James Heseltine who remained Grand Secretary until 1784—both these brothers were also signatories to the Charter of Compact. Thus while the Royal Arch remained a separate organisation it was no longer attacked from within the Grand Lodge, but rather kept at a polite distance.

The two books on Dunkerley tell his tale in much more detail. I suspect that both Grand Lodge and Grand Chapter were delighted to find an educated and personable man, who had enough money to survive and a 'grace and favour' apartment in a royal palace and no estate to have to manage. The chances of finding a brothers able to devote himself to a masonic life was (rightly) seized upon.

---

12 Henry Sadler, *Thomas Dunkerley: His Life, Labours and Letters.* Quoting a letter from a Bro John Gawler, pp. 51-52.

13 Dunkerley was also made Provincial Grand Master for other counties all at the same time. 1776 Essex, 1777 Superintendent of Lodges in Wiltshire and Dorset, 1784 Gloucestershire and 1784 Somerset. He used to travel with his wife and they would attend masonic banquets wherever they stopped.

How great was his influence in growing freemasonry where he travelled—that is harder to say (and the information needs searching for.

Abstract of Laws for the Society of Royal Arch Masons 1786

It has proved difficult to find much about developments in the Royal Arch in the years between 1770 and the publication of the Abstract of Laws in 1786. The intention seems to be to:

> ... we may only at present give you a few particulars, which, as they may serve for a foundation to your masonic studies, and also enable you to silence the cavils, and repel the irony of our common opposers (the vulgar, vicious, and illiterate) ought always to be retained in the memory of a Royal Arch Mason, ...

In the Section devoted to the Rules a couple will be quoted because they are relevant:

> Rule II
>
> That to this exalted degree, none are to be admitted but men of the best character and education; open, generous, liberal in sentiment, and real Philanthropies; who have passed through the three probationary degrees of Craft Masonry ; and have presided as Masters, and have been duly proposed and recommended by two or more Companions of the Chapter, balloted for, and approved of; the recommendation to be (unless on particular occasions) at least one Chapter previous to the ballot: Each brother to be not less than twenty-three years of age at the time of initiation, except the son of a Companion of the Chapter, or that he has been two years of the Master's degree in the Craft; and then, under the above regulations, may be exalted at twenty-one; but none to be admitted, if on the ballot there appears more than one negative.

This clause while it seems to accept the Dermott statement that one must be a Past Master seems to offer two alternatives—that is to be the son of a Chapter member, or a Master Mason of two years standing. An interesting set of options, but certainly an easier option that that of the Antients. But the Abstract of Laws goes on to add some administrative structure to the Grand Chapter:

> Rule XII.
>
> The business of the Grand Chapter More oft having encreased by frequent applications from Subordinate Chapters, according to the usage and customs of this Exalted Degree, We therefore the Most

Excellent, and Excellent Grand Officers and Companions, do hereby make known, that we have conflicted and appointed, besides the Officers necessary for every regular Chapter, the following, appertaining to the Grand Chapter, only, *viz:*. Our Most Excellent Companions and Past Matters, SIR HERBERT MACKWORTH, BART. PRESIDENT OF THE COUNCIL.—JAMES GALLOWAY, JOHN BROOKS, JAMES HESLETINE, AND JOHN ALLEN, ESQ TO HOLD THE GREAT SEAL OF OUR ORDER IN COMMISSION IN COMMISSION, AND TO BE OUR INSPECTORS GENERAL. And we hereby declare, that all Certificates granted by us, mail be sealed and signed by the three M. E. G. Matters, and the two Scribes for the time being; and also by one or more of the Inspectors.

This is an interesting rule because it indicates that they were very much aware, that for the first time in English Masonry, that it not only needed to put on a show of ritual, but that it also had to manage the business of the Grand Chapter itself. And they appointed four brothers to be Inspectors General to help achieve this. This was probably also an indication that they realised that this aspect of Grand Chapter had been less than satisfactory in the past

Rule XIII

We have also constituted and appointed Our Most Excellent Companions, JAMES HESLETINE, ESQ TO BE OUR CORRESPONDENT GENERAL; and FRANCIS CONST, ESQ TREASURER: and for the better governance of the several Chapters situated and held at a distance from the Metropolis, it is enacted, that Superintendants be appointed over the several Provinces in which Chapters are held; each with powers, according to the tenor of their deputation : an appeal nevertheless always reserved to the Grand Chapter. We do therefore constitute and appoint JAMES GALLOWAY Esq SUPERINTENDENT OVER THE COUNTY OF HANTS. THOMAS DUNKERLY, ESQ OVER THE COUNTIES OF WILTS, DEVON, SOMERSET and ESSEX; JOHN ALLEN, ESQ OVER THE COUNTIES OF LANCASTER and CHESTER; and RICHARD GARLAND, ESQ. OVER THE COUNTY OF YORK.

Rule XIII is another indication that there was a realization that they needed Grand Superintendents who were closely involved with the Province they were responsible for, and that it needed such involvement if the Royal Arch was to prosper.

It is interesting to see that even in 1786 Companions Galloway, French, Heseltine, Allen and Dunkerley, all signatories to the 1766 Charter of Compact, were still at the top of the Grand Chapter and in control some twenty years later. Looking at how long each office of the Grand Secretaries of the Grand Lodge was in office perhaps demonstrates that after Spencer died the Grand Chapter was able to issue warrants; and in particular also that once James Heseltine had retired from the post of Grand Secretary for the Grand Lodge of England that he had chosen to work to encourage the growth and prosperity of Grand Chapter.

Samuel Spencer	1757 – October 1768
Thomas French	October 1768 – May 1769
James Heseltine	May 1969 – 1784

Thomas Dunkerley continued to undertake his travelling lifestyle (usually accompanied by his wife) by being nominated at various times as Provincial Superintendent. The 1786 list in the 'Rules' is quite short but there is written evidence[14] that he held that position for many other counties as well.

The following is a List of the Counties presided over by
Dunckerley as Grand Superintendent of Royal Arch Masons,
And the period of service.

Bristol, 1782-1795.	Cornwall, 1793-1795.
Devonshire, 1780-1795.	Dorsetshire, 1780-1795.
Durham, 1788-1795.	Essex, 1776-1795.
Gloucestershire, 1782-1795.	Hampshire, 1778-1782.
Herefordshire, 1793-1795.	I. of Wight, 1778-1795.
Kent, 1785-1795.	Nottinghamshire, 1793-1795.
Somersetshire, 1782-1795.	Suffolk, 1786-1795.
Surrey, 1789-1795.	Sussex, 1787-1795.
Warwickshire, 1793-1795.	Wiltshire, 1780-1790.[15]

Dunkerley remained Provincial Superintendent for almost all of these of these counties until his death. With a few exceptions these positions were in the southern counties, and in particular Lancashire and Yorkshire had the most Chapters and continued to prosper. If one looks at the growth in the number of chapters it would seem that the new policy has a beneficial effect. The first 8 warrants were

---

14 Henry Sadler, *Thomas Dunkerley*. There are numerous mentions of these appointments throughout the book.

15 Henry Sadler, *Dunkerley*, p. 259.

granted in 1769 and that had grown to 85 by 1797[16] and then to 116 by 1800.[17]

The 1813 Union of Moderns and Antients Grand Lodges

It is not possible to ignore the Union of the two Craft Grand Lodges in England in 1813. Not only did amalgamate all the Craft lodges into one renumbered Grand Lodge, but it also had an effect upon both Chapter and KT. One of the issues in reaching an agreement was the insistence of the Antients that the Royal Arch must be included. They reached a 'political compromise' with a final agreement that became part of Article II:

II. It is declared and pronounced, that pure Ancient Masonry consists of *three* degrees, and no more; viz. those of the Entered Apprentice, the Fellow Craft, and the Master Mason, *including the* Supreme *Order* of the Holy Royal Arch. But this article is not intended to prevent any Lodge or Chapter from holding a meeting in any of the degrees of the Orders of Chivalry, according to the constitutions of the said Orders. [Words amended in authors italics]

The original draft handwritten clause was altered in several places even on the copy that was signed but eventually they found a form of words which only included three degrees but also stated that it also included "the Supreme Order of

---

16 Stephen Jones, *Masonic Miscellanies in Poetry and Prose*, pub Vernor and Hood, London 1797. Unusually, this lists lodges by county and also includes chapters. The inclusion of chapters would seem to indicate that the Royal Arch was prospering.

17 Freemasons Calendar for the Year 1800. Pub Stationers Hall under the sanction of the Grand Lodge of England. For the first time Chapters are also listed. It might be coincidence but this was the time when thoughts started turning towards a possible union of the Moderns and Antients Grand Lodges.

the Holy Royal Arch." It did not state that the 'Supreme Order' was a degree, but neither did it say that it included two other degrees, and therefore both parties felt able to sign the agreement. It is rare to find evidence of hard fought discussion and eventual compromise in writing—but here it is visible for us to read today.

The final sentence implied that it was still going to be possible to hold meetings of "any of the degrees of the Orders of Chivalry." This never happened, and it seems the Duke of Sussex conveniently forgot it (see later). Curiously is also *does not state* what those degrees were but as well as the Knights Templars, it could have included degrees like the Knight of the Sword, Knight of the East, and one needs to remember that De Lintots Rite of Seven Degrees had already been worked in London.

Chapter of the Order of Harodim, Free-mafons' Tavern, Great Queen-ftreet, Lincoln's-Inn-Fields, 3d Monday from January to April, and from October to December. Dine at Five exactly. Chapter opens at Seven. Vifitors admitted by Tickets, which may be had by applying to any Member of the Chapter. N. B. This is a Crafts' Chapter. See Prefton's Illuftrations of Mafonry, Ed. 1796, p. 342.

And if one looks in the 1796 edition of Preston's Illustrations one can see that perhaps the Duke of Sussex was wise to conveniently forget about any Chivalric orders and concentrate to ensuring that the new merged and now 'United' Grand Lodge of England became well established and all sources of new ideas put on hold.

> On the 4th of January 1787, was opened in London, the grand chapter of Harodim. Though this order is of ancient date, and had been patronised in different parts of Europe, previous to this period there appears not on record the regular establishment of such an association in England. For some years it was faintly encouraged, but since its merit has been further investigated, it has received the patronage of the most exalted masonic characters; and, under the patronage of Lord Macdonald, meets regularly at Free-Masons tavern on the 3rd Monday of January, February, March, April, October, November, and December; at which meetings any member of a regular lodge may be admitted by ticket as a visitor, to hear the lectures of masonry judiciously illustrated.

The Creation of the Grand Chapter in 1817

In England this was the occasion to create separate structures for the Royal Arch. This was done by UGLE creating a separate Grand Chapter for the Royal

Arch degrees (Excellent Masters and Royal Arch) within its control. So in 1817 the Duke of Sussex sent a message, read at the 3 September 1817 meeting of the Grand Lodge of England as follows:

> A Communication from the M. W. Grand Master was read, announcing that the two Grand Chapters of the Order of the Royal Arch existing prior to the Union of the Craft, had formed a Junction; that it being the Wish of the Members of that Order to render the Connexion between the Grand Lodge and Grand Chapter as intimate as Circumstances will permit, they had given Rank and Votes in their Meetings to all the Officers of the Grand Lodge, and they had, as far as possible, assimilated their Laws and Regulations to those of the Craft; and the Grand Master expressed his Hope that the Grand Lodge would be disposed to do whatever might be necessary on their Part to establish the Connexion between the two Bodies.

Practically this was achieved on 18th March 1817 when members of the two Chapters met, opened their own chapters, and then met together where they were joined as one, officers of Grand Chapter were elected and a committee formed to deal with laws regulations and other matter. One of the most significant decisions they made was that all Chapters registered before December 27, 1813, were to attach themselves to a lodge, take its number, hold meetings at different times to the Lodge and keep separate accounts and minutes.[18] It did however allow chapters to retain their own name while having to use the number of the lodge they were linked to. It must be pointed out that this practice of Chapters being linked to a Craft lodge only applies in England and nowhere else, especially not in either Ireland or Scotland. By 1823 around 200 Chapters had attached themselves to Lodges of which 38 were in Lancashire, 17 in London and in the three Provinces of West, North and East Yorkshire 19. In the same year there were 721 Lodges so about one in four lodges had a chapter attached to it.

The final act of the Duke of Sussex was, in 1834–35, to appoint a committee to examine the ceremonies for Installation of Principals. In addition it proposed that the ceremony of 'Passing the Veils' was abandoned. It is also worth mentioning that in this 1835 revision all Christian references were also removed. All these things were done, and this made the English Royal Arch ceremony the simplest Royal Arch ceremony in Great Britain.

In the Province of Bristol the Veils were formally acknowledged by Grand

---

18 It is believed that the renumbering of lodges at the 1813 union of the Antients and Moderns provoked many problems because some old lodges found themselves being given a higher number than a lodge founded maybe only a few years before the Union.

Chapter, seemingly around 1890, and it is worked in Exaltations in Bristol Chapters. The Passing the Veils ceremony is not worked anywhere else in England.

The Knights Templar become visible in England

The first appearance may have been in a scurrilous item in *Farley's Bristol Journal* of 25 January 1772 which refers to various individuals travelling between Bristol and Bath, and back again to spend the evening with the 'Knights Templars.'

However there are two other references to the conferral of other degrees in England, one for Mark and the second for KT.

> The earliest known reference to Mark masonry is in a cipher minute of the 'Moderns' Chapter of Friendship, in the year 1769. The minute, translated, reveals that:
>
>> At a ROYAL ARCH Chapter held at the George Tavern in Portsmouth on First Septr 1769 ... The Pro G.M. THOMAS DUNCKERLEY bro't the Warrant of the Chapter, and having lately rec'd the 'MARK,' he made the bre'n 'MARK MASONS' and 'MARK MASTERS,' and each chuse their 'MARK.'
>
> Further, under date July 21, 1771, it is learned that three Brethren were made Mark masons and Mark Masters, also R.A. masons and Excellent and Super Excellent masons. In this same chapter a minute dated October 21, 1778, records that the Z "read a letter from Com. DUNCKERLEY, that we might make KNIGHT TEMPLERS if we wanted and it was resolved to ..." (Two Brethren "took the MARK," and each chose his mark one of the two was "made ARCH next time.")[19]

But by 1780 we know that a body of Knights Templars in Bristol had created 'The Supreme Grand and Royal Encampment of Knights Templars of St John of Jerusalem, Knights Hospitaller and Knights of Malta etc etc' and produced a Charter of Compact dated 1780, and signed on 9th May.[20] The first sentence is worth reading:

> Whereas by Charter of Compact our Encampment is Constituted, the Supreme Grand and Royal Encampment of this Noble Order, with full Power, when Assembled, to issue, publish, and make

---

19 Bernard E Jones, *Freemasons Book of the Royal Arch* (1957), pp. 205-206.

20 Brian Price, *In the Steps of the Templars*. Lewis Masonic (2021). The full text of the Charter of Compact can be found in Appendix C, pp. 407-409.

known to all our loving Knights Companions, whatsoever may contribute to their knowledge, not inconsistent with its general Laws.

So yet again we see degrees appearing in England and initially often in ports which were either trading with Ireland and naval ports like Portsmouth and Plymouth. Naval bases were important because a significant proportion of the British Army were Irish and the only Grand Lodge issuing warrants for military lodges from 1732 till 1755 was in Ireland. Thus Chetwode Crawley's opinion is worthy of serious consideration.

> We have seen that the occurrence of Royal Arch Minutes in Bristol and in Youghal were almost simultaneous. Some connection of a similar kind might be traced in the spread of the Templar Degrees. For the prominence of the High Knights Templars of Ireland in the Dublin Freemasonry of 1774 was followed by the occurrence of the Degree in 1778 at Portsmouth in a quasi-military Lodge, and by that attempt at Templar organization in Bristol which is known as the Charter of 1780, while the revived York Grand Lodge, undoubt-edly in fraternal relation with Irish Military Lodges, almost simul-taneously recognised the "Five Degrees, or Orders of Masonry." The sequence seems too close to be accidental.[21]

We cannot improve upon Chetwode-Crawley's words. It might be worth not-ing that both the Royal Arch and Knights Templars appeared in English ports, and this was often around the same time the degree was known to be worked in Ireland. One is prompted to ask the question whether that degree had travelled from Ireland to England, or even in the other direction? So far no conclusive evidence has been found. The authors probably favour placing Ireland as the leader in the development of both the Royal Arch and KT in the British Isles—and that certainly was the case in Scotland with the Early Grand Encampment warrants. Circa 1770 seems to be a good approximate date for the Knights Templars establishing itself in the British Isles, but there are many mentions and claims for it being present from 1720 to around 1760. These are usually lacking sufficient evidence, but another source is perhaps indicated by all the early claims seem to appear in ports where there was significant commercial or military activity.

There seems little Templar activity in England between these early mentions with the exception of the Baldwyn Encampment and its 1780 Charter and it seems that it was only Dunkerley travelling around Britain that provided a focus. However when Dunkerley decided to form a Grand Conclave he only found 10 Encampments to join. Between York in the north, Redruth in the far south

---

21 WJ Chetwode-Crawley, "Some Early Irish Certificates and their story," *AQC* vol.16, pp. 78-79.

west and London in the south east that does indicate any great popularity at that time—and certainly very much less popularity than in Ireland.

Dunkerley wrote to John Knight on 27th January 1792[22] a most informative letter which sets out the scope of the early days of the Grand Conclave:

> Altho' Mrs. Dunckerley (the Lady Patroness of Kn[igh]t Templars) is near 80 years of age, and I am not far from 70, yet we intend (with God's permission) to visit the West of England next summer, and if we should winter at Plymouth, it is probable that I may have the happiness of conversing with some of the Knights Companions from Exeter, Redruth & Biddeford. I was selected Grand Master to revive the Order in England in February, 1791 and have had the pleasure to constitute the following Conclaves, viz:

CONCLAVES.	ENCAMPMENTS.
Of Observance of the Seven London Degrees	Coffee House, Ludgate Hill
Of Redemption.	York.
Royal Cumberland.	Bath. Bear Inn,
Fortitude.	First Regiment of Dragoon Guards.
Trine.	Biddeford. New Ring of Bells.
Naval.	Portsmouth.
Durnovarian.	Dorchester. Royal Oak.
Harmony.	Salisbury. Parade Coffee House.
Royal Edward.	Hereford. Bowling Green.
St. John of Jerusalem.	Redruth. London Inn.

The Baldwyn Encampment – Grand Conclave of Masonic Knights Templars – before 1780

There is one thing that does stand out in the list, and that is that Dunkerley's Grand Conclave did not include an Encampment from Bristol known as the Baldwyn Encampment. We do know Dunkerley was aware of this encampment, but it was absent from his 1791 list. What we can say is that Dunkerley was offered the position of Grand Master of the Bristol Encampment, and accepted the offer. But we can see from his letter of 22nd March 1791 to the Encampment at York—so almost a year before the letter he wrote to John Knight:

> Being Grand Superintendent of Royal Arch Masons at Bristol, I was requested by the Knights Templar in that City (who have had an Encampment time immemorial) to accept the Office of Grand

---

22 Henry Sadler, *Thomas Dunkerley* (1891), pp. 268-269.

Master, which I had no sooner comply'd with than Petitions were sent to me for the same purpose from London 1, Bath 2, the first Regiment of Dragoon Guards 3, Colchester 4, York 5, Dorchester 6, and Biddeford 7. I suppose there are many more Encampments in England, which with God's permission I may have the happiness to revive & assist. It has already been attended with a blessing, for I have been but two months Grand Master & have already 8 Encampments under my care.[23]

Fascinating that he accepted to be Grand Master of the Baldwyn Encampment in 1791 but a year later they were not mentioned in his list. It is also curious that Colchester has vanished. And we can see that more Encampments had joined during 1791, in Salisbury, Hereford and Redruth. Clearly something had happened in the time between the letter to York (which was before the Creation of the Grand Conclave in 24 June 1791. Price comments on this (p. 429) that did not find favour with Baldwyn.

But Dunkeley's letter to York perhaps offers some things to consider. Dunkerley says that he accepted to be Grand Master of Baldwyn, and then says he was asked by seven other Encampments to be their Grand Master as well. Even more curious in his letter to York of 24 March 1791 he states that he has "been but two months Grand Master"; and yet it was still three months before Grand Conclave was erected.

It must be worth considering that when Dunkerley accepted to be Grand Master of Baldwyn, who he describes as being 'Time Immemorial,' thinking that he was simply being a titular head of their Encampment; and that he maybe did not know of, or understand, their 1780 Charter of Compact. It might simply have been the case that Baldwyn expected to be the focus of the Grand Encampment and when they discovered that was not going to be the case they simply declined to join the Grand Conclave. Sadly we cannot know the cause, only the result.

What is well known is that Baldwyn continued to work as a separate body and only joined the Grand Conclave of Masonic Knights Templar of England and Wales in 1862. It did so by a Charter of Compact in 9th May 1862[24] and reserved its place as being a Time Immemorial Encampment for itself and appears at the top of the list of Preceptories. What is also of significance is clause 4, which is below:

---

23 Henry Sadler, *Thomas Dunkerley* (1891), p. 262.

24 Brian Price, *In the Steps pf the Templars* (2021). The full transcript of the 1862 Charter of Compact is reproduced on pp. 422-423. The dates of removal of Encampments can be found in Appendix L p. 430, and a list of Preceptories in Appendix N p. 433 et seq.

4. That the following Encampments established by and meeting under warrants granted by the said Encampment of Baldwyn at Bristol from time immemorial (that is to say)

> The Encampment of Antiquity at Bath (1791)
>
> The Encampment of Ascalon at Birmingham (1867) (removed before the 1868 renumeration)
>
> The Encampment of Holy Rood at Warwick
>
> The Encampment of the Vale of Jehosophat at Highbridge (1862) (removed before the 1868 renumeration)
>
> The Encampment of the Vale Royal at Salisbury (1862) (removed before the 1868 renumeration)
>
> And the Percy Encampment at Adelaide, South Australia (1858)

Note: Dates of formation and removal added by the authors

Shall from the day of the date hereof and hereby recognized and adopted and the several Knights Companions thereof affiliated by the Grand Conclave of Masonic Knights Templar of England and Wales and the said Encampments shall take precedence in the official Registers among the Encampments of the Grand Conclave of England and Wales according to the dates of their respective warrants.

It is fascinating to discover that England had two competing Grand Encampments just as did Ireland, and that they both continued to operate side by side for over seventy years. Interestingly when considers the number of Encampments in England is compared with those in Ireland it is very much smaller. Perhaps one can conclude that Ireland (and later in Scotland) benefitted from having the two orders where the Royal Arch and KT functioned together in the same Grand Encampment, rather than as a separate Grand Chapter and Grand Conclave?

The Grand Conclave after Dunkerley's Death in 1795

After the death of Dunkerley in 1795 the whole matter of who occupied the position of Grand Master took some work to resolve. Clearly Dunkerley was Grand Master from 1791 to his death in 1795, there was then an interregnum, and Lodge Rancliffe was elected and ruled from 1796–1800. The ruling body then seems to vanish till 1804 when it is awoken again by the Duke of Kent, as Grand Patron, issuing a Charter reconstituting the Grand Conclave. The Duke of Kent was then elected Grand Master, a position he resigned in 1807—once again becoming Grand Patron, when Waller Rodwell Wright was elected and served until 1812, when the Duke of Sussex took over until his death in 1843. It seems that whatever source one reads the details are all slightly different, and even this chronology and naming may not be completely accurate.

The Duke of Kent was appointed in 1804 and he became Grand Patron in 1807 at which point Waller Rodwell Wright was appointed till 1812 when the Duke of Sussex was appointed Grand Master. Sussex then remained as Grand Master until his death, however the Order was in practice managed by Robert Gill and John Christian Burkhardt. It was only in 1834 that Sussex added his name to a warrant for a new Encampment, 'Royal Sussex in Torquay.' The may also have been a few other new warrants issued, but by 1843 when Sussex died there may only have been around 30 Encampments remaining.

In 1846, Charles Kemey Tynte accepted to become Grand Master and the Templars became active again. It is just worth recording that the Grand Conclave also worked a couple of degrees that were included in the Ancient and Accepted that had to be resolved.

The period that followed the death of the Duke of Sussex resulted in an explosion of orders and degrees being worked in England and the Christian influence became more obvious in English Masonry. It is an interesting thought that the crisis in England for the 'higher degrees' lasted from 1813 until after the death of the Duke of Sussex in 1743 while in Ireland it was from 1805 until the formation of the Grand Priory of Ireland in February 1837. The adaption to and acceptance of more clearly defined system of orders was a painful process lasting over thirty years in both England and Ireland. Interestingly in Scotland the process was more or less completed in seventeen years.

The Royal Arch only for Masters Past the Chair

The attempt to limit membership of the Royal Arch was a requirement, as was reported by Fifield Dassigny in 1744. It was also a problem for Laurence Dermott once he started promoting the Royal Arch in England; indeed, discovered that his was a real problem. To get over this he quotes Dassigny word for word from the Dublin 1760 edition of Ahiman Rezon onwards.

> This is the Cafe of all those who think themselves Royal Arch Masons, without palling the Chair in regular Form, according to the ancient Custorn of the Craft: To this I will add the Opinion of our Worshipful Brother Doctor *Fifield D'Assigny*, printed in the Year 1744. "Some of the Fraternity (says he) have expressed an Uneasiness at this Matter being kept a Secret from them since they had already passed through the usual Degrees of Probation) I cannot help being of Opinion, that they have No Right to any such Benefit until they make a proper Application, and *I* (are received with due Formality: And as it is an "organized Body of Men who have passed the "Chair, and given undeniable Proofs of their Skill

in Architecture, it cannot be treated with too much Reverence; and more especially since the Characters of the present Members of that particular Lodge are untainted, and their Behaviour judicious and unexceptionable: So that there cannot be the lead Hinge to hang a Doubt on, but that they are most excellent Masons."[25]

The changed wording is the 1800 Ahiman Rezon is fascinating because it offers several ways, for the first time, that one could legitimately become a Royal Arch mason.

III. That no Brother shall be admitted into the H. R. A. but he who has regularly and faithfully passed through the three progressive degrees, and has performed the duties in his Lodge to the satisfaction of his Brethren; to ascertain which, they shall deliver to him in open Lodge, held in the Master's degree, a certificate to the following purport:[26]

"To the presiding Chief of the Chapter of Excellent Royal Arch Masons, under the sanction of Lodge No. Whereas our trufty and well-beloved Brother a Geometric Master Mason, and member of our Lodge, has solicited us to recom-. mend him as a Master Mason, every way qualified, so far as we are judges of the necessary qualifications, for passing the Holy Arch: We do hereby certify, that the said trusty and well-beloved Brother has obtained the unanimous consent of our Lodge, No. for the recommendation and signing this certificate.

Given under our hands this   day of 179

WM
SW

Secretary   JW

But further discovery made it clear that in reality this was probably a response not only to demand from Brethren but also in reaction to actions taken by the Grand Chapter of the 'Modern' masons. Their 1782 clause relating to who can be admitted is particularly interesting:

Who to be admitted

---

25 Laurence Dermott, *Ahiman Rezon*, 2nd Edition Chamberlain Dublin (1760), pp. 33-34.

26 *Ahiman Rezon*, 1800, printed by T Burton for the Editor, and in Rules and Regulations, p. 119 (rules as approved December 3, 1794).

II. That to this exalted degree, none are to be admitted but men of the best character and education; open, generous, liberal in sentiment, and real Philanthropies; who have passed through the three probationary degrees of Craft Masonry; and have presided as Masters, and have been duly proposed and recommended by two or more Companions of the Chapter, balloted for, and approved of; the recommendation to be (unless on particular occasions) at least one Chapter previous to the ballot: Each brother to be not less than twenty-three years of age at the time of initiation, except the son of a Companion of the Chapter, or that he has been two years of the Master's degree in the Craft; and then, under the above regulations, may be exalted at twenty-one; but none to be admitted, if on the ballot there appears more than one negative.[27]

And the date these regulations were approved in clearly stated:

Done from our ancient Code, and now revised in our Grand and Royal Chapter, this

10th Day of May, A. L. 5786, A.D. 1782.

John Allen, Z.

John Brooks, H.

Francis Const, J.

It is generally understood that the key requirement to become a Royal Arch mason was as described above 'and have presided as Masters.' The clause is equivocal in its meaning, and that is exacerbated by the unclear punctuation. The first half down to the semicolon is coherent. After that would seem to be a variety of condition except that one 'or that he has been two years of the Master's degree in the Craft.' It is the 'or' that only makes sense in the total context if it defines another category who may join. The next clause which starts with 'and then' implies other supplementary requirements for admission. The clause makes best sense (this century) if it is accepted as broadening the categories who can be admitted; but it might not have been intended to mean that.

Given the fact that there had always been pressure from brothers who had 'not passed the chair,' and that a nominal 'passing the chair' degree had been created, and because it was the tradition in many lodges for the most competent brother to be the master in the chair, and to keep that office for a significant number of year—thus minimising the number who could claim to be past the chair.

---

27 *Abstract of Laws for the Society of Royal Arch Masons*. London (1786), in the section entitled Rules and Regulations, p. 19. The date of approval is on p. 22.

Additional and Later Events *(provided for curiosity of the reader)*

1769 In the Royal Arch Chapter on Friendship in Portsmouth Thomas Dunkerley made Mark Masons and Mark Masters.

1769 Minutes for the early period of the R.A. (i.e., c. 1740 to 1760) are exceedingly rare and uninformative, but there is a record of an emergency meeting at Bolton in 1769, at which three men were successively installed as Master, and afterwards the actual Master of the Lodge was re-installed.[28]

1769 The Lodge of Unanimity in its minutes held a special 'Royal Arch night.' Its minutes record repeated such nights being held on Sundays.

1772 It needs to be remembered that it was also the year in which the three Grand Lodges (Antients, Ireland & Scotland) also agreed to be in 'constant correspondence' with each other. It is interesting to note that this friendship also seems to have extended to the Royal Arch even though in all these jurisdictions there was nothing formal to be in amity with.

1778 Letter from Dunckerley authorizing the Royal Arch Chapter of Friendship in Portsmouth to 'make Knights Templar' if they wished[29] (Smythe, *Brethren in Chivalry*, p. 24).

1799 Unlawful Societies Act. It seems not to be known how any warranted Royal Arch Chapters responded in order to comply (except in Scotland).

1823 Following the creation of the Grand Lodge of Wigan there was mention of creating a companion Grand Chapter—but no details remain of this.

1830 Duke of Sussex 'reopens' the Knights Templar and issues some warrants. Handfield-Jones[30] says that 'suddenly in 1839 the Duke threw aside the veil and openly assumed autocratic control.' Smythe[31] however paints a rather different picture, saying that after 1813 the Grand Conclave only met once on 31 January 1820, and in total it only consisted of the seven Time Immemorial Encampments that existed under Dunkerley in 1791. A further three Encampments were created, in 1824 (Hugh de Payens in Canada), 1826 (Cornubian in Falmouth/Torquay), and 1830 (Loyal Brunswick in Plymouth).

---

28 Harry Carr, "More Light on the Royal Arch," *AQC* 76 (1963), p. 215. Sadly Carr does not offer the name of the Lodge or any other details. Jones states this was in Anchor & Hope Lodge No. 37.

29 Frederick Smythe, *Brethren in Chivalry 1791–1991* (1991), p. 24.

30 R M Handfield-Jones, *The Origin and History of the United Religious and Military Orders of the Temple and St. John of Jerusalem*. London (1973), p. 11.

31 Frederick Smythe, *Brethren in Chivalry 1791–1991* (1991). Appendix I (pp. 142-156) gives a complete list of all Encampments / Preceptories.

There were another five Encampments before the Duke's death in 1843. The actual number of Encampments seems to vary according to which expert's writings one reads (authors apologies)

1845 George Claret published 'The Ceremonies of the Holy Royal Arch, also the passing of the Veils.' The same year Richard Carlile published his 'Manual of Freemasonry.'

1856 The February meeting of Grand Chapter receives a report which states that the Mark Masons degree does not form part of the Master Masons degree, and the question of its introduction into Masonry be left to the Grand Lodge of England.

1872 The idea of merging the Grand Conclaves of England, Ireland and Scotland was conceived, ratified in 1872, and the new Convent-General first met on 7th April 1873 and the Prince of Wales was elected Grand Master. Scotland withdrew early in the discussions, and it might have been that they thought it wiser not to be involved because they are already discovering territorial problems with the Supreme Council of England.

1895 On 19th July the Convent-General expired and vanished.

1819 In the County of Lancashire a Grand Chapter of Reconciliation was held at the Golden Lion, Dale Street, Liverpool on the 29 September. It might have been that the Union of the Grand Lodges took place in 1813, and a United Grand Chapter was formed in 1817, but the practical implementation of this took a few years before the integration of the various Royal Arch Chapters of a Grand Chapter of Reconciliation in Lancashire, one of the two strongholds of the Holy Royal Arch (the other being Yorkshire), took place at a meeting held on 28th September 1819. The General form of the meeting is below

> The G(rand) H(oly) R(oyal) Arch Chapter being duly formed, the Ancients on the one part, the Moderns on the other, they severally opened, according to their respective and usual customs, after which the sublime union was completed with all reverence & Humility to the Grand Architect of the Universe. The whole was united under the auspices of M(ost) E(xcellent) Prov^l Chiefs present for this County, over which was installed the R.W.P^l G^d Master Francis Dukinfield Astley Esq as M.E.G^dC. All adjustment & business being concluded this United Grand H.R.A. Chapter was closed with Solemn ceremony & ample Form.

> A Decent plain Dinner was prepared at the Golden Lion & both days were spent in convivial festivity.[32]

---

32 Minutes of the Provincial Grand Lodge (of Lancashire) from 19 August 1814 to 1 March 1860

England – A Summary Perspective

London in the 1730s and 1740s had a Grand Lodge that had grown rapidly, and London had become a centre of innovation in terms of what Andrew Prescott would describe as 'the invention of (masonic) history.' After the barriers to thought imposed by religion had significantly weakened, freemasonry was able to offer alternative ways to 'personal enlightenment.'

But right from the start the Grand Lodge in London had disapproved first of Masonry Dissected, then of Masters Lodges, the Scots Masons Lodge No. 115. This dislike, distancing Grand Lodge from these many other degrees did not stop them being created, being enjoyed by brothers and lodges all the way through the eighteenth century. Eventually life became chaotic enough that Grand Lodges actively sought to regain control over their own 'fiefdoms.' This happened in Scotland in 1800, in Ireland in 1805, in England in 1813 and at a similar date in the United States of America.[33]

The initial establishment of both the Royal Arch and later the Knights Templars in England seemed to be slow—if one considers only the lodges established under the 'official banners.' But perhaps it is exactly because there was a formally created Grand Chapter in 1766, based in London, while probably 90% of the Royal Arch activity was happening in Lodges outside and distant from London.

Activity from the centre was poor. Grand Chapter formed in 1766 did not issue any warrants until 1769 then only eight which were mainly in Lancashire and Dunkerley's Grand Conclave formed in 1791 only had seven Encampments. After all Dunkerley had started his KT campaign in Portsmouth in 1778 so progress (and maybe popularity) was poor.

In reading whatever came to hand one thing became apparent. Once outside London it is obvious that there was a predominance of interest in novel aspects of masonry in port towns, both commercial trading centres and naval harbours. While the preferred and often fastest means of travel was by boat, conditions were cramped, weather often poor and food probably monotonous; and the first thing once ashore would be to walk on firm land, find an alehouse for a beer or a coffee, and then a decent bed. And migrants such as the Huguenots coming from Europe would have arrived by sea as well. The appearance of the Royal Arch in Ireland was in ports, Yougall, Dublin and Coleraine demonstrates the spread by ordinary men and traders. It is worth noting that masonic lodges in port towns often recruited master mariners into the Craft—after all after unloading a ship cargo a return cargo was needed, and find this took time. Typically all three

---

inclusive, pp. .26-30.

33 John Belton, Brother, Just One More Degree, *Scottish Rite Journal* Mar/Apr 2013, pp. 7-9.

degrees would be conferred in an evening, and the application to Grand Lodge for a certificate might be back with the lodge before the boat sailed again.[34]

The role of military lodges is normally restricted to considering that regiments often created lodges where they set up camp, and usually Craft lodges. But there is another aspect to consider. That a visiting military brother over a beer or a glass of whisk(e)y would get to talking about other degrees that he has experienced. And that is a short step to another degree taking root far from home.

---

34 John Belton & Robert Cooper. *Scotland's Masons: Membership & Occupations 1800-2000.* Volume 3 of *Sheffield Lectures on the History of Freemasonry and Fraternalism* (2010), pp. 72-99.

1766 onwards: Neither Arch, Royal Arch nor Antient...

The attitude of the Grand Lodge of England towards both the Royal Arch and the Scots Master needs a good explanation, including the equivalent attitudes to other degrees in both Scotland and in Ireland and especially in France (where they were fully accepted, unlike Britain). There are plenty of sources to quote. Some recently published and others not but it does make the point that when the KT arrives matters will then get even worse.

Understanding the reaction of Grand Lodge towards all exposures and rituals is important in understanding that they were in both principle and practice opposed to all forms of innovation and because these alternative degrees made the governing of the Grand Lodge very much more difficult.. Thus all changes and higher degrees come inevitably from personal innovations either persons or groups of brothers, i.e., a lodge or members of a lodge. But let us start in 1730:

28 August 1730 Proceedings of the Grand Lodge of England

> Dr. Desaguliers stood up and (taking notice of a printed Paper lately published and dispersed about the Town, and since inserted in the News Papers, pretending to discover and reveal the Misteries of the Craft of Masonry) recommended several things to the Consideration of the Grand Lodge, particularly the Resolution of the last Quarterly Communication for preventing any false Brethren being admitted into regular Lodges and such as call themselves Honorary Masons.
>
> The Deputy Grand Master seconded the Doctor and proposed several Rules to the Grand Lodge to be observed in their respective Lodges for their Security against all open and Secret Enemies to the Craft.[1]

This was in response to the publication of *The Mystery of Free-Masonry* in the *Daily Journal* of 15th August 1730. But the problem of exposures came up again in Grand Lodge at the 15th December 1730 meeting after the publication of *Masonry Dissected* by Samuel Prichard. This on 20th October 1730, and again in the *Daily Journal*. The response of Grand Lodge was largely similar, and probably equally ineffective.

---

1   *QCA* 10, p. 128.

The Deputy Grand Master took notice of a Pamphlet lately published by one Prichard who pretends to have been made a regular
Mason: In violation of the Obligation of a Mason wch. he swears
he has broke in order to do hurt to Masonry and expressing himself with the utmost indignation against both hime (styling him an
Imposter) and of his Book as a foolish thing not to be regarded. But
in order to prevent the Lodges being imposed upon by false Brethren
or Imposters: Proposed till otherwise Ordered by the Grand Lodge,
that no Person whatsoever should be admitted into Lodges unless
some Member of the Lodge then present would vouch for such visiting Brothers being a regular Mason, and the Visitors name in the
Lodge Book, which Proposal was unanimously agreed to.[2]

We must all be indebted to Roberts Freke Gould for quoting two letters sent by
Thomas Manningham, Deputy Grand Master to the Provincial Grand Lodge
of Holland in reply to their letters.[3] The first, of 3rd December 1756, is briefly
quoted. The letter included to question whether they could have permission to
hold Scotch Lodges.

1st You desire the Grand Masters Permission to hold Scotch Lodges,
& institute the Brethren according to their method.

This cannot be allow'd, as we know no distinction of Lodges, Free
Masonry being the same in all parts of the world;...

...Of late some fertile Genius's here, have attempted considerable
Innovations, & their manner of working in Lodge, they term sometimes Irish, another Scotch Masonry, why, or wherefore they themselves best know; this I am certain off, all Innovations in our society
must tend to confusion.

In the second letter there is considerably more information about various degrees, where they were practiced and how news of them had been spreading to
England.

DR MANNINGHAM TO BRO SAUER AT THE HAGUE,
JULY 12TH 1757

...Amongst some of our lowest Brethren, I have met with, & fre-
quently heard of such Irregularities; Irregularities I justly call them,
because they deviate so much from our usual Ceremonies, & are so
full of Innovations, that in process of Time, the antient Landmarks

---

2   *QCA* 10, pp. 135-136.

3   Printed in the *Jaarboekja voor Nederlandsche Vrijmetselaren* of 1880 and in RF Gould, Masonic
    Celebrities: Thomas Manningham. *AQC* 5, pp. 106-109.

will be destroyd, by the fertile genius of brethren who will improve or alter, if only to give Specimen of their Abilities, & imaginary consequence; so that, in few Years it will be difficult to understand Masonry, as to distinguish the Points or Accounts of the Hebrew or Greek Language, now almost obscur'd by the Industry of Critiks & Comentators.

Three foreign Gentlemen & Masons lately visited the Lodge I belong to, & were introduc'd by me to the Grand Lodge & the Grand East; by discoursing with these Gentlemen I find Germany, Holland & Switzerland in some Places have Orders of Masons unknown to us viz. Knights of the Sword, of the Eagle, of the Holy Land, with a long train of etceteras; surely these points of masonry must be wonderful; I am certain they are very new; beside , these dignified & distinguish'd Order I find have Signs, Tokens, &c. peculiar to their respective Dignities, & adorn themselves with different colour'd Ribbons.

But perhaps it is the context of 1757 which is most significant. In 1743–44 the Royal Arch appears in Ireland, there was the Parfait Macon exposure in France with a section on the Scots Masters degree, and the 1744 Rules for the Clermont Grand Lodge include a clause relating to the powers of a Scots Mason. And the documents relating to the export of a HRDM of Kilwinning degree to Holland and a Maitre Ecossois to Berlin in Germany left London in 1740s. In 1757 Thomas Dunkerley tells us that he was exalted into the Royal Arch in a Lodge in Portsmouth in southern England—and we would probably be wise to remember that this was one of the major English naval bases in England through which regiments of troops passed—together with their masonic lodges, which were initially mainly Irish.

It is the nature of regiments of soldiers to travel, and to travel with and meet other regiments, and the nature of military life was long periods of training or inactivity, followed by savage sessions of fighting and death. Any repetitive occupation was thus welcomed by regiments. Warrants started to be issued quite early and the body issuing the warrants often did not relate to the origin of the soldiers. The starting sates were:

Irish warrants start in November 1732

Scottish warrants start in April 1747

Moderns commence in February 1755 and Antients in September 1755

It was during the Seven Years War (1756–1763) when fighting broke out in Quebec. This episode was part of an American attempt to invade Canada and rally French-Canadian support against the British. The key battle was won by the British in 1759. This was followed, mainly on 1759 by the Provincial Grand Lodge of Quebec issuing 13 warrants for British Lodges. This practice was copied by other provinces in the West Indies, who because of huge delays in correspondence across the Atlantic, simply chose to do their own administration.

For the period between the mid 1740s and mid 1760s Masonry in England was in a poor state, Grand Masters were indifferent, the Craft not popular, and evidence sadly lacking on many of the changes that did take place. Here is a letter from the Deputy Grand Master of England, are some facts. When Manningham says in 1757 that "These innovations are of very late years, & I believe the Brethren will find a Difficulty to produce a Mason, acquainted with any such Forms twenty, nay ten, Years." He is almost certainly correct.

And we need to remember that the Grand & Royal Chapter of the Royal Arch of Jerusalem did not appear in London till 1766 and that it warranted no chapters until 1769. Nor yet had the Knights Templars arrived in Ireland where they burst forth in 1773.

The disapproval of the Royal Arch by the Moderns Grand Lodge was particularly manifested by their Grand Secretary, Samuel Spencer. His letter in 1759 is well known. To an Irish brother seeking charity, and whose letter got delivered to the wrong Grand Secretary, he wrote:

> Your being an Antient Mason, you are not entitled to any of our Charity. The Antient Masons have a Lodge at the Five Bells in the Strand, & their Secretary's name is Dermott. Our Society is neither Arch, Royal Arch or Antient so that you have no Right to partake of our Charity.

Although Spencer was a signatory to the Charter of Compact in 1766 this did not stop him writing in 1767

> The Royal Arch is a society which we do not acknowledge and which we hold to be an invention to introduce innovation and to seduce the brethren.

The official attitude seems to have been summed up, in a kinder way, up by Grand Secretary James Heseltine, when he said, in 1774:

> It is true that many of the Fraternity belong to a Degree in Masonry which is said to be higher than the other, and it is called Royal Arch . . . I have the honour to belong to this Degree . . . but it is not acknowledged in Grand Lodge, and all its emblems and jewels are forbidden to be worn there . . . You will thus see that the Royal Arch

is a private and distinct society. It is a part of Masonry but has no connection with Grand Lodge and this is the only further degree known to us in England.

It is worth remembering that Grand Secretary Heseltine was a member and key supporter of the Royal Arch so he accepts the Royal Arch, but states that it is a separate part of masonry.

And going forward to November 1792 we can find the Proceedings of the GLE that "That this Lodge do agree with its Committee, that the Grand Lodge of England has nothing to do with the Proceedings of the Society of Royal Arch Masons."

The Structure of Freemasonry in the 18th Century

Today we are used to the idea that every order has some Grand Organisation governing it, and that every lodge, chapter or conclave must have a warrant of charter which allows it to operate; but I have to tell you that was only true on the 19th and 20th centuries. And we also normally expect there to be only one body for each order in one territory, although that can be vague and variously interpreted even today.

When the (1717/1721) Grand Lodge was formed in London it was the only one but as it expanded it found places that felt independent of it, Ireland (GL formed 1725), Scotland (GL formed 1736) and it was aware after 1725 of an independent body in York. In 1751 it met direct competition in the form of the newly formed *Most Antient and Honble Society of Free and Accepted Masons* (which is simply referred to as the Antients).

In Scotland Mother Kilwinning left the GL of Scotland in 1744 and did not return until 1807, and in the intervening years warranted lodges across Scotland and probably also for other degrees (although they seem to deny that). But it was only in 1756 that London felt it had no option but to accept that Holland would have its own GL of the Netherlands.

1766 was the year in which the Charter of Compact created the Grand and Royal Chapter of the Royal Arch of Jerusalem. This was the first Grand body created by the rulers of the Craft. However it only issued its first three warrants in 1769 and in total only chartered around 50 chapters by 1795. Maybe the problem was that lodges simply called an extraordinary meeting, worked whatever degrees they wanted, and the fee for the degree went into the lodge chest.

It is perhaps interesting to note that in Ireland where the Grand Lodge totally failed to exert control, the Royal Arch prospered. When the Knights Templars arrived they were able to increase their membership by making the Royal Arch another part of what they did. And when there was a competing second Grand Encampment was formed, then that competition boosted membership. Indeed one can almost see in the Irish practices an image not unlike the American York Rite, and which was created to solve exactly that problem.

The 1813 Union of Moderns & Antient Grand Lodges in England

Reaching this point readers will be well aware that the Moderns had always tried to keep other degrees at a distance; while the Antients has included the Royal Arch within their remit. Neither of these strategies had stopped other degrees appearing or becoming popular. But THE problem was that initially none of these were governed. The British Isles were surrounded by sea and Grand Lodges also faced problems caused by Lodge in port cities recruiting master Mariners, taking the money for their own account and getting the certificate from Grand Lodge to give to the Mariner before he went home. But of course the problem was that Grand Lodge only ever received any money once, because that brother has sailed off somewhere else to visit lodges in other ports.

When it became inevitable that the two Grand Lodges in England needed to get together there was considerable negotiation over how they would do this; and one problem area was that of the Royal Arch. Below is the original article 2 from the actual copy of the 'Articles of Union' that was signed. Look carefully at the 'scratch and rubbing' and it is clear that the final agreement was not what was first written.

The Moderns had only three degrees, while the Antients had four—and maybe that is what was written, and the degrees named. But they settles on three degrees and 'the Supreme Order of the Holy Royal Arch.' So here is the 'political' compromise —only three degrees (so the Moderns are happy), and a 'Supreme Order of the Holy Royal Arch' (so the Antients are happy). And they both signed. There were other complications which came later, but most importantly a deal was struck.

The Grand Lodge of England has had a Supreme Grand Chapter as part of its organisation. As such it has always encouraged its members to also become Royal Arch Masons, after all that means each member pays another annual fee to Grand Lodge. And as masonic membership has shrunk that financial imperative has increased.

The Grand Chapter website has the following explanation of the Royal Arch:

> Joining the Royal Arch (or 'Chapter') is the fourth and final stage in
> Pure Antient Masonry, as defined in the Act of Union of 1813 that

created the current United Grand Lodge of England.

Anyone who has been a Master Mason for four weeks can join—and should aspire to join the Royal Arch, because becoming a Companion of the Order continues their voyage of discovery.[4]

---

4   https://www.ugle.org.uk/about-us/royal-arch viewed 2024.

What others have said on Origins,
and Some Conclusions

The whole idea of researching the 18th century was to see what we could discover. The problem for masonic researchers over the last few decades has been that they see masonic developments in this period as chaotic, and with hundreds of degrees and no way of knowing how they differed. And writers have increasingly relied on re-quoting from past texts. Sadly the end result of this is a failure to think that there could be an alternative. But we thought this resume would be of value to readers; and we would say "do use the texts from the past, but be aware that there may be other contemporaneous information to be seen if one searches."

It is worth also reminding ourselves that all degrees, especially Masonry Dissected, were produced without any approval from anyone, or any Grand Lodge or 'Grand body'—simply because they did not exist.[1] It was the Brothers in Lodges who worked these new degrees, and the fees went into the coffers of the Lodge. In short it was a 'free for all' between 1730 and around 1800, when eventually all Grand Lodges took action to bring some sort of order into the (then) huge multiplicity of degrees that existed.

What others have said on origins

The famous **Robert Freke Gould**, in his *History of Freemasonry* (and his Concise History) says nothing more about the history of the Royal Arch than to mention the Arch at Yougall and Dassigny's Impartial Enquiry, but only with brevity.

When in 1894 **William James Hughan** analysed the origins of the Royal Arch, at length in his *Origins of the English Rite of Freemasonry,* there is for the first time a serious effort at investigation of other degrees:

> Having dwelt sufficiently on the debatable points connected with our subject, we have now to glance at the earliest *records* of Royal Arch Chapters in England and elsewhere. These are not quite so old as those of some others of the additional degrees, notably the minutes of the "Royal Order of Scotland," but that fact, which tends to lessen their value slightly, is more than counterbalanced by the typographical references to Royal Arch Masonry, which go back to

---

1   John Belton, "Brother, Just one more Degree?" *Scottish Rite Journal*, March-April, 2013.

a period earlier by several years than do any others, except the First Three Degrees. (p. 63)[2]

One cannot pass over the single best work on the English higher degrees without looking at the classic Bernard E Jones *Freemasons Book of the Royal Arch* first printed in 1957. It remains the best source of background information.

The redoubtable Harry Carr (1900–1983) also wrote on the subject in *AQC* in 1973 under the title "The Relationship between the Craft and the Royal Arch."[3] Carr was the preeminent masonic historian of his time. He wrote about the theories of ritual development, but he was wedded to the idea that there were no ritual developments in England between 1730 and 1760 but he tended to apply this only the Craft Freemasonry.

In his 1971 paper he accepts the events at Youghal in 1743, Dassigny's statement on the Royal Arch at face value and also notes the formation of Vernon Lodge No. 123 in Coleraine in 1745.

He quotes from Le Parfait Macon:

> *Le Parfait Macon* was another French exposure of 1744, designed, almost certainly, to mislead the non-Masonic public who might have acquired more reliable information from some of the better publications of that class.
>
> Its information on the three Craft degrees was a farrago of rubbish, but the book also contained a chapter on the *Ecossais* [Scots] Masons, from which the following extracts are drawn:
>
>> Those called *Ecossais Masons* claim that they form the fourth grade ... Instead of weeping over the ruins of the Temple of Solomon, as their brethren do, the *Ecossais* are concerned with rebuilding it.... Everyone knows that after seventy years of captivity in Babylon, the Great Cyrus permitted the Israelites to rebuild the Temple & the City of Jerusalem; that Zerubabel, of the House of David, was appointed by him [Cyrus] the Chief & Leader of that People for their return to the Holy City; that the first stone of the Temple was laid during the reign of Cyrus, but that it was

---

2   WJ Hughan. *Origins of the English Rite of Freemasonry especially in relation to the Royal Arch Degree*. Kenning London, 1894, p. 63 (Ch.4 Advent of Royal Arch Masonry pp. 46-85) http://www.tbm100.org/Lib/Hug84.pdf

3   Harry Carr, "The Relationship between the Craft and the Royal Arch," *AQC* vol. 86 (1973), pp. 36-54.

not completed until the sixth year of that of Darius, **King** of the Persians. It is from this great event that the *Ecossais* derive the epoch of their institution. . . .

The writer goes on to describe how Zerubabel chose the *Ecossais* from the most expert craftsmen; they were awarded higher pay and entrusted with particular words and a sign; these are described and they are quite worthless.

There are eight questions in the Catechism, all trivial, but one of the answers speaks of

> . . . the order given by Nehemiah to all the workmen at the time of the rebuilding of the Temple, to have swords always at their sides, & their bucklers near at hand during work, for use in case of attack by their enemies. . . . (Early French Exposures, pp. 197-9).

Here, in Le *Parfait Macon,* we have one of the Royal Arch themes linked specifically with the 'fourth degree' of *Ecossais* [Scots] Masons.

So here (p. 46) we find Carr almost writing a modern conclusion, but not able to personally accept it. Again further (p. 50) he writes "Let it be clearly understood that we are discussing secrets which pertained to the Craft of that period—i.e., *not* to the Royal Arch,...." Sadly Carr can only see these changes as being things despoiling the Craft degrees—rather than considering them to be parts of other non-Craft degrees or of a newly developing French set of degrees. It is worth ending this review of Carr's paper by adding his tenth conclusion:

> X. In some of the French exposures there are references to the *Ecossais,* usually described as the fourth degree, with brief hints which suggest that the ceremony embodied certain themes which may have belonged to the Royal Arch. In those instances in which the authors discuss the ceremony they always speak of it as a separate and, by implication, a higher degree; but there is never any hint that this fourth degree is a continuation or completion of the third; it was simply an additional degree of a supposedly higher grade.

Eric Ward's 1975 paper entitled "Dassigny, Youghal and All That"[4] is dealt with in the Chapter on Passing the Chair. Sadly he prefers not to like any of the Irish

---

4   Eric Ward, "Dassigny, Youghal and All That." *AQC* vol. 88 (1975), pp. 20-31. [It is perhaps worth mentioning that Ireland was considered to be inferior to England in the decades that followed WW2 and of course 'we all know freemasonry was invented in England.']

evidence. But it was clearly part of a period of interest in the origins of the Royal Arch in England.

Researcher **Roy A Wells** in *Freemasonry in London from 1785* (seen through the Antients' Domatic Lodge No.177 and its associates and published 1984) does however exhibit a sound grasp of the available information, and half the book is devoted to the Royal Arch. The early rules and regulation. He does not examine the origins but the book provides an excellent insight into the way the Antients worked.

It is perhaps useful to provide some comment upon the manner in which Irish Masons were viewed by the English (and earlier the Antients in England likewise). So I quote the words of Phillip Crossle when he went to talk to the Manchester Association in 1927 (and I would not dissent from his views of those days regarding how his propositions would be received). It is also worth noting that similar views were held in the USA:

> Whilst I endeavour to be impartial, my heart may run away with my head-so that by the time I shall have finished, probably you will put me down as one of those "insurgent Irish" who dares to come to 'Manchester to air his views.' "Insurgent" or not, I do feel that proper justice is not meted out to the memory of our Irish Craftsmen of the 18th century. For instance, according to "The New York Masonic Outlook" (March, 1927, p. 205), the Lodges of the "Antients" had "a considerable admixture of the proverbially insurgent Irish." "The Builder" (Feb., 1927, p. 61), too, would have us believe that the "Irish Lodges were apparently much more rebellious" than were those of other Masonic Constitutions.
>
> Given such a character, I exclaim: Poor Ireland, me countree-there goes another injustice to thee. Any contention that did exist among the Freemasons of Ireland, or of Irish descent, was to maintain their beloved Craft "according to the Old Constitutions."[5]

IRELAND – *Philip Crossle (1875–1953), John Heron Lepper (1878–1952), Redfern Kelly and the Irish Royal Arch Controversies of the 1920s*

First of all one must mention the publication of the History of the Grand Lodge of Ireland authored by John Heron Lepper and Philip Crossle and published by Lodge CC (aka Lodge 200) in 1925 to celebrate the bicentenary of the Grand Lodge of Ireland. Lepper later became the librarian at the Museum of Freemasonry in London after a career as a linguist. Philip Crossle was an Irish

---

5   Phillip Crossle, *The Irish Rite*, Manchester Association for Masonic Research 1927 (but published 1929), p. 65.

Historian and his legacy to Irish masonic history is also his library full of correspondence and information in the library at Molesworth Street. One must assume that most of the work they did on the History was in harmony but by the end of the 1920s it seems they fell out.

The year 1923 must have been a tumultuous one in Irish Freemasonry, for it was the year when the Red Cross Degrees, otherwise called Knight of the Sword, Knight of the East and Knight of the East and West was released from the control of the Knights Templars and became the (Irish) Grand Council of Knight Masons after having been largely officially absent for a century, although clearly well remembered, became (for the first time) an official part of the Irish masonic panorama once again. But in addition in 1923 there was a very public debate regarding the practice of the Royal Arch.

The same year of 1923 another of the heavyweight brothers in Irish masonry, Philip Crossle, came to speak at the Manchester Lodge of Masonic Research and wrote his own understanding under the title of 'The Early Practices of the Irish Craft', and this was later expanded with records from the Lodge in Birr added and later published in 1929 in the Transactions of Lodge 200.

Crossle's paper delivered in Manchester in 1927

The final stand-off took place between Philip Crossle and John Heron Lepper in respect of what Crossle calls 'The Irish Rite' also took place around this time. He wrote at length on 'The Irish Rite' and this was first published in the Transactions of the Manchester Association for Masonic Research in volume for 1927 which was actually published in 1929. In an extended format it was then published in the 1923 Proceedings of Lodge 200 (actually also printed in 1929).

Crossle was also the editor of the Transactions of the Lodge of Research No. 200. Lepper did not agree in any way with Crossle's opinions on the Irish Rite but was thus obliged to get his views in print in England in AQC.

The Irish publication was reviewed in *AQC*, volume 42 for 1930, by John Heron Lepper who was polite but utterly scathing. This debate is important because any and all Irish research on the Royal Arch since that date, always quotes, and always accepts without question, Crossle's theory—and is still absolutely relied upon by all Irish masonic researchers since then, and even in 2020. However, I remain unconvinced that many, if any, of the authors have ever read the complete Crossle paper AND the Lepper riposte. The result is that the Irish understanding of the Royal Arch has never moved on to consider alternatives to the Crossle opinion.

Belton has spent over a year trying to decide how to explain this issue. In the end the decision was reached that nothing could be more satisfactory that to quote directly from the Lepper review in AQC of 1930.[6]

This was a genuine duel between two Irish masonic giants. Philip Crossle was the Librarian of the Library in Molesworth Street, Dublin and also the editor of the Transactions of the Lodge of Research 200. One only has to sit in the library there and start to working through the nearly 50 volumes of the collected notes of Crossle to realise that legacy and stature of the brother. John Heron Lepper (1879–1952) was born in Ulster, suffered 'infantile paralysis,' was educated in Scotland, and went to Trinity College Dublin. He was called to the Irish Bar in 1903 but never practiced and moved to London in 1904 (aged 36). There he became a literary editor for the London publishers Cassells and one of the key publications upon which his name appears is their German-English dictionary. He became a member of Quatuor Coronati Lodge in 1922, in 1925 was awarded the Irish Grand Chapter rank of Past Grand Superintendent of the Tabernacle. After he retired be was appointed Librarian of the Library in Freemasons Hall in London.

But it was during these years that both Lepper and Crosse cooperated to produce the first volume of the History of the Grand Lodge of Ireland, published in 1925 to mark the bi-centenary of Grand Lodge. This is, and remains, one of the best masonic histories of freemasonry in Ireland—and evidence of differences of opinions seems absent from the text. However it was to end a very carefully crafted set of words by Lepper in riposte in 1930.

Lepper responded to this and chose as his medium of response *AQC*[7]—but alas this review seems not to have reached Ireland even to this day. Ideally Lepper would have responded in the Transactions of Lodge 200, but clearly he felt that would not be possible because Crossle was its editor.

Crossle – The Irish Rite and 'Royal Archism'

The essence of Crossle's thesis was that the names attached to degrees did not in any way reflect the content, and that content in Ireland was not known by the same name as in other places. This is thoroughly confusing, and the essence is quoted below:

> Forcibly struck by the reluctance, particularly in rural places, to depart from accustomed forms, I venture to describe the rise of our Irish Rite. Taking Pennell's book to represent the Rite in vogue be-

---

6   John Heron Lepper, "Review: The Transactions if the Lodge of Research No. 200 for the year 1929." *AQC* (1930), pp .115-123.

7   John Heron Lepper, *AQC.*

fore, and, according to local habitude, for many years after 1730, its rise falls into three periods.

First Period. From the methodical manner, right up to the year 1797 in which three distinct degrees were conferred at Birr, this was a local practice habitual from long usage. Possibly the very same practice, described by Pennell (1730):

1. Apprentice, or Brother.

2. Fellow Craft.

3. Master's part (M.M.), not confined to the Chair.

Nos. 1 and 2 seem to have embraced ceremonies up to and including the Hiramic legend. That is, Pennell's "Apprentice" synchronises with our present E.A. and F.C.; and his "Fellow Craft" with our present M.M. Indeed, if one thinks over it, our M.Ms. of to-day, when assembled, really are a Lodge of F.Cs. No. 3, Pennell's "Master's part," apparently, comprised the essentials of a ceremony subsequently elaborated into our present Irish Installed Master, Royal Arch, and Red Cross Mason degrees.

Second Period. According as conversion to Royal Archism took place, the precise date of which it is impossible to give, the above three degrees were maintained; but the names were changed. The change of the names seems to have taken place, in some Dublin Lodges, after 1744—possibly about 1750—60; at Birr as late as 1800, and still later in other rural places—thus:

1. Entered Apprentice and Fellow Craft (one degree), more often referred to as "Entered and Crafted."

2. Master Mason.

3. Royal Arch.

Here we have a system of three degrees only. No. 1, Pennell's "Apprentice," became known by a composite name. His "Fellow Craft," having lost its former significance, ceased to represent a specific degree. The name, only, was joined to the first degree, merely to preserve ·it from extinction. No. 2, Pennell's "Fellow Craft," was re-christened "Master Mason." It is important to keep this in mind. No. 3, Pennell's "Master's part" (M.M.), was re-christened "Royal Arch." It appears this change in name occurred according as subordinate Lodges obtained the requisite equipment, sometimes called an "encampment." The purport of the degree which we, in Ireland, now call 'Installed Master' must have been a portion only of Pennell's Master's part, and appears to have been merged in the ceremonies known by the general name of "Royal Arch" of the Second Period.

Third Period. The metropolitan ritualists, in order to keep abreast with the times—"as good out of the world as out of the fashion," as the saying goes—elaborated the Irish practice of Antient Craft Masonry into three groups. For want of precise evidence we cannot give definite dates when these elaborations occurred. They were gradual, possibly *circa* 1790 in Dublin. In many rural places, "Entered and Crafted" was not divided into two degrees until the 1840s.

Nos. 1 and 2, of the First and Second: Periods, were retained and expanded into our present three Craft degrees, and thus formed the first group.

No. 3 of the First and Second Periods was elaborated to such an extent that it expanded into groups two and three. (Many Irish Chapters conferred the R.A., group two, and the Red Cross Mason, group three, as one degree under the general name of "Royal Arch," with "Passed the Chair" subsidiary thereto. According to a minute, dated 14th July 1801, this was how Royal Archism was introduced to the Birr Lodge. A month or so afterwards, to accord with their accustomed practice, the Birr Brethren merged "Passed the Chair" in the Royal Arch; and it was not until 1818, that they definitely transferred it from the R.A.C. and began to confer it as a separate degree in the Lodge. (CC (1923), pp. 160-162)

This all takes some digesting because all the names of all the degrees are shuffled around. Crossle repeatedly in the text uses the phrase 'Royal Archism' which he defines more exactly for the reader as:

"'Royal Archism,' is a phrase of my own coining. It falls into the same category with 'Ritualism,' defined *inter alia:* 'excessive observance of forms in divine worship.'" (CC (1923), p. 144)

The phrase is repeatedly used as part of Crossle's diatribe and occurs some 24 times.

Lepper's Review of the Transactions of Lodge 200 for the year 1923

Lepper's words stand by themselves, so that is how they are quoted here almost in full, and from 'Review, *The Transactions of the Lodge of Research No. 200*' and published England in *AQC* volume 42 (1930).

(This will be a convenient place to give the warning that the J. Legend was not, in my opinion, in undisputed possession of the Royal Arch field in Ireland. Some of the R.A. seals illustrated in this book are sufficient proof to the contrary, were any needed, which is not the case.)

Having adopted his theory for better or worse, Brother Crossle sets out to attempt to prove it by citing a multitude of documents, which, however interesting and valuable in themselves, and they usually are so, bear better testimony to the wideness of his reading than to his success in either stating a case clearly or in drawing an obvious conclusion. When evidences clash with theory, as they are continually doing throughout, we are offered another theory to explain away the staggering inconsistency; and thus the airy fabric rises, improbability piled upon improbability, and cemented with ever-ready assertion in lieu of proof or logic.

We are told first of all that the three degrees mentioned by Pennell (1730)) viz. (1) E.A., (2) F.C., and (3) M.M. are not what we understand by the names now: that (1) included our present E.A. and F.C.; (2) our present M.M.: (3) our present Installed Master's degree, Royal Arch (Irish J. Legend) and the group of Red Cross degrees (for which see above). We are further told that at an indefinite period, but *circa* 1750, a conversion to what Brother Crossle calls "Royal Archism" took place in the Irish metropolis, since when pure unadulterated Irish Freemasonry has only been found sporadically preserved in isolated instances in remote country Lodges. I fear our Brother has left this very peculiar term of his own invention lying about too carelessly and that some will trip over it. After reading his definition of it at page 144, "that blessed word Mesopotamia" itself has more comfort, for me at all events. Yet, since I may be dense or unfair, I hasten to copy his words in full:

"'Royal Archism' is a phrase of my own coining. It falls into the same category with 'Ritualism,' defined *inter alia:* 'excessive observance of forms in divine worship.'"

But, if I have followed our Brother correctly, "Royal Archism" was rather an excessive lack of observance of forms, such a lack that its exponents failed to observe or preserve integral forms of the Irish Royal Arch degree, the existing Red Cross degrees. Thus the theory leads to a point where we must either fall into the jaws of a paradox or remain bogged in the slough of an inadequate definition.[8]

---

8 John Heron Lepper, "Review – *The Transactions of the Lodge of Research No. 200 for the year 1923* (Dublin 1929), published in *AQC* vol.42, pp. 115-120.

Lepper goes on to make certain points which show that Crossle's opinions are totally inconsistent with reality, and three examples are quoted:

> B. When the words Royal Arch occur in any old Irish connexion, they do not mean what we mean by Royal Arch, but something quite different. Thus the famous reference to the Royal Arch carried in procession at Youghal in December, 1743, "cannot be read to mean a degree bearing that name was conferred at Youghal in 1743." Similarly, Dassigny's equally famous reference (1744) "does not suggest that the Royal Arch Masons of York were anything more than M.M.s under another name." About Dassigny's further statement:
>
>> "it is an organised body of men who *have passed the chair*" (my italics) our Brother says: "This is an early reference to the expression passed the chair," used here in a colloquial sense; because no available evidence justifies the assertion that a separate degree, under that specific name, was conferred in Ireland before *circa* 1790."...
>
> C. The practice upheld by Laurence Dermott in England of conferring the Royal Arch upon only Installed Masters is not to be taken as indicating the Irish practice in 1746, when he received the degree in Dublin in Lodge 26.
>
> E. That Chetwode Crawley and subsequent scholars have been quite wrong in accepting in the ordinary sense of the words that Irish Grand Lodge Minute of 1786 which runs:
>
>> "Resolv'd that it is highly improper for a Master Mason's Lodge as such to enter upon their Books any transactions relative to the Royal Arch."
>
> Since the Master Mason's degree at this date contained the Royal Arch, the Words must bear some other meaning than that of prohibiting the record of Arch transactions in Craft Minute Rooks.
>
> What that other meaning may be. Brother Crossle does not make clear.

So there are the comments of Lepper upon the words of Crossle. We have to say that we agree with Lepper's conclusions. After spending several hours trying to find the words Crossle offers from (say) Pennel's 1730 Constitutions we can (eventually find and) read the words but cannot find the meaning he attributes to them. We also found it impossible to determine the dates offered by Crossle in relation to his claims.

Crossle's thesis runs through to the period when the Templars became active, but he never mentions them once. This is just another inconsistency present in the Crossle thesis.

Philip Crossle's article runs to 139 pages, sadly it is very convoluted and nearly impossible to understand well. What prompted him to propose this thesis can only be guessed at because it is so unlike his other work. By comparison the Crossle archives in the Grand Lodge of Ireland in Molesworth Street, Dublin are a superb and carefully indexed resource. It seems that in part he might have felt that the role played by Ireland in the development of freemasonry had been underplayed by non-Irish writers and that he wanted to correct that. We believe that we have given the Irish role a more dominant position in events, indeed one that it has long deserved.

It was published in a very scarce volume of the Transactions of Lodge 200 (IC) for 1923 but published in 1930; while the Manchester Association for Masonic Research paper was delivered in 1927 and only published in 1929. I tried for some years to locate a copy but eventually I asked the Library in Dublin if they had an old duplicate copy they could lend me to scan. The kind librarian Rebecca Hayes obliged, and they now also have a scanned pdf copy that can be emailed to any enquiring researcher. Both these volumes were printed some years after the papers were delivered, because membership of research lodges was not prospering at the time, so printing got delayed by some years.

Thee various ideas proposed over the last century have been very substantially dependent on viewing event as if past centuries were all the same as the 20th century. This has meant that matters have not moved forward with respect to the Royal Arch.

Conclusions

There never has been any doubt that the appearance in print in 1730 of *Masonry Dissected* changed the face of freemasonry for ever. There are of course odd earlier clues which demonstrate that other masonic thoughts were developing, but nothing so far of significance has been found. But probably the narrow Craft focus of Harry Carr when he announced that there had been no exposures in England between 1730 and 1760 was simply accepted by researchers as being the totality of what happened masonically in England, just the Philip Crossle's idea of an Irish Rite – both just wiped away any imagination from researchers in either England or Ireland respectively on either topic.

So this book started with the thesis that Masonry Dissected started the rush of freemasons towards 'higher degrees' so that eventually towards the end of the 18th century it was only the creation of a multiplicity of Grand bodies that brought order into freemasonry.

In all cases it was the actions of Grand Lodges that tried to control matters, but in many cases the task of creating more degrees lay in the hands of ordinary brothers and was totally outside the control of Grand Lodges. So in Scotland it was Grand Lodge who took the initiative in 1800 to exclude all degrees other that the first three – and this prompted Alexander Duechar to create a Grand Conclave in 1810 and then a Grand Chapter in 1817. In Ireland it was the infirmity and death of the Dep Grand Secretary and the failure to collect the dues that focussed the thoughts of John Boardman on creating Grand Chapters and Grand Encampments under the control of the Grand Lodge in order to generate cash flow. This produced a revolution in 1805 which split Irish freemasonry asunder, and the healing process took some twenty years. England needed to join the two Grand Lodges of Moderns and Antients and achieved this in 1813. It also brought the Royal Arch within the control of UGLE and the Knight Templars were put 'on hold' until 1830. It was only after the death of the Duke of Sussex in 1843, that control was removed and other orders were then created.

These attempts to bring order into freemasonry were often driven by highly motivated individuals. In England of course it was the Duke of Sussex, in Scotland Alexander Deuchar and in Ireland it was John Fowler' but there were of course others. It is worth recounting the activities of Fowler, if only to see the breadth of his activities.

It is worth expanding a little upon Bro John Fowler's Masonic life. He was born in Ireland in 1769 and initiated in February 1792 at the age of 23 and in

December 1793 installed as Master of his lodge. At almost the same time, 1793, he set up a school and continued in that profession until 1836 when he retired to became a full time Freemason. He was Deputy Grand Master from 1818-1824 and Deputy Grand Secretary from 1827-1856. However before that he had become known as the leading exponent of the rituals of every other Masonic Order known in Ireland. In June 1802 under a French Constitutional Warrant he formed the Dublin College of Heredom (the 24° of the Order of the Royal Secret or the Rite of Perfection, known nowadays as the 30° of the Ancient and Accepted Rite). He corresponded with Frederick Dalcho from 1801 until the war between Britain and the United States in 1812 made that temporarily impossible. As if that was not enough, he was also behind the introduction into Ireland of the Rite of Misraim in 1820 and the formation of the Supreme Grand Royal Arch Chapter of Ireland in 1829. It seems that whatever was going on with ritual, Fowler was always at the centre of it. He was truly a brother who could not resist the lure of "just one more degree," but also a brother who really influenced Masonic affairs in Ireland.

In France, the situation was a little different. When the first public mention of the "maîtres écossois" was made, in December 1743, the Grand Lodge reacted negatively by denying their legitimacy. A little later, a printed disclosure revealed that these newcomers were claiming special privileges in the Lodges of the three first degrees. Finally, we know that at the same time, in Paris, in his personal lodge, the Grand Master, the Count of Clermont, practised at least four degrees above the Master's degree, and even a knightly degree. Throughout the next three decades, dozens of high degrees were to appear, escaping the control of the Grand Lodge - but without provoking its hostility - while several organisations competed to ensure the control of these new degrees. In many respects, France, before the French Revolution of 1789, was a veritable paradise of the high degrees, relegating the first three to the level of a mere masonic passing introduction. However, in the early 1780s, the Grand Orient of France, created in 1773, established its power over all the high degrees by creating within itself a "Grand Chapitre Général".

This book has not looked at developments in the United States. The two key players there were Henry Fowle and Thomas Smith Webb[1]. The need for organization was possibly identified earlier in the United States by Henry Fowle (1766-1837) of Boston. He was initiated in 1793, appointed Junior Warden in November of the same year, and had taken most of the available degrees in the next couple of years. Fowle clearly saw the need for organization, and in 1798 (after only five years a brother!) he founded with Thomas Smith Webb

---

1   John Belton. Brother Just One More Degree. Scottish Rite Journal March/April 2013 p.7-9. This explores the topic in more detail.

and others the General Grand Chapter Royal Arch Masons and later the Grand Encampment of Knights Templar of the U.S.A. So in the move to create order from the chaos we find Webb and Fowle; and indeed they were also ahead by a couple of years of the foundation of the first Supreme Council in South Carolina.

When this enterprise between Belton and Dachez started it was almost a clean sheet of paper and shelves full of the books from the past full of the same identical quotations. It also seemed that the last century was devoted to researching Craft Masonry and in terms of the higher degrees it was the Ancient and Accepted that was the focus. We have explored and discovered a great variety of fascinating information and tried to paint a very different picture; that is not to say it is complete - because it is not.

It could never be complete, but perhaps most novel in the approach to the research; that of taking a holistic view and a forensic approach. And this has shown that freemasonry travelled across Europe and found brothers with keen minds, imagination and libraries. And perhaps it really displays the exceptional role played by the Union French Lodge No.98 in London and its members.

The role played by French Freemasonry and the interchange of ritual and ideas has proved the surprise we always hoped for. On this point, the main achievement of our research has undoubtedly been to show that we cannot understand the development of Freemasonry between 1725 and 1760 without systematically cross-referencing British and French developments, which then shed light on each other. This is particularly true of the period from 1744 to 1760: while English Masonic scholarship has always deplored the absence of sources on Masonic practices in this period, this is the time when printed exposures multiplied in France, and it is thus a period for which we also possess numerous manuscript rituals. It is also worth remembering that from 1725 to 1745, the British element was very influential in French Freemasonry, particularly in Paris, and that Masonic practices in London and Paris were very similar – often involving the same actors, some of whom crossed the Channel several times.

Many of our findings are different to the established norms of masonic history. We have endeavoured to exercise caution in our claims, and maybe on some points we will be proved wrong, if so we will still be delighted to have stimulated thoughts in other minds on a period of masonic history previously much ignored.

What we have discovered is that there is real and dateable evidence to be gleaned by a careful, even if fast, reading of 18th century materials that are available to all via book.google. One can read the 1749 views of Louis Travenol on ritual developments or of Thomas Lansa on the state of singing. Such contemporaneous views are invaluable, and also often offer an especially rare insight on those around them at the time. And such detailed, and especially accumulated researches, on individual brothers in various countries have enabled us to place the Union French Lodge no.98 of London at the very forefront of the spreading of freemasonry from London into Europe. We probably also accept that researchers will find that Dublin also played a significant role when they hunt for facts.

The idea for this research, and thus the book, was the realisation that in trying to bridge the gap between Masonry Dissected and the more organised freemasonry which appeared from the early 19th century that masonic researchers had simply assumed that there was no more evidence to be found. Thus there was almost a whole century when nothing was found to 'write a better history' of the masonic 18th century. We believe we have proved them wrong.

The authors started from the position of knowing no more than what had been written, and set out on the journey to see what evidence there was to be found. Doing again what others before us had done was not going to produce results. So we went back to examine and fully read all the available old documents and manuscripts. And you have read what we have discovered.

Digital Resources & Acknowledgements

The majority of this research was done during the period of the covid-19 pandemic which both limited access to libraries and limited our ability to travel. During this period John Belton never once entered a masonic library in person, but thanks to various librarians is given elsewhere. The breakthrough was provided as a result of Google Books[2] and also by Gallica (the digital function of the Biblioteque National de France), Bodleian Library in Oxford, Bayerische Staatsbibliothek in Munich and also several French city libraries. What they have enabled is the ability to download scanned historical printed documents and this has enable transnational research to be undertaken while sitting at one desk at home. We must express our undying gratitude to these organisations for the broad minded view of their librarians who have comprehended that a book scanned as a pdf is as real a book as one printed on paper.

In a more traditional style we must extend our thanks to various Masonic Libraries and Librarians: Martin Cherry of Museum of the Grand Lodge of England, Pierre Mollier of the Grand Orient of France, and the librarians of the Grand Lodge of Ireland, and Grand East of the Netherlands. Our thanks also to the Quatuor Coronati Lodge for permission to use the English transcripts of French rituals produced by Harry Carr and to Bro Bob Bashford for his permission to use his images of the Vernon Lodge jewels as used in his paper in

---

2   https://en.wikipedia.org/wiki/Google_Books

AQC. And finally our thanks to Paul Rich for his interest and for agreeing for Westphalia Press to publish our discoveries—and fittingly in 21st century style it is print on demand. There have been numerous researchers both living and dead upon whose shoulders we have been able we have been able to see a different view of this previously under-researched part of masonic history. We thank them one and all.

Index

The authors are indebted to Dr David Harrison for
his labours in producing this index

Note: *Degree names in italics*

Related Titles from Westphalia Press

Ancient Mysteries and Modern Masonry: The Collected Writings of Jewel P. Lightfoot, Edited by Billy J. Hamilton Jr.

Jewel P. Lightfoot. Former Attorney General of the State of Texas. Past Grand Master of the Masonic Grand Lodge of Texas. From humble beginnings in rural Arkansas, he worked to become an educated man who excelled in law and Freemasonry. He was a gentleman of his time, well-known as a scholar, public speaker, and Masonic philosopher.

Essay on The Mysteries and the True Object of The Brotherhood of Freemasons
by Jason Williams

This isn't a reprint of a classic. It's a new rendition with new life breathed into it, to be enjoyed both by the layperson trying to understand the Craft and Masonic scholars taking a deeper dive into the fraternity's golden years—when the concepts of liberty and equality were still fresh.

Female Emancipation and Masonic Membership:
An Essential Collection
By Guillermo De Los Reyes Heredia

Female Emancipation and Masonic Membership: An Essential Combination is a collection of essays on Freemasonry and gender that promotes a transatlantic discussion of the study of the history of women and Freemasonry and their contribution in different countries.

Freemasonry, Heir to the Enlightenment
by Cécile Révauger

Modern Freemasonry may have mythical roots in Solomon's time but is really the heir to the Enlightenment. Ever since the early eighteenth century freemasons have endeavored to convey the values of the Enlightenment in the cultural, political and religious fields, in Europe, the American colonies and the emerging United States.

Freemasonry: A French View
by Roger Dachez and Alain Bauer

Perhaps one should speak not of Freemasonry but of Freemasonries in the plural. In each country Masonic historiography has developed uniqueness. Two of the best known French Masonic scholars present their own view of the worldwide evolution and challenging mysteries of the fraternity over the centuries.

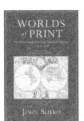

Worlds of Print: The Moral Imagination of an Informed Citizenry, 1734 to 1839
by John Slifko

John Slifko argues that freemasonry was representative and played an important role in a larger cultural transformation of literacy and helped articulate the moral imagination of an informed democratic citizenry via fast emerging worlds of print.

Why Thirty-Three?: Searching for Masonic Origins
by S. Brent Morris, PhD

What "high degrees" were in the United States before 1830? What were the activities of the Order of the Royal Secret, the precursor of the Scottish Rite? A complex organization with a lengthy pedigree like Freemasonry has many basic foundational questions waiting to be answered, and that's what this book does: answers questions.

The Great Transformation: Scottish Freemasonry 1725-1810
by Dr. Mark C. Wallace

This book examines Scottish Freemasonry in its wider British and European contexts between the years 1725 and 1810. The Enlightenment effectively crafted the modern mason and propelled Freemasonry into a new era marked by growing membership and the creation of the Grand Lodge of Scotland.

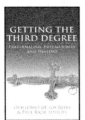

Getting the Third Degree: Fraternalism, Freemasonry and History
Edited by Guillermo De Los Reyes and Paul Rich

As this engaging collection demonstrates, the doors being opened on the subject range from art history to political science to anthropology, as well as gender studies, sociology and more. The organizations discussed may insist on secrecy, but the research into them belies that.

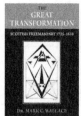

The Great Transformation: Scottish Freemasonry 1725-1810
by Dr. Mark C. Wallace

This book examines Scottish Freemasonry in its wider British and European contexts between the years 1725 and 1810. The Enlightenment effectively crafted the modern mason and propelled Freemasonry into a new era marked by growing membership and the creation of the Grand Lodge of Scotland.

Getting the Third Degree: Fraternalism, Freemasonry and History
Edited by Guillermo De Los Reyes and Paul Rich

As this engaging collection demonstrates, the doors being opened on the subject range from art history to political science to anthropology, as well as gender studies, sociology and more. The organizations discussed may insist on secrecy, but the research into them belies that.

Freemasonry: A French View
by Roger Dachez and Alain Bauer

Perhaps one should speak not of Freemasonry but of Freemasonries in the plural. In each country Masonic historiography has developed uniqueness. Two of the best known French Masonic scholars present their own view of the worldwide evolution and challenging mysteries of the fraternity over the centuries.

Worlds of Print: The Moral Imagination of an Informed Citizenry, 1734 to 1839
by John Slifko

John Slifko argues that freemasonry was representative and played an important role in a larger cultural transformation of literacy and helped articulate the moral imagination of an informed democratic citizenry via fast emerging worlds of print.

Why Thirty-Three?: Searching for Masonic Origins
by S. Brent Morris, PhD

What "high degrees" were in the United States before 1830? What were the activities of the Order of the Royal Secret, the precursor of the Scottish Rite? A complex organization with a lengthy pedigree like Freemasonry has many basic foundational questions waiting to be answered, and that's what this book does: answers questions.

A Place in the Lodge: Dr. Rob Morris, Freemasonry and the Order of the Eastern Star
by Nancy Stearns Theiss, PhD

Ridiculed as "petticoat masonry," critics of the Order of the Eastern Star did not deter Rob Morris' goal to establish a Masonic organization that included women as members. Morris carried the ideals of Freemasonry through a despairing time of American history.

Brought to Light: The Mysterious George Washington Masonic Cave
by Jason Williams MD

The George Washington Masonic Cave near Charles Town, West Virginia, contains a signature carving of George Washington dated 1748. This book painstakingly pieces together the chronicled events and real estate archives related to the cavern in order to sort out fact from fiction.

Dudley Wright: Writer, Truthseeker & Freemason
by John Belton

Dudley Wright (1868-1950) was an Englishman and professional journalist who took a universalist approach to the various great Truths of Life. He travelled though many religions in his life and wrote about them all, but was probably most at home with Islam.

History of the Grand Orient of Italy
Emanuela Locci, Editor

No book in Masonic literature upon the history of Italian Freemasonry has been edited in English up to now. This work consists of eight studies, covering a span from the Eighteenth Century to the end of the WWII, tracing through the story, the events and pursuits related to the Grand Orient of Italy.

westphaliapress.org

Policy Studies Organization

The Policy Studies Organization (PSO) is a publisher of academic journals and book series, sponsor of conferences, and producer of programs.

Policy Studies Organization publishes dozens of journals on a range of topics, such as European Policy Analysis, Journal of Elder Studies, Indian Politics & Polity, Journal of Critical Infrastructure Policy, and Popular Culture Review.

Additionally, Policy Studies Organization hosts numerous conferences. These conferences include the Middle East Dialogue, Space Education and Strategic Applications Conference, International Criminology Conference, Dupont Summit on Science, Technology and Environmental Policy, World Conference on Fraternalism, Freemasonry and History, and the Internet Policy & Politics Conference.

For more information on these projects, access videos of past events, and upcoming events, please visit us at:

www.ipsonet.org

Printed in Great Britain
by Amazon

42170509R10236